WIL

WILL SMITH is an actor, producer, and musician, and an Academy Award, Grammy, and NAACP award winner, who has enjoyed a diverse career encompassing films, television shows, and multiplatinum albums. He holds many box office records, including the most consecutive $100 million-grossing movies (eight). He and his wife founded the Will & Jada Smith Family Foundation to accelerate the growth of initiatives that focus on deepening individual and collective empowerment in the areas of arts and education, social empowerment, health and wellness, and sustainability.

MARK MANSON is the number one *New York Times* bestselling author of *Everything Is F*cked: A Book About Hope* and *The Subtle Art of Not Giving a F*ck: A Counterintuitive Approach to Living a Good Life*. Manson's books have been translated into more than fifty languages and have sold over twelve million copies worldwide. Manson runs one of the largest personal-growth websites in the world, markmanson.net, with more than two million monthly readers and half a million subscribers.

WILL

WILL SMITH

WITH MARK MANSON

PENGUIN BOOKS

PENGUIN BOOKS

UK | USA | Canada | Ireland | Australia
India | New Zealand | South Africa

Penguin Books is part of the Penguin Random House group of companies
whose addresses can be found at global.penguinrandomhouse.com

 Penguin
Random House
UK

First published in the USA by Penguin Press in 2021
First published in the UK by Century in 2021
Published in Penguin Books 2023
001

CONTENTS

THE WALL

hen I was eleven years old, my father decided he needed a new wall on the front of his shop. It would be a big wall: roughly twelve feet high by twenty feet long. The old wall was crumbling, and he was "sick-o'-lookin' at it." But rather than hire a contractor or construction company, he thought it would be a good project for my younger brother, Harry, and me.

Daddio did the demolition. I remember looking at that gaping hole in excruciating disbelief. I was utterly certain that there would never be a wall there ever again.

Every day for nearly a year, my brother and I would go to my father's shop after school to work on that wall. We did everything ourselves. We dug the footing, mixed the mortar, and carried the buckets. I still remember the formula: two parts cement, one part sand, one part lime. Harry was in charge of the hose. We'd mix the pile with shovels out on the sidewalk and then fill two-gallon buckets and lay our separate bricks. We did it without any rebar or wood forms, just one of those levels with the water bubble in the middle.

If you know *anything* about construction, you know this is a loony-ass way to do this. If we can keep it real, this is chain-gang kinda labor. Today we would just call Child Protective Services. This is a job so tedious and unnecessarily long that what ended up taking two kids most of a year would have only taken a team of grown men a couple of days, at most.

My brother and I worked weekends, holidays, vacations. We worked through the summer that year. It didn't matter. My father never took a day off, so neither could we. There were so many times I remember looking at that hole, totally discouraged. I couldn't see how this was ever going to end. The dimensions became unfathomably large in my mind. It seemed like we were building the Great Wall of West Philly— billions of red bricks stretching infinitely into some distant nowhere. I was certain that I would grow old and die still mixing concrete and carrying those buckets. I just knew it.

But Daddio wouldn't let us stop. Every day, we had to be there, mixing concrete, carrying buckets, laying bricks. It didn't matter if it was raining, if it was hot as hell, if I was mad, if I was sad, if I was sick, if I had a test the next day—there were no excuses. My brother and I tried to complain and protest, but it made no difference to Daddio; we were trapped. This wall was a constant; it was permanence. Seasons changed, friends came and went, teachers retired—but the wall remained. Always, the wall remained.

One day, Harry and I were in a particularly stank mood. We were dragging our feet and grumbling, "impossible this" and "ridiculous that."

"Why'd we have to build a wall for, anyway? This is impossible. It's never gonna get done."

Daddio overheard us, threw down his tools, and marched over to where we were yapping. He snatched a brick out of my hand and held it up in front of us.

"Stop thinking about the damn wall!" he said. "There *is* no wall. There are only *bricks*. Your job is to lay *this brick* perfectly. Then move on to the next brick. Then lay *that brick* perfectly. Then the next one. Don't be worrying about no wall. Your only concern is *one brick*."

He walked back into the shop. Harry and I looked at each other, shook our heads—*This dude's a kook*—and went back to mixing.

Some of the most impactful lessons I've ever received, I've had to learn in spite of myself. I resisted them, I denied them, but ultimately the weight of their truth became unavoidable. My father's brick wall was one of those lessons.

The days dragged on, and as much as I hated to admit it, I started to see what he was talking about. When I focused on the *wall*, the job felt impossible. Never-ending. But when I focused on *one brick*, everything got easy—I *knew* I could lay one damn brick well. . . .

As the weeks passed, the bricks mounted, and the hole got just a little bit smaller. I started to see that the difference between a task that feels impossible and a task that feels doable is merely a matter of perspective. Are you paying attention to the wall? Or are you paying attention to the brick? Whether it was acing the tests to get accepted into college, hitting it big as one of the first global hip-hop artists, or constructing one of the most successful careers in Hollywood history, in all cases, what appeared to be impossibly large goals could be broken down into individually manageable tasks—insurmountable walls comprised of a series of conceivably layable bricks.

For my entire career, I have been absolutely relentless. I've been committed to a work ethic of uncompromising intensity. And the secret to my success is as boring as it is unsurprising: You show up and you lay another brick. Pissed off? Lay another brick. Bad opening weekend? Lay another brick. Album sales dropping? Get up and lay another brick. Marriage failing? Lay another brick.

Over the past thirty years, like all of us, I have dealt with failure, loss, humiliation, divorce, and death. I've had my life threatened, my money taken away, my privacy invaded, my family disintegrated—and every single day, still, I got up, mixed concrete, and laid another brick. No matter what you're going through, there is *always* another brick sitting right there in front of you, waiting to be laid. The only question is, are you going to get up and lay it?

I've heard people say that a child's personality is influenced by the meaning of their name. Well, my father gave me *my* name, he gave me *his* name, and he gave me my greatest advantage in life: my ability to weather adversity.

He gave me will.

It was a cold, overcast day, nearly a year after my brother and I had begun. By that time, the wall had become such a fixture in my life that thoughts of finishing it felt like delusions. Like, if we ever *did* finish, there would tragically be another hole, right behind it, that immediately needed to be filled. But on that frigid September morning, we mixed the final pile, filled the final bucket, and laid the final brick.

Daddio had been standing there watching the last few bricks being set into place. Cigarette in hand, he stood quietly admiring our work. Harry and I set and leveled the final brick, then silence. Harry kinda shrugged—*What now? Do we jump, do we cheer, do we celebrate?* We gingerly stepped back and stood on each side of Daddio.

The three of us surveyed our family's new wall.

Daddio plucked his cigarette to the ground, twisting his boot to put it out, exhaled the final drag of smoke, and, never taking his eyes off the wall, he said, "Now, don't y'all *ever* tell me there's something you *can't* do."

Then he walked into the shop and got back to work.

WILL

ONE

FEAR

've always thought of myself as a coward. Most of my memories of my childhood involve me being afraid in some way—afraid of other kids, afraid of being hurt or embarrassed, afraid of being seen as weak.

But mostly, I was afraid of my father.

When I was nine years old, I watched my father punch my mother in the side of her head so hard that she collapsed. I saw her spit blood. That moment in that bedroom, probably more than any other moment in my life, has defined who I am today.

Within everything that I have done since then—the awards and accolades, the spotlights and the attention, the characters and the laughs—there has been a subtle string of apologies to my mother for my inaction that day. For failing her in that moment. For failing to stand up to my father.

For being a coward.

What you have come to understand as "Will Smith," the alien-annihilating MC, the bigger-than-life movie star, is largely a construction—a carefully crafted and honed character—designed to protect myself. To hide myself from the world. To hide the coward.

My father was my hero.

His name was Willard Carroll Smith, but we all called him "Daddio."

Daddio was born and raised in the rough and rugged streets of North Philadelphia in the 1940s. Daddio's father, my grandfather, owned a small fish market. He had to work from 4:00 a.m. until late at night every day. My grandmother was a nurse and often worked the night shift at the hospital. As a result, Daddio spent much of his childhood alone and unsupervised. The North Philly streets had a way of hardening you. You either crystallized into a mean motherfucker, or the hood broke you. Daddio was smoking cigarettes by eleven and drinking by the age of fourteen. My father developed a defiant and aggressive attitude that would continue all his life.

When he was fourteen, my grandparents, fearing where his life was headed, scraped together what money they could and sent him to an agricultural boarding school in the Pennsylvania countryside where kids learned farming techniques and basic handyman work. It was a strict and traditional place, and by sending him there they hoped to introduce some much-needed structure and discipline into his life.

But nobody was going to tell my father what to do. Other than working on some of the tractor engines, he couldn't be bothered with what he described as "that hillbilly bullshit." He would skip classes; he smoked cigarettes and kept on drinking.

At age sixteen, Daddio was done with this school and ready to go home. He decided to get himself kicked out. He started disrupting classes, ignoring all the rules, and antagonizing anyone in a position of authority. But when the administrators tried to send him home, my grandparents refused to take him back. "We paid for the full year," they said. "You're getting paid to deal with him, so *deal* with him." Daddio was stuck.

But Daddio was a hustler—he was going to find his way out: On his seventeenth birthday, he snuck off campus, walked half a dozen miles to the nearest recruiting office, and enlisted in the United States Air Force. This was classic Daddio—he was so hell-bent on defying authority and rebelling against both his parents and the school that he jumped out of the frying pan of an agricultural boarding school and directly into the fire of the United States military. He ended up in the exact structure and discipline my grandparents had desperately hoped to instill in him.

But as it turned out, Daddio *loved* it. It was in the military that he discovered the transformative power of order and discipline, two values that he came to worship as the guardrails protecting him from the worst parts of himself. Wake up at 4:00 a.m., train all morning, work all day, study all night—he found his lane. He discovered that he could outlast anybody, and he began to take pride in that. It was another aspect of his defiant attitude. Nobody could force him to wake up with a bugle horn because he already *was* up.

With his passionate work ethic, boundless energy, and undeniable intelligence, he should have quickly risen through the ranks. But there were two issues.

First, he had a brutal temper, and superior officer or not, if you were wrong, he wasn't doing it. Second, his drinking. Let me tell you, my father was one of the smartest people I've ever known, but when he was angry, or drunk, he became an idiot. He would break his own rules, subvert his own objectives, destroy his own things.

After about two years in the military, this self-destructive streak peeked through the veil of order and ended his service career.

One night, he and the guys from his platoon were gambling. (Daddio was sweet with a pair of dice.) He took those dudes for almost a thousand dollars. Once he'd stashed the winnings in his footlocker, he headed out to get something to eat, but when he returned from the mess hall, the guys had stolen back the money. In his fury, Daddio drank himself into a frenzy, took out his service pistol, and lit up the barracks. Nobody got hurt, but it was enough for the air force to show him the door. He was fortunate that he wasn't court-martialed—instead, they just discharged him, put him on a bus, and invited him to never come back.

This was a tension that ripped through my father's entire life—he demanded such rigid perfection from himself and the people around him, yet after too many drinks, or if he snapped, he would burn everything to the ground.

Daddio moved back to Philly. Undaunted, he took a job in a steel mill while putting himself through night school. He studied engineering and showed a real aptitude for both electricity and the science of refrigeration. One day, after being passed over for a promotion at the steel mill for the third or fourth time because of his race, he simply walked out the door and never went back. He knew refrigeration, so he decided he'd start his own business.

Daddio was brilliant. Like many sons, I worshipped my father, but he also terrified me. He was one of the greatest blessings of my life, and also one of my greatest sources of pain.

My mom was born Carolyn Elaine Bright. She's a Pittsburgh girl, born and raised in Homewood, a predominantly Black neighborhood on the east side of the city.

My mother, a.k.a. "Mom-Mom," is eloquent and sophisticated. She has a petite frame, with long, elegant, piano player's fingers, perfectly sized to deliver a gorgeous rendition of "Für Elise." She had been a standout student at Westinghouse High School and was one of the first Black women to ever study at Carnegie Mellon University. Mom-Mom would often say that knowledge was the only thing that the world couldn't take away from you. And she only cared about three things: education, education, and education.

She loved business—banking, finance, sales, contracts. Mom-Mom always had her own money.

Life moved quickly for my mother, as it often did in those days. She married her first husband at the age of twenty, had a daughter, and was divorced less than three years later. By twenty-five, as a struggling single mom, she was probably one of the most educated African American women in all of Pittsburgh, yet she was still working jobs beneath the level of her true potential. Feeling trapped and craving bigger opportunities, she packed up the baby and moved to live with her mother—my grandmother Gigi—in Philadelphia.

My parents met in the summer of 1964. Mom-Mom was working as a notary in the Fidelity Bank in Philly. She was rolling out with some girlfriends to a party, and one of them told her she just *had* to meet this man. His name was Will Smith.

In many ways, Mom-Mom is the total opposite of my father. Whereas Daddio was the boisterous, charismatic center of attention, Mom-Mom is quiet and reserved; not because she's shy or intimidated, but because she "only speaks when it improves on silence." She loves words and always chooses them carefully—she speaks with an academic sophistication. Daddio, on the other hand, was loud, spewing the lingo of a 1950s North Philly hood rat. He loved the poetry of his profanity—I once heard him call a man a "dirty rat, cocksuckin', low-down, mangy pig fucker."

Mom-Mom doesn't use profanity.

It's important to note here, that back in the day, Daddio was the *man*. Six foot two, smart, good-looking, the proud owner of a fire-engine-red convertible Pontiac. He was funny; he could sing; he could play the guitar. He could *lock* people into him—he was always the dude standing in the middle of a party with a drink in one hand and a cigarette in the other, a master storyteller who could keep a room buzzing.

When Mom-Mom first saw Daddio, he reminded her of a tall Marvin Gaye. He was savvy and knew his way around people. He could talk his way into a party, get free drinks and a table near the front. Daddio had a way of moving through the world like everything was under control, it was all going to be fine. This was comforting for my mom.

My mother's memory of their first days together is just a blurred montage of restaurants and clubs, strung together by a stream of jokes and laughter. Mom-Mom couldn't get over how funny he was, but most important to her, he was ambitious. He had his own business. He had employees. He wanted to work in white neighborhoods, with white people working for *him*.

Daddio was going places.

My father wasn't used to interacting with women of my mother's educational accomplishments—*Man, this bird's smart as a muthafucka*, he thought. Daddio was the *street* smarts to Mom-Mom's *book* smarts.

My parents had a lot in common, too. They both had a passion for music. They loved jazz, blues, and, later, funk and R&B. They lived through the glorious Motown days and spent much of it dancing together in musty basement parties and jazz clubs.

But there were strange commonalities, as well—the stuff that startles you and makes you think, *This must be God's plan.* Both of my parents had mothers who were nurses who worked night shifts (one was Helen; one was Ellen). Both of my parents had short-lived marriages in their early twenties, and they both had daughters. And in perhaps the strangest coincidence, they had both named their daughters Pam.

My parents got married in a small ceremony at Niagara Falls in 1966. Soon after, Daddio moved into my grandmother Gigi's house, on North Fifty-Fourth Street in West Philadelphia. It wasn't long before they combined their very different strengths and talents into an effective team. Mom-Mom ran Daddio's office: payroll, contracts, taxes, accounting, permits. And Daddio got to do what he did best: work hard and make money.

Both of my parents would later speak fondly of those early years. They were young, in love, ambitious, and they were movin' on up.

My full name is Willard Carroll Smith II—*not* Junior. Daddio would always correct people: "Hey! He ain't no mutherfuckin' Junior." He felt like calling me "Junior" diminished both of us.

I was born on September 25, 1968. My mom says that from the moment I showed up, I was a talker. Always smiling, yapping, and babbling away, content to just be making noise.

Gigi worked the graveyard shift at Jefferson Hospital in Center City, Philadelphia, so she'd take care of me in the mornings while my parents were at work. Her house had a huge porch, which served as my front-row seat to the drama of North Fifty-Fourth Street, and a stage on which I could join in the theatrics. She'd prop me up on that porch and watch me jibber-jabber with anybody and everybody who walked by. Even at that age, I loved having an audience.

My twin brother and sister, Harry and Ellen, were born on May 5, 1971. And counting Mom-Mom's daughter Pam, just like that there would now be six of us under one roof.

Fortunately, the North Philly entrepreneur in Daddio was alive and well. He had gone from repairing refrigerators to installing and maintaining refrigerator and freezer cases in major supermarkets. Business was taking off—he was expanding beyond Philly into the surrounding suburbs. He started to build a fleet of trucks and hire a crew of refrigeration and electrical technicians. He also rented a small building to use as his base of operations.

Daddio was always hustling. I remember one particularly frigid winter, cash got tight, so he taught himself how to repair kerosene heaters. They were all the rage in Philly at the time. He put up a bunch of flyers, and people started bringing him their broken heaters. Daddio figured out that once he'd fixed a heater, he'd have to "test" it for a couple days, to make sure it was working. At any given time, he'd have ten or twelve kerosene heaters "being tested for the quality of his work." That many heaters will easily warm a West Philly row home, even in the coldest of winters. So Daddio canceled our gas service, kept his family warm and toasty for the winter, *and got paid for it.*

By the time that I was two years old, Daddio had established his business firmly enough to buy a house about a mile away from Gigi in a middle-class neighborhood of West Philly called Wynnefield.

I grew up at 5943 Woodcrest Avenue on a tree-lined street of thirty grayish-red brick row homes, all connected. The physical proximity of the houses cultivated a strong sense of community. (It also meant that if your neighbor had roaches, you had roaches, too.) Everybody knew everybody. For a young Black family in the 1970s, this was as American dream as you could get.

Across the street was Beeber Middle School and its majestic concrete playground. Basketball, baseball, girls jumpin' double Dutch. The ol' heads slap-boxing. And the second the summer hit, pop goes the water plug. Our neighborhood was thick with kids, and we were always outside playing. Living within one hundred yards of my house, there were almost forty kids my age. Stacey, David, Reecie, Cheri, Michael, Teddy, Shawn, Omarr, and on and on—and that's not even counting their siblings, or the kids on the next blocks. (Stacey Brooks is my oldest friend in the world. We met the day my family moved to Woodcrest. I was two, she was three. Our mothers pushed our strollers up to each other and introduced us. I was in love with her by the time I was seven. But she was in love with David Brandon. He was nine.)

Times were good, and people were clearly having sex . . . a lot.

My middle-class upbringing contributed to the constant criticism I took early in my rap career. I was not a gangster, and I wasn't selling drugs. I grew up on a nice street in a two-parent household. I went to a Catholic school with mostly white kids until I was fourteen. My mom was college educated. And for all of his faults, my father always put food on the table and would die before he abandoned his kids.

My story was very different from the ones being told by the young Black men who were launching the global phenomenon that would later become hip-hop. In their minds, I was somehow an illegitimate artist; they would call me "soft," "whack," "corny," a "bubblegum rapper," criticisms that violently infuriated me. Looking back, I realize I may have been projecting a little, but the reason I hated it so much was that they were unknowingly poking at the thing I most hated about myself, my sense that I was a coward.

Daddio saw the world in terms of commanders and missions, a military mind-set that informed every aspect of his life. He would come to run our family as though we were a platoon on a battlefield and the Wood-crest house was our barracks. He didn't *ask* us to clean our rooms or to make our beds—he commanded, "Police your area."

In his world, there was no such thing as a "small thing." Doing your homework was a mission. Cleaning the bathroom was a mission. Getting groceries from the supermarket was a mission. And scrubbing a floor? It was never just about scrubbing a floor—it was about your ability to follow orders, to exhibit self-discipline, and to complete a task with the utmost perfection. "Ninety-nine percent is the same as zero" was one of his favorite sayings.

If a soldier failed his or her mission, it had to be repeated until perfected. And to disobey a command meant you faced a court-martial, and the punishment usually came in the form of a belt to your bare ass. (He'd say, "Take 'em off, I ain't gon' beat my clothes.")

In Daddio's mind, everything was life or death. He was preparing his children to thrive in a harsh world—a world that he saw as chaotic and brutal. The instilling of fear was—and still is to a large degree—a cultural parenting tactic in the Black community. Fear is embraced as a survival necessity. It is a widely held belief that in order to protect Black children, they must fear parental authority. The instilling of fear is viewed as an offering of love.

On May 13, 1985, Daddio came into our rooms calling for us to get on the floor. A couple of miles south of Woodcrest, the Philadelphia Police Department had just dropped a pair of one-pound bombs on a residential neighborhood. We could hear the faint *ka-ka-ka-kaaaaa-ka-ka-kaaaaaa* of automatic gunfire. Five children and six adults would die that day in what is now known as the MOVE bombing. Two entire city blocks—sixty-five homes—were burned to the ground.

The news always seemed to reinforce Daddio's point of view. Daddio's ideology was centered on training us mentally and physically to handle life's inevitable adversities, but what he unwittingly created was an environment of constant tension and anxiety.

I remember one Sunday afternoon, Daddio was taking a rare day off and sitting in the living room watching TV. He called me over: "'Ey, Will?"

Popping straight to attention, I said, "Yes, Daddy?"

"Run up to Mr. Bryant's and grab my Tareyton 100s."

"Yes, sir!"

He handed me five dollars, and I was off to the corner store. I was maybe ten years old at the time, but this was the 1970s, back when parents could send their kid to buy cigarettes.

I ran down the street directly to Mr. Bryant's without stopping. Totally out of breath, a perfect soldier.

"Hi, Mr. Bryant, my dad sent me to pick up his cigarettes."

"How you doin', Will?" Mr. Bryant said. "They didn't come in today— tell Daddio they should be here tomorrow. I'll hold a carton for him."

"OK, thank you, Mr. Bryant. I'll tell him."

Still a good soldier, I headed home. On my way back, I ran into David and Danny Brandon, who had just gotten this weird new thing called a Nerf football. It was a football, but it was soft.

Any soldier would have stopped.

This thing was *amazing*—I got lost in the ingenuity of this extraordinary object. *You could throw it in the winter, but it wouldn't hurt your fingers if you caught it! You could miss it, it could hit you in the face, and you'd be fine!* One minute turned into five, and then five became ten, ten became twenty . . . Suddenly, David and Danny freeze. Their eyes lock over my shoulder.

I turn, and my stomach drops. Daddio, bare-chested, striding up the middle of the street right at me.

"WHAT THE HELL ARE YOU DOIN'?"

David and Danny evaporated. I quickly try to explain.

"Daddy, Mr. Bryantsaidthecigarettesdidn'tcomeinand—"

"WHAT DID I TELL YOU TO DO?"

"I know, Daddy, but I—"

"WHO'S IN CHARGE?!"

"Whadda you mean—"

"WHO'S IN CHARGE?! YOU? OR ME?"

My heart pounding out of my chest, my voice quivers: "You are, Daddy—"

"BECAUSE IF TWO PEOPLE ARE IN CHARGE, *EVERYBODY DIES*! SO, IF YOU'RE IN CHARGE, LET ME KNOW BECAUSE I WILL DEFER TO YOUR LEADERSHIP!"

His nostrils flaring, the vein in his left temple pulsing madly, his eyes burning through my fragile, ten-year-old innocence.

"When I send you on a mission, there are two possibilities—one, you complete the mission. Or two, YOU. ARE. DEAD. Do you understand me?"

"Yes, Daddy."

Daddio grabbed me by the back of the neck and dragged me home.

I didn't think I deserved a whuppin' for that. Most of the times I got hit during my childhood, I didn't think I'd earned it—it felt like an injustice. I wasn't the kind of kid you needed to spank. I already wanted to please you. David Brandon needed a beatin'. Matt Brown needed a beatin'. If I got in trouble, it was usually because I was distracted—I would forget something or my mind would drift. I think the corporal punishment of my childhood just convinced me I was bad.

The constant fear during my childhood honed my sensitivity to every detail in my environment. From a very young age, I developed a razor-sharp intuition, an ability to attune to every emotion around me. I learned to sense anger, predict joy, and understand sadness on far deeper levels than most other kids.

Recognizing these emotions was crucial and critical for my personal safety: a tone in Daddio's voice, a pointed question from my mother, a twitch of my sister's eye. I processed these things quickly and profoundly—a missed glance or misinterpreted word could quickly deteriorate into a belt on my ass or a fist in my mother's face.

Daddio had a black leather key pouch hooked on his utility belt that held about thirty keys, which for me served as an alarm system. The second he'd walk through the door you could hear his keys jingling as he placed them back into their case and reset them at his hip. I became so in tune that I could discern his mood from the rhythm and the intensity with which he handled his keys. My bedroom was at the top of the stairs, directly facing down to the front door. If he was in a good mood, they would jingle effortlessly, as though they were lighter than usual. If he was pissed, I could hear the jolt of pressure as he reattached them to his hip.

And if he was drunk, the keys didn't matter.

This emotional awareness has stayed with me throughout my life. Paradoxically it has served me well as an actor and performer. I could easily recognize, comprehend, and emulate complex emotions long before I knew that people would pay me for it.

My father was born on the heels of the Great Depression. He was a poor Black kid living on the streets of North Philly in the 1940s. He basically had a tenth-grade education. Yet, over the course of his life, he built a business with a dozen employees and seven trucks, selling thirty thousand pounds of ice per day to grocery stores and supermarkets in three states. He went weeks without taking a day off, decades without taking a vacation. My mother has memories of Daddio coming home in the middle of the night from the shop; dumping thousands of dollars in cash onto the bed, saying, "Count that"; and then immediately heading out into the night to get back to work.

My father tormented me. And he was also one of the greatest men

I've ever known. My father was violent, but he was also at every game, play, and recital. He was an alcoholic, but he was sober at every premiere of every one of my movies. He listened to every record. He visited every studio. The same intense perfectionism that terrorized his family put food on the table every night of my life. So many of my friends grew up either not knowing their fathers or not having their fathers around. But Daddio had my back and never abandoned his post, not even once.

And while he never learned to overcome his own demons, he would cultivate in me the tools to confront my own.

As much as we all suffered under Daddio's militaristic views of love and family, nobody suffered more than my mother. If two people being in charge meant everybody dies, then that meant my mother could never be in charge.

The problem was that my mother wasn't the type of woman to be commanded. She was educated, proud, and stubborn, and as much as we begged her to please be quiet, she refused.

Once, when Daddio slapped her, she egged him on.

"Oh, you're such a man! You think that hitting a woman makes you a man, huh?"

He hit her again, knocking her to the ground.

She stood right back up, looked him in the eye, and calmly said, "Hit me all you want, but you can never hurt me."

I have never forgotten that. The idea that he could hit her body but somehow *she* was in control of what "hurt" her? I wanted to be strong like that.

Everybody in my house could fight.

Except me.

My older sister Pam was strong like our mother. She was six years older than me, and she was kinda my childhood bodyguard. She would stand up to anybody at any time. There were multiple situations where somebody would take my money or I would get bullied or come home crying, and Pam would grab me by the hand, walk me straight outside, and scream, "WHO DID IT? Point to 'em, Will!" Then she'd proceed to casually whoop the whole ass of the unfortunate kid I pointed at. It was a sad day when she left for college.

Harry turned out to be strong, too. While I took extra special care to please my father every chance I got, Harry mimicked my mother's behavior. Starting at a young age, he preferred to just stand up and take the beatings. He once yelled at my father, "You can hit me, but you can't make me cry. [*Smack*.] I'm not crying! [*Smack*.] I'm not crying." Eventually, realizing he couldn't break him, Daddio laid off Harry altogether. All along, Harry's courage—the fact that my little brother was able to stand up to "the monster"—just reinforced my shame. In a family of fighters, I was the weak one. I was the coward.

In acting, understanding a character's fears is a critical part of understanding his or her psyche. The fears create desires and the desires precipitate actions. These repetitive actions and predictable responses are the building blocks of great cinematic characters.

It's pretty much the same in real life. Something bad happens to us, and we decide we're never going to let that happen again. But in order to prevent it, we have to *be* a certain way. We choose the behaviors that we believe will deliver safety, stability, and love. And we repeat them, over and over again. In the movies, we call it a character; in real life, we call it personality.

How we decide to respond to our fears, *that* is the person we become.

I decided to be funny.

Each of my siblings remembers that night in that bedroom with our mother. Each of us was incredibly scared, but each of us responded differently, in ways that would go on to define who we were for much of our lives.

Harry, despite being only six years old, tried to intervene and protect our mother—he would do so many times over the coming years, sometimes successfully. But that night, Daddio just shoved him away.

My brother intuitively got my mother's lesson about pain: Harry had discovered that untouchable place within himself, that place where you could hit him as much as you wanted, but you could never hurt him. I remember him once yelling at my father, "You'll have to kill me to make me stop."

That same night, my sister Ellen responded by running to her bedroom, curling up on the bed, covering her ears, and crying. Later, she would recall Daddio walking by her room and, hearing her sobbing, coldly asking, "Now what da fuck *you* crying about?"

Ellen withdrew. Not only from Daddio but from the rest of the family. Years later, her withdrawal would result in outright rebellion. She'd stay out all night drinking and smoking and wouldn't even bother to call to say where she was.

If Harry was "fight," Ellen was "flight," and I became a pleaser. Throughout our childhood, my siblings and I judged one another harshly for our different reactions, and those judgments hardened into resentment. Ellen felt like Harry and I didn't support her; Harry felt that, as the older brother, I should have been stronger, I should have done something. And I felt like their responses only inflamed the situations and made it worse for all of us. I wanted everybody to just shut the fuck up and do it my way.

I wanted to please and placate him, because as long as Daddio was laughing and smiling, I believed, *we would be safe.* I was the entertainer in the family. I wanted to keep everything light and fun and joyful. And while this psychological response would later bear artistic and financial fruits, it also meant that my little nine-year-old brain processed Daddio's abusive episodes *as somehow being my fault.*

I *should* have been able to keep my father satisfied. I *should* have been able to protect my mother. I *should* have been able to make the family stable and happy. I *should* have been able to make everything all right.

And it's in this compulsive desire to constantly please others, to keep them laughing and smiling at all times, to redirect all the attention in the room away from the ugly and uncomfortable, toward the joyful and the beautiful—it's there that a true entertainer is born.

But that night, in that bedroom, with me standing there in the doorway, watching my father's fists collide with the woman I loved most in this world, watching as she collapsed on the ground, helpless, I just stood there. Frozen.

I had been scared my whole childhood, but this was the first time I had been aware of my own inaction. I was my mom's oldest son. I was less than ten yards away. I was the only chance she had for help.

Yet, I did nothing.

It was then that my young identity congealed in my mind. It became encased in a hard sediment, an unshakable feeling that no matter what I have done, and no matter how successful I have become, no matter how much money I've made or how many #1 hits I've had or how many box office records I've broken, there is that subtle and silent feeling always pulsating in the back of my mind: that I am a coward; that I have failed; that I am sorry, Mom-Mom, so sorry.

Do you know what happens when two people are in charge? When two people are in charge, everybody dies!

That night, in that bedroom, at only nine years old, watching the destruction of my family as my mother collapsed to the floor—in that moment, I decided. I made a silent promise. To my mother, to my family, to myself:

One day, I would be in charge.

And this would never, *ever* happen again.

TWO

FANTASY

ow, I know y'all were thinkin' I was going to start this book off with, "Iiiiiin West Philadelphia, born and raised . . . ," not with stories of domestic abuse and violence.

I was tempted, I mean, how could I not be? I'm a make-believer. And not just any ol' make-believer, I'm a Legendary, Bad Boy, Man in Black kind of make-believer: I'm a *movie* star. My first impulse is always to clean up the truth in my mind. To make it better. To shine it up a little bit so it doesn't hurt as much. I redesign it and replace it with whatever suits me. Or really, whatever suits *you*: I'm a crowd-pleaser. It's my *actual* job. The "truth" is whatever I decide to make you believe, and I *will* make you believe it: That's what I do.

I'm a master storyteller. I thought about showing you the pretty me, a flawless diamond; a swaggy, unbreakable winner. A fantasy image of a successful human being. I'm *always* tempted to make-believe. I live in an ongoing war with reality.

Of course, there's the red-carpet-walking, fly-car-driving, tight-fade-wearing, box-office-record-breaking, hot-chick-marrying, *I Am Legend*–pull-up-doing, jiggy-ass "Will Smith" . . .

And then there's me. This book is about me.

Iiiiiin West Philadelphia, born and raised
On the playground is where I spent most of my days

Chilling out, maxing, relaxing all cool

I got my ass beat and bullied every day after school . . .

That's how the song *should* have gone. OK . . . I can admit I was a weird kid. Kinda skinny, sorta goofy, with a bizarre taste in clothes. I was also the unfortunate owner of a prominent set of ears that made David Brandon once say that I looked like a trophy.

As I think back, I probably would have made fun of me, too. It didn't help that I liked math and science; they were my favorite subjects in school. I think I like math because it's exact; I like when things add up. Numbers don't play games or have moods or opinions.

And I talked a *lot*—probably too much. But, most important, I had a wild and vivid imagination, a fantasy life that was much broader and lasted way longer than most children. Whereas when most kids just played around with plastic army men, Nerf balls, and toy guns, I would construct elaborate fantasy scenarios and then get lost in them.

When I was about eight or nine, Mom-Mom sent me and Pam to Sayre Morris day camp in Southwest Philadelphia. It was the usual, bargain-basement thing: rec room, swimming pool, arts and crafts. I came home after the first day and ran into the kitchen, where my mom was sitting with our next-door neighbor, Miss Freda.

"Hey, baby, how was camp?" Mom-Mom asked.

"Aw, Mom, I *loved* it. They had this big jazz band with trumpets and violins and singers and drums, and they had one of those horn things that do like this." I mimicked the back-and-forth movement of a trombone.

"And then we had a dance battle, and like fifty people were doing choreographed moves together. . . ."

Miss Freda looked at my mom—*A full jazz band? Fifty choreographed dancers? At a children's summer camp?*

What Miss Freda didn't know was that she was caught in the cross fire of a playful game between my mother and me, one that still goes on even to this day. The rules are, I describe the most colorful, vivid, outlandish scene that I can come up with, which I then superimpose over the reality of my actual experience, and Mom-Mom's job is to determine how much of it is actually true, and in which case, does she need to do something?

My mom paused and came nose to nose with me. Her gaze served as a sort of old-school, mother-wit lie detector, looking for the slightest wobble in my commitment to my story. I didn't flinch.

She'd seen enough.

"Willard, stop playing. There was no jazz band at Sayre day camp."

"No, Mom, I'm telling you—it was *crazy*."

Miss Freda, confused, said, "But, Carolyn, he didn't even know the word for a trombone—he had to have seen it, right?"

"No. He does this mess all the time."

Just then, Pam walked into the kitchen, and my mother said, "Pam, was there a full jazz band, a dance contest, and a trombone at camp today?"

Pam rolled her eyes.

"What? No. It was a *jukebox*, Mom. Will stood there and listened to the jukebox all day—he didn't even get in the pool."

Mom-Mom looked to Miss Freda. "I *told* you."

I burst into laughter—Mom-Mom won this round, but at least I beat Miss Freda.

My imagination is my gift, and when it merges with my work ethic, I can make money rain from the heavens.

My imagination has always been the part of me that Mom-Mom loved the most. (Well, that and when I got good grades.) It's a weird mix of love that she has for me. She loves my silly side, but she needs me to be smart.

At some point in her life, she decided that she was only allowed to talk about important stuff: educational reform, generational wealth, the new misleading national health guidelines. She doesn't "entertain foolishness." Her and Daddio debated *everything*.

"Integration is the worst thing that ever happened to Black folks," Daddio said emphatically.

"You don't believe that, Will—you're just sayin' it to pluck my nerves," Mom-Mom said dismissively.

"Listen to me, Car'lyn! Before integration, we had our own. Black businesses were thriving because niggas had to patronize niggas. The cleaners, the restaurant, the hardware store—everybody needed everybody. As soon as Black folks was allowed to eat at McDonald's, our entire economic infrastructure collapsed."

"So are you suggesting that you'd prefer to be raising these children in slavery, or in Jim Crow?" Mom-Mom said.

"I'm suggestin' that if there was a nigga water fountain, niggas would be gettin' hired to fix it."

Mom-Mom would never say it to Daddio, but she would repeat all the time, "Never argue with a fool, because from a distance, people can't tell who's who." So when she would stop arguing with you, you knew what she thought of your position.

When I say silly stuff, it makes the world *lighter* for her. But she needs me to say smart stuff, too. That makes her feel safe. She thinks that the only way I'll be able to survive is if I'm intelligent. She likes about a sixty-forty ratio of smart to silly. She's the best audience I've ever had. It's like there's some hidden part of her that even she's not aware of that's always egging me on.

Come on, Will, sillier, smarter, sillier, smarter . . .

I like to hit her with stuff that, on the surface, is super silly, and I hide the smart under it to see if she can find it. I like the look on her face when she thinks something is just stupid, and then the smart part sneaks up on her. (That's *my* favorite, too.)

Comedy is an extension of intelligence. It's hard to be really funny if you're not really smart. And laughter is Mom-Mom's medicine. In a way, I'm her little doctor, and the more she laughs, the more silly, smart, spectacular shit I make up.

As a child, I would disappear into my imagination. I could daydream endlessly—there was nothing more entertaining to me than my fantasy worlds. There *was* a jazz band at camp; I *heard* the trumpets; I *saw* the trombone, the zoot suits, the big dance scene. The worlds that my mind created and inhabited were as real to me as "real life," sometimes even more so.

This constant stream of images and colors and ideas and silliness became my safe place. And then, to be able to share that space, to be able to transport someone, became the ultimate bliss. I love the ecstasy of a person's rapt attention, taking them on a roller-coaster ride of their emotions locked in harmony with my fantasy creation.

For me, the border between fantasy and reality has always been thin and transparent, and I've been able to step in and out of each effortlessly.

The problem is one man's fantasy is another man's lie. I developed a reputation in the neighborhood as a compulsive liar. My friends felt like they could never trust what I said.

This is a strange quirk about me and even continues to this day. It's a running joke among my friends and family that you have to dial back my stories two or three notches to know what *actually* happened. Sometimes I'll tell a story and then a friend will look at Jada and say, "OK, so what *really* happened?"

But as a child, what the other kids didn't understand was that I didn't lie about my perceptions, my perceptions lied *to me*. I would get lost; sometimes I would lose track of what was real and what I had made up. It became a defense mechanism—my mind wouldn't even contemplate what was true. I would think, *What do they need to hear to be OK?*

But Mom-Mom got me—she *delighted* in my peculiarities. She made space for me to be as silly and creative as I could be.

For instance, for much of my childhood I had an imaginary friend named Magicker. A lot of kids go through the imaginary-friend phase—usually between four and six years old. Those imaginary friends are amorphous identities that don't really have any shape or personality. The imaginary friend wants whatever the child wants, hates what the child hates, and so on. It's made up to affirm the child's thoughts and feelings.

But Magicker was different; even as I write this book, the memory of Magicker is as vivid and resonant as any of the actual experiences of my childhood. He was a full-blown *person*.

Magicker was a little white boy with red hair, fair skin, and freckles. He always wore a little powder-blue polyester suit, with a fire-engine-red bow tie. His pants rode just a little bit too high, exposing poorly chosen white socks.

Whereas most other children's imaginary friends served as projections and affirmations, Magicker had distinct preferences and opinions about what games we should play and where we should go and what we should do. Sometimes, he would disagree with me; other times, he'd make me go outside when I didn't want to. He had strong ideas about certain types of foods and the character of people in my life. Even as I'm sitting here recalling our relationship, I'm thinking, *Damn it, Magicker, this is* my *imagination!*

Magicker was such a significant presence in my childhood that my mom would sometimes set out a separate plate for him at the dinner table. And if she wasn't making any headway with *me*, she'd talk to Magicker instead.

"OK, Magicker, are you ready to go to bed?"

Fortunately, this was the one thing that Magicker and I always agreed on—we were never ready to go to bed.

A side effect of being lost in a fantasy life was that I had a lot of eccentric ideas about what was fly, fashionable, or funny. For example, I'm not sure how it developed, but I stumbled into an unfortunate but passionate cowboy-boot phase. Man, I *loved* cowboy boots; in fact, I refused to wear anything else on my feet. I'd wear them with sweatsuits; I'd wear them with jeans.

Hell, I even wore them with shorts.

Now, a Black kid in West Philly in cowboy boots might as well just put a bull's-eye on his back. Kids would make fun of me and tease me mercilessly, but I didn't understand *why*. "These boots are *dope*!" And the more they laughed, the deeper my commitment to cowboy boots grew.

I was always a bit of an oddball. Things that felt normal to me could seem strange to others, and things that other people celebrated sometimes didn't inspire me in the least.

Back in the day, Huffy mountain bikes were on fire; every kid wanted one. And one Christmas, all my friends on my block got together and we agreed to ask our parents for Huffy bikes that year. The plan was we would all ride our matching bikes to Merion Park, a small park just far enough outside our neighborhood to feel like we were on an adventure.

Well, Christmas came, and Santa made good on ten brand-new, matching Huffys. Noon rolled around, and everybody was out front.

Everybody, that is, except me.

See, I didn't ask for a Huffy. Huffys were for suckaz! And they were about to witness what a *real* bike looked like. Because while they had all asked for stock, standard, run-of-the-mill Huffy mountain bikes, I ain't no sheep. I had asked for . . . a bright red Raleigh Chopper. Choppers were those low-rider bikes with a big wheel in the back and a tiny one up front, with the handlebars that stuck way up in the air, with the three-speed gear shift and an L-bucket dragster saddle, a.k.a. the banana seat. They were like the Harley-Davidson of kid's bikes. You felt like you were on a *motor*cycle on that thing. It was the undisputed coolest bike on earth.

I couldn't sleep the night before imagining my entrance. I had worked out my big reveal: I would wait for everybody to line up out front, ready to go, but I would come out from the *back* driveway, maintaining the element of surprise. I even planned and practiced what I was gonna say when they saw me on my Chopper. "Whaddup, suckaz, what y'all waiting for? Let's go!" and then I'd just ride past them so they would have to catch up with me: Will Smith, the leader of the pack, the king of the neighborhood.

The moment arrived. I had been watching them from behind the curtains in my living room; I could tell they were all waiting and wondering, *Where's Will at?* And just then I rolled out from the driveway, handlebars scraping the heavens, peddling smoothly in my cowboy boots—that Raleigh Chopper first gear was *butter.*

I was *the man.*

I float on by, all eyes on me. I throw the nod, then hit them with the line: "Whaddup, suckaz, what y'all waitin' for? Let's go!"

It was quiet for a few seconds. I figured I had 'em shook.

Then I was nearly knocked off my Chopper by the roar of laughter that emerged behind me. Teddy Allison literally laid on the ground laughing.

Through his tears he managed to say, "What the *fuck* is that jawn?"

I hit the brakes and turned to scan the rest of the crowd to see if Teddy was just bussin', or if he was speaking for everybody.

"Nigga, are you in a biker gang?" said Danny Brandon. "You can't even see over them handlebars!"

Michael Barr said quietly, "This what happens when you go to white schools."

But it didn't matter what they thought, because to me, I was *hot.* That's one of the things about having an overactive imagination: I could make my mind believe *anything.* I was able to cultivate an almost delusional level of confidence.

And while this somewhat skewed perception of myself would often end in ridicule or getting my ass kicked when I was young, on many occasions throughout my life it served as a superpower. When you are unaware that you shouldn't be able to do something, then you just do it. When my parents told me I couldn't be a rapper because there were no careers in hip-hop, it didn't deter me, because I knew *parents just don't understand*. When television producers asked me if I could act, I said, "Of course," even though I had never acted a day in my life—I thought, *How hard can it be?* When movie studios said they couldn't cast me because African American leads don't sell to international audiences, I wasn't necessarily offended, I just couldn't understand how a mother-fucker *that* wrong could have *this* job. It wasn't just the racism that bothered me, it was the *stupidity*. People would tell me how I was supposed to be, and it just didn't make any sense. I felt like their rules didn't apply to me.

Living in your own little world with your own rules can be an advantage sometimes, but you have to be careful. You can't get *too* detached from reality. Because there are consequences.

My consciousness was an infinite playground that I delighted in exploring.

But when I was a kid, the benefits of my fantastical delusions were still far off in the future, and the consequences were front and center. Tolerance and open-mindedness weren't the most common schoolyard virtues in West Philly. Kids could be cruel. And the more eccentric you are, the less mercy you will be shown.

The playground is a hunting ground where every little boy is testing the limits of his own budding masculinity, attempting to prove himself as stronger and dominant, constantly flexing and challenging other boys, measuring himself against them, and punishing those weaker than himself.

I was skinny and profoundly unathletic. My limbs and my torso had a sadly dysfunctional relationship. In addition, I had an overactive imagination and, from what the other kids could tell, I lied incessantly.

All this meant that I was singled out by the other boys as an easy and justifiable target on which to prove their dominance. I got pushed around, picked last for games, hit, and spit on—you name it, I got it.

One day, when I was probably twelve or thirteen years old, a bunch of us were playing basketball in the schoolyard. I was fresh to death in my bright green shorts and my favorite cowboy boots. In my *mind*, I was Magic Johnson, but on the actual court I was more like a figure skater—cowboy boots don't necessarily provide the requisite grip or ankle support you might otherwise find in a standard basketball shoe.

Basically, I was stumbling all over the place.

At some point, the universal basketball bragging began, everybody trying to demonstrate how they could replicate the moves of their favorite players. One guy shouted out "KAREEM!" as he slung up a sky hook. Another screamed out "BIRD!," throwing up a three. But this was Philadelphia in the early eighties—how dare they disrespect these Philly streets? There's only one name to yell out on these courts: Dr. J, Julius Erving.

So, I said, "Watch out! Here comes the DOC! Move, y'all, I'm about to dunk!"

Matt Brown bust out laughing. "Nigga, you can't dunk."

Granted, I had never dunked before, but as soon as I said it, I believed it. As I made my way back to half court, I licked my fingers and wiped the bottom of my cowboy boots for traction. As I prepared to take a running start, I swear to the Almighty I had no doubt I was about to dunk this ball.

As I stretched my shoulder to prepare for full extension, the guys started throwing out bets.

"I bet you three dollars you can't do it, Will!"

"Bet!" I clapped back. "Get my money ready!"

"I'm in for five!" somebody said.

"I'll take all-a y'all's money! Bring it!"

And I'm agreeing to all of them, because in my mind, this ball is already dunked. The guys all fan out. There's a moment of anticipation;

I steady myself, as the murmuring settles. And then, *boom!* I take off running down the court. I'm seeing the Julius Erving "Rock the Baby" cradle dunk in the 1983 finals sweep against the Lakers. Cowboy boots clomping, feet flailing, I hit my stride. About to take off, I'm up, I'm flying, the cameras are flashing, the crowd is going crazy.

And then . . . silence.

And somehow, I'm falling. Backward? Something has gone wrong.

SLAM!—reality hits with the force of paved asphalt.

I am not Julius Erving.

I am out. Cold.

The bigger the fantasy you live, the more painful the inevitable collision with reality. If you cultivate the fantasy that your marriage will be forever joyful and effortless, then reality is going to pay you back in equal proportion to your delusion. If you live the fantasy that making money will earn you love, then the universe will slap you awake, in the tune of a thousand angry voices.

And if you think you can dunk like Julius Erving in cowboy boots, then gravitational reality will invoke a painful and divinely perfect retribution.

Let's rewind and see what actually happened:

I had clomped my way from half court; all was still going well as I accelerated past the foul line. I took my last dribble; liftoff was smooth—not perfect—but I was airborne. As I ascended, I got just high enough to hit the rim with the ball, completely halting my forward momentum, thereby causing my legs to fly out from under me. (The slang terminology for this particular sporting mishap is "hanging yourself on the rim.") As I think back, the added weight of the cowboy boots may have exacerbated the torque.

I came down hard, directly on the back on my head and neck, knocking myself unconscious.

When I wake up, my friend Omarr is standing over me. I can see the strobing lights of an ambulance, there's blood in my hair, and I have no idea where my left cowboy boot is.

I can hear Omarr's voice.

"He's awake! He's awake!"

Omarr is my oldest friend—well, except for Stacey Brooks. When he was little, he was so pigeon-toed that he'd be tripping himself and falling and scuffin' himself all the time when we were playing. His parents decided that he should have corrective surgery. When he was five, the doctors broke both of his legs and reset them. Omarr had leg braces all summer, but when it was time to go to school, all of a sudden, he was the fastest kid on the block *and* the best dancer. It made us all want the magical surgery!

As my vision slowly sharpens, Omarr's face slips into focus. I can see in his eyes that my fall must have been pretty bad. He isn't laughing; he's scared.

"Yo, man, you alright?"

I do a quick inventory—I can move my hands, my arms, my legs, my feet. Nothing broken. I muster an affirmative nod.

As they strap me to the stretcher and slide me into the ambulance, I catch a final glimpse of Omarr.

"Yo, O! It went in, right?"

Make-believe is a normal part of psychological development. But as we grow up, we start to let go of our fantasy life simply because we discover that living in the *real* world is more valuable to us than clinging to our fantasies. We have to learn how to deal with others, how to succeed at school and at work, how to survive in the material world. And it's hard to do that if you're unable to perceive reality accurately.

As such, we all have to learn to make a distinction between what is real and what is not. In fact, some people make the distinction so well that, as adults, they unfortunately lose the ability to embrace anything other than concrete, material reality.

But, for some reason, I didn't go through this process. Or, perhaps, I *refused* to go through this process. That's because my fantasy life is what protected me from the world. Offered the choice between the infinite playground of my imagination and a reality filled with constant threat, my mind chose fantasy.

We all delude ourselves a little bit around the things that scare us. We're afraid of not being accepted by people at work, or at school, or on Twitter, so we convince ourselves that they're stuck-up or ignorant or cruel. We concoct entire narratives about other people's lives when in fact we have no clue what they're thinking or feeling or struggling with. We invent these stories to protect ourselves. We imagine all sorts of things to be true about ourselves or the world, not because we've seen evidence for it, but because it's the only thing that keeps us from collapsing back into fear.

Sometimes we'd rather blindfold ourselves than take a cold, hard look at the world *exactly* as it is.

The problem is delusion works like poisoned honey—it tastes sweet in the beginning but ultimately ends in sickness and misery. The stories we tell ourselves, which are designed for our protection, are the same stories that create the walls that prevent the very connections we so desperately crave. I told myself that I had a friend named Magicker because it made me feel less alone. But that fantasy was also a part of why I was disconnected from the other kids in the neighborhood. Later in my life, I would invent the fantasy that becoming rich and famous would solve all of the other problems in my life. But the pursuit and maintenance of that fantasy only drove the people I loved further away from me.

As a child, I told myself that if I kept Daddio entertained and made him laugh then he wouldn't hurt my mother. But that fantasy only caused me to feel like a coward, an unworthy son, despite the fact that none of it was my fault.

My fantasy life, while in some ways protecting me, also caused me to feel more guilt and shame and more self-loathing. All fantasies eventually fail. No matter how hard you fight, the truth is undefeated; reality remains the undisputed champ.

Daddio only took one summer vacation in my entire childhood. When your family sells ice, you are trapped at work from the first week of June, when you get out of school, to just after Labor Day, when you go back.

But in the summer of 1976, Daddio decided to take off two months, rent a camper, and drive the family cross-country. There was a family reunion from Gigi's side in Los Angeles. We took the northern route out to LA, and the southern route back to Philly.

I have seen every nook and cranny of the United States of America. We left Philly and headed west to Pittsburgh to see Mom-Mom's childhood home. Her father—we called him Pap Pap—still lived there. He seemed like a really old version of Daddio. Legend had it that Pap Pap would get so angry sometimes that his nose would bleed—and that could be just watching the Steelers.

Next stop, Cleveland, to see Aunt Tootie and Uncle Walt. Then Chicago to the Great Lakes, then on to Minneapolis and the Dakotas. We saw prairie dogs, but I don't know why they call them that. They look like tall hamsters that stand upright—think Timon from *The Lion King*. Harry got a handmade drum from a Sioux tribal leader in South Dakota. He banged that thing all the way through Mount Rushmore, the Devils Tower, and into Yellowstone National Park. We saw Old Faithful—I couldn't believe they could tell you down to the second exactly when it was going to erupt. The ranger would point and then *abracadabra!* Huge jets of boiling water shooting up out of the ground. The smell was nasty—Daddio said it was sulfur (I was glad to find that out because for a second, I thought it was Ellen).

Mom-Mom woke us up at sunrise on the top of a mountain in Wyoming. We were *above* the clouds. *This is what heaven must feel like.* But then we got stuck for an hour because a black bear walked out into the middle of the road and headed straight for our camper. It was a park rule that you had to turn off your vehicle if there was a bear within fifty feet of your vehicle. Daddio slammed the window closed with both hands—it's the only memory I have of him ever being scared of anything.

After about two weeks, Daddio started commenting that this was the longest period in his life that he'd gone without seeing any Black people. (Apart from us, of course—we're Black.) Daddio was suffering from Negro Withdrawal Syndrome, or NWS, but one day at a rest stop in Wyoming, he saw a Black couple driving away, and he chased them and pulled them over just to shake their hands and say hi. They thought it was very funny.

Daddio drove all day to the Craters of the Moon National Monument in Idaho—it looks just like the moon, and you actually *feel* like you're on it. He was exhausted, but Mom-Mom didn't want to be on the moon— she didn't feel comfortable there—so we never checked into the motel, and Mom-Mom drove us south to Salt Lake City. When Daddio woke up, he took us out into the Great Salt Lake. He explained how buoyancy works in salt water versus the fresh water of the Great Lakes; he showed us how easy it is to float. He made ice, so he knew everything about water.

But the most incredible thing I'd ever seen in my young life was the Grand Canyon.

"This entire canyon was carved by water," Mom-Mom said.

I was in total awe, but I was too scared to approach the edge. I remembered Peter Brady on *The Brady Bunch* also being amazed about how water could possibly make this canyon. "Wow!" he said. "No wonder you don't like us to leave the water faucets dripping."

And just when I thought the day couldn't get any better, Harry accidentally dropped his drum into the canyon. It seemed like it fell for about three days. I was so sick of hearing him bang that thing it felt like the heavens had answered my prayers.

This trip expanded and detonated my imagination. Every person we came across seemed like a new and fascinating character; every destination was a dreamland; and I felt like life was just waiting for me to make up the story. The American landscape was so diverse and beautiful—there were mountains and prairies and valleys and white-water rivers and regular deserts and painted deserts and green forests and petrified forests and corn into infinity and sequoias or redwoods—whichever ones we saw—touching the sky, which was filled with sun sometimes and tornadoes in the distance and funny clouds and scary clouds and all the clouds in between.

These were the best eight weeks of my childhood—everybody was happy.

We were the perfect family.

About a block away from Woodcrest, at the end of Graham Street, there was a known sex offender. All the kids in the neighborhood knew about him, and our parents told us to never go anywhere near his house. We rarely saw him—he was like a ghost or an urban legend.

One day, I saw a little girl going up the front steps to his house—he was standing in the open doorway, inviting her in. My heart started pounding in my chest; I thought about calling out to her, but I froze—she was too far away, and I could *see* him. I was terrified.

I ran home, up the steps to my bedroom, and slammed the door. Nobody was supposed to go into that house. That was the Bad Man's house. *Did he see me? Is he coming to get me?*

Needing to get as far away as possible, I hid in the closet, shaking. I could feel Magicker with me.

You have to tell an adult, Will.

"But I can't. What if the man found out it was me? What if he tries to hurt me for telling on him?"

Will, go tell your parents right now.

"I can't I can't I can't."

Will. Go. Right now.

But all I could do was curl up on the floor of the closet and cry.

WILL! GET UP! You have to go tell your parents!

Magicker was angry now. He never got angry.

You have to tell someone! You have to get up, NOW!

I closed my eyes and buried my head in my hands.

"I can't."

Just like I couldn't face my father. Just like I couldn't face the neighborhood bullies. I couldn't even *tell* someone that somebody else was potentially being hurt. What was wrong with me? Why was I always so afraid? Why was I such a coward?

I just laid there, trembling. Ashamed. Weak. Moments passed. I took my hands away from my eyes.

Magicker was gone.

There's a moment when your fantasies recede and you realize that you are still *you*. Imaginary friends or dunking basketballs won't make the fear go away. They may help you forget for a moment, but reality remains undefeated. Fortunately, someone else had seen the girl enter the house and had intervened. But what if they hadn't?

I never saw Magicker again.

THREE

PERFORMANCE

S unday morning at Resurrection Baptist Church and the monotone voice of Reverend Claudis Amaker echoed across old rickety wooden ceilings, raining down the infallible word of God upon us.

My grandmother Gigi (pronounced "Jee-Jee") always dressed up for church. To her, the Sunday presentation of yourself was an intentional act of devotion to the Lord. She wore one of those pristine, floral, church-lady dresses, perfectly accessorized with the church pearls and the church hat with the giant satin flower pinned to it. During the sermons, she'd fan herself, eyes closed, shaking her head in agreement, chiming in, "Preach, Pastor, say it again!" or just a simple "*Mmm-hmmm!*" Every once in a while, she would glance down at me, checking to make sure I was paying attention.

But I was just nine years old. People clapped and swayed and cried and prayed, all the while my nine-year-old mind couldn't help but wonder if this service was ever going to end.

Except every third Sunday when the visiting Reverend Ronald West would take the pulpit.

Reverend Amaker was our *home* pastor, and he would *talk* about the power of God, but all I could hear was the voice of the adults in *Charlie Brown*—"Wah, waaah, wah, wah." Reverend West, though, would *show* you God's power. He wore stylish red CAZAL glasses with a matching three-piece suit, punctuated with the standard bleached-white Baptist pocket hanky—he was six foot three, 210 pounds of God's glory.

And do not let him near your piano, because after Reverend West played it, you could just wheel that thing out to the trash.

Reverend West led the choir. He always started off seated, playing the piano with his left hand, directing the choir with his right, calmly leaning into some slow, Mahalia Jackson–style ballad to warm up the elders.

This was just the calm before the storm.

Slowly, he would transform, allowing the music to carry him into a trance. Tears would fill his eyes, sweat building on his brow, as he rummaged for his hanky to clear the fog from his glasses. The drums, the bass, the voices, all rising at his command, as if imploring the Holy Spirit to show itself. And then, like clockwork, an ecstatic crescendo, and . . . *BOOM!* The Holy Ghost fills the room. Reverend West explodes from his seat, kicking over the stool, both hands possessed, banging in praise on the piano. Then, with a guttural roar, he blazes across the stage to the three-tiered electric organ, demanding that it do what God intended it to do, swirling massive orchestral Baptist chords, all the while sweat flying; the congregation erupting, singing, dancing; old women passing out in the aisles, weeping; Reverend West pointing, directing, never once losing control of the choir and the band . . . until his body would collapse in surrender and gratitude for the merciful bliss of God's love.

As the music settled, Gigi returned to her seat, dabbing tears from her eyes, and my little heart pounding—not even totally sure what that sweet vibration was inside my body—all I could think was *I wanna do THAT. I want to make people feel like THAT.*

Now I lay me down to sleep,
I pray the Lord my soul to keep;
If I should die before I 'wake,
I pray the Lord my soul to take.

It's always been funny to me that the first prayer my grandmother taught me was actually a rap.

Gigi was Jesus's homegirl. I've met many people who say they are religious. But I've never met anyone who lived out Christ's gospel the way my grandmother did. She walked and talked and *embodied* the example of Christ. This was not a Sunday thing for her. It was a 24-7-365 thing. Everything she said, everything she did, everything she *thought*, it was to glorify God.

Gigi worked the graveyard shift at the hospital, which allowed both of my parents to maintain full-time jobs. She watched my siblings and me during the day and worked at night. At the young age of four or five, hearing the phrase "the graveyard shift" filled me with images of ghouls and demons and my superhero grandmother slaying vile creatures just so she could feed me—while I lay in bed, safe and sound, caressing the silken edges of my cream-colored puffed blankie.

I used to beg her, "Please don't go, Gigi! Please stay here with me!" I felt such guilt. My impressionable mind twisted the situation into a sense of personal failure and weakness. I thought, *What kind of kid stays in bed while his grandmother has to fight monsters in a graveyard at midnight?*

It felt as though she was risking her life to protect me. And in some sense, maybe she was—not her *life*, but she was certainly sacrificing a big part of herself for me, my siblings, and my parents.

"One day, I'm gonna take care of you, Gigi," I said.

"Aww, thank you, Lover Boy." That was her nickname for me.

One day we were sitting on Gigi's front porch. She was crocheting a sweater—which at some point I was going to be forced to wear—when a homeless woman walked by. Her clothes were filthy; her face was darkened and haggard, a mix of dirt and sunburn. Her front teeth were missing. And even though she was down on the street, I could smell the pungent reek of urine. I'd never seen a homeless person before. She looked like a witch to me, and I prayed she'd just walk on by.

But Gigi stopped her.

"Excuse me, miss, what's your name?"

I was horrified—I thought, *Gigi, what are you doing? Just let her go!*

This woman was clearly not used to being asked her name, or at least not recently. She seemed to almost have to *remember* it.

After a long pause, as she sized up my grandmother, she said, "Clara."

"Will, this is Miss Clara," Gigi said, as though they were old friends.

With that, Gigi walked down off the porch and put her arm around Clara.

"I'm Helen," Gigi said, and *invited her into the house.*

My mind was furiously flip-flopping between disgust and terror. But it was about to get way worse.

First, they went to the kitchen. Gigi didn't give Miss Clara food that was already prepared in the refrigerator; she cooked her a fresh meal, from scratch. While Clara ate, Gigi handed her a robe, took all of her clothes, and washed and folded them.

"Will?" Gigi called out.

What could she possibly want with me? I thought.

"Yes, Gigi?"

"Go run Miss Clara a bath."

As I think back, this may be the moment where one of my most famous movie catchphrases was born: *OH HELL NAW!* I thought.

I ran the bath.

Gigi then took Miss Clara upstairs, bathed her with her bare hands, brushed her teeth, and washed her hair.

I wanted to scream, *Gigi! Stop touching that dirty lady! She's gonna stank up our bathtub!* But I knew better than to say that.

They were both about the same size, so Gigi took Clara to her closet and began holding up clothes in front of her in the mirror to see which ones would fit.

Miss Clara was gasping with gratitude. Through tears, she kept saying, "This is too much, Helen, way too much. Please stop. I don't deserve this."

But Gigi wasn't having it. She held both of Clara's hands, gently shaking them to get Clara to look into her eyes.

"Jesus loves you, and so do I," Gigi said. That was the end of the discussion.

Gigi didn't make a distinction between your burdens and her own. She truly believed the message of the Gospel. She saw loving and serving others not as a responsibility but as an honor. I never heard her gripe about working the graveyard shift. Never heard her say a negative word about my father, even though he had beaten her daughter. With her Bible in hand, her arms were open not only for us but for everyone. She was joyfully her brothers' and sisters' keeper.

Gigi was the moral compass that has guided my entire life. She was my conduit to God. If *Gigi* was happy with me, that meant that *God* was happy with me; but if she was unhappy, that meant that the universe was displeased. Gigi's approval of me meant that the universe approved of whatever I was doing. In my mind, she had a direct line to God. When she was talking, I felt like I was getting explicit instructions *from God*. So her approval wasn't simply the adoration of a loving, gentle grandmother—her approval was how I would access and harness the power and favor of the Lord.

Gigi personified my understanding of holiness and divinity. To this day, when I ask myself, *What makes a person* good?, my mind immediately pictures my grandmother. When I sat in those hard wooden pews at Resurrection Baptist as a kid, I didn't understand the meaning of the sermons or the intricacies of scripture. But I got Gigi. She lived as Christ taught her to live. She walked the walk. And through her, I saw God's love. I *felt* God's love. And that love gave me a sense of hope. Gigi was light. She illuminated the possibility that life could be beautiful.

When I think back to my childhood, I visualize my father, my mother, and Gigi arranged as a philosophical triangle.

My father was one side of the triangle: discipline. He taught me how to work, how to be relentless. He instilled in me an ethic that "It's better to die than to quit."

My mother: education. She believed that knowledge was the irrevocable key to a successful life. She wanted me to study, to learn, to grow, to cultivate a deep and broad understanding, to either "know what you're talking about or be quiet."

Gigi: love (God). Whereas I tried to please my mother and father so I wouldn't get into trouble, I wanted to please Gigi so that I could bathe in that transcendent ecstasy of divine love.

These three ideas—discipline, education, and love—would fight for my attention throughout the rest of my life.

Gigi was obsessed with this one Broadway play from the 1960s called *Purlie Victorious* that was turned into the musical *Purlie* in 1970. Written by Ossie Davis, it was the story of a Black preacher named Purlie who went down to Georgia, opened a church, and began saving enslaved people from an evil plantation owner. One year, Gigi decided all the kids at church had to perform *Purlie*. We had to learn every word, and every song, front to back. She would have my siblings and me practice in the living room, record player blaring, as we sang and danced along.

Forty years later, I can still sing you every song from *Purlie*.

Gigi was always encouraging me to perform. She was the self-appointed head of special events at Resurrection Baptist Church and organized all of the Easter recitations, nativity reenactments, the Thanksgiving feeding of the poor, holiday talent shows, post-baptism potluck dinners, and on and on—you name it, she planned it. As soon as my brother and sisters and I could talk, Gigi had us up in front of the congregation giving a rendition of some biblical something, for all to see and "enjoy."

Both my parents encouraged music as well. We all took piano lessons as kids because Mom-Mom played. My brother, Harry, blew a saxophone badly for a while, and I took drum lessons briefly in middle school, including a thankfully forgettable stint abusing a snare in the Our Lady of Lourdes marching band. But the piano was the only instrument that actually liked me.

One of the more famous moments on *The Fresh Prince of Bel-Air* was the final scene of the pilot, where after an argument with Uncle Phil, he leaves the room and I sit down on the piano bench. The producers had originally planned on me sitting with my back to the piano so they could push the camera in on my face as I pondered the profundity of Uncle Phil's closing words. But when I sat down, I *faced* the piano, and began playing Mom-Mom's favorite, Beethoven's "Für Elise." James Avery, stunned, stepped back around the corner. The set went silent as everyone realized this show was about to be special. The whole point of the scene had been to never judge a book by its cover. The producers were so inspired by this improvisational moment that they kept it, and it became the defining thematic premise of the entire series.

But my greatest piano performance had come a decade earlier.

I was eleven years old, and Gigi had organized a children's talent show, followed by an Easter-egg hunt in Resurrection Hall. I had been practicing the Morris Albert song "Feelings" as a part of my piano lessons. Gigi had made me play it for her every night for a month. Then she sprung it on me.

"Lover Boy, I want you to play this song for everybody at church on Easter."

At the time, it was the only song I knew how to play, and I had never played the piano in front of anybody except my family.

"Wait, Gigi, no, I can't, I'm not ready," I said. "I'm gonna mess up the notes."

She smiled.

"Aw, baby," she said, gently caressing my cheek, "God doesn't care if you hit the notes right."

Gigi had a magical, invisible power; she would never apply force, yet no one could resist her overwhelming energy.

And so it was that two weeks later I found myself dressed in a cream, pin-striped three-piece Easter suit, sitting at the piano in Resurrection Hall. Gigi beaming in the wings. My hands trembling. Two hundred faces gazing. Silence. Anticipation. My heart pounding out of my chest—it felt like it wanted to leave whether I decided to or not. And Gigi gave me the nod.

I took a deep breath, somehow found an F, and began.

The way the piano was situated onstage, I had eye contact with Gigi the whole time. Morris Albert's "Feelings" was ringing through Resurrection Hall for an audience of two hundred people. But I was only playing for one person. And the look on her face . . . I still struggle to describe it. The words "pride" or "approval" are pale and inadequate. I can only say that I have been chasing that look in the eyes of every woman I've ever loved ever since. I've never felt more certain of someone's adoration. All my career, my performances, my albums—everything—has been a relentless, unbroken quest to relive the delicious purity I felt when I played "Feelings" at Resurrection Hall for my Gigi.

I didn't have to *do* anything different; I didn't have to *be* anything different. In that moment, just as I was, bum notes and all, I was enough.

I began to perform all the time.

Whether I was making up skits for my parents, or reenacting a movie for my friends, or singing songs at church for Gigi, performance became my little secret oasis of love. It gave me the warmth of affection but behind the protection of a mask. It was perfect: I could hide myself *and* be loved at the same time, mitigating the risk of vulnerability but gaining everything.

I was hooked.

But it would take me another forty years before I understood that I had misinterpreted my grandmother's deepest lesson. If I had understood what she was *truly* trying to teach me, this book would end right here. But as you can see, there are nineteen more chapters.

One year, during Christmas Eve services—Resurrection Hall decorated from entry to altar, adorned to a level that even Jesus may have thought was a bit too much—Gigi was peacefully swaying to the choir's soothing rendition of "Blessed Assurance." I watched her rock and hum, and I found myself becoming hypnotized by her tranquility. She was not quite smiling, but the soft rise in the corners of her mouth betrayed an invincible serenity. I would later come to recognize this look as the look that people have when they know things that the rest of us don't.

She caught me staring.

"Yes, Lover Boy?"

"Gigi, why you so happy all the time?" I whispered.

Now she was fully smiling. She paused, like a gardener preparing to sow essential seeds. She leaned over and whispered in my ear, "I trust God. And I am *so* thankful for his grace in my life. I know that every single breath I take is a gift. And it's impossible to be unhappy when you're grateful. He put the sun in the sky, and the moon. He gave me *you*. And our whole family. And for *all* of that, he only gave me one job."

"What's your job, Gigi?"

"To love and care for all his children," she said. "So everywhere I go, I try to make everything I touch better."

Then she reached out and touched the end of my nose.

"Boop. . . . See?"

I've been called "nigger" to my face five or six times in my life—twice by police officers, a couple of times by random strangers, once by a white "friend," but never by anyone who I thought was *smart* or *strong*.

I once heard some of the white kids at school "joke" about "catch a nig-ger, kill a nigger" day, an apparently well-known "holiday" in their neighborhoods. Back in the early 1900s, some of Philly's white commu-nity members would pick a specific day to assault any Black person they saw walking around their neighborhood. Seventy years later, some of my Catholic school classmates still thought it was funny to joke about it. But every encounter I've ever had with overt racism was with people I estimated to be weak enemies at best. They always seemed unintelli-gent, angry, and to me, easily circumvented or defeated. So, consequently, *overt* racism—although dangerous and ever-present as an external threat—never made me feel inferior.

I was raised to believe that I am inherently equipped to handle any problems that may arise in my life, racism included. Some combination of hard work, education, and God would topple any and all obstacles and enemies. The only variable was the level of my commitment to the fight.

But as I grew older, I started to become more aware of the silent, unspoken, and more insidious forms of prejudice lurking around me. I'd get in more trouble for doing the same things my white classmates would do. I got called on less often, and I felt like teachers took me less seriously.

I spent most of my childhood straddling and navigating two cul-tures: my Black world of home and the neighborhood, Resurrection Baptist, and Daddio's shop; and the white world of school, Catholic church, and the prevailing culture of America. I went to an all-Black church, lived on an all-Black street, and grew up playing with mostly other Black kids. But at the same time, I was one of only three Black children attending Our Lady of Lourdes, the local Catholic K–8.

At school, it was impossible to not feel like an outcast. I didn't dress like the white kids. I didn't listen to Led Zeppelin or AC/DC, and I *never* got my head around lacrosse. I simply didn't fit in. But back in the neighborhood, I didn't quite fit in, either. I didn't talk like the other kids or use the slang they did—my mother didn't even allow us to say "ain't" at home. Mom-Mom worked for the school board of Philadelphia, and she was a stickler for words. One day, she heard me yell out to my friends, "Hey, where y'all gon' be at?"

Her head whipped around in disbelief, like that girl from *The Exorcist*. "I hope they're going to be behind that preposition," Mom-Mom said.

At Catholic school, no matter how well-spoken or intelligent, I was still the Black kid. In Wynnefield, no matter how up I was on the latest music or fashion, I was never quite "Black enough." I became one of the first hip-hop artists who was considered "safe" enough for white audiences. But with Black audiences, I was labeled "soft" because I wasn't rapping about hard-core, gangster shit. This racial dynamic is something that has plagued me in various forms throughout my entire life.

But just like at home, performance and humor became my sword and shield. I was your classic class clown, telling jokes, making silly noises, being all-around ridiculous. As long as I was the "funny kid," it meant I wasn't just the "Black kid."

Funny is color-blind; comedy defuses all negativity. It is impossible to be angry, hateful, or violent when you're doubled over laughing.

But I started to notice that a joke that would kill at Our Lady of Lourdes would garner blank stares in Wynnefield—and vice versa. I realized that white people and Black people responded differently to my humor.

My white friends tended to lean into my bigger, broader moments, when I was light and silly and displayed a cartoonlike physicality. One of the white boys in Lourdes once tried to light his fart in the bathroom; I thought that was a little far to get a laugh, but it worked. They also liked puns and word play, witty sarcasm, and they *demanded* a happy ending—everyone had to come out OK.

My Black friends preferred their jokes more real and raw and demanded a gritty slice of truth at the core of the comedy. They saw my silliness as weakness—I would have got the whole shit kicked out of me if I'd tried to light a fart in Wynnefield. They responded better when my humor sprang from strength, from more of a battle mentality—put-downs, insults, disses, and nothing played bigger than smashing some-body who was talking shit. They loved it when someone got what was coming to them—karmic justice—even if the somebody was *them*. As Black people, we love laughing at ourselves. When we can joke about something—our pains, our problems, our tragedies—it makes them just a little bit more bearable.

I learned to move between these two worlds. If I was making the kids on the corner laugh, I wasn't getting my ass kicked. If I was mak-ing the white kids at school laugh, I wasn't a nigger. If I was making Daddio laugh, it meant my family was safe. I began to equate laughter with safety.

The little scientist in my head started searching for what I called "the Number One Answer." "The Number One Answer" is the perfect, mythical joke that obliterates everyone who hears it, no matter their race, creed, color, age, nation of origin, sexual orientation—no one would be safe from the power of this joke. Throughout my career, and quite honestly, my entire life, this has been an obsession for me. I am forever seeking the perfect wording, the perfect tone of voice, the per-fect delivery, the perfect physicality, the perfect *swagginess*, all of which would coalesce into a perfect moment of comedic nirvana and unalloyed human harmony.

But despite my high aspirations, life at Our Lady of Lourdes grew more and more difficult. I've always been reluctant to ascribe the esca-lating issues between myself and the school to racism. The subtle forms of disrespect, the multiple suspensions in seventh and eighth grade, exclusions from parties and school events . . . I've often wondered if it was more about me being Baptist in a Catholic school than being Black in a white world. The school wanted my parents to have me baptized Catholic, but they refused, even though doing so would have meant a 20 percent reduction in the yearly tuition. They knew that Lourdes was so much better academically than the local public schools, so they insisted that I tough it out.

The breaking point came halfway through my eighth-grade year. I played on my middle school football team, and I had proven myself as the top defensive back of the season—seventeen interceptions in ten games.

Each year, the football team would have a banquet where all the players, parents, and the coaches hosted a dinner to honor the team at the end of the season. The kids who won awards were supposed to sit at the front and then walk up onstage and be recognized. Since I had the most interceptions on the team, I was set to receive my trophy: Defensive Player of the Year. But a week before the banquet, I was informed by Sister Agnes that because I had been suspended from school (before the football season had even started), I wouldn't be allowed to sit up front or receive an award onstage. I was disappointed, but I figured that was fair—it was a rule, and everybody knew I won anyway.

But on the night of the banquet, I saw my white friend Ross Dempsey sitting at the front, preparing to receive his trophy, even though we had gotten suspended together.

This injustice *infuriated* me. I leaned over to Mom-Mom and Daddio and told them what was going on. Without a word, they looked at each other, and in a moment of rare but potent agreement, they stood up, and we left.

We drove home that night in silence. A few days later, over dinner, without looking up from his meal, Daddio said, "We're done with that school."

And that was that.

That summer was hot.

Business was booming and cash was flowing, so Daddio treated himself to a Kodak Super 8 home movie camera and projector. This was dope as hell. It had one of those big rubber eye pieces and a little leather strap for your wrist so you didn't drop your whole summer's worth of money off your back patio.

Had Daddio grown up in a different time or place, he definitely would have been an artist. When he was a teenager, one of his school-teachers loaned him a camera and he fell in love with photography. He ran all over North Philly snapping photos and later learned to develop film in a darkroom.

But when it started to consume all of his time and attention, his parents and teachers reminded him that he needed to work and make money. Photography was an expensive hobby. So when he was sent to boarding school, they made him give the camera back. His heart was broken, but Daddio never lost his love for photography.

His new Super 8 camera turned him into one of "those" dads, the kind who, at birthday parties and barbecues, would follow all the kids around filming everything they did, making us smile, do tricks, or be funny. Because the camera didn't have sound, he encouraged us to wildly overexaggerate our movements—Charlie Chaplin–style—to communicate his narrative without words.

Daddio let go behind the camera. When there was work to be done, he was all about order and discipline. But when his camera was rolling, he wanted to see me jumping around and being silly. I ate up the attention—you could not keep me out of his picture frame, even when he was not trying to shoot me. (I invented photobombing.)

After we would shoot, Daddio would rush down into the basement, throw a sheet up on the wall, and carefully feed the delicate reels of film into the projector. Following a series of frustrating snags and mis-fires, the sheet would suddenly light up . . . with us! A road trip here, a birthday party there. These were our family's highlights.

Daddio would sometimes play the guitar, too. Glass of Chivas Regal on the side table, a Tareyton 100 dangling out of his mouth, his eyes squinting from the dancing smoke, he'd pick the chords to Andy Williams's "The Shadow of Your Smile," or attempt some intricate jazz riff that his workingman's hands were just too battered to perfect. He'd pluck, strum, and even sing. It was *always* something romantic; love songs seemed to put him in a good mood. My mom, too.

The music and home movies brought peace to the house. I think our home movies depicted Daddio's dream of a perfect, happy family. And by a strange alchemy, what was true on the screen became true in the basement as we all watched together. In every image we were all smiling, laughing, having fun. There was no fear, no tension, no violence. For those brief moments, Daddio's life imitated his art, as we all smiled and laughed and sang along.

Psychologists have written about how our relationship with our parents in childhood and early adolescence creates our "map" for understanding love in adulthood. When we interact with our parents as children, some behaviors and attitudes win us attention and affection and other behaviors and attitudes cause us to feel abandoned, unsafe, and unloved. The behaviors and attitudes that win us affection often come to define what we understand as love.

Daddio appreciated when I worked hard and performed his directed orders with intensity and precision. He applauded when I was disciplined in laying a perfect brick toward the construction of a perfect wall. Mom-Mom loved when I used my brain—*she* applauded the thinker within me, when my wit and intellect were most on display. My mom is my prototype: patient, brilliant, formidable, nurturing. She'd prefer to do things together, but she's going to be fine with or without you. Mom-Mom can carry it all for a while if you need to take a break.

With Gigi, there was something majestic and empowering about how she loved me. Whenever I performed for her, I felt like I was plugged into the *Force*, like I couldn't lose. She was like the sun to me. If I could just make the world see me the way Gigi saw me when I played "Feelings," then that was it. That was the mountaintop.

The concepts of love and performance became fused in my mind. Love became something earned by saying and doing the right things. In my mind, great performances got you love; bad performances left you abandoned and alone. An exquisite performance secured affection. But if you sucked, you sucked by your damn self.

I performed to placate my father to quell his fouler moods. I performed to distract my family from the growing tension and resentment that was consuming our home. I performed to get the kids in my neighborhood to like me. As such, I began to see happiness for myself and my loved ones as a function of my ability to perform. If I performed well, we would all be safe and happy. If my performance faltered, we were in trouble.

Daddio was at his most loving either behind a camera or projector. Therefore, I always wanted to be in front of his camera, and he always wanted me in front of it. It was one of the few times in my childhood where he and I were perfectly aligned. I loved being in my father's home movies. It brought me closer to him. And that deep craving for his love and approval undoubtedly played a role in my desire to perform on film later on in life.

Throughout my life, I have been haunted by an agonizing sense that I am failing the women I love. Over the years, in my romantic relationships, I would always do too much. Coddling, overprotecting, desperately trying to please them, even when they were totally fine. This insatiable desire to please manifested as an exhausting neediness.

To me, love was a performance, so if you weren't clapping, I was failing. To succeed in love, the ones you care for must constantly applaud. Spoiler alert: This is not a way to have healthy relationships.

When I was thirteen years old, Daddio hit Mom-Mom for the last time. She'd had enough. She went to work the next morning and didn't come home. She didn't go far—just a few blocks to Gigi's house—but the message was clear: She was done. This was the first of only two times in my life that I contemplated suicide. I thought about pills; I knew where a boy had lost his legs on the train tracks; I had seen people cut their wrists in a bathtub on TV. But what kept ringing in my mind was a faint memory of hearing Gigi say that killing yourself was a sin.

Daddio reverted to full military protocols. He was now in absolute command; he was going to do it all. He woke up at four that next morning to prepare breakfast. He was determined to prove that he didn't need Mom-Mom.

By five thirty, the plates were on the table: half an apple, sunny-side eggs, and a slice of scrapple. A pitcher of orange juice and a pitcher of milk. Mom-Mom never did pitchers.

By six, Ellen and I were sitting at the table. Harry knew he was supposed to be down by six. I guess 6:04 was my brother's silent protest. Daddio let it go (he would never have ordinarily let it go; 6:04 would usually have meant no breakfast for Harry). The food had been sitting out for thirty minutes, so the eggs were cold, and the half apple was turning brown. Ellen and I ate quietly.

"The eggs are hard," Harry said.

Daddio seemed to not even hear him; he was washing the dishes. *Start clean, stay clean* was one of Daddio's maxims. He used it for cooking and at work. You clean up as you go along, not leaving one big mess for the end.

Harry's nose turned up at the food.

"The apple is all brown," Harry said.

Please, Harry, just leave him alone. . . .

"And what's this mess?" Harry said, poking the scrapple with his finger.

Without a word, Daddio snatched up Harry from the chair and carried him to the front door, opened it, and deposited Harry outside. He then handed Harry his book bag and slammed the door.

Harry didn't come home that day after school. He went to Gigi's house and moved in with Mom-Mom.

When Harry left, it was just as painful for me as Mom-Mom leaving. I wanted to be with her, too, but I was too scared to leave. It only solidified my deepest insecurity. I could no longer deny the truth: I was a coward.

Mom-Mom lived at Gigi's for three years. We saw Mom-Mom every day. She would bring us lunch, and we would stop by Gigi's, sometimes spend the night. The houses were close enough that we maintained our outward proximity, but on the inside, our family was broken.

It was during this time that I began to escape into television. I found solace and joy in the perfectly crafted family narratives of my favorite sitcoms: *Happy Days*; *Good Times*; *The Brady Bunch*; *Laverne & Shirley*; *Mork & Mindy*—and Jack Tripper on *Three's Company* was the truth. I idealized the families I saw on TV. They were doing exactly what I had been trying to do—they'd have a problem, Mr. Cunningham would be pissed; Richie would be scared; it would look bad for a minute, but then the Fonz would say something funny, bang the jukebox, everybody laughed, and they all lived happily ever after.

Yes. Exactly. It's not that fuckin' hard!

I wanted to be the happy-go-lucky teenager who always got along with his parents. I wanted to have a mother and father who loved each other. I wanted to live with two beautiful girls against Mr. Roper's rules. At a minimum, I felt I deserved a quirky alien who would come down from Ork and solve all my problems.

Instead, I was trapped in chaos.

But my *biggest* obsession as a kid was the television show *Dallas*. The Ewings were a large, wealthy Texas oil family, led by J.R., the iron-willed patriarch. He ruled the Ewing clan much like Daddio ruled the Smiths. Except J.R. Ewing was hella rich. People give you a whole lot more leeway when your family compound has a *name*. That blew my *mind*. Their house had a *name*! "Southfork" was a three-hundred-acre ranch in North Texas. The entire Ewing family—brothers, sisters, parents, grandparents, in-laws, aunts, uncles, nieces, nephews—everybody lived at Southfork. I wanted *my* whole family to live together like that.

I will never forget the scene that changed my life. In retrospect, it was just a small moment: It was a normal sunny day in North Texas. The Ewing family was assembling for the mandatory family meal. They cut to an exterior shot of the palatial mansion, and Sue Ellen, J.R.'s wife, came to breakfast on a *horse*. My young mind would never be the same. She came from *her* house on the property to the *family* house on the property on a *fucking horse*? To me, Southfork was heaven: a property where everybody lives together and my wife could come to breakfast on a fucking horse.

Meanwhile, in the real world, I buried my shortcomings further under layers and layers of performance. I adopted a personality that was indefatigably cheery, upbeat, and positive. I responded to the dissonance of my world by remaining purely constant: I was always smiling. Always fun and ready to laugh. *Nothing wrong in my world.*

One day, I would be in charge, and everything was going to be perfect. *We are going to have a big house on a huge property and everybody's going to live together, and I'll take care of everybody.*

I would be the golden child. My mother's savior. My father's usurper. It was going to be the performance of a lifetime. And over the next forty years, I would never break character. Not once.

POWER

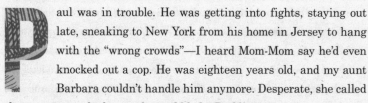aul was in trouble. He was getting into fights, staying out late, sneaking to New York from his home in Jersey to hang with the "wrong crowds"—I heard Mom-Mom say he'd even knocked out a cop. He was eighteen years old, and my aunt Barbara couldn't handle him anymore. Desperate, she called the one person she knew who could help: Daddio.

It had been a few years since any of us had seen my cousin Paul. We all remembered him as a sweet but serious kid. But when he showed up in Philly in the summer of 1983, he was a grown-ass man.

Paul was tall now, his shoulders were broad, and he was *shredded*. This dude was a brick. The knuckles on his hands had scratches and cuts and keloid scars that he clearly did not get from cooking. He sported a *huge* Afro with a Black Power–fist pick stuck in the top. But *his* pick was the special edition that had the peace sign cut out of the wrist/handle. And if that didn't get your attention, Paul also went everywhere with an attack-trained German shepherd named Duke.

Paul had recently achieved his first-degree black belt in kung fu, and proudly walked around West Philly dressed in his gi and kung fu slippers. He was full-on into his militant Black Power phase. He was like the no-bullshit, real-life version of Bruce Leeroy from the movie *The Last Dragon.*

Paul never said much, but when he did speak, he was unfailingly polite—he would karate bow all the time and end every sentence with either a "yes, sir" or "no, ma'am." He stayed to himself, and he didn't bother anybody, but if you fucked with him, and he snapped . . . two words: Scorched. Earth.

By this time, Daddio's business, ACRAC (Air-Conditioning, Refrigeration, Air Compressors) was poppin'. It had expanded and morphed beyond just refrigeration repair. When he would sell his clients new refrigeration equipment, they would often *pay* him just to get the old ones out of their stores. His shop became a sort of graveyard for refrigerators and ice machines. But instead of sending them to the junkyard, Daddio would work day and night to refurbish and rebuild them. Before he knew it, he had the capacity to produce thousands of pounds of ice each day from machines that had been thrown away as trash. And just like that, our family was now in the cubed-ice business, manufacturing, packaging, and delivering bags of ice throughout Philadelphia, into Jersey, and even as far as Delaware.

The problem was that bagging thousands of pounds of ice each day required labor. A *lot* of labor. And because ice is cheap, you need the labor to be cheap. It started with me and Harry and Ellen and both my sisters Pam, and then all of our friends. And then Daddio started recruiting extended family and all of *their* friends. Child labor laws were very different back in the day, so pretty soon, every kid in the neighborhood was bagging ice. ACRAC was the way kids stayed off the street and made a little money for the summer. Daddio had become a kind of kid whisperer in Wynnefield. Because he was so military-minded, he was instilling structure and discipline to the level that most of these kids had never experienced. And he paid cash! If a kid was late, he sent them home. If someone cursed or fought, they were out. The kids' parents loved it—their kids were earning cash money and learning respect and discipline. Daddio was in his lane.

So, when Paul started getting in trouble, my aunt Barbara shipped him to Philly hoping that the structure (and cash) of Daddio's ice house would change his life's trajectory.

But it was *my* trajectory that would end up being forever changed.

Paul moved in with us in late May, just in time for the summer ice rush. He had me walk him around the neighborhood. I showed him where Mr. Bryant's was, and I introduced him to my friends—I was showing off my cool-ass cousin. Paul loved hanging with me—he thought I was *hilarious*. He started showing me how to connect with Duke, and even shared the secret attack commands—which were in *German* (a German shepherd, trained *in German*—I thought that was hot). And best of all, he was teaching me kung fu. That summer, he became a kind of big brother that I never had.

Daddio ran ACRAC the same way he ran our house: as a commander. He would yell and rant and curse; we'd all be terrified, walking on eggshells, hoping he wouldn't explode. But Paul was the first person I ever met who wasn't bothered in the least by Daddio's anger or outbursts. When Daddio would flip, Paul would get totally calm and still, never taking his eyes off Daddio. Paul's body language was very clear: *You can say anything you want, old man, as long as you say it over there. But if you come over here, two words . . . Scorched. Earth.*

I was amazed—Paul and Daddio got along perfectly. The idea that someone could be confronted by the Daddio ogre, stand in the storm of his rage and fury . . . and disarm him with nothing more than a look and a laugh? I had never experienced that kind of power. Paul's martial arts training allowed him to submit to Daddio's authority. He respected him, but he was not afraid of him, because deep down inside, Paul knew that if he needed to, he could kill him.

And Daddio knew that, too.

For the first time in my childhood, Paul made me feel safe in my own home. He was powerful. If Paul was around, no one would mess with me. Not the neighborhood kids. Not the white boys from school. Not even Daddio.

And just when I thought it was impossible for my cousin to get any cooler, he unlocked the world of hip-hop.

Back then, hip-hop wasn't what it is now. There had been a couple of hits, but for the most part it was still underground. There were no albums or singles, no radio play, no videos—you had to know somebody who knew somebody who could get you a cassette tape of one of the live performances exploding from the epicenter: New York City. People would literally go stand in the audience at a party and hold up a boom box over their heads to record the performers. That's how mixtapes were created—people physically going to a party and holding a big-ass radio up in the air for an hour, two hours, then making copies of the tape and giving them to their friends. People in New York would cut a tape of some of their favorite hip-hop artists, make a copy, then take it to their friend in Boston, mail one to their brother in LA, or play one for their little cousin in Philly. These tapes got traded, sold, copied, and traded again. This hand-to-hand exchange across the country was what drove the rocket-fueled expansion of hip-hop. It was grassroots. It was viral before anyone knew what "going viral" was. It was straight from the street to the heart.

Back in the 1970s in New York City, Black communities would throw block parties. They'd shut down their block, and a DJ—short for "disc jockey"—would bring out a turntable and a box of records and play on the street for everybody to dance. Given that this was the 1970s, most of what they played was funk and disco music.

The songs in both funk and disco always featured instrumental sections somewhere in the middle. The song would be jammin' along, and then it would begin to rise, until it reached a soaring crescendo with every instrument at full blast, and then *BOOM!* Nothing but the drummer. This became known as the "break." Break beats were designed to have a little extra *spladow* to 'em. The break was the time for performers like James Brown to show off their dance moves, but as it turned out, the breaks became the hottest part of the song and always set the party on fire.

Because everybody loved dancing to the breaks so much, one day at a block party in the Bronx, a guy named DJ Kool Herc came up with the idea to bring out *two* turntables and have *two* of the same record. That way, he could switch back and forth between them, playing only the break, and keeping it going indefinitely. Two turntables and a mixer also meant that he could blast between James Brown and the Winstons and back to Brown then to Sly and the Family Stone—from break to break to break, only playing the favorite ten seconds of everybody's favorite records. This created a frenzied, new-style dance party. And modern DJing was born.

Because the DJ now had two turntables and a mixer, another innovation emerged: scratching. Scratching was done by moving a record back and forth, creating a wild new sound in music. One of the records could be scratched while the other played the break. The record being scratched would then be released, perfectly on beat, and then the process was flipped so that the break could continue for as long the people wanted to hear it.

And the only thing that was missing from the equation to make it hip-hop was rapping.

DJs now had two turntables and twice as many records. The demands of the craft consumed more and more of their attention, preventing them from being able to interact with the crowd as much as they used to. So they started bringing their brother or one of their friends along to be on the mic to engage with the crowd. These "masters of ceremonies" would talk to the audience, hype 'em up, brag about the DJ, and generally entertain the audience: "Ladies, lemme hear ya!" "Who got a hundred dollars in they pocket?" "Where Brooklyn at?"

Eventually, the most creative MCs started to talk in rhymes to the rhythm of the break beats—a flavor imported from Jamaican immigrants known as "rapping."

The block parties began to *blaze*. Especially when the rhymes were clever, funny, poetic, or, best of all, when they shouted out your neighborhood.

The equation was now complete: DJing + MCing = Hip-Hop.

And the world was *not* ready.

Paul's "troublesome" escapes to New York City had given him access to *all* the mixtapes. He knew people who were down with a crew called "the Zulu Nation," an early collective of hard-core hip-hop enthusiasts based out of the New York/New Jersey area. He could get me any tape: Grandmaster Flash; Melle Mel and the Furious Five; the Treacherous Three; Kool Moe Dee battling Busy Bee Starski; and my all-time favorite, Grandmaster Caz and the Cold Crush Brothers.

Grandmaster Caz was single-handedly, undeniably, the greatest influence of my hip-hop life. He was the prototype for the Fresh Prince. He was one of hip-hop's first storytellers. Caz was witty, he was clever, his verses took you on a journey; you'd be on the edge of your seat listening to him rap, always wondering what was gonna happen next. And most of all, my dude knew how to land a punch line. I wanted to be just like Caz. In fact, my first hit single, "Girls Ain't Nothing But Trouble," was inspired by—wait, no, *influenced* by . . . OK, basically, I studied every single line of a Grandmaster Caz mixtape freestyle called "Yvette" and then wrote my own version of his story. I guess why I connected to him so much was that I had had a similar experience to what he describes in "Yvette," but it never dawned on me to write a rhyme about it. In a way, Caz validated and unleashed a creative part of me that I never thought anybody would care about. He made it OK to be me.

It was a long time ago, but I'll never forget
I got caught in the bed with this girl named Yvette
I was scared like hell, but I got away
That's why I'm here talking to you today . . .
I was outside of my school, shootin' up the rock
A crowd of people gathered round listenin' to my box
It was me, the L, the A, and the Al'
And then I slipped away to make a phone call
And to this very day it was a move I regret
But I didn't know it then, so I called Yvette.

GRANDMASTER CAZ, "YVETTE"

There's probably no need to point out the similarities, but to gild the proverbial lily: I always loved that Caz was on a *basketball* court when he makes the call to Yvette. So in the theme song for *The Fresh Prince of Bel-Air*, I put my character on a basketball court, too—a quiet homage to the legend.

I'm not exactly sure when I became "a rapper." Back then, hip-hop wasn't something we *did*—it was what we *were*. Hip-hop was not just our music—it was dance; it was fashion, street art, politics, social justice. It was everything; it was life; it was us. Outsiders didn't see it as a legitimate genre of music to pursue and perfect, but we weren't even thinking about it in those terms. It was something new, fresh, fun, and exciting that was growing around us and within us. None of us thought it was going to blow up and dominate the world like it does today, and if someone had asked, "Where do you think hip-hop will be in forty years?," I probably *wouldn't* have said, "Oh, it'll be one of the most impactful forms of music in the history of humankind." We simply loved what we were doing, so we kept doing it.

I still remember the first rhyme I ever wrote; I was twelve years old:

At the age of one, I had just begun, on my journey to the T-O-P.
And at age two, everybody knew, that I was a hellafied [huh] MC.
At age three, any sure shot could see, I was a bona fide lover at heart.
I got an IQ of 142 and, like my name, I'm a work of art.

Fortunately, I got better. With Paul's tapes and encouragement, I became obsessed. I was already an incessant talker and performer. But now I was walking around *all day*, quietly babbling and rapping to myself, constructing new rhymes, reciting my favorite verses, trying to freestyle on whatever was going on around me. I went out and bought one of those black-and-white speckled composition notebooks and started writing down my rhymes and practicing them in my room in the mirror.

My fantasy-driven mind would splash all over those pages, sometimes even surprising me by what came out. My creative river was raging. Rapping was the most natural thing in the world to me.

And from the cocoon of a bullied, awkward kid, emerged a natural-born killer MC.

Overbrook High School was located less than a mile away from Our Lady of Lourdes. But it may as well have been on another planet. The environments could not have been more different. Whereas Lourdes bordered the wealthy white neighborhood of Lower Merion, Overbrook was the center of a section called Hilltop, which anchored the poorer Black neighborhoods of West Philadelphia.

Our Lady of Lourdes was a small, intimate Catholic school with only a few dozen kids per grade, most of them white. I had been one of only three or four Black kids in the entire place.

But Overbrook was nicknamed "the Castle on the Hill." It was gigantic, an absolute monster of a structure. Built in 1924, back when they used *real* materials to build buildings, it spanned two square city blocks and loomed over the neighborhood like a stone fortress. You had to ascend a mountain of thirty stairs just to make it from the sidewalk to the front door, and if you survived the climb, what you found inside was nearly twelve hundred students, 99 percent of them Black.

Swarms of kids buzzed through the city-block-long hallways. At Lourdes, everyone had known who I was, but when I walked into Overbrook on my first day, I was completely anonymous.

I was intimidated and terrified. As I look back with today's understanding, I was probably on the edge of a panic attack. My heart was racing, my hands were shaking, but by this time I had developed an infallible strategy for coping with my fear: performance. If I could get them laughing and smiling, then I would feel safe.

I'm still not exactly sure why I did what I did that first day. It was a reflex, some bizarre automatic defense mechanism, as though my emotional immune system had kicked in and took control of my mouth.

I was talking before I knew what I was going to say, and thereby started my high school career with maybe the stupidest thing I had done in my life up until that point.

Just before 8:00 a.m., EST, a couple hundred kids gathered in the sprawling cafeteria for orientation. We were the new kids, there to get acclimated, to get our class assignments, and to be officially welcomed to Overbrook High School. As I entered the cafeteria, the mounting pressure of my anxiety finally became too much. I put my hands up into the air and shouted:

"'Scuse me, 'scuse me, may I have everybody's attention please?"

The room quieted; two hundred students all turned and looked—at *me*.

"He's here," I said, pointing to myself. "Y'all can relax, because he's here. . . . You're welcome. Go 'head back to what y'all doin'. . . . I'll be here if y'all need me."

There was a strange silence—clearly, this was an educational first for most of the kids. A couple of them chuckled, then most just went back to doing what they had been doing before they were so bizarrely interrupted. I'm not sure what response I had hoped for from the crowd, but the outburst had at least purged most of my anxiety and tension.

As I ventured deeper into the room, I slid past a dude who had clearly not been impressed by my announcement. Without looking up, he said, "Man, don't nobody give a *fuck* that you here."

Without missing a beat, I leaned down to him and said, "'Ey, just gimme ten minutes, your *girl* gon' care."

Ooooohhhh! The voices around us rang out; there were even a couple claps.

The kid looked at me for a second but didn't say a word. He gave this stiff-chinned nod—not a nod of agreement—but a nod of *A'ight, so that's how it's gonna be.*

I moved on victoriously, thinking, *Maybe this high school thing ain't gon' be so bad.* At 8:31, orientation was complete, and the students were all released into the Overbrook halls to juke and fumble and stumble around until we located our homeroom classes.

My homeroom was 315, and as I was rounding the stairs between the second and third floors, I saw the dude from the lunchroom out of the corner of my eye, sneaking up behind me. Then there was a blue flash, a sharp pain to the right side of my head . . . and then nothing.

The next thing I remember is the taste of blood, then a clamor of voices, my top lip is swollen, and my front teeth are loose, and I have the worst headache I've ever had. This guy had taken one of those old-school combination locks—the kind that everybody used for their lockers. He'd put the lock in the palm of his hand and the steel loop over his middle finger, creating a makeshift form of brass knuckles. As he passed, he cracked me on the right side of my head with the lock. I went down instantly; as I fell, I hit my mouth on the stairs. Blood everywhere, kids screaming, teachers running, everybody trying to figure out if I had died or not.

The lights in the principal's office are killing my eyes. I'm holding a towel over my mouth as Daddio walks in. Pretty soon, the police are there, and I mumble through my recollection. Daddio is furious; the police are talking to the principal about pressing charges. In my haze, all I can think is *Wait, wait, everybody slow down. This is all happening too fast.*

I just wanted to hit pause and then rewind. I wanted a do-over. I didn't want to be here; I didn't want any of this to be the truth.

"Come on," Daddio says, "let's go."

He stands me up.

The hallways are empty now. Daddio feels like a lion that can't find anything to kill. We exit the side door. I'd only been at Overbrook for an hour and a half. It's weird to be out of school in the middle of the day. The Sugar Bowl convenience store is across the street. I wanted a water ice and a pretzel. It just seemed like Daddio wasn't in the mood, so I didn't ask.

As we drove away, I saw the kid being led in handcuffs from his first day of high school and discarded into the back of a paddy wagon. He was later expelled, and I never even knew his name.

Night. The moonlight glints off my swollen, Vaseline-caked lips. The first moment of solace in a day of complete and utter insanity. As I lay in my bed (on my left side), I wonder, *What the hell happened? How did I get here?*

Just then, Gigi came in to check on me. She changed out my ice pack, plumped up my pillow, and reset the bandage on my head. I gotta say, it's not too bad having a nurse for a grandmother.

I told her the whole story. She didn't lecture or scold. She simply said, "You know, if you stopped talking so much, maybe you could see some of those hits coming."

Then she kissed me and went on her way.

I couldn't stop thinking about Gigi's words. She was right—I *was* always talking, always joking—I never shut up. I talked not because I had anything particularly important to say, but because I was afraid. It began to dawn on me that my overcompensation and fake bravado were really just another, more insidious, manifestation of the coward.

My thoughts were swirling. My mind drifted to the time when Gigi found my first rap book.

Like most young kids emulating their hip-hop idols, I had been writing verses full of curse words and slick, slangy vulgarities, and I had accidentally left my book out in the kitchen.

Gigi found it and read it. She never said anything to me, but she wrote me a note on the inside front cover.

> *Dear Willard,*
>
> *Truly intelligent people do not have to use language like this to express themselves. God has blessed you with the gift of words. Be sure you are using your gifts to uplift others. Please show the world that you are as intelligent as we think you are.*
>
> *Love,*
> *Gigi*

Lying in my bed, I was overcome with shame. Had I used my words to uplift others? I thought about this kid sitting in a jail cell somewhere— *What is* his *grandmother doing right now?* He had potentially thrown his whole life away, a demise maybe not caused but certainly provoked by my words. I knew for certain I didn't want to be *that* kinda person.

But my shame slowly began to give way to a staggering realization of the power of words. I knew that I had unconsciously caused my whole day—I didn't know exactly how, but I knew for damn sure I had done it. I sensed for the first time that I *wasn't* weak; in fact, I was *infinitely* powerful—I just had no control over it. My imagination was running wild with the possibilities. God had indeed blessed me with the gift of words. And that night, I was getting my first glimpse of the power of those words to alter and shape my reality.

And then I asked myself, *If I have this much power, shouldn't I use it for good?* Words can affect how people view themselves, how they treat each other, how they navigate the world. Words can build people up, or they can tear them down. I decided that night that I wanted to use my words to empower others, to help rather than hurt.

I never cursed again in my rhymes. And I got criticized and smashed for years for that choice. But there was no peer pressure that even came close to overriding Gigi pressure.

Those first months of high school were a little rocky, but I was certainly no longer anonymous. And in the same way that the power of my words had almost destroyed me, I was now starting to see their power painting my dreams.

By the middle of that school year, hip-hop had really started to bubble in Philly, and now everyone had their own cousin Paul—somebody they knew in New York who could get them mixtapes. The success of "Rapper's Delight" by the Sugarhill Gang was putting major dents into mainstream barriers. Everybody was listening to that song all the time.

Walking the halls of Overbrook that year was like walking through a hip-hop battleground. Hip-hop may not have been on TV, it may not have been on the radio, but at Overbrook High, everybody was rapping. Nobody knew it yet, but I had been writing rhymes every day for the past eight months. I had pages and pages of different concepts and punch lines and stories. I started to keep a stash memorized and ready to go. I would walk up on groups of kids rapping and join in, and I slowly started to develop a reputation as a pretty good rapper.

The new thing was freestylin'. Somebody would beatbox with their mouth and then the rapper would improvise in the moment about whatever was around them—some kid's funny shoes, the test you failed in math class, the girl you liked, whatever.

This was always my biggest strength. I had been cracking jokes my entire life. Now all I had to do was make them rhyme and people were flippin'.

The best beatboxer in the whole school was a guy named Clarence Holmes—everybody called him Clate. Not only could he generate the most bass, but he could mimic the actual sounds of popular breakbeats. And on top of *that*, Clate could do sound effects—he could make a bird noise in the hallway that was so realistic people would be turning around to see who let a bird in here. I soon realized that every time Clate beatboxed for me, he always made me sound better. I started seeking him out every day after class. I'd roll up and hit him with our standard greeting: "'Sup, C, you ready to rock?"

"You know what it is," he'd say.

Clate was always ready to rock. *Always.* So much so that we all started callin' him "Ready Rock C."

Pretty soon, what started out as just casual freestyle sessions—rhymin' and flowin' and trying to one-up each other—morphed into what became known as battles. I would step up and do a verse, then the other kid would try to one-up me. Maybe he'd make fun of my hair or my clothes. Then, when his verse finished, I had to step back in and freestyle a response. The judge of who "won" was determined mainly by who got the biggest laugh or cheer from the crowd. If you won the crowd, you won the battle.

I was *invincible*—two words: Scorched. Earth.

There were some guys who were cleverer than me, who had tighter flows or better voices, or more developed poetic sense. But *nobody* was as funny as me. Nobody could rock the crowd with a punch line the way I did. What nobody seemed to ever understand was that you *can't beat funny.* You can spit all the tough gangster shit you want—you can rip rhymes about all the money and women in the world—but if your pants are just a little bit too far above your shoes, and somebody says,

Look at you, homey, pretendin' you all fly
looks like your shoes went to a party and your pants *got high*

and forty people laugh? You're done. It's over.

Rapping changed everything for me. For the first time in my life, I was popular. I was getting attention and respect. Ready Rock and I were from Wynnefield, but Overbrook was in Hilltop. Many times, in these battles, we'd be reppin' for Wynnefield. So a lot of the same neighborhood guys who used to pick on me and make fun of me were now getting hyped when *I* showed up. I was making new friends; girls were starting to feel me. Ready Rock and I became inseparable.

The other reason I never lost a rap battle was because I had been raised in the house of Daddio, molded and chiseled by his unrelenting work ethic. I practiced incessantly. Unlike the other kids, who were starting to smoke weed and cut class, I spent hours and hours filling notebooks with rhymes every day. I'd stand in the mirror and practice my verses, making sure my face and my body language were perfectly matched to reinforce and punctuate the punch lines. I was tightening my delivery and trying to deepen my tone. Every break between class, and before and after school, I was always looking for some sucker who was slippin'. I'd battle anybody—in the lunchroom, in the parking lot, at the Tustin Playground or the Beeber schoolyard. In class, I started having fun with my teachers, rhyming answers back when they called on me. I'd rhyme to my parents. I'd answer the phone in rhymes. A lot of adults pretended they hated it, but I knew they loved it.

The combination of hip-hop and humor made me untouchable. I had found my voice. I was choosing my words poetically and comedically. And now, for the first time, I was experiencing a surge of power over my own life. My teachers loved me. I'd be late for a class or miss my homework or get caught being silly in the back of the room. They couldn't yell at me because they were laughing.

I started noticing that I was never getting in trouble. One of my favorite teachers was Miss Brown. She taught algebra II, elementary functions, and trig. She had flawless, chocolate skin and big, steady brown eyes. Her body was just under five feet tall, but she was six eight on the inside. She knew exactly what I was doing. By this point, I was at least a foot taller than her, and when I would do something that she needed to check me for, she'd walk right up into my chest and say, "Come down here so I can talk to you."

Learning is really easy when you can feel that your teachers love you. Miss Brown began to jokingly call me "Prince Charming." She'd sarcastically say things like, "Oh, look, Prince Charming has graced us with his homework this Monday morning. How kind of him."

The kids would laugh, and I would eat it up. As long as everybody's laughing, I'm good.

Back in the eighties, the word "fresh" was the new hip-hop slang. Everybody was sayin' it every other word—like "fly" in the seventies, or "dope" in the nineties; in the eighties, if something was hot, you'd say, "Man, that's fresh." One day I came running into Miss Brown's class literally only forty-five seconds after the bell, and, looking at her watch, she said, "His Highness, the Prince, two minutes late . . ."

I quickly corrected her.

"Nah, Miss Brown, we both know I am barely thirty seconds late. And if you don't mind, thenceforth and hitherto do I demand to be known as the *Fresh* Prince." The classroom burst out laughing.

The name stuck.

In order to feel confident and secure, you need to have something to feel confident and secure *about*. We all want to feel good about ourselves, but many of us don't recognize how much work that *actually* takes.

Internal power and confidence are born of insight and proficiency. When you understand something, or you're good at something, you feel strong, and it makes you feel like you have something to offer. When you have adequately cultivated your unique skills and gifts, then you're excited about approaching and interacting with the world. And what I learned from Paul was that being good at something allows you to be calm in a storm, knowing that you can handle whatever comes. There is a great Bruce Lee quote that resonates with me. One of Lee's students once asked him, "Master, you constantly speak to us of *peace*, yet every day you train us to *fight*. How do you reconcile these conflicting ideas?" And Bruce Lee responded, "It is better to be a warrior in a garden, than a gardener in a war."

Rapping didn't just win me the approval I desperately craved from my peers; it gave me a sense of power. But I knew it was fleeting; it demanded my constant attention and nurturing. I knew I was good, but I also knew that I had to work.

It wasn't going to just *come* to me. I had to go get it.

I kept seeing her in the hallways—I'd even had a dream about her—but we were from two different cliques. I was rappin' now, so I was rollin' with the cool kids, but she wore big-ass glasses, and her and all of her friends were in the art program and lugged around those big-ass portfolio bags.

But Melanie Parker was beautiful. She noticed me soon after the unfortunate lock incident. She was a mochaccino-flavored cutie—she had that sort of goofy-gorgeous-genius thing, a beguiling mixture of insecurity and quirkiness surrounding a simmering core of artistic brilliance.

We had been sniffin' around each other for a few weeks, and I could tell she was far too much of a lady to speak first. She had gorgeous mahogany eyes, and a springtime smile that I would come to understand was painted on top of hidden layers of sadness. Melanie was a broken angel, and from the moment I saw her, I wanted nothing more than to take care of her.

So, I pressed up on her.

"Wassup, cutie. I'm the Prince," I said.

She smiled politely, and said, "What does your *mother* call you?"

I was thinking, *Damn—my mother calls me by my government name.*

"Well, she calls me Willard," I said, "but you can call me—"

"Willard," she interrupted. "Nice to meet you, *Willard*. I'm Melanie."

She never called me *Will*, she never called me *Prince*—she called me *asshole* once or twice. But to this day, she calls me Willard.

"Look, that's a big-ass art bag," I said. "May I carry it for you to your next class?"

Melanie paused; I sensed that she already liked me, but she felt like she had to make it difficult. She handed me the bag without a word and walked off to class. I followed her, already completely in love. When we reached her classroom, I handed her the bag.

"I think you should let me carry it home for you, too, this afternoon," I said. "You should rest your art muscles."

I would walk Melanie home from Overbrook every day. She took easily to wonder and awe—everything was interesting to her. She was one of those people who could stop and look at a tree for ten minutes. Melanie lived in the opposite direction from Woodcrest, so I'd walk ten minutes to her house—carrying her big-ass portfolio all the way—then twenty minutes back to mine, thinking about those eyes all the way home.

Melanie was born and raised in Minneapolis. Her household was filled with violence to a tragic extreme: Her mother ended up killing her father and went to prison for it. Her mother incarcerated, Melanie moved to Philly to live with her aunt, a strict Muslim who opened her home to her niece but who maintained very strong opinions about how a teenage girl should behave.

I never quite got the whole story, but on one occasion, Melanie and her aunt had a very serious disagreement about something, which esca-lated to the point that her aunt threw Melanie out of the house. Legally, without a place to stay, Melanie could have been sent back to Minneap-olis and placed into foster care. I was panic-stricken. I told Mom-Mom the whole story and begged her to let Melanie stay with us.

"Mom, it will only be for a little while," I said. "I'll get a job, do what-ever I have to do to get a bunch of money, and me and Melanie will get our own place. I love her, Mommy. Please can she stay with us till I can figure it out?"

Mom-Mom's eyes welled, her tears a complex emotional mixture. On the one hand, this was *exactly* the kind of son she had hoped to raise—loving, responsible, committed. But on the other hand, she knew from personal experience the fragile realities of young love.

"Oh, hell no!" Daddio said. "Car'lyn, you know exactly what they gon' be doin'."

But I had already promised my mother: "No sex." Melanie would stay in the basement; I would sleep in my room two floors up. It was only temporary. Daddio protested, but Mom-Mom won this one.

I'm still not exactly sure why I did what I did that night. To this day, I have no idea what I was thinking. Of all the experiences I am sharing in this book, this is the individual moment of personal behavior that makes the least sense to me.

Before I reveal what happened, I would like to preface my remarks by making it unequivocally clear that I was *deeply* and *totally* in love with Melanie Parker. We were going to be married; we were going to have four beautiful mochaccino-flavored children; and our union would live alongside the epic tales of romance: Romeo and Juliet, Tristan and Iseult, Tupac and Janet, even Eddie and Halle in *Boomerang*.

But at 4:00 a.m., less than three months into our star-crossed love affair, Mom-Mom should have been asleep but tragically decided she wanted a cup of coffee. And wearing slippers far too quiet to defend her delicate sensibilities, she approached the threshold of the family kitchen. Still innocent, she flipped the light switch as she had done tens of thousands of times before. But this time, her eyes landed upon her eldest son and his girlfriend deep in the throes of reckless lovemaking. As a teenager, outside of physical injury, you can*not* feel worse than having your mother catch you and your girlfriend doggy-style on her kitchen floor.

"OH, *WILLARD*!" Mom-Mom growled, slapping the lights off. Stomping furiously up the stairs, the slamming of her bedroom door functioned as a disastrous exclamation point.

Now she wants to make noise!

By the grace of God, those few days at Woodcrest allowed Melanie's aunt to calm down and let her move back in. I was only sixteen, but I was all in—I was determined more than ever to get us our own place so Melanie and I could build a life together.

I had gotten my driver's permit just before my sixteenth birthday. Ready Rock and I loved to drive around West Philly after school every day, looking for people to battle. They were pretty easy to find back then. It would be a bunch of dudes standing on a corner in a circle, one of them with their hands cupped around their mouth, bopping their head back and forth—the universal human beatboxing posture.

We'd pull the car over, step out, strike the B-boys' stance, and it was *on*. It didn't take but a minute for me to start schoolin' fools. I'm dropping punch lines, people waving and screaming—"AWWWWW SHIT! YOU HEAR WHAT HE SAID?" The smart guys just quit when they realized I had won the crowd, because once the crowd is against you, anything you say just makes you look stupider. But some suckaz didn't—they would try to keep going, and then two words: Scorched. Earth.

By my junior year, I had developed a reputation around West Philly.

I joined a crew of slightly older guys—we called ourselves "the Hypnotic MCs." The design of the group was based on Grandmaster Caz and the Cold Crush Brothers: We had a DJ and four MCs. DJ Groove on the tables; Jamie Fresh; Sheihkie-D; my friend Mark Forrest, a.k.a. the Lord Supreme; and me, the Fresh Prince. (Ready Rock would pop in and out, but he wasn't really feeling these dudes.)

I took my role in the Hypnotic MCs very seriously. I attacked it with the discipline Daddio had instilled in me. But back then, I hadn't learned yet that most people didn't have the same work ethic as me.

I wanted to rehearse every day, on a specific schedule. They were looking at it more casually. Sometimes they would show up late to rehearsal, and other times not at all. I wanted us to perform at all the block parties and pool our money to buy equipment, pass out flyers to advertise ourselves, create our own cassettes. Because I was the youngest, they always kind of laughed at me and dismissed my ideas. I did finally convince everybody to put up $200 a piece so we could purchase the brand-new SP-12 sampling beatbox. I dug in for a few weeks at the ice house and came up with my share. We now had a beatbox, four microphones, two turntables, and all the records we'd ever need. Because Groove was the DJ, we agreed to keep all the equipment at his house.

We did a handful of pretty good shows together over about a six-month period, but mostly the equipment just sat there in Groove's basement unused. I was getting frustrated—nobody wanted to grind and go get it. My work ethic and constant pushing slowly drove a wedge between me and the group. They resented me for always bugging them and ruining what to them was just supposed to be a fun hobby. I resented them for not putting the effort in to make this thing as good as it could possibly be.

I remember being at rehearsals with them and finding myself barking out a Daddio axiom: "Ninety-nine percent is the same as zero!"

We started having arguments and fights over everything: over lines, over which break beats went best with what harmony, over who would take which verse—every decision became a chore. Knowing what I know now, I can see that there was no way it could have worked, but back then, my mind-set was that *everything* could be fixed.

But finally, after months of no progress on recording anything, I went to Groove's house and told the guys that I was out. To them, I was the obnoxious kid who was killin' everybody's vibe anyway. They sorta shrugged, shared a laugh between themselves, and threw me deuces.

So I grabbed my mic and my headphones, and, in the honor of fairness, I offered to buy the SP-12 back from them.

"It's not for sale," Groove said. There was a new coldness in his voice.

"C'mon, man, y'all not even usin' that thing," I said. "My dad will help me with the cash. . . ."

They just ignored me and kept talking among themselves. It wasn't about the SP-12; it wasn't even about resentment. It was about power—they were disrespecting me because they could. They knew I couldn't do anything.

"A'ight, fine," I said. "Just give me my two hundred dollars and y'all can keep it."

They all kinda smirked at one another and then Groove said, "Nope."

No argument. Nobody raised their voice. Just no after no.

Outwardly I stayed cool, but a fury was beginning to churn inside me. I had suffered bullying and abuse in my home and all through my childhood. And I was sick of that shit.

"OK," I said calmly. "I'll see y'all later." But as I started to leave, I realized that the SP-12 was sitting right there. So I walked over to it, I paused, then I snatched it up, violently ripping the cables from the wall, held it high over my head with the knobs facing down, and *CRASH!* I slammed it down onto the concrete basement floor. That thing *disintegrated*—knobs, plastic, transistors, spraying everywhere.

"What tha fuck are ya *doin'*?" Groove screamed.

And then I hauled ass up the basement stairs and out into the street. They were right on me in the beginning, but I was the young one. Back in the day, how I was running was known as "bookin'." I put my head down and didn't look back for eight blocks. When I finally slowed down, there was no one behind me.

I was on my own now.

All of the windows were broken out of Daddio's brand-new Chevy van. The radio, and all of his tools, were gone.

Paul had the van when it happened. And he was almost in tears apologizing to Daddio. Daddio was trying to calm him down.

"This shit happens, man—that's why we have insurance," Daddio said.

But something about Paul's inner code made this unforgivable. He felt like the van was in his possession and he had been entrusted with it. I had never seen him like this. Paul felt like he had somehow failed and dishonored Daddio. Daddio could see *that thing* rising up in Paul, the thing that led to him being in West Philly in the first place.

"Hey, Paul, look at me," Daddio said. "You know how many times niggas done broke in and stole my shit?"

"I know exactly who did it, Uncle Will," Paul said.

"Fuck them niggas, Paul," Daddio said. "We got too much shit to do. Leave it alone."

But Paul couldn't let it go. He was messing with a girl named Shelley who used to mess with this ol' head named Black. Black ran Wynnefield. He was always on the corner in front of Mr. Bryant's store with seven or eight of his friends. Black was about six foot four and always had his shirt off. He didn't give a *fuck*. He would smoke weed *outside* in the *daytime*.

Paul walked straight into the middle of the crowd, right up to Black.

"Did you touch my uncle's van?" Paul said. Everybody on the corner laughed.

"Yeah, I did it, what you gon' do about it—"

BLOOP.

Within a couple of seconds, Black's nose was broken. But he didn't know yet. He wouldn't find out until later, when he regained consciousness.

I'd never seen a fight like this except in the movies. Paul beat up everybody. Every dude on the corner either bleeding, running away, or asleep.

Paul didn't come home that night. Or the next. He had disobeyed Daddio. I guess that was too much for him to bear.

It would be thirty-five years before I saw him again.

HOPE

om-Mom and Harry moved back into Woodcrest. My family wasn't one that talked about things. I was never privy to what she and Daddio had decided—I didn't ask; they didn't tell. But whatever it was, he never put his hands on her again.

It was midway through my senior year. I had just gotten my SAT scores: low twelve hundreds. This was far from a perfect score, but for a Black kid from an inner-city school in Philadelphia, those numbers were more than good enough to get me really good options for college. Mom-Mom was ecstatic. She was dancing around the house, calling all her friends at Carnegie Mellon and MIT—you would have thought *she* was going back to college.

My strong subjects were math and science. By 1986, more and more schools were beginning to offer computer science and engineering courses. Mom-Mom set up a war room. She had a map of the United States; she was cross-referencing "engineering schools" with "cities and states where we had family members," "cost of living" with "distance from Philadelphia." With that information at hand, she narrowed down my options to her top five or six schools, organized in order of most likely to least likely acceptance. She then filled out all of the applications, handled all of the housing logistics, and weighed all of the travel and financial-aid issues. At the time she worked for the school board of

Philadelphia, so when it came to education, her organization and execution made even Daddio applaud.

We had family friends in Wisconsin, and suddenly Mom-Mom decided we were going to take a quick family trip to see them. (The patriarch, Walter McCallum [we called him Uncle Whatchamacallit], was tight with the admissions officer at the university's College of Engineering.) She had already gotten my sister Pam into Hampton University, and I was up next. Her wildest dreams as a parent were coming true—all of her kids were going to college.

Mom-Mom was the commander in charge of the "Will Getting into College" mission. All of a sudden, she was very comfortable with the idea that *if two people are in charge, everybody dies.*

It was a Friday night, and my girl Judy Stewart was having her birthday party up the block. I met up with Ready Rock after school.

"Yo, you goin' to Judy's party tonight?" he said.

"Nah, man, she played me. I DJ'd her party for the last two years and she got somebody else and didn't even tell me."

"Well, she didn't just get *somebody* else, man. She got Jazzy Jeff."

"Word?! I've been hearin' about him, but I never saw him cut."

"Yeah, man. He's *ill*," Ready said. "He's from Southwest, though, and he's gonna be in *our* hood! We gon' stand for that?"

Ready Rock always knew how to gas me up for a battle. Not that I needed much fuel.

"Yo, what's his rapper's name?" I said.

"MC Ice. He can't touch *you*, though."

"*Nobody* can touch me."

Ready Rock loved when I talked dirty like that. He gave me a pound. My mind was churning with battle rhymes organizing themselves for tonight's slaughter.

"You know what, we're gonna hit that party tonight and *smash* these fools," I said. "We gotta rep Wynnefield."

"Bet!" he said. "Ready Rock C and the Fresh Prince versus Jazzy Jeff and MC Ice! I'll meet you there at eight."

"A'ight, bet. Later."

Jeffrey Allen Townes grew up on Rodman Street in southwest Philly, about four or five miles from Wynnefield. Jeff came from a musical family. His father used to emcee for the jazz legend Count Basie. His older brothers played in funk and fusion bands, and his sisters were always singing Motown tunes. He was the baby of the family and was a musical sponge, absorbing and processing all of the incredible talent that was happening around him.

At the age of fifteen, Jeff was diagnosed with cancer, non-Hodgkin's lymphoma. After various painful and difficult treatments, he managed to beat the illness, but his mother became understandably overprotective, and Jeff found himself spending his days in the family basement surrounded by ten thousand of his father's and brothers' jazz, funk, and blues records. Jeff would spend all day digging through them, listening to everything from John Coltrane and Charlie Mingus to Stevie Wonder and James Brown, noting the different styles, the musicianship, the instrumentation.

When he was ten, Jeff had begun DJing. His encyclopedic knowledge made him a musical marvel. Everyone called him "Jazz" because of his ability to seamlessly blend complex jazz tunes with modern funk, disco, or hip-hop rhythms. Eventually, that got extended to "Jazzy Jeff."

A lot of you young guns might not know this, but back in the day, DJs were actually more famous than MCs. Rapping was still pretty rudimentary. We hadn't developed the rhythmic or linguistic ingenuity that we have today. Instead, *DJing* was the innovative and exciting center of attention.

It's hard to explain to people who aren't familiar with old-school cuttin', but Jeff's ability to scratch out rhythms and blend sounds was, and still is, for the most part, unparalleled. He pioneered techniques and styles in those Philly basement parties as a teenager that are still used by thousands of DJs all over the world today. He could manipulate records in ways that no one had seen or heard before. He could bend keys and time signatures and alter sounds, one of which I later named "the Transformer Scratch," because it reminded me of the sound effect from the *Transformers* cartoon. He could make the vocal lines of two records "talk" back and forth to each other, creating "conversations" from two completely different songs.

I could go on and on. But I'll stop and just say there's a reason why many, including myself, consider Jeff to be the GOAT of hip-hop DJing. Even today, over thirty years later, he's revered by DJing experts as one of the best in the world.

The point is: I know I am the big famous movie guy, but back in the eighties, *Jazzy Jeff was the star.* It was *me* backing *him* up.

That night at Judy's, I showed up early. I made my entrance into her basement: two-tone Lee jeans, black on the back, white on the front, with "Fresh Prince" down the left leg in red letters and a matching two-tone Lee jacket. I had taken the Lee patch off the waistband of the pants and had attached it to a silver rope chain around my neck.

I was almost too fly for this party.

As I stepped into the room, my mind flashed to the last time I had been in Judy's basement. The harrowing events documented in my first single, "Girls Ain't Nothing But Trouble," actually happened right here. I was with one of Judy's girlfriends in that basement one night when Judy's father woke up at around 2:00 a.m. to the unmistakable sounds of exquisite lovemaking (my sounds, not hers). From the top floor I heard him bellowing and tearing down the stairs.

"WHO THE FUCK IS IN MY HOUSE?"

I bolted up and scrambled naked through the narrow back hall, snatching open the door to the rear driveway, which to my horror had since disappeared under twelve inches of snow.

It was thirty-one degrees, and I had a choice to make.

"Where is he? WHERE IS HE?" Judy's father roared.

Decision made.

I ran a full city block, butt naked, back to my house, in the snow. I was outside for over ten minutes making snowballs, trying to hit Harry's bedroom window. Finally, the window goes up, and Harry looks down.

I had not heard my brother laugh harder before, or since.

It also happens that Judy's basement was where I met Jeff for the first time. Whatever magic juju Judy had going on in her basement in the mid-eighties, apparently Jeff and I owe our careers to it. Thanks, Judy.

When I arrived, Jeff was still setting up. Judy introduced us.

"What up, man, I'm Jazz," he said.

"Prince," I said, pointing to my leg.

I was thinking, This *is Jazzy Jeff?* He was wearing these big-ass glasses, and he didn't have his name on his clothes anywhere—how was anybody supposed to know he was Jazzy Jeff? There was a Band-Aid around the middle scratching finger on his left hand. Apparently, he had been scratching so much that the top knuckle of his finger now had a bend in it. Everybody was raving about this dude, but I was *thoroughly* unimpressed. *If this joka is the best DJ in the city, I'm sad for Philly.* A lot of the famous DJs back in those days were flashy, doing backflips and jumping over their turntables and all of that. Jeff was quiet, skinny, soft-spoken, and looked more like a science nerd than a samurai on the wheels of steel.

I sat down and chilled while Jeff continued to set up. It's always good to show up early before a battle so you can clock your material. I was plotting all the punch lines I was gonna kick about his glasses and his Band-Aid, but I was really going to be battling Ice. A few minutes go by and I say, "Yo, Jazz, where's Ice?"

Jeff didn't even look up. I could tell this was a sore subject.

"Good question. I called him like five times. He never hit me back."

Back then there were no cell phones—you couldn't get in touch with people like today. Judy's guests were arriving now, but there was no sign of Ready Rock. The party was starting. I could see that Judy was getting nervous, and I could sense that Jeff wasn't feeling too great, either. My "pleaser" kicked in, full steam.

"Hey, I'll rock wit' you till Ice gets here if you want," I said.

Jeff, relieved, said, "Aw, that would be dope. Thanks. I *hate* having to talk on the mic."

"I got you," I said. "There's *nothing* I enjoy more than talking on a mic."

We both laughed. Judy squealed and clapped her hands.

There are rare moments as an artist that you cannot quantify or measure. As much as you try, you can rarely reproduce them and it's near impossible to describe them. But every artist knows what I'm talking about—those moments of divine inspiration where creativity flows out of you so brilliantly and effortlessly that somehow you are better than you have ever been before.

That night with Jeff was the first time I ever tasted it, the place that athletes call "the zone." It felt like we already existed as a group and we just had to catch up to ourselves—natural, comfortable, home.

Jeff could sense my rhyme style. He always knew when my jokes were coming, when to drop the track out so people could clearly hear the punch line, and I could tell by which hand he was using what type of scratch was coming. He preferred different scratches with his left hand than with his right. Sensing this, I could draw the audience's attention to which scratch was coming by which hand he was transitioning to. He was choosing the tracks and adjusting the tempos based on what he felt best accentuated the narrative structure and the flow of my rhymes. And just as the music crescendoed, I'd throw down a dagger of a line and Jeff would drop the beat into the funkiest, hottest, party-rocking shit these Philly kids had ever seen in their lives.

That night was crazy. When the party was over, me and Jeff stood out in the driveway catching our breath and cooling off. We were still hyped.

"Yo, the Truck Turner echo thing you did was *blaze*," I said.

"Your flow sits *perfect* locked to that Chic bassline!" Jeff responded. "Next time, we'll use the 'Bounce, Rock, Skate, Roll' and then *transition* to Chic . . ."

"Word! Word!"

Ideas poured out of us like a fire hose, creativity ricocheting back and forth between us. Everything *he* said set off *three* ideas in my mind, and my responses had him holding his head and walking around in circles.

We never really talked about it, never really made it official, but that wild November night in Judy Stewart's basement, he became my DJ, and I became his rapper. From then on, we were DJ Jazzy Jeff and the Fresh Prince, just two kids from West Philly—partners, friends, brothers.

And we still are today.

Over the next couple of months, me and Jeff dug in *hard*. We practiced every day, performed every weekend. He *lived* in his mother's basement. It was his sanctuary, his magic workshop. When you entered, it felt like you were getting a sneak peek behind the curtain of the wizard.

Jeff was the first friend I'd ever had who plain and simple outworked me. I think it would be a misrepresentation to say that he "practiced a lot." It wasn't that he was *practicing*—it was that he *didn't do anything else*. You'd never catch Jeff in the kitchen or watching TV. You wouldn't show up at his house and see him walking up the front steps coming back from the store. He didn't *go* to the store; I guess wizards don't do their own shopping. Jeff was standing in front of his turntables fourteen to eighteen hours a day, seven days a week, 365 days a year. It's literally the only image I can conjure of Jeff in his childhood home.

Jeff was a mad scientist, and he loved technology. He was always waiting for a new gadget to arrive in the mail that you could only get from some seventy-eight-year-old guitar builder of questionable history in Vienna. Jeff was moving from solely DJing into beat making and recording. He got a TASCAM four-track recorder, and he was experimenting with creating his own records. He now had a mini studio.

Jeff is three years older than me, so he had already graduated, but I had to still go to school *and* work at the ice house. So by the time I'd get to rehearsal around 4:00 p.m., Jeff had already put in ten hours of work. He'd give me two tracks to write to; I'd show up the next day with one written, and he'd hand me six more tracks. This went on for the first few months of our partnership. DJ Jazzy Jeff was a hip-hop terminator. *He didn't eat, he didn't sleep, and he absolutely positively would not stop until you were* dead.

I tried to keep up—I would stay as late as I could, until Mom-Mom or Daddio would call asking me if I knew what time it was. Those early months in Jeff's basement were among the most creative times I've ever experienced. Everything was cutting-edge, everything was hot; it was experimental and inspiring. I never wanted to leave. We were seeking our sound, but we found ourselves.

One night, we were rehearsing in Jeff's basement and some random dude wearing a Lacoste polo shirt, tan khakis with a razor crease, and Adidas shell toes crawled through the basement window. He calmly went and took a seat in what he clearly thought of as *his* corner. The music was playing, and Jeff and I were deeply engaged in our artistic banter, so I guess he didn't want to interrupt us. Jeff didn't react to his presence at all. This went on for a few minutes, until I tried to break the awkwardness that obviously only I was feeling.

"Hey, man, you gotta watch wearing those shoes with them pants. If khakis touch shell tops, they could blow your ankles up."

I was just trying to break the ice, but the dude looked at me, perceiving a challenge, and said, "Oh, is *that* what we doin'? We *bussin'*? Because we can get started with those car-door ears of yours. . . ."

"Nah, nah, nah, homie, I'm just messin' wit' you. I'm Will. They call me Fresh Prince."

Jeff finally popped out of his nutty-professor trance and snapped his headphones off.

"Oh damn! Whaddup, JL?" Jeff said. "When did *you* get here?"

James Lassiter was Jeff's best friend from childhood. JL grew up one block over, on Hazel Avenue. When Jeff was sick as a child, his mother wouldn't allow him to go off his front porch, so JL would come over and sit for hours and hours with Jeff, keeping him company. This routine continued long after Jeff's recovery and well into their adult lives.

JL was a serious cat. When I met him, he was putting himself through Temple law school. He was studying during the day and working at the University of Pennsylvania hospital at night. He would stop at Jeff's for the last two hours of his day, part habit, part unwind, part front seat to the evolution of the greatest DJ who has ever lived.

Our rise in the Philly hip-hop scene was nuclear. We had done every show we could: block parties, school dances, proms, basement parties, birthdays, fundraisers in church parking lots—you name it, we did it. We had established a rep as fun, creative, captivating party rockers. Eventually, in early 1986, we scored our first real gig at a major venue, the famous Wynne Ballroom. "Wynne" was short for Wynnefield—my hood, my people, with my new DJ. And we smashed it. We were the hottest hip-hop duo in these Philly streets.

But our big break came in September 1986, when Jeff was invited to compete in the New Music Seminar Battle for World Supremacy.

The Battle for World Supremacy was an old-school DJ and MC battle competition held annually in New York City. All of the legends of hip-hop had performed and competed in it: Grandmaster Flash, Busy Bee, Mantronix, Melle Mel, and so on. It was like the Olympics of early eighties hip-hop.

Local radio DJ Lady B is an iconic pioneer of Philly hip-hop. She was playing rap music before anybody in the city, back when it was only on WHAT AM radio. She called Dave "Funken" Klein, who was one of the event coordinators, and told him that she had a DJ in Philly who was changing the game. Lady B pressed Funken Klein to put Jeff in the competition.

Even though it was just two hours away by car, the drive felt like a pilgrimage. New York City was the mecca of hip-hop. I had never been to New York. To me, the idea that music could be my passport to new worlds excited and inspired me. Here I was, *right now*, walking through New York City, headed to the coolest event on the planet. And all because of rap music.

The Battle was being held in the grand ballroom at the Marriott Marquis in Times Square. We rolled up, ten-deep, full swag; red Phillies baseball caps filled the room. We were intimated and in awe, but you couldn't tell it from all the noise we were making—Philly was now officially in the building.

Jeff approached the sign-in table. I was standing behind him, arms crossed, chin high, B-boy stance on swole. Melle Mel walks by to my left, entering the ballroom. My B-boy stance got just a little less swole. And then Grandmaster Flash entered right behind him. For comfort, I put my arms by my side. And then I heard a sound over my shoulder, that outburst you hear when old friends haven't seen each other for a while. I vaguely recognized one of the voices. *Where do I know that voice from?*

And then it hit me. I had never seen him in person before, but I knew it was him. He wasn't rocking a B-boy stance, no flashy clothes, no entourage, but the crowd still parted when he walked through. The undisputed favorite for the MC competition: Grandmaster Caz.

As he passed, it took everything I had not to squeal, "I LOVE YOU, CAZ!" Fortunately, he passed quickly, and I didn't play myself, but I'm not sure how much longer I could have held out. Jeff finished signing in, I put my hands in my pockets, and went quietly to find a seat.

There were two sections of the Battle for World Supremacy—the MC competition, and the DJ competition. Eight competitors in each; three elimination rounds; last man standing wins. The battle was set up so that each competitor had three thirty-second slots in each round to do their thing. They would go back and forth with their routines, and at the end, the judges would score them, partially based on their techniques and overall performance, but also on the reaction of the crowd.

The MCs were up first, and it wasn't even a fair fight: round after round, rapper after rapper fell to the wit and charisma of my idol. Grandmaster Caz was crowned the World Supreme MC, and I could hold out no longer:

"I LOVE YOU, CAZ!"

The DJs were up next. Back in the day, this was the battle people *really* came to see.

As the newcomer, in the first round, Jeff was paired against DJ Cheese, the previous year's champion. Most DJs had worked out two or four routines and repeated them throughout the competition. But Jeff had spent the previous week preparing nine separate thirty-second routines. He realized that if there were three rounds, each round having three slots, that he would be able to go through the whole tournament without ever repeating a single routine. But he took it even further: Each routine was timed perfectly to end in thirty seconds. So, whereas other DJs were looking sloppy getting cut off by the buzzer, or they had a twenty-second intro and never really got their routines started, Jeff's perfectly timed routines had punch lines right at twenty-nine seconds— the effect was that Jeff's buzzer became a signal to the crowd to erupt.

The first round is set to begin. Jeff walks across the stage, maybe a little overeager, just a bit too happy to be there, and extends a hand of greeting to DJ Cheese. Cheese looks Jeff up and down and flags him (refused to shake his hand). As Jeff returns to his DJ setup, his cheerful demeanor is gone, and his eyes have turned icy. If Cheese would have known what was coming, he would have just shaken Jeff's hand, or better yet, tried to break it off.

Cheese was up first—he came out strong. But Jeff fired back with one of Philly's favorites, a tricky rhythm scratch. People were looking at one another and murmuring, not quite sure what they had just seen. DJ Cheese is eyeballin' Jeff, sensing that this is just the beginning. Nobody had ever seen cuttin' like this. The crowd was inching up on to the edges of their seats.

DJ Cheese unleashed his second routine and once again nailed it. The crowd *cheers*—big scores from all the judges. Then the audience settles down to see what other artillery the Philly kid has brought with him. And with no announcement and no fanfare, Jeff introduces the world to his "Transformer Scratch." In 1986, that was the illest thing anybody had ever heard. And that was just the first ten seconds. He finishes the routine slicing "Pump Me Up" by Grandmaster Flash and the Furious Five. There's a verse at the end of that song that goes:

I'm the bow-legged brother, there'll never be another
I bought a mansion for my mother

Jeff did a breakdown, cutting the last line into syllables:

And I bought

a

man-

sion,

for

my

And then he held it, letting the clock run out, and at twenty-nine seconds, right before the buzzer, he released the last word:

mother

The buzzer sounded, and the crowd lost it. The judges were jumping up out of their seats and walking around with their hands on their heads. Jeff's scratches were so clean, sharp, and calculated that people realized they were witnessing the evolution of the art form. DJ Jazzy Jeff was now serving notice that the road to World Supremacy rolled through Philly.

Jeff was flawless that night. And when it was all said and done, the 1986 World Supreme DJ was a kid who spent most of his life in a basement in Southwest Philly: *my* DJ, DJ Jazzy Jeff.

Afterward, we all piled into our single room at the Marriott Marquis. We knew something big had just happened—Eric B. & Rakim even came to the room to personally congratulate Jeff. We weren't quite sure where this was all going, but we had the sense that some important fuse had just been lit.

We stayed up all night, laughing, dreaming, plotting, planning. That night was the first night I realized that the possibilities hip-hop presented me far outstretched anything else I had dared hope for. My whole life, my parents' hopes for me had been predicated on education and hard work. I was supposed to go to college. I was supposed to get a good job. I was supposed to move up in the world. And as the self-designated golden child, I had always committed to living up to my parents' hopes and dreams. I couldn't imagine it otherwise.

But by the time we drove home the next morning, New York disappearing behind us, I was struck with an overwhelming conviction: *I am not going to college.*

Dana Goodman had cash.

He was about five six and heavyset, not fat, but thick in a way that he could hurt you if he had to. Approaching forty, he was a Wynnefield ol' head. When you would see him standing on the corner it was only briefly, because he was *above* those fools—he was doin' *real* shit.

Dana was the little brother of *Lawrence* Goodman, founder of Pop Art Records, one of the first New York–based hip-hop labels. Lawrence was from Philly, but he was killing them in NYC.

Those first few months back in Philly, me and Jeff were on fire. Jeff was now spending 80 percent of his time making records and 20 percent DJing. We had finished six or seven songs on Jeff's TASCAM four-track. He had mixed them as best he could, but Jeff was becoming increasingly frustrated that his equipment couldn't quite reproduce the sounds that were trapped in his head.

I had recently purchased a Sharp 777, the original hip-hop boom box. It was one of the first times I noticed a major corporation responding to the demands of our burgeoning art form. The 777 was a loud-ass, heavy-ass radio. You had to be strong to carry that thing around, and you had to carry it, because for some reason, if you sat it on the ground, it drained your expensive ten D batteries way faster. Best of all, the 777 had dual, high-speed cassette replication capabilities, so I would take the cassettes that me and Jeff made home with me, and I would stay up all night high-speed-dubbing our demos. This was the old days where you had to do one tape at a time. It was dull and monotonous—you know, like, building a brick wall when you're fucking nine—but it needed to be done, so I did it.

I then handed those tapes out to *everybody*. I didn't care if you even knew what hip-hop was, if you got two ears and a tape deck, then my name's the Fresh Prince—it says it right here on my pants—and I've got a tape you gotta hear.

Overbrook High was situated in Hilltop, and Hilltop was run by about thirty dudes who called themselves "the Hilltop Hustlers." One of the top rappers in that crew was Steady B, and Stead' was Lawrence Goodman's nephew. The word on the street was that his uncle had just given him a deal and he had music coming out later that year. I wanted Stead' to get my tape to Lawrence—the problem was, I was from across the bridge in Wynnefield, and if there was one thing that a Hilltop Hustler would *never* do, it's help a nigga from Wynnefield.

But then it hit me: Dana Goodman lives in *Wynnefield*! Maybe he'll pass our tape to Lawrence.

Dana and Lawrence, like many brothers, had a bit of a sibling rivalry going on. Dana saw the money his brother was making with his record label, and he hoped to start a label of his own. He called up me and Jeff and said he wanted to meet. So we invited him over to Jeff's to hear us perform.

Dana was wearing a dark blue velour Sergio Tacchini sweatsuit, the one with the red and white elasticated wrist- and ankle bands. The sweatsuit was zipped open just low enough to reveal his seven or eight slim gold chains bouncing off the Afro on his chest. He was that older dude who *almost* got away with dressing like the kids, except he had dress socks on. Dana always wore sunglasses—indoors, outdoors, noon, midnight, basketball court, church. You never caught Dana not rockin' his shades.

That day, Dana pulled up in front of Jeff's house in a brand-new, four-door, steel-blue Audi 4000 CS Quattro 5-Speed, and for the first time in my life, I saw a phone in a car. It was the first car phone ever—it was a rotary-dial, house phone that somehow worked in his car. Dana stepped out on Rodman Street; he was a *boss*. He was loud, he was a showman, and the sun was bangin' off his pinkie ring. Me and Jeff were standing on his mom's porch; Dana saw us, threw his arms wide open, and in his low, weathered baritone voice, yelled out to the kids playing, and the neighbors passing, "YOOOW! Dere they go!" pointing to me and Jeff. "That's *them*, y'all. You better get they autographs *now*! That's DJ Jazzy Jeff and the Fresh Prince! Them boys 'bout to *do* sumpn'!"

He called me and Jeff down.

"Come 'ere, y'all. Gimme some love!" Me and Jeff stepped down to the sidewalk, and Dana hugged us like a proud father.

"Love what y'all did up in New York, holdin' it down for *Philly*!"

Me and Jeff smiled.

"Well, you know, that's what we *do*," I said.

Just then, one of Jeff's neighbors, a dude a few years older named Keith, called out: "'Eyy! Dana! Dat you, man?! Oh, shit, it's Dana Goodman—what you *slummin'*, man?"

Keith and Dana shook hands—one of those long, elaborate handshakes with multiple steps from a previous generation, which also didn't go with Dana's sweatsuit.

"What brings you 'round these parts?" Keith asked.

"Oh, you know. I'm here to talk to these boys about a little business," Dana said.

"*Business?*" Keith looked at me and Jeff. His energy shifted slightly, but our youth and our excitement blinded us to the subtleties.

Keith pulled Dana aside, put his arm around him.

"You know this is Jimmy Townes's little brother, right?"

Dana looked over at Jeff.

"Jimmy Townes's brother?"

Keith got up real close to Dana and whispered something in his ear that we couldn't hear.

Dana looked down, then started nodding, "Yeah, yeah, I got you, man, this jus' business. *I'm* tryin' to help *them*."

"*Fam*-ily," Keith said, loud enough for us to hear this time. He then said his goodbyes and went back down the street.

Dana came down to the basement. Me and Jeff let him hear everything we had. Dana picked the two songs he liked the most: the first was called "Just One of Those Days." "Just One of Those Days" features a slow, 92 BPM groove where I rapped about having one of those days where everything goes wrong. For the chorus, Jeff sampled Irving Berlin's "Puttin' on the Ritz," a 1928 ragtime joint that was the first song ever performed in a film by an interracial ensemble. It was pure Jazzy Jeff, mixing old-time, high-brow music with the scratches and rhythms of hip-hop. It crystalized our musical dynamic: Jeff's musical sophistication and in-depth knowledge married to my natural storytelling and humor.

The second song was "Girls Ain't Nothing But Trouble," the one inspired by Grandmaster Caz's "Yvette." This time, Jeff sampled the theme song from the famous 1960s sitcom *I Dream of Jeannie*. He used the brand-new Roland 909 drum machine, and he de-tuned the toms to make them sound like a bassline. I told the story of the night in Judy Stewart's basement when my exquisite lovemaking almost got me frostbitten. Dana loved it; he was cracking up.

"Yo, did that really happen? Tell the truth: That happen for real?"

"Yeah, man," I said, "that was a rough night."

He burst out laughing.

"Boy, y'all sum talented, funny niggas," he said.

Hip-hop has evolved so much over the decades that listening to those songs now I cringe—they sound so simplistic and repetitive. But back then, what we were doing was revolutionary. Jeff and I played with the structure of songs in a way that no one else in hip-hop had up until that point. We had lyric-less choruses; we had verses that were half samples, half raps. I was building verses that constructed a full story—each verse leading into the next, begging the listener to finish the song to find out what happened by the end. It was a new day—dare I say . . . it was fresh.

Dana was bobbing his head to the beat, clapping his hands, stomping.

And then finally, playing as if he couldn't take it anymore, he said, "That's enough, that's enough, turn it off!"

Jeff hit the stop button on the four-track.

If we had been in a cartoon, Dana would have had spinning dollar signs in his eyes. But in real life, he thumbed the gold chains on his chest, and said, "Aw, man! What y'all say we make a *record*?"

Me and Jeff snapped—we were *hyped*. Jumpin', high-fivin', yellin'— we were so naive, we thought that was *it*. You just invite a guy to your house, and he says, "Let's make a record!" and boom, you're a star!

We didn't realize that Dana didn't even have a company yet. He had no distribution, very few connections in radio or television.

And DJ Jazzy Jeff and the Fresh Prince were his first foray into the music business.

A week later, we walked into Studio 4, a professional recording studio that Dana found in downtown Philly.

It's hard to describe what Jeff's face looked like when he entered the main control room. It was as if he were a seventeen-year-old virgin walking onto the set of a porno movie and finding out that he was the star. Dana presented us with a recording contract, and we signed it.

We had never been in a real recording studio before, so we weren't really sure what to do or how it worked. Dana had at least been in with his brother on many of the Pop Art hits. He had ideas of how it should be and what he wanted to hear. The contract dictated that Dana was the producer and co-songwriter of our music. He started telling Jeff to change tempos, to shift pitches, to add cuts and adjust sounds. Jeff disagreed with many of Dana's creative choices, but in Dana's mind, since he paid for the studio time, he was in charge. Jeff was fuming, but this was our big shot, our one chance, so we didn't want to mess it up.

"Just One of Those Days" got mangled in that recording session. The tempos between the verse and chorus were different. The song inexplicably changed keys. The mix was awful. Jeff still hates that track, even though we rerecorded it later.

But "Girls" got through the recording sessions mostly unscathed and still held up as a song. Despite Jeff's grumblings, it was decided that "Girls" would be our first release as a single, and "Just One of Those Days" would be the B side. We'd release them to build up some hype while we recorded our first full album.

The "Girls Ain't Nothing But Trouble" single "came out" in March 1986, although nobody knew it, because it was on Dana's new record label, Word-Up Records. No offices, no employees, no distribution—the single wasn't even in stores; Dana was selling the vinyl out of the trunk of his car. Nothing was happening. To his credit, he was doing everything he knew how to do. He was a hustler—he spent his own money, and he absolutely believed in DJ Jazzy Jeff and the Fresh Prince.

Even though nobody knew we had a record out, Jeff's win at the Battle for World Supremacy meant that promoters started calling to put him on shows, and I came as a part of the package deal. We started hitting the nicer clubs around Philly; we played Delaware and Atlantic City.

The shows were getting big enough that there were contracts, and on one occasion, we needed to sign and fax one back by 5:00 p.m. the same day or we'd lose the gig. Jeff and I were scrambling—who the hell do we know with a fax machine?

JL was sitting in "JL's Corner" of Jeff's basement, in his own world, "reading" the back of an Ohio Players album cover, the one with the naked girl on the inside with the honey all over her. Jeff and I were getting more and more frantic, trying to prevent this $1,500 from evaporating as 5:00 p.m. approached.

Neither of *us* had a fax machine; I figured Mom-Mom might have access to one at work, but it was already late on Friday. Daddio didn't like that "newfangled shit." And Word-Up Records only had a rotary-dial car phone in its mobile business office.

JL sat there quietly, as Jeff and I became aggravated with each other.

"You got all of this computer shit down here but you don't have a damn fax machine?" I said. "You can get a sampling guitar pedal from a Nazi in Vienna and you don't have no way of faxing a damn contract?"

"How is it *my* job? What do *you* do in the group?"

JL never looked up; and in a bored monotone voice, he said, as much to the Ohio Players girl as to me and Jeff, "I have a fax machine. . . ."

And that's how James Lassiter became our manager.

There's a great concept from Jim Rohn:

"Look at the five people you spend the most time with because that's who you are."

This is an idea I've always understood innately. Deep down inside, I knew that my dreams would be made or broken by the people I chose to surround myself with. Confucius had it right: It's nearly impossible for the quality of your *life* to be higher than the quality of your *friends*. And by the grace of God, there has never been a single moment in my life when I have looked to my left or to my right and not seen an extraordinary friend, someone who believed in me and was down for whatever.

JL was in his final year of law school, and while it may have been a casual act of convenience for Jeff and me to hire him as our manager, we quickly realized that JL was not a casual kinda guy. He started making contact with all of our venues and concert promoters and began requesting documentation and financial information about record sales and studio costs from Dana. And when he wasn't satisfied with the responses, he hired a New York City attorney to oversee all of our business dealings. JL was one of those guys who didn't care about fame or money; he wasn't flashy, and he didn't want fancy clothes or sparkly jewels. He prided himself simply on defending the people he loved.

JL read the recording contract we had signed with Dana. He had highlighted and circled and x-ed out clauses, which didn't really matter because we had already signed it. Perched in "JL's Corner," with a perplexed look on his face, he asked, "Did you two *read* this contract?"

Jeff and I kinda glanced at each other.

"I didn't read it, did you?" I said.

Jeff shook his head, and then to JL said, "Nah. What does it say?"

That was not the answer JL was hoping for.

"It says that y'all are *stoopid*."

Dana was always upbeat, telling us how hard he was working and how much money he was spending to promote the record. Jeff had heard it a couple of times on WHAT around midnight, and a few friends and family members had caught it, but it was getting spotty airplay at best.

"You gotta bribe radio stations; you gotta wine and dine people. You know, it's *competitive*. They be trying to jawn me up! They playin' it, though, y'all just not catchin' it! Just give me some time, y'all gon' be HUGE!"

Since I had secretly decided that I wasn't going to college, I stopped doing homework, I didn't study for tests, and I didn't even show up for a lot of my classes. As far as Daddio was concerned, if I was disciplined at the ice house, performed my tasks impeccably, and wasn't getting myself arrested or killed, he was cool. But Mom-Mom was friends with all of my teachers at Overbrook, and she snapped.

Mom-Mom's super-most parenting mission was for me, and for all of her children, to go to college. For her, college was *everything*. It was what she had picked up and moved to Philly for. It was why she tolerated Daddio's drinking and violence. It was a big part of why she moved back to Woodcrest. To her, a college education was the fundamental bedrock of a successful life. And without it, I was doomed.

Hope sustains life. Hope is the elixir of survival during our darkest times. The ability to envision and imagine a brighter day gives meaning to our suffering and renders it bearable. When we lose hope, we lose our central source of strength and resilience.

My mother's hopes for her kids had sustained her through the darkest years of her marriage. But now, I had developed hopes of my own. I had hip-hop hopes. I had hopes for albums and being onstage in front of fifty thousand people shouting "Hoooooo!!" when I told them to. These hopes were now empowering and sustaining *me*. I would have *died* if I had to give them up. I couldn't; I wouldn't.

It came to a head one afternoon toward the end of my senior year. I hadn't come home after school; I had gone straight to Jeff's to rehearse. It was about 10:00 p.m. when I finally made it home. I could feel Mom-Mom before I even put my key in the front door.

Sure enough, Mom-Mom was in the kitchen, waiting for me.

"Hey, Mom!" I said, mock-joyfully.

"Are you having a problem?" she said evenly.

"Nah, I'm good, Mom."

"No, apparently, you're having a *big* problem. Or, at least, you're about to."

"What's up, Mom, what happened?"

"I just talked to Mrs. Stubbs. After four years you've forgotten where your classrooms are?"

"No, Mom, I'm just doin' a lot of stuff."

"What are you doing that's more important than getting into college? You know these schools are going to look at your final senior grades? We have come too far for you to throw your life away now. What is your *problem*?"

Mom-Mom's voice and her posture denoted anger, but I saw something else beneath that: She was terrified. My heart melted.

"Mom. I've been working with Jeff for almost a year. People say he is the best DJ in the world. Rap is blowin' up. It's on the radio, it's on MTV, and Run-DMC went to *Japan*. I'm tellin' you, Mom, we are making songs that are as good as what anybody else is doing. Every time we perform, people go *crazy*. We found a record producer who's puttin' up money; we have a manager. Nobody in Philly can rap as good as me. Everybody says we're gonna be stars. I just need some time to make it happen."

"No. You can't be a rapper," she said bluntly.

"What? Why not?"

"Because I don't know what that is. You listen to me right now: You will not cut another class; you will not miss another test. You will complete every single piece of homework that is assigned to you. You are going to college in the fall. Period."

"Mom, just listen to the *music*. . . ."

"I've been hearing you hippity-hopping around here your whole life! That is a *hobby*; that is not a *career*. Good night."

She stood up from the kitchen table, turned to walk away, and I stopped her with probably the worst thing I ever said to my mother.

"Mom, I'm not going to college."

I was here on the backs of generations who had struggled through hardship and sacrifice—the blessed recipient in a long lineage of striving African Americans to have a stable, educated, middle-class life in America. Mom-Mom and Daddio's generation grew up in the throes of segregation and immense poverty. Gigi's family had escaped the Jim Crow South. My mother had fought through decades of school district bureaucracies, financial uncertainty, and Daddio's bullshit to get me to this point. And she was going to be damned if I didn't go to college because of some music I was doing at basement parties with homeboys named Jazz and Ready Rock.

Our hopes had finally collided. And these hopes were inherently incompatible with each other. One had to give way. One of us was going to have our heart broken.

The thing I've learned over the years about *advice* is that no one can accurately predict the future, but we all think we can. So advice at its best is one person's limited perspective of the infinite possibilities before you. People's advice is based on their fears, their experiences, their prejudices, and at the end of the day, their advice is just that: it's *theirs*, not yours. When people give you advice, they're basing it on what *they* would do, what *they* can perceive, on what *they* think *you* can do. But the bottom line is, while yes, it *is* true that we are all subject to a series of universal laws, patterns, tides, and currents—all of which are somewhat predictable—you are the first time you've *ever* happened. YOU and NOW are a unique occurrence, of which you are the most reliable measure of all the possibilities.

I've always loved the scene in *The Pursuit of Happyness* on the basketball court, in which Jaden's character shoots the ball and yells, "I'm going pro!" My character, Chris Gardner, discourages him from pursuing basketball but catches himself: "Don't ever let somebody tell you you *can't* do something, not even me. . . . You got a dream . . . you gotta protect it. People can't do something themselves, they want to tell you you can't do it. If you want something, go get it. Period."

My mother's college education saved her life, which solidified for her a fundamental premise: A college education is the only armor against the brutality of this world. And without a college education, I would be condemned to certain destruction. This was not her *advice* to me—this was "the truth." To her, being a rapper was impossible.

But I am not my mother. Just as her education saved and defended her from the hardships of her early life, performance and hip-hop had saved me from *mine*. It's clearer when I look back now. While we were gridlocked and colliding and arguing, the reality was, both things were true—one was true for *her*, and the other was true for *me*.

But at the time, neither of us could compromise because it would mean destroying everything we stood for.

Daddio was caught in the middle. Mom-Mom was *demanding* that he make me go to college, and I was begging him to please understand what *I* was saying.

It was clear that he was going to have the final word. Daddio was going to be the judge, the jury, and the executioner of the hopes and dreams of either his wife or his son.

Daddio deliberated for about a week. He would take me for a drive, Mom-Mom for a walk; he'd ask questions and listen to us talk. In the meantime, Woodcrest was as cold as the ice house. My mother and I were cordial—we kept it on "hi" and "bye." And then one evening, Daddio called us both into the kitchen. My mother and I sat at the table, and Daddio leaned against the stove.

Daddio had been here before, except the last time he was sitting in *my* seat, when he was being told by his parents what he could and couldn't do, when he had so loved his camera, but he'd been told it was just a hobby, not a career. At his heart, Daddio was an artist who had been robbed of his dreams and his passions because they were "unrealistic" and "impractical." But he also knew firsthand the viciousness of this world against an uneducated Black kid. Everything Daddio ever did, somebody had told him he couldn't do it. He was supposed to get a job because there was no way he could start his own business; people told him there was no way white people would work for *him*; there was no way real supermarkets would buy ice from a Black man. He lived against a ferocious headwind of doubt and discouragement, but he did it all anyway.

"So, here's what we gonna do," Daddio said. "You got one year. Your mother said she can get all them schools to hold your acceptance till next September. We're gonna help you and support you to do anything you think you need to do to succeed. But in one year, if it ain't happenin', you're going to go to whichever one of them school's your mother choose. That work for you?"

In my mind a year was forever. I was ecstatic.

He turned to Mom-Mom. "That work for you?"

Mom-Mom clearly didn't love it, but this was a compromise that kept her dreams alive. She only said one word.

"Yup."

And with that, Daddio went back to work.

My experiences with my father are a mixed bag, to say the least. But that night, in the kitchen at 5943 Woodcrest Avenue, he displayed the most exquisite leadership I had ever seen.

That was how a father was supposed to be.

A few weeks later, my mother called the dean at the University of Wisconsin, a school where my application had been accepted. She told the dean everything.

"It's terrible," she said. "My son wants to take a gap year. He's doing something called 'rapping.' He's got a manager, and some company is paying him to record an album. It all sounds suspect to me, but we were wondering if you could hold his place until September '87."

The dean listened patiently. "I think that's incredible, Mrs. Smith."

"What?" Mom-Mom said.

"For a young man his age? He would *never* get that kind of life experience here. He should *absolutely* do it."

My mother was floored.

"And certainly we'll hold a spot for him. If his album doesn't work out, he can attend next year. That's no problem."

A few weeks later, in early May, about a month before my graduation, I was bagging ice at ACRAC. In case you were wondering, bagging ice is just as dull and monotonous as it sounds. And you *always* hurt your back. The aluminum scoop held about four pounds of ice; two and a half scoops into a ten-pound bag, which you would then spin to twist the top and then drop it into the tie machine and then toss the bag into the shopping cart. If you stacked them correctly you could get about twenty-four bags into one shopping cart. Then you roll the cart into the freezer, take the bags out one at a time, and stack them. In a four-hour session, one person could do 200–250 bags. It's repetitive and you just kinda zone out for a few hours while you do it.

I always liked to do it at night because that's when Power 99 played hip-hop. I'd listen to the "Power 9 at 9" countdown, getting lost in my own world and staying up on the new hip-hop jawns. I would rap along, memorizing my favorite songs, and shovel on beat, inventing my own rhymes.

But that night, I was quiet. For the first time I understood the old saying "Be careful what you wish for because you just might get it." I had held my ground against my parents, and they gave in. But now I had to prove it.

"Number five—five—five—*five!* We got Kool Moe Dee's brand-new track, 'Go See the Doctor.'"

I . . . was . . . walking down the street, rocking my beat,
clapping my hands and stomping my feet.
I saw a little lady, so neat and petite,
she was so sweet, yes, I wanted to meet—

I mean, I'm as good as Kool Moe Dee, I thought, trying to psych my-self up. But Mom-Mom had gotten into my head. *What if she's right? What if a rapper isn't really a thing? And only one year? Is that enough? This last year just blazed on by. Maybe I should go to college. I did do all of this with Jeff while I went to high school—maybe I could go to college and still do music.*

Scoop, bag. Scoop, bag. Scoop, bag.

I am not tryin' to be livin' at home. I need my own spot, my own money, my own car. . . .

"Number FOOOOURRR!!! The Beastie Boys are back with 'Hold It Now, Hit It.'"

Now I chill real ill when I start to chill,
When I fill my pockets with a knot of dollar bills
Sippin' pints of ale outta da windowsill
When I get my fill I'm chilly chill

Scoop, bag. Scoop, bag. Scoop, bag.

Man, I'm definitely as good as the Beastie Boys. Except they're on the radio, and I'm baggin' ice. Maybe baggin' ice is my destiny. But, man, if I'm stuck here with Daddio in ten years, I'm-a sever my own head with the dull end of this ice scoop.

I mean, Run-DMC and Beastie Boys had to have their own versions of baggin' ice, right? Or maybe they were flukes, one in a million . . .

"Number—number—number THREE!!! Check it out, y'all—hot off the presses from Stetsasonic's debut album, *On Fire*, this is a new one, you guys been asking for it, it's called 'My Rhyme.'"

But I'm one in a million. Jeff's one in a million. Mom-Mom is not my target audience. How she think she gonna tell if a rapper is good or not? She judgin' stuff she don't even understand. And what about Melanie? You can not keep a girlfriend if you runnin' off to some college somewhere. She'll be tossed up with some other joka in two weeks.

Scoop, bag. Scoop, bag. Scoop, bag.

"And we're back, with number TWOOOOO!! It's yo' boys' old favorite, that's right, RUN! D! M! C! 'My Adidas!'" This was my *jam*; it snapped me out of my funk. I was back to shoveling on beat and rappin' along.

My. Ahhhh-didas walk through concert doors
And roam all over coliseum floors
I stepped on stage, at Live Aid
All the people gave, and the poor got paid

My shoveling picked up pace, completely involuntarily.

That's *the power of hip-hop*, I thought.

My Adidas touch the sand of a foreign land
With mic in hand
I cold took command

But my reverie was short-lived. I couldn't get my mind off Mom-Mom. I'd failed to protect her from Daddio. I wasn't brave enough to go with her when she left. And now, the hopes she had for me, the dreams that had sustained her through all her pain and trouble, I was spittin' in the face of that. I couldn't shake the sense that I was failing her again.

"My Adidas" finished playing, and Power 99 went to a commercial break. I realized I had missed the end of the song.

Damn, I thought. *Not even "My Adidas" could pull me out of this one.*

I rolled the final cart into the freezer. I was done for the night. I counted the bags while commercials blared—new mattress sales, "everything must go."

Maybe I could sell mattresses, I thought. *That shit can't be hard. I could do hip-hop mattress raps.*

Get a good night's rest, good sleep routines
Got twins and fulls, got kings and queens

I threw the shovel on the side, closed the machines up.

"And we're back, with the 'Power 9 at 9' Countdown! Tonight, we have a newcomer to the countdown—"

Shutting off the lights, I realized I couldn't find my keys. I'd lost my keys a few times before, and Daddio had had to come pick me up. I was dreading the thought of having to call him to come get me. Here I am, demanding my independence, about to have to call my daddy to pick me up because I can't find my damn keys.

"The phones have been off the *hook* all day from y'all wanting to hear these guys, so get ready for our hometown boys, Philly's very own, *DJ Jazzy Jeff and the Fresh Prince*. This is . . . 'Girls Ain't Nothing But'—"

I totally froze. My mouth was hanging open, for some reason my heart was pounding. I wanted to scream, I wanted to jump, but at the same time I didn't want to do anything to bump into the universe and knock my record off the radio. Then those words. Those words I knew so well and had repeated hundreds, maybe thousands, of times before, were coming out of the radio:

> *Listen, homeboys, don't mean to bust your bubble*
> *But girls of the world ain't nothin' but trouble!*

It was my voice. That was me. On the radio. *Me. My rhymes. My voice!* I wanted to call people, but I didn't want to miss it.

> *Just last week when I was walking down the street*
> *I observed this lovely lady that I wanted to meet*

I ran outside; I wanted to grab somebody, to tell somebody, "THAT'S ME, Y'ALL, THAT'S ME."

But it was ten o'clock; nobody was out there. I started giggling, a knee-jerk reaction that I still have to this day when I find myself in extreme emotional circumstances. I couldn't stop laughing. It was a joyous, blissful laughter. The pure joy of a child waking up on Christmas morning. The joy of discovery. Of renewed hope. Of a new life.

The joy of being right about me.

SIX

IGNORANCE

We didn't know shit.

The tour bus pulled up on Woodcrest. We'd all agreed we'd meet at my house because my street was the widest. My whole family assembled to see us off. Mom-Mom, Daddio, Gigi, Ellen, Harry; Pam was home now, too. But Melanie said she couldn't bear to see me drive away—we had said our goodbyes the night before.

The neighborhood kids had never seen a tour bus before, so they buzzed around, checking the tires, peering into the luggage bays, and talking to the driver.

Somehow, Dana had done it. "Girls Ain't Nothing But Trouble" lit up local radio in May 1986—finally. When it first came out in March it had stumbled, but by late May it caught fire. We were hearing that it was getting played in Delaware, New Jersey, and even New York City.

I graduated from high school in June, which meant I had an entire month as a senior with a hit record on the radio (that's too much power for one seventeen-year-old to have). As I ran offstage in my cap and gown, waving my diploma, I ran to hug Mom-Mom. But she jokingly refused to hug me, snatched the diploma out of my hand, and said, "Boy, this is MINE."

By July, Dana had me and Jeff locked in Studio 4 in downtown Philadelphia recording our debut album, *Rock the House*. Because Jeff and I had been making songs since the day we met, we finished the album at light speed. But Dana kept messing with the songs, remixing and reengineering them, and ultimately ruining the production. Our relationship with him was already souring, but we didn't have time to focus on that. We had a hit song, and we had to figure out how to capitalize on it right now.

We did a few shows up and down the East Coast with LL Cool J and Whodini, including a couple of sold-out gigs in New York City. Then we booked our first full tour: We would be opening for Public Enemy and 2 Live Crew, two of the biggest hip-hop acts in the country at the time.

We fed our luggage into the belly of the tour bus. My biological family ceremoniously presenting me unto my new hip-hop family. JL was the new "father"—he was the mature one; he was the adult in the room. He gave Mom-Mom and Daddio our itinerary, complete with bus routing, hotel names and phone numbers, venue addresses and dates, agents' names and contact info.

JL was twenty-one, going on twenty-two. He was the oldest, and Mom-Mom and Daddio were relieved he was in charge. Omarr was the youngest—he was only sixteen, and even at that age his fashion sense was fire. He always had the hottest gear and was the only person I've ever known who traveled with an iron. Most groups had at least two dancers for the symmetry, but Omarr's leg surgery had been so effective that we only needed him. He and I had grown up about ten doors from each other; he had been a witness to most of the major events of my life so far. He had seen me through Raleigh Choppers, cowboy boots; he'd bagged more than his share of ice; he'd even lied to me as I was being deposited into the back of an ambulance.

"Oh yeah, man, definitely, you *definitely* dunked it."

Omarr wouldn't be graduating high school until next year, so JL had to walk up the street to his house to promise his mother that he would take responsibility for Omarr getting his homework done and maintaining his honor roll status (Miss Brown—who had already played a key role in the naming of the Fresh Prince—had made this a condition of Omarr being allowed to go on tour with us).

"Mrs. Rambert, you don't have to be concerned," JL said to Omarr's mom. "*I* graduated from Overbrook; *Will* graduated from Overbrook; and I give you my word: I will make sure that *Omarr* graduates from Overbrook."

Over the next year, JL helped Omarr do his homework in hotel rooms, on tour buses, at rest stops, and they even missed our day at Six Flags Over Georgia because of Pythagoras.

Ready Rock had stayed out partying the night before; he was exhausted. He threw his bags on the bus and was fast asleep in his bunk before we even pulled off.

Jeff had just gotten brand-new Anvil cases to transport his turntables, records, and beatboxes. At the time, because of my excitement, I didn't notice, but Jeff was quiet and to himself that day. In subsequent years he would confide in us that because of his sheltered childhood, every time we would have to leave Philly, he suffered extreme anxiety attacks and other physical reactions. He would have thirty- to forty-minute vomiting spells, but for the longest time, he never said a word.

We had all decided that if we were going to be traveling around to all of these strange towns and cities, it would be unwise to go without security. And in the early days of hip-hop, "security" was defined as your biggest and tallest friend who didn't smile. Ours was Charles Alston, a.k.a. Charlie Mack.

Charlie Mack was raised in South Philly, one of the rougher sections of town. His parents were separated, and he lived with his mom. They moved a lot during his early childhood, until the chaos of his home life pushed him into the streets.

Charlie started hustling on the corners when he was just eleven years old. Not too long after, he graduated to gun totin' and more serious drug dealing. By the time we met him, he was six foot seven, almost three hundred pounds, and nobody messed with Charlie Mack.

He showed up that day with a green trash bag full of ones and fives—clearly the previous evening's revenues from his purveying of neighborhood pharmaceuticals. He had the trash bag slung over his shoulder like a ghetto-ass Santa Claus.

"Charlie. You can*not* walk around carrying a Hefty bag full of cash," JL said.

"Wha'chu mean, wha'chu mean, wha'chu sayin'? I'm not goin' nowhere wit'out my money," Charlie grumbled.

Charlie's voice is way too deep, and he speaks *way* too fast to be nearly seven feet tall. And when he gets excited, he has no problem saying the same word or phrase as many times as necessary until you submit. "My man my man my man my man, and again, and again, hold up hold up hold up hold up hold up." This will stop *anybody* in their tracks—the timbre and speed of repetition are barely comprehensible but magically induce compliance on the part of the listener.

So we let him calm down—me, Jeff, and JL spoke to him later. We talked about our dreams and what we all hoped to build together. We offered Charlie a choice: He could continue to be a drug dealer, or he could take this shot with us to build real lives. We couldn't pay him as much as he could make on the streets, but when we could, we promised we would.

Charlie paused; I could tell he was weighing the whole of his life. He had dreams, too. And in some deep, hidden part of his soul, he knew he was living beneath himself—he had just needed someone to say it out loud.

"I think I can fuck wit' y'all," he said.

He ultimately devoted his life to DJ Jazzy Jeff and the Fresh Prince. It would prove to be a commitment that was not without twists and turns. But one thing was true from that day on: He never sold drugs again.

Bags are finally loaded. Everyone has said their goodbyes. The posse is mounted. I hug my family and step into the tour bus doorwell. Three dirty rubber stairs, the threshold into my new life, a stargate, the portal out of my childhood and into the infinitely unknowable—on my own, where Daddio could no longer hurt me, but he could no longer protect me, either. Away from the shame of failing my mother, away from the fear in her eyes that seemed to say, *He's ruining his life*.

As the doors began to close, I caught eyes with Gigi. She smiled that smile I'd seen in Resurrection Baptist Church every single Sunday of my life.

"Jus' remember, Lover Boy," she said, "be nice to everybody you pass on your way up, coz you just might have to pass them again on your way down."

The sun was setting as our bus rattled across the Chesapeake Bay Bridge. Pennsylvania had turned into Delaware, Delaware had turned into Maryland, and the initial excitement had settled. The hum of the road lulled my heart into a reverie.

The thought washed over me: *I am in charge now.*

I had never been in love like I was with Melanie Parker. I wanted to build a life for us, to shield her from the chaos in the world. I wanted to do it right.

From the time I was five years old, I always wanted to be married. I wanted my own family. Even my childhood games with my siblings: We used to play "White Family." Ellen was "Kathy," Harry was "Dickie," and I was "Junior."

Later, my fantasies as a teenager never involved having multiple girlfriends or wild orgies. My fantasies always involved *one* woman. I wanted to ravish her with my complete, undivided devotion and affection. I wanted to be the best man she's ever known—I wanted to fulfil all of her dreams, solve all of her problems, take away all of her pain. I wanted her to *adore* me. I wanted to be so trustworthy and emotionally reliable that I would cleanse her impression of *all* men. And if I could have killed a dragon for her, climbed up her hair, entered the heavily guarded castle, and then have my kiss work as an antidote to the poison she'd ingested, that would have just been a little icing on my love cake.

I was eighteen.

From the day I met her, Melanie had been the center of my life. Healing the pain of her trauma became my constant preoccupation. The look in Melanie's eyes became the substitute for Gigi's approval. I've always needed a woman to achieve for. When I performed, I was now performing for Melanie. When I started making money rapping, in my mind, I was making money for her. I bound my self-esteem to the sliding scale of her happiness. If she was happy, that meant I was a good person. If she was unhappy, that meant I was a monster.

We arrived in Tallahassee on the first leg of our southern run. The rest of the guys would go to the venue early to set up and sound check, and because all I had to do was rap, I could arrive forty-five minutes before showtime. On that first night, I walked into the dressing room to find the whole squad sitting around with six or seven girls. Jordache jeans and bamboo earrings everywhere. The dressing room smelled like the perfume section of a Merry-Go-Round.

I politely asked Keisha, Mercedes, and Cinnamon 'n' them to leave. And I called a crew meeting.

"We gotta get these rules straight," I said. "I don't want no girls in the dressing rooms; no girls on the bus; and whatever floor we're staying on in the hotel, I don't want no girls there, either. I don't wanna be smellin' no perfume and hearin' no giggling 'n' shit. I'm in love with Melanie, we're in a *relationship*, and I am not out here for no foolishness."

The guys all kind of looked at one another as if to say, *He can't be serious.* Ready Rock raised his hand, and I pointed to him.

"What, man?"

Ready Rock, somewhat confused, said, "So, where we supposed to fuck all the groupies at?"

"Hopefully, you'll be fucking them behind that preposition," I said.

"Will, that's crazy, man," Charlie Mack said. "You're not out here by yourself. This is all of us. How you makin' lateral decisions?"

"Look, man, I'm about to *propose* to this girl; we're getting *married*. And I am *not* messin' it up because of a bunch-a horny-ass ghetto hyenas."

"Big bro, I respec' that you in love 'n' all that," Omarr said, "but that don't make me no hyena."

I was going full choirboy. And the guys didn't like it *at all*. But when my mind locks onto an idea—when I commit to a system of beliefs—there are only two options: one, I complete my mission.

Or two, I'm dead.

We didn't know shit.

We didn't realize you had to pay the bus driver yourself, and if you didn't, he might just go home. We didn't know that some venues would skim money off the top—that they'd lie to you about how many tickets they'd sold. We didn't know that unruly audiences would throw things at you onstage if they didn't like you—pennies, bottles, batteries, shoes, and even an M-80 explosive in Oakland one night. We didn't know there were all kinds of curfew laws and union rules in different states that meant your show would get shut down if you didn't shut up and get offstage quick enough. We didn't know that you had to grease the security guys at the venue if you didn't want your stuff to come up missing. We didn't realize that one inch on a map could equal twelve hours on a tour bus.

People often say *ignorance is bliss.*

Maybe . . . right up until it's *not*.

We punish ourselves for not knowing. We always complain about what we could and should have done, and how much of a mistake it was that we did *that* thing, that *unforgivable* thing. We beat on ourselves for being *so* stupid, regretting our choices and lamenting the horrible decisions we make.

But here's the reality—*that's what life is*. Living is the journey from not knowing to knowing. From not understanding to understanding. From confusion to clarity. By universal design you are born into a perplexing situation, bewildered, and you have one job as a human: figure this shit out.

Life is learning. Period. Overcoming ignorance is the whole point of the journey. You're not *supposed* to know at the beginning. The whole point of venturing into uncertainty is to bring light to the darkness of our ignorance. I heard a great saying once: Life is like school, with one key difference—in school you get the lesson, and then you take the test. But in life, you get the test, and it's your job to take the lesson.

We're all waiting until we have deep knowledge, wisdom, and a sense of certainty before we venture forth. But we've got it backward— venturing forth is how we gain the knowledge.

Over the next few years, while our ignorance would rain down a deluge of pain and suffering, when I look back, I see clearly it could have been no other way. The universe only teaches through experience.

So, even when you haven't the slightest clue what you're doing, you just have to take a deep breath and get on the damn bus.

You couldn't have found three more different groups to put on the same stage than DJ Jazzy Jeff and the Fresh Prince, Public Enemy, and 2 Live Crew. But hip-hop was like that back then.

I found myself studying the audience even more than the performers. We were all tapping into totally different aspects of the human spirit.

Public Enemy would ignite social consciousness—people would

stomp and yell and cheer, venting their dissatisfaction with authority. I noticed how the security energy in the building—particularly in the South—would heighten as Chuck D riled the audience to rail against our shared sense of injustice.

As part of their show, they had a stunt man dress up as a KKK member. They played out a scene in which he was sentenced for his crimes against humanity, and then in the most shocking moment of their entire show, they put a noose around his neck and hung him on-stage. For thirty seconds his body jerking and convulsing in mid-air, while the crowd watched until his last shudder. And then silence, his lifeless body swinging above center stage . . . and then:

YES! The rhythm, the rebel!

Chuck D would drop into "Rebel Without a Pause," as *chaos* and *pandemonium* was unleashed. And while I have experienced other performers who have *matched* the level of intensity Public Enemy could conjure, I have *never* seen it surpassed.

2 Live Crew tapped into an entirely different kind of energy. Luther Campbell, a.k.a. Luke Skyywalker or Uncle Luke, came out onstage and screamed to the crowd, "Heeeeeeeeyyyyyyyyy!?" and fifteen thousand people screamed "WE WANT SOME PUSSYY!!" including the probably eight thousand women in attendance. (I still haven't totally figured that one out.) We had never heard of 2 Live Crew, yet in Florida they were the headliner. Their hit single was called "We Want Some Pussy." They were giving the crowd permission to unleash, at least verbally, their inner hyenas. This was further amplified by the simulated lewd sex acts they included in their shows. And if I can keep it real, some nights they just skipped the *simulated* part.

But what really caught my attention was how smart everybody was. This was an era when "authority"—be it government, business, law enforcement, even many parents—was skeptical and fearful of the growing influence of hip-hop and hip-hop artists. Rap concerts were met with stringent scrutiny, particularly when we toured through southern states. When you're on tour with Public Enemy and 2 Live Crew in Georgia, South Carolina, Mississippi, and Alabama, rest assured your ass was gonna get stringently scrutinized.

Before the concerts in the South, there were always meetings with local sheriffs and chiefs of police to inform us of the local laws and statutes that governed the behavior that would be tolerated onstage. We were informed that any infringement would lead to an immediate ending of the show, and we would be forcibly pulled offstage and arrested. Needless to say, both public fellatio and hanging Klansmen were frowned upon in Mississippi.

Given the high stakes, these meetings would inevitably escalate into social debate and legal interpretation. Chuck D knew the law—he had local advocates, community leaders, and legal scholars arming him with the counterarguments and information necessary to defend his First Amendment rights. And when all else failed, he had bail money preorganized. But what was *not* gonna happen was some local sheriff telling him he couldn't perform his show exactly the way he wanted to perform it. He hung a Klansman every single night of that tour.

Luke Skyywalker, on the other hand, *wanted* to get arrested. He saw it as supremely effective publicity. Uncle Luke was a brilliant entrepreneur; he owned his own record company, distributor, agency, and merchandising group, not to mention barbershops, supermarkets, and nightclubs. He hadn't yet worked out how to expand his businesses beyond his regional foothold. But he knew that if he got arrested in Macon, Georgia, that Baton Rouge and Shreveport, Louisiana, would sell out within twenty-four hours of the headline. (And on top of it, he'd had a perfectly lovely time onstage.) He was also well aware of the growing national and international spotlight that was shining on the question of art versus morality. At the time, Tipper Gore, then the wife of the senator, Al Gore, was leading the charge against profanity in entertainment. Back then, FCC rules forbade broadcasting profanity, and 2 Live didn't have a single record that didn't have profanity in it. (Even record store owners were getting arrested for crimes of obscenity for selling their albums.) So, Uncle Luke got a boat, built a radio station on it, and kept it offshore in international waters where he could legally broadcast back to the mainland. Luke saw 2 Live Crew being at the explosive center of this battle, and he aimed to harness this fuel to expand his business globally.

Eventually, the US Court of Appeals ruled that rap was protected by the First Amendment. (More than twenty years later, Luther Campbell ended up running for mayor of Miami-Dade County.)

I remember sitting in those meetings, wanting to raise my hand so bad and say, *Excuse me, Mr. Sherriff Officer sir, you don't need to look at me, coz my grandmother agrees with you. But honestly, you can probably just arrest them right now. Coz Chuck is definitely gonna hang a Klansman tonight, and Luke never gets past the first chorus before his balls are all the way out.*

Now, our show, Mr. Officer sir, is good, wholesome, family fun! Jeff is the best DJ on earth. Ready Rock C can make the theme from Sanford and Son sound like it's underwater! Omarr couldn't even walk till he was six, but now he's the best damn dancer since . . . Who might you know? . . . Who's a good white dancer? . . . Fred Astaire! And if there was ever a Black kid you wanted your daughter, Becky Sue, to bring home, I promise you it's me. You won't have no problems out of us. Are we free to go now?

I don't remember JL speaking once in any of those meetings. Instead, he filled legal pads with notes. He studied every single word; he later went back to research the statutes; he met with Public Enemy's managers; made friends with tour promoters; picked Luke Skyywalker's brain about major labels versus self-distribution. JL spent less and less time going with us sightseeing, to clubs, or to amusement parks, and more and more time studying the music business from any and every angle.

Touring had opened our eyes to the industry and the intricacies of how it actually worked. Public Enemy had a management company, accountants, A&R reps, and road managers. We just had JL. Word-Up Records, Dana's record label, still didn't have any other artists signed to it; Dana didn't tell us how many records we sold. Our record still wasn't available in any stores outside of Philly.

But the breaking point for me happened when we found out that Dana had not been returning calls from Russell Simmons.

Back then, Russell was arguably the single most important person in the hip-hop world. He had been representing artists and producing records since 1977. He cofounded Def Jam Records, the biggest hip-hop label in the eighties. And he had groomed, managed, and produced all of the biggest acts, such as the Beastie Boys, Run-DMC, LL Cool J, and Whodini.

Apparently, Russell had been trying to contact us for months already, but none of his messages were getting to us because he was trying to reach us through Dana.

We were pissed.

Russell absolutely *loved* DJ Jazzy Jeff and the Fresh Prince. He was raving about the first line of "Girls Ain't Nothing But Trouble" where I say, "Aw my eye, my eye / Man this guy just walked up to me and punched me in my eye, man / Talkin' 'bout how I was just trying to talk to his girl, man / I don't even know her, man!"

"That's the illest shit I've ever heard," Russell said. "What rapper admits they got punched in the eye?"

Russell recognized our honesty, vulnerability, and self-deprecating humor—unheard of in hip-hop at the time—as a passport to places rappers had never gone. Russell wanted to work with us; unfortunately, Dana refused to talk to him.

I've always marveled at JL's and Dana's opposite reactions to Russell's enthusiasm. Whereas Dana was threatened by Russell's interest, JL saw Russ as a potential teacher and a gateway to new opportunities.

And JL had a plan: Even though Dana controlled the recording of our music, JL controlled the management of our career. He agreed to turn over the management of DJ Jazzy Jeff and the Fresh Prince to Russell Simmons and Lyor Cohen at Rush Management under three conditions: (1) they would put Jazzy Jeff and Fresh Prince on tour with their biggest artists; (2) they would hire JL to oversee our account; and (3) they would teach JL the business.

Russell agreed.

It is so painful when people I care about miss the opportunity to elevate. I've been in this kind of situation maybe fifty times in my career. I am trying to climb and fly as high as humanly possible, and I want to take the people I love with me. But invariably, at critical moments, when the necessity to level up presents itself, some people—like JL— rise to the occasion and others fold. Whether they don't see the grander vision, or can't take the heat of the fresh challenge, or they're trapped by some hidden, self-defeating narrative, over and over I have suffered the pain of waving from the bow of the new ship as they're left behind, standing on the shore.

"You gotta get us out of this Dana deal," I said to JL.

"It doesn't work like that," JL said.

"So he can just hold us back and there's nothing we can do? Doesn't he have some legal responsibility?"

"He has a *contract*," JL said. "You just make the records. Let me figure this out."

Hip-hop was now a global business, and DJ Jazzy Jeff and the Fresh Prince were primed to be packaged and sold to the world. We needed national and global distribution.

Jive Records was based out of London. (Jive would later become famous for masterminding the careers of Britney Spears, NSYNC, and Backstreet Boys, but back in the eighties, they were the biggest hip-hop label in Europe.) With Dana controlling our record in the United States, JL orchestrated an international distribution deal with Jive to sell *Rock the House* overseas. Jive hired Dana's Word-Up Records to be the official distributor of DJ Jazzy and Jeff and the Fresh Prince in the United States.

On the surface, this appeared to be an easy win for Dana. He'd get to keep selling our records in the States while we'd gain a bigger profile worldwide and go into the studio on Jive's dime. Basically, Jive would cover all the costs, but Dana would still get a revenue stream at home. Dana couldn't wait to sign *that* contract. Dana got a big check and sold our international rights to Jive.

Jive immediately remastered and rereleased *Rock the House*, in March 1987, with a new cover and a new burst of energy, and it became a significant global hit. They were also able to sell this new version as an import in the United States. Dana realized that he had opted for a one-time payment instead of a royalty, and he could do nothing about the imports. So he demanded more money and threatened to refuse all cooperation with Jive.

A legal battle ensued. And as soon as the lawyers started digging into our paperwork, they figured out that I had been seventeen when I signed the contract with Dana. Under Pennsylvania law, anyone under the age of eighteen cannot legally sign a contract without a parent or guardian present. I had signed mine in the lobby of a studio before a recording session, therefore, in legal terms, our contract with Dana never existed.

Just like that, Dana Goodman was out of the DJ Jazzy Jeff and the Fresh Prince business.

Dana was furious. At first, he blamed Jive and Russell Simmons. But lacking the lawyers and money to go after them, he decided to exact revenge on the next best thing: me.

People in the neighborhood started pulling me up: "Hey, man, Dana's really upset. Just watch your back."

Then, one night, he pulled up outside our house, parked his car on the street, and just sat there. I was terrified, but Daddio never flinched. Not saying a word, he opened the front door, walked up to Dana's car, and leaned down into the open passenger-side window. Daddio saw a gun on the dashboard.

"Can I help you?" Daddio said.

"Where's that muthafucka at?" Dana gruffly responded.

"Well, if the muthafucka you're looking for is Will, he's in the house. You're welcome to come in and kill him now. And the whole family's home, too, coz if you touch Will, you gon' have to kill us all. . . . But we ain't acceptin' no fuckin' threats from you."

Daddio immediately turned his back on a man who could easily have shot him and strolled into the house. I'm not sure if it was his military training or his upbringing on the streets of North Philly, but he taught me a valuable lesson that day: It's better to die than to walk around scared.

I was in the living room, peeking from behind the curtain. I watched as Dana put his car in drive and drove away.

SEVEN

ADVENTURE

f this book were a movie, we've now reached the montage scene where the music kicks in ("For the Love of Money" by the O'Jays), and everything goes great.

Our hero can't miss; he's on the come-up. Every shot goes in; every kiss burns with the passion of a thousand suns; he can't get to the bank fast enough to cash all the checks. His name dances off the lips and rings in the ears of the high and the mighty—no longer emblazoned on the side of his pants, his moniker now bounces off his chest in twenty-four-carat herringbone gold littered with ethically sourced diamonds.

It became clear in this year that he was *never* going to college.

Our debut album, *Rock the House*—led by "Girls Ain't Nothing But Trouble" as the first single, and now plugged into the international distribution system of Jive Records—ended up going gold (selling more than 500,000 copies) and would eventually reach #83 on the Billboard 200 chart. And while that wasn't necessarily considered earth-shattering at the time, Cinderella had made it to the ball.

Now, I don't want to be the old guy at the end of the bar yapping about how much better music was in *his* day. How these kids don't know nothin' about *real* rap. There is actually brain science that theorizes that the songs you hear in your teenage years become embronzed in your emotional memory, heightening their nostalgic power beyond any other period in your life.

That's not what's happening here. I get that that's what happens with other people. But this is not some dopamine-induced opinion, blinkered by wistful memories of a fairy-tale adolescence. No! What *I'm* saying is *objectively*, and **factually true:** The late 1980s was the greatest time in hip-hop history, period, full stop, amen.

Please be seated; allow me to make my case.

From the moment Jeff and I stepped on that tour bus in late 1986, through summer 1988, we performed nearly two hundred shows. And I would like to list just a few of the hip-hop icons with whom we shared a stage (imagine this in my "trying not to be an asshole" voice):

Run-DMC

LL Cool J

Whodini

Public Enemy

2 Live Crew

Salt-N-Pepa

Eric B. & Rakim

N.W.A

EPMD

UTFO

J.J. Fad

Beastie Boys

The Geto Boys

Heavy D and the Boyz

Sir Mix-A-Lot

Kid 'n Play

MC Lyte

Queen Latifah

Grandmaster Flash

Ice-T

Mantronix and Just-Ice

Eazy-E

Too Short

MC Hammer

Doug E. Fresh and Slick Rick

Big Daddy Kane

Biz Markie

Roxanne Shante

MC Shan and the whole Juice Crew

A Tribe Called Quest

Leaders of the New School

Naughty by Nature

Shall I continue, or we good?

This was one of the greatest periods of my life. Everything was new—we were defining the culture. We were a part of the wave, the tsunami that was carrying hip-hop across the globe. Every artist was unique—something happened every show that was a first in hip-hop. We were playing in front of crowds where sometimes 50 percent of the audience had never seen someone rap before. They were in awe. There was an intoxicating energy of discovery and adventure.

This was a time in my life rich with first encounters and mind-expanding new experiences. The executive who ran our account at Jive was a Japanese woman named Ann Carli. At first, Jeff and I were a little confused at how she was going to direct our careers, and then she spoke. She had been at the heart of the initial bursts of hip-hop in New York City. She fed Jeff and me a global diet of the world's hip-hop colorings. I could feel my spirit of adventure awakening. I discovered the vital importance of travel—it lends critical perspective. Things that had been debilitating problems in my mind on the streets of West Philly barely existed in a rodeo arena in Omaha, Nebraska. I made a promise to myself that I would eat anything that the locals ate. I've eaten blackened alligator, sea slugs, camel, and chocolate-covered crickets. (Everything tastes like chicken. It doesn't—I just always wanted to say that.) I wanted to see and do everything.

On the back of the moderate but solid success of *Rock the House*, Jive Records was eager for us to record a follow-up album as soon as possible. In the fall of 1987, our first-ever trip out of the United States was scheduled—six weeks in London, where Jive was headquartered, to record in their company studios.

But two weeks prior to our departure date, JL called me with that 1:00 a.m. phone call where even the tone of the ring makes your heart jump.

"Jeff was in a car accident," he said.

Disoriented, I responded, "What happened? Where is he? Is he cool?"

"I don't know; I'm going to the hospital; I'll hit you back."

Back then, there were no texts, no reaching people in their cars, no minute-to-minute reports on how your loved ones were doing. You just made sure everybody stayed off the landline, you kept checking the phone for a dial tone, and you waited. And the longer you waited, the more graphic and disturbing the pictures your mind painted—until you were absolutely certain that you'd never see them again.

At about 3:15 a.m., the phone rang again. This time the ring was louder than it should have been, like it was ringing *at* me instead *for* me.

I answered.

"Yo."

"He's cool," JL said. "His right leg is broken, and he has a cast from his hip to his ankle. Other than that, he's fine. But the doctor said he shouldn't fly. We need to postpone the trip for about eight weeks."

In the background I heard Jeff scream out, "I don't give a fuck WHAT that doctor says. In two weeks, I'm-a be on a plane to London."

And true to his determined spirit, two weeks later, we were checking in to the Holiday Inn, Swiss Cottage. It was me and Charlie in one tiny cramped-ass hotel room, and JL, Ready Rock, and Jeff and his full-length cast in another. Just five Philly kids, dreary English days and dank English nights, but a private recording studio set aside just for *us* on Jive's dime.

We spent more than a month in London, and I couldn't have told you a single thing about the city. We didn't walk through Hyde Park or visit Westminster Abbey. We didn't see Buckingham Palace or climb the Tower of London. We didn't sit in a thousand-year-old pub and eat fish and chips. And we sure as hell didn't go to no soccer match.

We never even adjusted from our jet lag. We woke up at 4:00 p.m. every day, hit the studio by 6:00 p.m., worked until about 6:00 a.m., grabbed some free breakfast from the Swiss Cottage buffet, and went to bed around 7:00 a.m. We kept that schedule up for almost six weeks.

And it was *bliss*.

Well, except for the one night that Jeff decided he wanted his cast taken off. His six-week appointment to have it removed fell while we were still in London, and his leg was starting to itch, but he didn't trust Britain's National Health Service to take it off. He was more comfortable if me and Charlie Mack did it.

As a general rule, if someone asks me if I can do something, the answer is always yes, a delusional trait that both Charlie Mack and I share wholeheartedly.

"It's a cast, I'm sayin', it's just a cast. Let's just take it off," Charlie said indifferently.

I, too, felt confident in the basic simplicity of the operation. It was just a cast.

I called room service and requested a steak knife. Little did I know that British hotels didn't carry steak knives (this would make the process of cutting a piece of steak far too easy for them). Undeterred, I said, "Well, can you send up thirty butter knives, please?"

The Swiss Cottage butter knives had a tiny serrated edge at the tip (which suggests that they weren't actually butter knives). My plan was, I would give Charlie fifteen knives, and he would begin cutting at Jeff's ankle, and I would take fifteen knives and start cutting at Jeff's hip.

The way the math played out in my mind, by the time we'd worn out the serrated edges of the "butter knives," we should have met at Jeff's knee for a quick high-five celebration before making the last ceremonial cut. I had a vague memory that this two-ended, meet-in-the-middle process was successfully employed in the building of the Panama Canal and equally in the construction of the United States railroad system.

The cutting began. Or the lack thereof. Butter knife after butter knife bent and fell, as confusion grew into frustration on Charlie's sweat-moistened face.

"Yo, these knives ain't doin' shit," he said.

I was twelve years old the last time I'd had a cast, and at the time they were made of plaster of paris. Apparently, cast science had advanced since then, and Jeff's was made out of some new alien material that I later learned was fiberglass.

About six knives in, I called a halt. Undeterred, I suggested that Jeff get into the bathtub. We'd make the water as hot as he could take it, thereby softening this puppy up. I assured Jeff it would come right off. He agreed.

Me and Charlie helped Jeff into the bathtub, both legs fully submerged, and then we waited. Pretty soon, a look of concern washed over Jeff's face.

"Yo, man, y'all need to get this shit off, it's tightenin' up," Jeff said.

I remember thinking, *What would MacGyver do?* MacGyver was a hit 1980s TV show where the lead character, Angus MacGyver, would get into all kinds of predicaments, only to come up with some ingenious solution. As I was attempting to channel my inner Mac, I heard the door to the hotel room open—a few seconds later, JL pokes his head into the bathroom.

By this point, Jeff is squirming and moaning in the bathtub, while Charlie Mack and I are on our knees holding two "butter knives" with twenty-eight others scattered all over the bathroom floor. JL takes a long pause, presumably trying to puzzle out what he's seeing.

Stumped, he shouts, "WHAT THE FUCK ARE Y'ALL DOIN'?"

"JL, JL!" Jeff squealed. "You gotta get this shit off my leg!"

"WHY ARE YOU IN THE TUB?"

JL had spent the previous two years working at a hospital. So, while it was not his expertise, either, he at least knew that you don't soak a fiberglass cast in hot water while it's still on somebody's leg.

"YOU CAN'T GET THAT CAST WET LIKE THAT."

"Just get it off, y'all," Jeff wailed.

"Stop bitchin', man, it can't be that bad," Charlie said.

"GET HIM OUT THE GODDAMN TUB," JL barked.

"YOU DON'T NEED TO BE YELLIN' AT US, JL, THAT DON'T HELP *SHIT*!" Charlie snapped back.

Me and Charlie got Jeff out of the tub as instructed and laid him on the bathroom floor. We had been keeping canned foods in our hotel rooms because Swiss Cottage room service wasn't all it could have been. JL immediately went over and opened a can of beef stew. With the jagged edge of the aluminum lid, he came over to Jeff's cast, and whereas Charlie and I had been trying to cut vertically up and down the cast, JL made gentle horizontal moves *across* the cast, and like Grant through Richmond, in less than ninety seconds, he had made a full-length incision, which Charlie and I were able to easily pry fully open.

Jeff was free.

Angrily, JL threw the top of the beef stew can into the trash, and as he exited, he grumbled, "Y'all are as stoopid as shit."

In medical scenarios, we may have been dumb and dumber. But in the studio, we were *fire*. Those recording sessions were probably the purest creative experiences I have ever had in my career. We recorded so many songs, and the record company loved so many of them, that they decided to attempt something that had never before been tried in the world of rap: DJ Jazzy Jeff and the Fresh Prince would release hip-hop's first double album.

Jeff and I had no concept of what this album was going to do, whether it was something fans would want to hear, whether MTV would like it, whether radio stations would play it, whether hip-hop heads would diss it. None of this crossed our minds—all we cared about was that we were inspired and inflamed by the creative process. We were having *fun*—we were best friends at the center of our new family, and we were on the cutting edge of a burgeoning global art form.

We were riding high, but in hindsight, imperceptible seeds of impending discontent were being sown.

Some people thrive at high altitudes, but others can't breathe. And what do people do when they climb a mountain and realize the air is too thin? They try to get back down as fast as possible. Quincy Jones called it "altitude sickness."

In high school, Ready Rock and I had been best friends. We would ride around every single day battling and creating. We were inseparable. But as DJ Jazzy Jeff and the Fresh Prince began to take shape, human beatboxing was becoming less and less of a core art form within our group. The record company was also not interested in songs featuring human beatboxing. The result was that Clate was being pushed to the fringes of our new family. I was telling him to not worry—"I got you," I said. In hindsight, it was too much change too fast, and the experience demanded emotional maturity that was far beyond what *any* of us possessed.

And to make matters even more painful and complicated, Charlie Mack and I were becoming locked at the hip. We weren't just sharing a hotel room together—we were sharing every aspect of our lives. There's even a song on the album celebrating my relationship with Charlie, "Charlie Mack (The First Out the Limo)." The song developed from Charlie overdoing his security job—he would sit in the front of the limo with the driver, and he would be pissed if me or Jeff got out before *he* did. He would bark, "Gotdam, y'all, lemme secure the perimeter before y'all step out!"

There are no songs on the album about Ready Rock.

From 1987 until 1990, I did not step outside without Charlie Mack with me. Whereas Jeff and JL were quiet, introspective homebodies, Charlie and I were loud, raucous, center-of-attention party-starters. We were always looking for something to get ourselves into. We both loved to party; we loved to talk; we loved traveling and gambling and fast cars; and women loved us. Charlie not only matched but also challenged my adventurous spirit. This joka never wanted to sleep. If we were only in a town for ten hours, he didn't see any reason to spend a single minute in the hotel room. Many a day he *literally* dragged me out of bed to go to Paisley Park in Minneapolis, or to go hear a speech given by some activist in Chicago, or demand that we take a picture on "the Strip," which is what Charlie calls the Champs-Élysées in Paris.

"C'mon, man," he'd say, "you get to sleep all you want when you dead."

The other part of our chemistry was that Charlie and I are both incredibly competitive and absolutely delusional in our high self-regard. We'd spend entire days arguing about who could run faster, who's a better driver, who could throw a football farther, who was more handsome, who was funnier, who was smarter, and, most of all, which one girls liked more.

Charlie absolutely hated it when a woman walked past him to flirt with me. He could *not* figure out why a woman would want to waste time with *me* if she could have *him*. He finally begrudgingly concluded, "Man, the only reason girls wanna get wit' you is coz you're famous."

To which I replied, "Nah, Charlie, you got it *backward*: I'm *famous* because all the girls wanna *get* with me."

We were the yin to each other's yang; we filled in the gaps in each other's life experience. We saw each other's blind spots and augmented each other's deficiencies.

Charlie, like Daddio, had sharp streetwise instincts—he used to call it his "ghetto radar." Charlie just *knew* when something bad was about to happen. We'd be out somewhere, everything would be going great, and out of nowhere, Charlie would whisper in my ear, "Let's go."

I'd be like, "What? Yo, we just go here."

And then, more forcibly, "Get up. *Right. Now.* I said, 'Let's *go.'*" I remember thinking that Charlie Mack was the human equivalent of an overly sensitive smoke alarm that keeps going off at 2:00 a.m. when there's no fire. And because it's a smoke alarm, you can't ignore it, because one day there may actually be flames. But Charlie Mack was an *infallible*, perfectly calibrated hood smoke alarm. Every single time, I'd be grumbling in the parking lot as the sound of gunshots rang out from the party we'd just left.

We compensated for each other's weaknesses. Charlie knew the streets, and I understood broader emotional patterns. I was book smart and mainstream-friendly. Whereas Charlie's physical appearance was scary and intimidating, I knew how to smile, make people feel safe, and get us in anywhere.

Both of us were wildly deficient, but together we made one really capable person.

I was Charlie's ticket into rooms into which he would never have been invited. And Charlie was the hammer that came down on anybody who dared to talk shit about me. He emboldened me to defend myself physically. Around this time, the chorus of criticism that I was "corny" and "soft" was beginning to rise. I didn't curse; I rapped about my high school experiences; I used a lot of humor. The shit-talking was that I wasn't a "real MC" or—the worst—that I wasn't "Black enough" and my music wasn't "real hip-hop."

"Jus' punch the muthafucka in the *face*!" Charlie would say. "He won't say that shit next time."

So, with him having my back, I started doing exactly that: If somebody talked shit, I punched them in the face . . . (and then jumped behind Charlie).

He's the DJ, I'm the Rapper was released on March 29, 1988. Anchored by "Brand New Funk" and "Parents Just Don't Understand," the album would eventually reach #4 on the Billboard 200, going triple platinum (selling more than three million copies).

What was so groundbreaking about the record was that half was a DJ-centered tour de force, a "scratch album" in which Jeff absolutely massacred the wheels of steel. And the other half was the rapper side, where I was allowed to let the hyper-creative, poetic playfulness of my nineteen-year-old mind run wild.

Then, the unimaginable happened: It was announced that the 31st Annual Grammy Awards would be the first to include a rap category. And "Parents Just Don't Understand" was nominated alongside Salt-N-Pepa's "Push It," "Going Back to Cali" by LL Cool J, Kool Moe Dee's "Wild Wild West," and "Supersonic" by J.J. Fad.

This was the first time I ever saw Jeff cry. I was excited beyond anything I'd ever experienced, but I'm not an "accomplishment cryer." I wasn't mature enough to ask back then, but I always wanted to know exactly what part of it was so emotional for Jeff. Was he thinking about his cancer as a child? Was it his mother and his musical family who had been reaching for this for so many years and he was the one bringing this honor? Was he scared? Did he realize there was no going back—that his old life was gone forever—and that the bar was now set so high?

Charlie Mack, who had recently joined the Nation of Islam, said, "This the will-a God. Y'all aligned with the will-a God. You won! I'm tellin' you, you won. None of them records gonna beat your record. What God ordains, no man contains."

Charlie Mack had been speaking in spiritual rhymes for a few months now. But in pure Charlie Mack form, on February 22, 1989, Bobby McFerrin won Record of the Year for "Don't Worry, Be Happy;" Album of the Year was George Michael's *Faith*; Tracy Chapman won Best New Artist; and the winner for Best Rap Performance was DJ

Daddio in 1971, in the ACRAC office. He's probably not talking to anybody—he just knows he's fly.

Mom-Mom and Daddio, pictured here right before they were about to make me.

The Woodcrest house in West Philly. This is where I grew up.

My full name is Willard Carroll Smith II. I was born on September 25, 1968. I'm nekkid under that blanket.

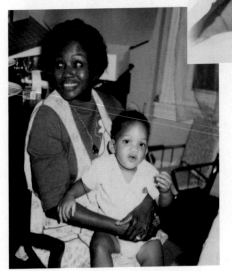

Me and my Gigi in her house on North Fifty-Fourth Street.

Daddio was always teaching—he wanted us to be able to build and create with our hands.

Mom-Mom with my twin siblings, Harry and Ellen. Dig the 'fro.

In the Woodcrest house with Pam, Harry, and Ellen. Early smile practice.

The ACRAC fleet, blocking what is now "Will Smith, Sr. Way" in West Philly. (The dark-blue van with the white lettering is the one Paul had when it was broken into.)

With Mom-Mom, Daddio, Pam, Harry, and Ellen at Woodcrest in the early 1970s.

In the kitchen at Woodcrest. I was a very fearful child.

On the great road trip of my childhood in 1976.

The Grand Canyon was the greatest thing I'd ever seen.

Overbrook High School was nicknamed "the Castle on the Hill." It spanned two square city blocks, and loomed over the neighborhood like a stone fortress.

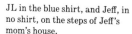

JL in the blue shirt, and Jeff, in no shirt, on the steps of Jeff's mom's house.

The crew who set out from West Philly on our first major tour in 1986. Clockwise, from top right: me, dancer Omarr, beatboxer Ready Rock, manager James Lassiter, DJ Jazzy Jeff, and security in the form of Charlie Mack Alston (who, if you haven't noticed, is holding me and Jeff up in his arms).

In the early days of hip-hop, "security" was defined as your biggest and tallest friend who didn't smile. Charlie Mack was off-duty in this photo with Jeff.

With JL in London in fall 1987. This was about as tourist as we got.

Gold records for DJ Jazzy Jeff and the Fresh Prince. From left: JL, Jeff, Russell Simmons, and Lyor Cohen. Russell absolutely loved DJ Jazzy Jeff and the Fresh Prince.

Bucky Davis was five foot one, and the one is a stretch. There was absolutely no reason for him to bend over in this photograph.

Mimi Brown is one of the most iconic DJs in Philadelphia history. She was the seductive, sultry voice of our childhood imaginings, and seeing her in person did not disappoint.

Me and Tanya back in the day. I'm cool with everything in this photo except my pants being rolled up . . . and how I'm standing . . . and not having a shirt on . . . and shades at night . . . and what am I looking at?

Me and Quincy Jones, season one, on the living-room set of *The Fresh Prince of Bel-Air*.

Friday night tapings of *The Fresh Prince of Bel-Air* were as hot as any club you've ever been to. Standing, from left: Benny Medina, Joseph Marcell, Alfonso Ribeiro, James Avery, Tyler Collins, Kadeem Hardison (the star of *A Different World*), me, Quincy Jones, Al B. Sure!. Sitting, from left: Tatyana Ali, Janet Hubert, and Karyn Parsons.

Me and Karyn on the set of the *Fresh Prince*. Don't hate the player, hate the game.

Sheree Zampino is from New York. Not real New York—Schenectady
(damn near Canada.) Here with our respective parents on our wedding day in 1992.

With Sheree and Trey in 1993. He got his mom's eyes and his dad's ears.

Hey, I found this baby in the pool. Says his name is Trey. I can't swim, so somebody should probably take him.

Seems like my tailor used all the extra fabric that was left over from Jada's outfit.

Surrounding every strong man are generations of strong women.
With Fawn, Gammy, Gigi, Mom-Mom, and Jada.

"Marty Maaaar!"
"Big Will-aaaay!"

This is the shot from *Bad Boys* that made me a movie star,
despite my novice acting mistake: finger on the trigger.

Jazzy Jeff and the Fresh Prince for "Parents Just Don't Understand," making us the first rappers *ever* to receive a Grammy Award.

We ultimately ended up boycotting the actual ceremony because NARAS, the Grammy committee, refused to televise the presentation of the rap award. We felt like that was a slap in the face—rap music had outsold the industry that year; we deserved to be there. Russell Simmons and Lyor Cohen organized the boycott for Jazzy Jeff and the Fresh Prince, along with Salt-N-Pepa, Ice-T, Public Enemy, Doug E. Fresh and Slick Rick, Stetsasonic, and many others.

And even though we weren't at the Grammys, Jazzy Jeff and the Fresh Prince were everywhere else. Life changed forever—well, almost. Jeff's mom planned a celebration dinner for Jeff and me after our first American Music Award. We showed up on the block as returning hometown heroes—people were coming out of their houses to cheer and applaud and shake our hands. It took us twenty minutes to get into Jeff's mom's house. When we finally made it in she threw her arms around us, gushing pride and joy. Then she handed Jeff five dollars and a shopping list.

"Jeffrey, I want you to go to the corner and get me some bread, some baking soda, and see if they got them yams that come in a can."

"But, Mom . . . ," Jeff started.

"But nothing, boy, go get that stuff I told you to get."

So, DJ Jazzy Jeff and the Fresh Prince had to walk through our adoring fans up to Looney's.

They didn't have the yams.

Russell Simmons was orchestrating the global destruction of all barriers to hip-hop, and me and Jeff were one of his battering rams. We were the "clean" group, the "respectable" group—for Russell, we were the perfect weapon against all naysayers. We were at the tip of the spear. We launched *Yo! MTV Raps*, blasting hip-hop into daytime television.

When the Four Seasons Hotels would not allow rap artists to stay during their tours, Russell convinced them to allow DJ Jazzy Jeff and the Fresh Prince, opening the doors for future hip-hop artists to use the chain. Daytime radio was terrified to put rappers on live, so they always forced rappers to prerecord interviews to make sure we didn't say anything crazy. Me and Jeff were among the first wave to be allowed to speak live on the radio during the day.

Our shows were getting bigger, the crowds were getting louder. One night in Detroit, at the Joe Louis Arena, I got overexcited and forgot the words to "Parents Just Don't Understand." This had never happened to me before. My heart dropped into my stomach. There are few things more embarrassing than forgetting the words to the one song that eighteen thousand people spent their hard-earned money to come and hear. But something miraculous happened: The entire crowd began to sing the lyrics back to me. Every person knew every word. I held the mic out to the crowd, and they finished the song. It took everything I had not to burst into tears. Thousands of people saying *my words* back to me. I felt loved, protected, and cradled by a crowd of strangers.

We were red-hot, and unstoppable.

At twenty years old, I was a world-famous rapper, a Grammy Award winner, and a Freshly minted millionaire (pun intended).

I *would* drop the mic, but I need it for the next chapter.

For months, Gigi had been saving up to move to a sixteenth-floor apartment overlooking the Main Line. It was a beautiful building set up for senior-friendly living. Her house on North Fifty-Fourth Street had become a burden for her—too many stairs, and generally inconvenient for her advancing years. With my first money, I surprised Gigi with the apartment she'd been saving up for. She had thought we were just going to *look* at it, but then the real estate agent handed her the keys.

"Lover Boy?" she said, with a gasp. "How'd you do this?"

"Well, Gigi, see, there's this thing called rap music . . . ," I said, putting my arms around her.

Melanie and I moved into Gigi's old house on North Fifty-Fourth Street. My childhood home was now our new home. I had promised Melanie that I would take care of her, and here I was, providing the first safe home of her short life.

I'd won. All of my dreams were blossoming into vivid THX sound and Technicolor.

I had conquered life.

EIGHT

PAIN

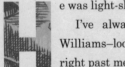e was light-skinned, with light eyes. I hated dudes like that. I've always been intimidated by those Christopher Williams–lookin' jokas. Women have always shoulder-surfed right past me to gawk over Al B. Sure! or El DeBarge.

I had just come home from a two-week run in the Pacific Northwest: Seattle, Portland, and a bunch of the little ones in between. I used to run right offstage, into the car, straight to the airport, to get back to Melanie as quickly as possible. I didn't want to leave any room for my inner hyena to grab the wheel and drunk-drive through my life.

I was meeting Melanie at her aunt's house; I had the car drop me off there directly from the airport. We were going to walk from her aunt's to our new home. For old time's sake, we were going to pass Overbrook High and hit the Sugar Bowl convenience store for a water ice and a soft Philly pretzel, just as we'd done a thousand times before.

I always loved how much Melanie missed me. Even weekend gigs . . . when I came home Monday mornings, she acted like I'd been gone for months. She knew how to make a dude feel glad he was home.

When I walked in after the Northwest trip, she and her aunt were in the kitchen, cooking, just as they'd been so many times before. Being on the road can be excruciatingly lonely—it feels almost like it dehydrates your heart. Her aunt was in her usual dark blue hijab with her glasses way down on the tip of her nose so she could see into the pots.

The smell of the food seemed to soften and quench my parched soul. Melanie was in one of her art smocks that doubled as an apron. (I always thought that was weird; paint is *chemicals*—that smock did not belong in a kitchen.)

I looked at Melanie. Everything was the same except something wasn't. Her energy was odd; something was off. Because of my upbringing, it's almost as if I have a shock collar wrapped around my central nervous system. When I perceive that something is askew, that someone's external behavior is out of sync with what is going on in their heart and mind, my body experiences what I can best describe as a gradual rising electrical current. I feel a *bzzzzzz*. And then it's like I'm shivering, but I'm not cold.

The kitchen was hot, but I had the chills.

We sat down. We ate dinner. We talked about the neighbor's dogs. Melanie's aunt had once been to Portland. She didn't like that section of the country—too rainy. Melanie was laughing too much.

Bzzzzzz.

After dinner we watched *Trading Places*. I know every word Eddie Murphy says in that movie; he was my idol. Melanie and I had seen it at least ten times, but tonight she kept laughing too hard.

BZZZZZZZZZZ.

Her aunt went to bed. We were finally alone. Melanie snuggled into me; I had missed her a lot on this trip. We kissed. But her kisses felt less like affection and more like something she thought she'd better do if she was going to successfully hide the fact that she had fucked somebody.

BZZZZZ. BZZZZZ. BZZZZZ. BZZZZZ.

To this day I don't know how I knew. Or how I felt so confident to commit wholeheartedly the way I did to my instinct. Taking her arm from around my neck, pushing away, I stood up and yelled, "You think I'm STUPID?"

"What?" Melanie said.

But not strongly enough.

"I know what the fuck you did. Stop looking at me like I'm stupid."

I was all in, every chip on the table. I was holding nothing, but she folded.

"I'm sorry," she said, bursting into tears. "It only happened one time. But I don't love him, I'm so sorry. I love you. We were just friends, and then . . . you were gone! I didn't know what you were doin' out there. I was missing you. I swear to God, I won't do it again."

What? I was *right*? But no. Why?

I had been knocked unconscious in the past. My first day at Overbrook High when I was hit in the head with that lock: there is a blue flash, and then you're in a strange, alternate universe where all of the things you once believed are now up for grabs. Gravity, cause and effect, love, whether or not it rains in Southern California.

This is impossible. I've done everything right. I'm winning. I'm the best. I've made a home for us. I've spent months arguing and fighting with a ravenous, slathering pride of ghetto hyenas to keep girls off the buses and out of the hotel rooms. I haven't touched or kissed or barely even glanced at another woman. I come straight home from the airport. We've talked about babies and making a better home than either of us had grown up in. How could you possibly do this to me? How could you do this to us?

On the outside, though, I was strangely calm, because none of these thoughts were registering as actual feelings. I *wanted* to be angry—I mean, you're supposed to be pissed when somebody cheats on you, right? But I *felt* nothing.

Melanie was covering her face, crying on the couch.

Dan Aykroyd was attacking Eddie Murphy. Eddie was pleading for his life: "It was the *Dukes*. It was the *Dukes*."

And I just stood there, numb. When somebody cheats on you, you have to *do* something. But what? I didn't feel any emotions, but I was not going to be a coward. Not this time.

What do you do when somebody cheats on you? I knew I had to do the storm-out thing. But I also knew I had to do something violent to punctuate my departure. I scanned the room for possibilities. Next to the fireplace I noticed one of those forged-iron pointy things that you poke the logs with. But what will I do with it? *I sure wish I had some emotion to give me a little direction. . . .*

Nevertheless, I picked it up. The front entry to Melanie's aunt's house was a beautiful wooden atrium holding a hundred glass panels. I stood for a moment, looking at Melanie weeping, deeply uncommitted to my as-yet-undetermined but-absolutely-mandatory hissy fit. I calmly carried the iron pointy thing toward the front door and began to break the windows out one by one.

I guess I smashed about twelve, maybe fifteen, before I felt I had sufficiently done my performative duty as a cuckolded twenty-year-old. I slammed the pointy thing to the ground—it scared the hell out of me: It clanged a lot louder than I thought it would. *Shit—what if Melanie's aunt heard that?* I thought. *I should probably go.*

Melanie and I were supposed to be walking home together, but instead I decided to walk to Woodcrest alone.

Mom-Mom had finally had enough. She had kicked Daddio out while I was on tour, this time for good. Daddio had moved into the apartments above the ACRAC office. I knew Mom-Mom would be home alone.

It was about a twenty-two-minute walk. I could not believe I had just broken all those windows. I couldn't locate where it had come from within me. It seemed so strange to me to break things because I thought I *should*, not because I was at all emotionally impelled to do so. This discordance was hilarious to me. Out of nowhere I began to chuckle, replaying the scene in my mind. I was thinking, *Will, you are an absolute lunatic.* And that made me laugh even more. This whole shit was hysterical.

By the time I got to Woodcrest, Mom-Mom was sitting on the front step. Clearly, she had spoken to Melanie's aunt; she never sat on the front step. Her eyes were brimming; she was hoping to God that I was OK, but she was bracing for the storm. She knew her boy.

When I saw her eyes, I felt how completely in tune she was to my pain. It wasn't just mine anymore, it was *ours*. And like a blast of dynamite demolishing the dam holding back the river of my agony, I collapsed on the sidewalk, ten feet from where the tour bus had borne me away from her.

Mom-Mom runs down, throwing her arms around me, as I wail. My childhood home mutely staring down upon my anguish. I had believed that leaving Woodcrest would mean I'd never have to feel this way again.

"How could she *do* this, Mommy? Why did God let this happen?"

Mom-Mom said nothing; she just held me. I was an adult now; my problems were beyond her fixing. I could feel her tears falling on the back of my neck.

She picked me up and took me home.

Heartbreak should be considered a disease—it induces a debilitating state akin to mental illness. The pain I was suffering was so intense I would have preferred to have been stabbed or beaten or have a tooth pulled without Novocain.

My girlfriend had cheated on me, which was proof to my shattered mind that I was a piece of shit—I reasoned that she wouldn't have cheated if I had been good enough. I had failed *another* woman.

I desperately needed relief. But as there's no pill for heartbreak, I resorted to the homeopathic remedies of shopping and rampant sexual intercourse.

Shopping: That next week, I flew ten of my friends from Philly to Atlanta and I closed down the Gucci store.

"Whatever y'all want, I got it," I said, slinging my Amex down on the counter.

I had an Amex card now. And unlike my heart, *it* was unbreakable. Money was flowing like the Nile. We had just launched the "DJ Jazzy Jeff and the Fresh Prince Rap Hotline." 1-900-909-JEFF was the first-ever 900 number. Premium-rate telephone numbers were a revolutionary new way to connect with fans (and, basically, the predecessor to modern social media). Fans called our number, and we would leave daily messages—a few minutes long—about where we were and what we were doing. It cost two dollars for the first minute, and forty-five cents for each additional minute. At the height of the popularity of the line, we were getting five thousand calls a day.

Do the math. My Amex card wasn't just unbreakable, it was invincible.

Rampant sexual intercourse: Up until this point in my life, I had only had sex with one woman other than Melanie. But over the next few months, I went full ghetto hyena. I had sex with so many women, and it was so constitutionally disagreeable to the core of my being, that I developed a psychosomatic reaction to having an orgasm: It would literally make me gag and sometimes even vomit. In every case, though, I had hoped to God that this beautiful stranger would be "the one"—the woman who would love me, who would heal me, who would make this pain go away.

But invariably there I was, retching and wretched. And the look in the eyes of the woman even further deepened my agony. I was doing the very thing I hated Daddio for—hurting women.

I was miserable, so I purchased my first house, a mansion facing Merion Park, in the rich neighborhood across City Line. I had seen it in my dreams—bleached white hardwood floors, two-story ceilings in the living room, and a Jacuzzi in the master bedroom (not in the *bathroom*—in the *bedroom*). The first thing I bought for the place—before beds, couches, towels, or even silverware—was a pool table.

I eventually got a bed. It was the first time I'd ever slept in a king-sized. Me and Harry had slept in the same bed most of our childhood. Me and Charlie Mack had roomed together on the road. I realized that first night on Merion Road that I had never really slept alone. I didn't like it. My heart was bleeding—I was dying in love with Melanie Parker.

I wanted her back.

My mind at the time still correlated performance with love. The entire basis for my self-esteem was foundationally dependent upon whether my woman was happy. My self-image was inexorably bound up in women's opinion and approval of me. I figured that since I was not receiving the love I so deeply craved, it had to be because of a deficiency in me as the lead character. If I had performed the role of "boyfriend" better, she wouldn't have cheated.

As you can probably imagine, that bought me a first-class ticket on a bullet train to agony.

Melanie worked at the Merry-Go-Round in the Gallery, a mall in downtown Philly. I had it all planned: a grand, romantic gesture of forgiveness. I was going to walk in, our eyes would meet, I would forgive her, and she would fall into my arms, gushing tears of gratitude and remorse. Then I would tell her that I wanted to marry her and that no wife of mine has to work in a shit-ass Merry-Go-Round. We would give her boss the middle finger, hop into my brand-new Benz 300CE, and I would take her to her new Merion Road mansion, the one with the Jacuzzi in the bedroom, not the bathroom.

Parking at the Gallery was rough, so Charlie Mack drove us. That way he could sit in the car and keep it parked right in front of the store so I could Romeo-flex into the Merry-Go-Round, sweep her off her feet, and carry her over the threshold to the awaiting Benz.

Beep beep! Charlie hit the horn.

"Yo, man, you know I don't have no license. So, if the cops come, I'm-a just dip," Charlie said.

This joka was messing up my whole production.

"Why don't you just get your gotdamn license?" I yelled.

"You know I got a gun charge! I can't get it yet! Jus' go get Melanie, man, hurry up before 5-0 roll up!"

I ran into the store. It was a quiet day; the place was mostly empty.

Melanie was behind the counter, folding Jordache jeans. She didn't see me—I got to watch her for a few (I would have watched her longer, but Charlie didn't have a license). In those few moments, I knew I didn't want to be without her. Whatever was empty inside of me felt full when I saw her. All that ached was soothed; all that was thirsty was quenched.

She looked up, and our eyes met. There was a brief but undeniable moment of clarity. Melanie absolutely loved me. And I loved her.

Bzzzzzzz.

Shit. My damn shock collar. I don't know what it is, but I trust it. I let my attention tunnel deeper inside of her. I walk up to her; we hug. Still not right.

BZZZZZZZ.

I let go of her. We smile. I scan the store.

He was light-skinned, with light eyes. I hate dudes like that.

BZZZZZZZZZ.

I look back to Melanie. She pretends to fold the clothes quicker.

"My lunch break is in fifteen, we can go get something to eat," she says.

BZZZZZZZZ.

I look back to him. He won't make eye contact with me now.

I see you, motherfucker.

I charge across the store. He tries to get away—guilty. But there's nowhere to hide in a Merry-Go-Round. I'm all over him. Melanie is screaming. Somehow, Charlie Mack appears, and pulls me off him. The store is a wreck; so are his pretty green eyes. Charlie is dragging me, and I am dragging Melanie. We scramble into the getaway car.

"Nigga, I told you I had a gun charge. What are you *doin'*?" Charlie barked as we peeled away.

That was Melanie's last day at the Merry-Go-Round. She promised to never see that guy again. I took her home to her new mansion on the Main Line. The one with the Jacuzzi in the bedroom, not the bathroom.

We vowed to make it work. My secret, unspoken oath was, *If you come back, I promise I'll be good enough.*

The JBM stands for the Junior Black Mafia. Their motto in Philly was "Get down, or lay down." Meaning, you were either with them or against them; you were either a part of them or you were dead.

When you're a twenty-year-old rapper from the inner city of Philadelphia who's just made his first million dollars, the only people who can afford to hang with you are other rappers, professional athletes, or drug dealers.

I picked drug dealers.

Bucky was five foot one, and the one is a stretch. He was a former Golden Gloves champion, and he was one of the top lieutenants in the JBM. When he was in the room, he commanded the first and the last word. If you had a disagreement, he was more than happy to take off his $30,000 worth of jewelry and meet you in the street. But if you were disrespectful, the jewelry didn't matter, because he never wore a ring on his trigger finger.

Bucky loved to laugh. He reveled in my sense of humor. With today's eyes, I can see that he was coming to Merion Road to get a break, a little breather from the stress and brutality of the street. I was his personal court jester. He loved to hear me buss on people—insult comedy was his favorite; coincidentally, it was my forte.

I made the mistake, though, one night, of cracking a joke about Bucky's height.

"Yo, Buck, you wanna boost, or maybe a stepstool for that next shot?"

Nobody even snickered. Buck stayed calm, which was a terrible sign; the room fell silent. He walked over to me, his chin barely reaching my chest. He just stood there. I knew that meant I had to bend down so he could talk to me. I lowered myself like a silverback in the wild surrendering to the alpha.

Buck whispered in my ear, "Just coz you a *star*, don't mean I won't make you *see* some."

The logic of his analogy wasn't entirely flawless, but the underlying point was well taken. I never joked about Buck again.

Merion Road was now party central. At any given time, there would be twenty or more people in the house, blasting music, shooting pool, thousands of dollars' worth of Philly cheesesteaks littering the kitchen. (I probably could have just bought Overbrook Pizza for how much money I spent there.) There were boxing matches in the backyard, and a basketball court . . . in the living room.

And nonstop gambling on *everything*. Needless to say, this environment was not conducive to Melanie's artistic aspirations.

"Willard, can you turn the music down a little bit?" she'd say.

"My bad, babe, give me about a hour. I'm schoolin' these fools. . . ."

I felt like my forgiveness had been such a gigantic gesture of love that she should be grateful to even be here.

The truth was, I never actually forgave her.

The weekends were when it really turned up.

It was not uncommon for $150,000 to change hands between Friday night and Sunday morning. My boy Bam was the best pool shooter; he was always taking our money on the table. But one Saturday night, I caught fire on the pool table; I could not miss. Full-length bank shots, combinations, 8-ball spot shots, perfect English dropping the cue ball into sweet positions, everything went exactly where I was calling it. Buck found himself on the short (sorry!) . . . I mean *unfortunate* end of a $30,000 losing streak. He sent one of his boys to go get more cash. But Buck lived in Southwest—that was at least a forty-five-minute round trip—so he threw his car keys on the table. The room erupted—"Ooooooh *shit!*" My heart jumped for a minute, but I ain't no bitch. I threw the keys to my brand-new sea-foam green Benz 300 right next to the keys to his custom black convertible BMW 325i.

"Rack 'em up," I said.

I ran four balls off the break; high balls. The room was church si-lent. Bucky sized up his first shot—easy 2 ball in the corner; left him-self great position on the 7 in the side. A little too aggressive, though, left himself out of position in the corner; he had to bank the 4 back under. But Buck ain't no bitch, either. He ran the entire rack, and all I could do was watch helplessly, chalking my custom pool cue for a shot I may never get to take.

Bucky lined up the 8 ball. Bank shot, cross corner. The 8 was sailing in slow motion toward the corner pocket. The gravity of the 8 ball was preparing to snatch my car keys with it into the abyss. A roar brewing as the ball approached: "Awwwwwwwwww . . ."

But . . . No! The 8 ball clips the titty just enough to rattle it around and stand up in the jaws of the pocket. The room explodes.

I've got new life. But I gotta do some real shootin'. I've still got three balls to pocket before I get a shot at the 8-ball duck in the corner—and if I miss one, Bucky's back on the table, and *he's* not gonna miss.

My first ball is the dreaded straight shot, full-length of the table. I don't play with it—I line it up, dead center of the pocket, two to go. Sec-ond shot would be in the side pocket, but my third shot's in the corner, meaning I gotta put some English on the cue ball ("drawz," meaning hitting it low to cause it to spin backward). If not, it could roll straight into the corner pocket, scratching and ensuring Bucky's victory.

My concept around shooting pool was to never ponder the shots too long. Line it up, hit it. Line up the next one, hit it. No time to let my mind punish me with doubt or indecision. Charlie Mack always used to say, "Scared money can't make no money." That would become a motto for my life. But that night, it was an ice-cold mind-set that made me unbeatable.

And just like the rest of the night, I couldn't miss. All Bucky could do was watch helplessly, chalking his pool cue, for a shot he would never get to take. I ran the table, tapped in the 8 ball, and respectfully picked up both sets of car keys.

Bucky was furious, but he was way too gangsta to let you see it. He stormed out of the house, slinging the door open, only to realize he might need to call a cab.

I ran out behind him.

"Yo, Buck," I said.

"Not now, nigga, gimme a minute," he said, with all the gangsta that a dude preparing to hitchhike could muster.

"Buck, here." I held out his car keys. "I'm not takin' your damn car."

"What?" he said, confused.

"You're my boy. I'm not keepin' your *car*," I said.

"You serious?" he said, looking at me like I had four heads.

"Buck, I'm not gonna invite you to my house and then take your car. I'm an asshole, but not *that* much." I shoved the keys into his hand.

I didn't recognize it in this moment, but I would see clearly later, that this was a gesture of humanity that was nonexistent in the environment in which Bucky was forced to survive. He noticed it, and he became visibly emotional.

"Why you trippin, Buck? It's not that serious . . . ," I said.

He gathered himself, shook the keys in his hand, and said, "Coz I would have kept *your* car."

I turned to go back into the house. Bucky chirped his car open, and yelled to me, "Hey! If anybody ever fuck wit' *you*, they got a problem wit' *me*."

And he meant it.

At the time, I didn't correlate my cravings and my generally erratic behavior with the wounded state of my heart. When I bought a candy-apple-red IROC-Z and dipped the rims in a matching candy apple, I wasn't perceiving that as a medicinal reflex. Nor did I connect the purchase of my custom Suburban with four eighteen-inch woofers taking up the entire back half to my feelings of inadequacy, loss, and betrayal.

I just thought it was fun that when I was picking up someone, I wouldn't have to call ahead—I would just put my volume on about seven, and they knew who was coming.

I was *spun* out and I was *acting* out. I bought my first motorcycle: a blue Suzuki Katana 600. I didn't even know how to ride, and I crashed it in the first week. But I was ballin' way too hard to drive a banged-up bike, so I bought a new one, the red one.

JL crashed *that* bike; the damage wasn't too bad: just some scuffs on the side panels. But then, not to be outdone by JL, Harry totaled it. I figured this was a sign—maybe bikes weren't for me—so I bought a turquoise T-top Corvette.

I lined all of my cars and motorcycles up in front of the house and invited Daddio over so he could see how well I was doing. Daddio pulled up in his two-tone blue Chevy work van. He always believed that vehicles should have a utility. I stood proudly out front as he got out of the van. We hugged.

"I just got the 'Vette last week," I said.

"These are *all yours*?" he asked, looking disdainfully at my fresh new fleet.

"Yup," I said proudly. My arms were respectfully by my side, but in my mind my B-boy stance was on swole.

"Boy, why you need *three* cars?" he said. "You only got *one* ass."

This wasn't exactly the response I'd been hoping for. But his mathematical opinion fell on deaf ears, because the 1988 Grammy for Best Rap Performance went to DJ Jazzy Jeff and the Fresh Prince for "Parents Just Don't Understand."

Melanie and I weren't having sex anymore.

Something had been broken. We both wanted nothing more than for it to be fixed, but we were barely twenty years old. Our romantic dreams were far too fragile to survive the brutality of our immaturity.

I started going to Los Angeles a lot. It was the first time I realized the vibrational power of a city. As soon as the plane would touch down at LAX, something inside of me would awaken and align. Something *I was*, and something *LA was*, clicked into harmonious agreement. The energy of the town excited me. I needed less sleep; I was always refreshed; my skin looked better; I was eating right; I wanted to work out. I was inspired. I have since realized the critical importance of environment. Choosing the city you live in is as important as choosing your life partner.

And I had just met Tanya Moore. She embodied the sunshine and the possibilities that defined LA: the quintessential West Coast rider. Fine as hell, sophisticated, but sharp in the streets. She knew what neighborhoods to walk in, and which ones to drive around. She knew that my red Phillies baseball cap should come off at LAX, and I could put it back on as soon as the flight home crossed the Mississippi.

Pooh Richardson was the star shooting guard for UCLA, which, next to millionaire rapper, was about as good a gig as a twenty-two-year-old Black kid could get. He was born and raised in the heart of South Philly, and he walked around UCLA like the damn mayor. Pooh was everything on that campus, and when his Philly homeboys showed up, he laid it out.

Pooh was dating Tanya's cousin Tgia, who basically managed Pooh's life. She handled his food, his press; she would clear the room when he needed to get ready for practice. It was a relationship mind-set that to me at the time seemed so mature. Pooh was the star, but he literally wouldn't know where his sneakers were. His one job was to play basketball *well*—Tgia did *everything* else. When I saw them together I knew I wanted *that*. They were partners in the "Pooh Richardson Going to the NBA Business." (He ended up playing ten years in the league.)

Me and Charlie Mack rolled up to Pauley Pavilion where UCLA was playing Stanford. We saw Pooh in the locker after the game.

"Philly is in the building!" he screamed.

The first thing a Philly dude notices when one of his homeboys moves to another city is how bad his fade haircut looks. Philly is known for the fade—we invented it, and we do it right.

"Yo, man, your barber is slippin'," I said obligatorily. I probably would have said it no matter what it looked like. When you're from Philly, and somebody gets their haircut in another city, you *have* to say it looks bad.

"Yeah, we haven't figured that one out here yet," Pooh joked, touching the sides of his fade. If you're from Philly, you have to say something like that, too.

He introduced me to Tgia and her cousin Tanya. I must have been too obvious in my appreciation of Tanya's beauty, because Pooh grabbed a towel and held it up to my mouth.

"Yo, man, you slobberin', I don't want you to slip and fall on your spit."

I shoved the towel away, slightly embarrassed but keeping my smile and my charm on blaze.

"C'mon, man, go ahead wit' that shit." I laughed, turning to introduce myself to Tanya.

"There must be something in the water in Philly," Tanya said. "They're growin' y'all real nice out there."

Pooh jumped in.

"Yo, Tanya, I'm tellin' you, this nigga is the *next one*. You better lock him up now coz he's going from here to the *moon*!"

I was thinking, lock *me* up? Shit, she had me at *real nice*.

JL was the only one of my friends who'd ever seen me cry. On a train ride to New York one day, I'd broken down when I told him the story about Melanie, sobbing into his chest. JL is *not* an emotional guy, and I was *not* holding back. (He would later tell me that in that moment, he devoted his life to me. JL said he *knew* he needed to protect me.)

JL pulled me up one day.

"Hey, man, you gettin' into a lot of fights lately. Wassup?"

There was a couple of months stretch when I literally got into a fight every weekend. I'm not sure if it was knowing that Bucky had my back, or that Charlie Mack was standing right beside me—or if it was the only elixir that could satiate my raging heart—but I started sucker punching everybody and anybody who even looked at me sideways. I was angry, because even a Grammy, millions of dollars, and a candy-apple-red IROC didn't even begin to fill the holes inside of me.

The thing about money, sex, and success is that when you don't have them, you can justify your misery—*shit, if I had money, sex, and success, I'd feel great!* However misguided that may be, it psychologically permeates as hope. But once you *are* rich, famous, successful—and you're still insecure and unhappy—the terrifying thought begins to lurk: *Maybe the problem is* me.

Of course, I dismissed that foolishness quickly. I just needed more money, more women, more Grammys.

The record company was ready for our follow-up album to *He's the DJ*. Three million records sold, first-ever Grammy Award in rap, but this *new* album was gonna smash all of that.

JL wanted us to do preliminary recording in Jeff's mom's house. Whereas I had bought cars, clothes, and houses, Jeff had converted the basement into a *Star Trek*–level home recording studio. JL thought it would be the most cost-effective approach to get our ideas down in southwest Philly, and then go for the final recording back to London. Jive owned the recording studios there, and we got preferred rates.

But me and Jeff had other ideas. Jeff had heard of a famous recording studio in the Bahamas—Compass Point Studios in Nassau. He suggested we record there. After all, Mick Jagger, Grace Jones, David Bowie, Sade, even Iron Maiden had all recorded at Compass Point. Since we were big-time now and had a multiplatinum album of our own, it only seemed fitting that we record where multiplatinum artists record. Jeff couldn't wait to dig into the studio and check out the tech. I couldn't wait to check out the two massive casinos that had just been built in Nassau.

We were hyped. JL protested, but he was outvoted two to one. No filibusters in Jeff's mom's basement. That next Friday, we were off to the Bahamas . . . all *ten* of us.

I had never been to the Bahamas.

It was ninety degrees and sunny when we landed. Our luggage and equipment got held up in customs, so we hit the beach. Rum punch and chicken fingers until the sun set, then we hit the casino—till sunrise. And that's how the "recording" of our new album went for about the first week or so.

We had scheduled six weeks to record, and we had locked out the studio, meaning, we had to pay whether we used it or not. Our first full session in the studio—day nine in the Bahamas—was more like a night in a club: Jeff was DJing while we all sat around with girls and food and drinks. Occasionally, I would get up on the mic, more performing for the crowd than trying to innovate or create new music.

After that first session, JL pulled Jeff and me aside and warned us that we were burning through $10,000 a day, and that if we didn't start recording, he was pulling the plug. Me and Jeff were kind of offended.

"You don't understand the creative process," I said. "This environment, the people, all the stuff we're doing is our inspiration."

"Yeah, J," Jeff chimed in, "don't block the flow."

"Just let us do what *we* do, and you do what *you* do," I said.

JL nodded, very slowly, as if to say, *OK, I see how it is.*

One month, and a couple of hundred thousand dollars into our "process," and the red recording light hadn't come on once—we had still not completed a single song.

I guess JL was justified in doing what he did. At the time, I couldn't believe he did it. I would never have done it to him. But I guess he felt that the times were desperate, so he employed equally desperate measures.

It was a Friday night. About twenty of us were lounging around in the studio. Our LA squad had flown in to help with the "creative process." I was about five rum punches in, and I had graduated beyond chicken fingers into *jerk* chicken, black beans, and rice. I guess it was hot in there because I had my shirt off.

It doesn't matter how old you get—there are some childhood images that will always bring a chill down your spine or make your stomach drop. I was holding court in the middle of Compass Point Studio A when the door started to open. I first caught a glimpse of JL pushing the door wider, and then . . .

Daddio.

The room froze. Those who knew, *knew*—the other guests *guessed*. Daddio calmly took in the scene. His eldest son, topless. Rum punch and jerk chicken stinkin' up the room. Bahamian bikinis bouncing and misbehaving. And we were "at work." To Daddio, this was Sodom and Gomorrah.

He paused. Then:

"Everybody get the fuck out," he said. "I need to talk to Will and Jeff."

We landed at Philadelphia International Airport at 2:38 p.m. I slept the entire flight. I don't remember takeoff, or landing. I'm not sure it's an actual medical condition, but I'm pretty certain I was in an embarrassment coma. James "JL" Lassiter had dropped a dime on me and tattled to my daddy. The whole shit was a debacle.

But within two weeks, our third album, *And in This Corner . . .* , was at least finished.

In the tragic aftermath of his grim reaper–like appearance at Compass Point, Daddio had made an aggressive, but nonetheless convincing, assessment of our behavior.

"You boys are fucking off an opportunity that most people can't even *dream* about. You got a major corporation financin' your project, and you got girls and shit sitting around in the studio? Keep your dick out them people's money. You can *bullshit*, just don't *bullshit* while you on the *clock*. This shit ain't gonna last forever."

While Daddio's Bahamian intervention had saved us from further immediate catastrophe, the first domino had already been tipped. With no budget left, we quickly cobbled together the best tracks we could come up with. But there was no real vision or continuity to the album. Me and Jeff were unfocused, and out of sync.

And in This Corner . . . was doomed from the start.

NINE

DESTRUCTION

The downward spiral had begun.

And in This Corner . . . came out Halloween 1989 and achieved full crickets. In a desperate attempt to salvage something from the mess, we sprinted out onto the road to perform and promote and do anything we could to inject some life into the album, but it was dead on arrival.

The winter of 1989 was a progressively abominable shit show.

It began with Ready Rock. He had recorded a bunch of songs, none of which ended up making the album. He was one of the best beatboxers there ever was, and in our live shows he definitely got some of the biggest cheers. But hip-hop was changing—beatboxers were becoming less central to the art form. He felt disrespected and disregarded.

As a result, our disagreements became division, division became open conflict, until Ready and I were damn near at war.

Clate started showing up late for everything: flights, sound checks, meetings. He'd sleep all day and be in a stank mood all night. Throughout the tour, our arguments escalated in both frequency and intensity. In his mind, he and Jeff were the main attractions, and *they* were carrying *me*.

"Me and Jeff are the only talented ones around here, the rest of y'all just riding our coattails," Clate shouted, during one of our innumerable collisions.

It all came to a head one night in Kansas City. During our show, we would introduce Ready Rock at about the halfway point. He'd come out, and me and him had a fifteen-minute routine before he'd go off and me and Jeff would close the show. He had a grand entrance—I'd be rapping, and at the end of my verse I'd shout, "Ready Rock C, Give Jeff a hand!" I'd dramatically point to the side, the spotlight would come on, and he would do a helicopter sound effect with his mouth that would shock the hell out of the crowd. He could open and close his hand around the microphone, shifting the frequency to give the illusion of the helicopter passing from left to right.

The crowd loved it.

But this night, I shouted, I pointed, the spotlight panned, but no Ready Rock. Jeff just kept the beat going, and after another four bars, I said it again: "Ready Rock C! Give Jeff a hand!"

Clate didn't come out.

Without missing a beat, Jeff launched into the next track and we continued the show as if nothing had happened.

It is unbelievably painful for me as I write this chapter because these conflicts and misunderstandings had such simple solutions, yet our immaturity demanded that we had to suffer excruciating consequences in order to learn the most basic lessons of human relating. It's so obvious to me today how hurtful it must have been for Clate to go from being my best friend and my creative right hand to someone who was increasingly being excluded and alienated and asked by photographers to step out of pictures. And what's worse, we never even talked about it.

But that night, we were two young rams.

After our set, I went raging backstage.

"*Where the fuck is Clate?*" I screamed. I blast into the dressing room, and there he is, sitting in *my* chair, sunglasses on, calmly eating a bag of Doritos.

"*Man, where the hell were you at?*"

Clate didn't respond—he just sat there crunchin'.

"Why you ain't come out?" I roared.

He continued crunchin'. After a few seconds, he swallowed and said, "I just didn't feel like performing tonight."

I was shocked and incensed; but I said nothing.

We stared at each other. Each second our new reality was hardening. In my heart, he had about ten seconds before the concrete set.

Nine, eight, seven, six.

Crunch. Crunch. Stare.

Five, four, three.

Crunch. Stare.

Two.

"A'ight, cool," I said, as I turned and walked out.

I never called for Ready Rock again.

The next night, Jeff and I altered the set. Clate was standing there at the side of the stage. The part in the show came where he'd usually be called out; we skipped over it and went to the next song. Same thing in Dallas, same thing in Houston, same thing in San Antonio.

We stopped speaking. Clate started riding on other groups' buses, and when he rode with us, he stayed in his bunk. One day, near the end of the tour, we heard a strange sound coming from his bunk.

Click-clack, snap. Click-clack, snap.

Charlie Mack's bunk was directly above Clate's. Charlie, irritated by the sound, leaned out of his bunk to investigate. He opened the curtain to Clate's bunk.

"Yo, man, what the hell is you doin'?" Charlie screamed, jumping down from his bunk.

Clate was cleaning a semiautomatic Uzi submachine gun. He didn't have any bullets, but he was practicing chambering a round and pulling the trigger.

Click-clack, snap. Click-clack, snap.

Gone was my high school friend—the easy laugh, the excitement of battling on the street corners around Overbrook, the joy of stumbling onto a new sound. Left in his place was a person I no longer recognized.

In my entire life, few things have been more painful than watching someone I love self-destruct. Daddio used to say, "You can stop a homicide, but you can't stop no suicide." Ready Rock was making good money doing what he loved. He was performing in front of thousands of people and seeing the world. He had a crew of friends who would die for him. Yet, there was some blind or broken part of him that, for some reason, couldn't perceive the full scope of the opportunity stretching out before him. He had made his way into the abundant part of the Great River only to scratch and claw his way back to the desert.

Throughout my career, I have seen this pattern over and over again. I have given hundreds of jobs to people, many of whom have ultimately cracked and crumbled under the pressure of the possibilities. As the great Negro poet Charlie Mack once put it, *"Pressure busts pipes, homie."*

We all have to contend with the natural processes of destruction. Everything is impermanent—your body's going to get old; your best friend is going to graduate and move to another city; that tree you used to climb in front of Stacey Brooks's house is going to crash down in a storm. Your parents are going to die. Everything changes; it rises, and it falls. Nothing and no one is immune to the entropy of the universe.

That is why *self*-destruction is such a terrible crime. It's hard enough as it is.

When we got back to Philly, Ready Rock grabbed his bag, I grabbed mine. There were no goodbyes, no eye contact. I watched him walk off down Woodcrest; he never looked back even once.

Because of my childhood experiences with Daddio's destructive streak, I've always had very low tolerance when I recognize similar energies within people around me. The funny thing is, it's always crystal clear to me when I perceive them in others, but I'm blind as a bat to those same energies within myself.

The first (and only real) single from the third album was called, "I Think I Can Beat Mike Tyson." I've often used Mike's invincibility at the time as a metaphor to explain the distinction between natural destruction and self-destruction.

Imagine you were to secure a title fight against Mike Tyson in his prime. Fearful for your life, you hire legendary trainer Freddie Roach, you commit to the perfect diet, the perfect training regimen, you do everything within your power to prepare yourself to face Iron Mike. You step into the ring in impeccable physical and mental condition, and Mike destroys you within fifteen seconds. You did everything you could possibly have done, and still lost. You're just not as good a fighter as Mike Tyson. That is a *bearable* loss; that is what I'm calling *natural* destruction.

But if you were lollygagging during training, didn't really eat right, and let your boy Pookie train you—and *then* Mike knocks you out in fifteen seconds—now you have to face an *unbearable* loss. You have to live the rest of your life not knowing what might have happened had you done your best. In the back of your mind, forever, you will know that you didn't only lose to Mike Tyson, you lost to *yourself.* The fight wasn't you versus Mike—it was you *and* Mike versus *you.*

That's how I feel about *And in This Corner . . .* The music business is fickle—some records work; some don't. Sometimes there's a track that you think is going to be a hit, and no one feels it; then the one you weren't even thinking about becomes a monster. That's the natural way, the inevitable ebb and flow of the universe. But if you piss away $300,000 on rum punch and chicken fingers, and your father has to fly in and drag your ass home, and then you throw together a bunch of tracks in your best friend's mother's basement, you're manifesting an unfair fight. It's two against one: it's you *and* the universe versus *you.*

It's respectable to lose to the universe. It's a tragedy to lose to yourself.

And in This Corner . . . flopped, hard. We were coming off three million records sold—triple-platinum sales—and the first-ever Grammy Award in rap. Expectations and investments were very high. And we crashed and burned.

We knew the album was a swing and a miss. But it didn't become real until we went out on tour again. The crowds were thinner. People weren't as hyped to see us. They were no longer singing my lyrics back to me. And our performance fees were cut by almost 70 percent. We made it OK in our minds by thinking of it as "promotion."

In retrospect, I could feel the impending onslaught, but I couldn't figure out what to do, or how to stop it. And I certainly didn't think it was going to get as bad as it did.

By this time, Melanie and I were living in that dreadful demilitarized zone between the bliss-filled old days of romance and hopeful possibilities, and the fast-approaching inescapable days of resentment, rage, and destruction. Trapped in that awful quiet lovelessness where two people coexist in the same house but rarely in the same room. Where the air is filled with apathetic words, not yet dipping into vitriol but purposely devoid of kindness. That unique hell where you know it's done but it's not over yet.

*M*e and Charlie were spending more and more time in LA.

The second I would land, Tanya would be at the airport with a rental car, keys to the hotel, dinner reservations, whatever I needed. LA girls always seemed organized and business-minded. They were always fly, and always pursuing some kind of dream or opportunity. There was something about the culture of Los Angeles that bred an upwardly mobile mentality. Tanya never asked me for anything; this was just how she got down. She made me feel at home.

We knew each other for almost a year but we never even kissed.

I could faintly sense that Tanya and Los Angeles were about to play some significant role in my survival. I guess I was kind of unconsciously locating the lighthouse and the lifeboat for the storm that was darkening on the horizon. Gigi's words were ringing in my mind: *Jus' remember, Lover Boy, be nice to everybody you pass on your way up, coz you just might have to pass them again on your way down.*

Becoming famous is about as much fun as the material world has to offer. *Being* famous, bit of a mixed bag; but *fading* famous sucks ass.

I could read the writing on the walls—some of it was in my own handwriting. I saw the crowds' silent faces at the end of our sets. I noticed how business calls that once got returned in two hours were now taking two weeks or didn't get returned at all. And most alarmingly, my Amex wasn't quite breaking, but it was bending like a muthafucka. And in the middle of all of that distortion, the subtle compass within me kept pointing west.

Charlie could feel it, too.

He took it upon himself to push and to dig and to cajole—everything within his power to excavate and manifest a more positive future. Charlie was shameless. He would introduce me to absolutely anybody within shouting distance, even people he didn't know.

"Little Richard! Little Richard!" he bellowed across the Soul Train Awards.

Then, excitedly to me, "Will, that's Little Richard, he wit' Diana Ross. . . . Come on, get the picture."

"Damn, Charlie, they *talkin'*! Jus' leave them alone," I said, wildly embarrassed.

"You want the picture, or you don't want the picture? You gotta be *seen* wit' people." Then he dragged me over to Little Richard and Diana Ross, and basically listed my entire discography for them.

"I know y'all heard it—he got a Grammy. Y'all, like, in the Grammy Club together!"

Charlie Mack is bigger than most human beings, and certainly bigger than most people's security. So, once he decided he wanted something—like a picture, or a conversation—things tended to gravitate out of his way.

LA illuminated the limits to my fame. I was huge in the world of hip-hop, but in Hollywood, I was nobody. At a Lakers game, I was nobody. At the Roxbury, I was *extra* nobody. When Eddie walked in, he shut it down. It was humbling, it was embarrassing, and it was frustrating.

I remember one night in LA, the DC go-go band EU (Experience Unlimited) was playing at the Palladium. They had opened for us in 1988 and '89 and we had developed a friendship with the lead singer, Sugar Bear, and the rest of the group. Spike Lee had just put their song "Da Butt" in his movie *School Daze*, and EU was now the hottest group in the country. Charlie and I planned to take a break from the emotional battery of being nobodies in Hollywood and just for a night retreat to the world of music.

We headed to the Palladium and rolled up to the backstage entrance. Hordes of groupies and fans all pleading with the bouncers about how their cousin left a ticket, but the will call is closed—the usual crap that makes security guards just look over their heads and ignore them. Charlie does his usual thing, stepping up to the front and speaking for me.

"Hey, my man, I'm here with the Fresh Prince."

"The who?" the security guard says, looking past Charlie to me.

I always hate these kinds of moments where I have to stand there and try to look recognizable. Because now, everybody is staring at you to see if you're famous enough to pass the "bouncer test." You're out on a limb. And when you just flopped an album, it's a thin and rickety branch.

"The Fresh Prince, man. The Fresh Prince. You know, Jazzy *Jeff* and 'em," Charlie clarified.

The bouncer looked at me with the universal glare that signifies *I'm foraging through my visual Rolodex and . . . nope, you're not in there.*

"If y'all ain't got tickets, y'all gonna need to move to the back."

Just then, the door opens, and Sugar Bear from EU sticks his head out and looks around. I made a rookie error—I overcommitted. But when I saw a familiar face, he felt like one of those round life preservers being thrown to me as I was drowning in a deepening sea of insignificance and irrelevance. Before I could stop myself, I blurt out, "Hey! Sugar Bear!"

Sugar Bear looks *right at me*. There's a moment of recognition. I point at the security guard as if to say *Yo, man, tell this dude to move and let us in.*

Sugar Bear pauses, looks at the security guard, subtly shakes his head. He scans the crowd to see if the person he was really looking for is out there. They're not, so he turns and goes back inside.

I turned and gracefully made the ex–famous person's walk of shame. Inside, I was raging, but as is my habitual emotional way, on the outside, I was totally calm. I didn't know where I was going, but block after block, I just walked. Charlie said nothing but kept step right behind me. We walked for miles in silence.

What the hell was happening? Since we came off tour, Jeff had retreated to his mom's basement. His reaction to the looming winter of our careers was to hibernate—he had turned down a chance to do a show in Africa and a tour in Australia. I was pissed that he was hiding—it seemed like cowardice on his part. And it activated my most violent trigger: I'd been fighting my entire life to not be a coward. I believed that we needed to go head-to-head with the obstacles that were building against us, but I couldn't do it without him. I felt like he'd betrayed me.

JL was complaining about me and Charlie being in LA so much.

"Y'all are wasting your time—you need to come home so we can get back into the studio, writing and recording," JL said.

Melanie and I were barely speaking. And here I was, in the empty streets of Hollywood, on a Thursday night, anonymous and adrift.

Charlie Mack was like an old-time boxing trainer whose fighter had just got his whole ass handed to him in the previous round. If we weren't on Hollywood Boulevard, he definitely would have been pouring ice water down my shorts. I was hurt bad. But I knew I had another round in me.

We approached a crosswalk, the red hand beckoning directly to *me*. Halt. Stop. Breathe. Think. My rage settled. Contemplation churned into passion, then . . . a decision.

"That will never, *ever*, happen again," I said. "I promise you that."

Charlie didn't open his mouth; he just nodded his head. He knew something profound was happening inside of me. And he was down for whatever.

The light changed, and we walked on.

I didn't pay my taxes.

It's not like I forgot, it was more like . . . I just didn't pay my taxes. In January 1990, Uncle Sam decided that I'd had enough fun and he wanted his.

I owed the IRS taxes on around $3 million of income. I think somewhere above a million dollars, Uncle Sam shifts from ornery to irritable and everything north of about $2.3 million makes him aggressive and cantankerous.

So, as was my general approach to problem-solving during this period of my life, I dumped it on JL.

"Wait, you didn't pay *any* taxes?" he said. He was on the phone, but I could tell that he sat down.

To this day, JL is the most frugal, sensible, and fiscally responsible person I've ever met. He doesn't spend any money on anything ever. No fancy cars, no jewelry, no trips, no Jacuzzi in his bedroom nor his bathroom. While Jeff and I were spending our spoils wildly, JL never moved from his childhood bedroom. He was taking this very phone call in his mother's kitchen.

"Nah, nothing," I said.

"Like, *nothing* nothing?"

"Yeah. No. I mean, yeah. Nah."

"Y'all are stoopid as shit," JL said. "Y'all understand this is a *big* problem, right?"

I didn't notice in the moment, but JL kept saying "y'all," denoting a plurality of stupidity. I would later discover that Jeff hadn't paid his taxes, either. And to make matters worse, JL had been lax on billing us for his commissions, so not only had we spent all of *our* money, we had spent JL's cut, too.

We were all broke.

JL hired a tax attorney (for me and Jeff—he paid *his* taxes), scheduled a meeting, showed them the notices from the IRS. He also engaged an accounting firm, Gelfand, Rennert & Feldman, to oversee our hypothetical future earnings.

First went all the cars. Then my motorcycles. Stereo systems are very expensive when they go in—they're worth damn near nothing when they come out. Then the excruciating decision was made—IRS, attorney, and accountants unanimously agreed: I would have to sell the Lower Merion house, pool table included.

I was rich and famous, minus the rich, and minus the famous.

I was *worse* than broke—I was in the *hole*. The walls were tumbling down. I had enjoyed Sodom and Gomorrah way more than I was enjoying Jericho.

There's a strange thing that happens when someone falls: Your demise somehow proves to everyone you've ever disagreed with that *they* were right, and *you* were wrong. They develop a smugness and seem to get a brutal enjoyment out of the fact that God is finally punishing you. People tend to have a schizophrenic relationship with winners—if you're down too long, you become an underdog and they feel impelled to root for you. But if you're ever unfortunate enough to be *up* too long, you better get a helmet.

One night, in the middle of what would become the final racks of 8 ball ever played on my first pool table on Merion Road, Melanie came down the stairs. She was looking fine as hell, wearing a royal-blue miniskirt and matching leather jacket. She had on three-inch heels— she never rocked heels. Big bamboo earrings I had bought her that she'd never worn before. Her makeup was perfect, no glasses tonight; eyeliner. Her cleavage would certainly not have been approved of in her aunt's house. So why did she think it would be approved of in mine?

She pranced through the gauntlet of me, Charlie, Bam, Bucky, and a couple more of my JBM boys. Everybody looked, but nobody made a sound. The JBM had a code—they were always respectful of each other's women.

"Where you goin'?" I asked, as I missed an easy 11 ball in the side.

"Out," Melanie said.

All I could think was, *Why the fuck is she doing this right now? Is she really going to challenge me in a room full of Philly's hardest gangsters and killers? In the middle of the IRS seizing all my shit? Wearing clothes that I paid for? Making me miss an easy-ass 11 ball in the side? BZZZZZZZZZ.*

"Where's 'out'?" I said, as Charlie lined up his next shot, about to take a hundred dollars that I didn't have.

"I don't know." She shrugged. "Out."

"I think you're not going out," I said, drawing a line in the sand and trying to save face. "You should go ahead back upstairs."

"Whatever, Willard," she said, as she moved toward the door.

"If you walk out that door, I promise you it's gonna be a bad look."

We stared at each other. Each second our new reality was hardening. In my heart, she had about ten seconds to go back upstairs before the concrete set.

Nine, eight, seven, six.

Charlie sunk a high ball in the side.

Five, four, three.

Eyeliner. Cleavage. Bamboo hoops.

Two.

"I'll see you later, Willard."

Melanie walked out.

An hour later, I was in the house alone. Melanie and I were no longer in that loveless demilitarized zone. The bliss-filled old days were finally giving way to the days of resentment, rage, and destruction.

Melanie's taxi pulled up around 2:00 a.m. I was waiting for her out front. I had collected everything I'd ever bought for her—clothes, shoes, bags.

Anything that would burn.

I had drenched everything in lighter fluid.

Our eyes met.

I struck the match.

WHOOSH.

As I write this chapter, I have never seen or spoken to Melanie again. I've reached out on multiple occasions over the years with no response. She was the victim of one of the lowest points in my life. Yes, we were young, yes, we hurt each other, but she did not deserve how I treated her; she did not deserve how it ended.

Charlie Mack was in love with Mimi Brown, one of the most iconic DJs in Philadelphia history. She was the seductive, sultry voice of our childhood imaginings, and seeing her in person did not disappoint. Charlie missed no opportunity to get me to the station. I kept finding myself doing interviews at WDAS FM, on Mimi's show. It was like Charlie was now my publicist, and he had one contact in the music industry: Mimi Brown.

This was my third interview with Mimi in the span of two weeks. She had launched a show called *Rap Digest*—I was running out of things to talk about, but Charlie felt we weren't quite hitting the critical points we needed.

"Mimi, oh my god, oh my god—I'm tellin' you! The people just love hearin' y'all talk! Y'all lightin' them phones *up*! We gotta keep doin' this!" Charlie gushed romantically.

Mimi had been an early supporter and advocate for DJ Jazzy Jeff and the Fresh Prince. She was one of the first to ever play our records, and she was one of the Philly pioneers pushing hip-hop onto daytime radio. And she loved a hometown boy. It was always the same with Mimi, whether we were hot or cold, big record or no record—she wanted her studio to feel like home. We were always welcome.

It was a win-win-win—Mimi got a great interview, I felt respected and appreciated, and Charlie got to shoot his shot.

The studio was a cozy little soundproof room with glass on two sides. People within the station could walk by and look in on the interviews and talent who showed up. Mimi and I were always a particularly appealing attraction—we laughed and joked a lot, and we played an interesting mix of hip-hop and R&B that was revolutionary at the time. It felt like a live show as we interacted with the staffers behind the glass.

One afternoon, I started rapping live, which doesn't sound like much today, but I *promise* you it was jaw-dropping back then—this was one of the first times it had ever happened on Philadelphia radio. You have to understand, this was a time when many radio stations' promotional taglines were "*All* music—no rap!"

Behind the glass, the crowd grew and started going crazy—some because they realized they were witnessing the birth of a new era, and others because they probably thought they were witnessing the death of

Mimi Brown's career. As I play and perform to the glass, I'm stopped in my tracks as I realize . . . I'm face-to-face, eye-to-eye, with Dana Goodman. He had heard me on the radio and decided to show up.

If the motherfucker you're looking for is Will, he's in the house. You're welcome to come in and kill him now.

Dana stares, emotionless, and whispers into the ear of the dude with him. The dude nods and moves toward the door of the studio. I keep performing, my eyes steady on Dana. I try to signal to Charlie, but he's staring at Mimi.

The door opens. The man enters the booth and stands beside Charlie. Charlie's ghetto radar is once again on point. Charlie slides almost imperceptibly into striking distance—he's no longer looking at Mimi. I finish rapping; the crowd applauds; Mimi and I sit down to continue our interview.

"You need to thank Dana Goodman," the man yells out.

"Yo, my man, they're live on the radio. Cool out," Charlie whispers.

"You need to thank Dana Goodman," the man yells out, louder this time.

"Homie, we can do whatever you wanna do *outside*. But you gon' be quiet in here," Charlie said, more forcefully.

The dude put his palm on Charlie's chest to shove him away.

"Tell your man to thank Dana G—"

Before his lips could form the first *o* of Goodman, Charlie cracked him with a straight right hand dead on the button, and dude's head explodes like a watermelon. It was as if Charlie had shot his fist out of a cannon. The guy crashed into the metal rack holding the eight-track cassettes, scattering them all over the room. Dude was down and *out*. Charlie grabs me, and Mimi and runs us toward the back parking lot.

"Charlie, Dana's out there," I shout.

"Just keep goin', keep goin'," Charlie says. We exit into the back parking lot as station security grabs Mimi. Charlie throws me into the car, and we're out.

I had never been in a jail cell before. It was way too small, and there were way too many of us in there. Frankly, I felt like we all deserved better.

Apparently, there is an arcane law in Pennsylvania—the "master/slave clause"—that states that if one person commits a crime *under the control or direct influence of a master*, then the "master" is legally liable for the actions of the submissive/slave party. The man's legal team argued that because of my "dominant" relationship with Charlie, I was culpable for his actions. Charlie was never even arrested, even though it was he who had broken the man's left eye socket and irreparably damaged his cornea. Clearly, the man's legal team thought that I was a "deep pocket" and logically reasoned that I was a bigger financial target than Charlie.

The joke was on them. I didn't have a dime to my name. But as I sat in that jail cell, facing aggravated assault, criminal conspiracy, simple assault, and reckless endangerment charges for a punch I hadn't even thrown, I finally understood a term I'd heard many times before: Rock. Bottom. I was literally lying on a cold stone floor. Everything I had, everything I built, the woman I loved, was gone. I was broken. And as I lay there in the fetal position, trying to figure out *How the fuck did I get here?*, I made the horrific error of clinging to the universal, rock-bottom axiom of hope: *Well, I guess it can't get any worse than this. . . .*

Hopefully none of you will ever need this information, but if you can at all avoid it, do *not* get arrested on a Friday. I was released on Monday morning (no one gets let out on a weekend). I went straight to Woodcrest to see Mom-Mom; I hadn't spoken to her; I was sure she'd be a mess.

The crazy thing is, when I saw the police car in front of Woodcrest, it never even crossed my mind that they were there because of me.

One of my childhood friends, Lil' Reggie, had recently become a cop. He had the kind of heart that everybody wanted in a police officer. Reggie was the Man in the neighborhood; Mom-Mom loved him, and everybody respected him.

When I walked in, Mom-Mom and Reggie were sitting in the kitchen. She hugged me. . . .

BZZZZZZZZ.

Damn it, my shock collar. What the hell has Reggie been saying to my mom?

I gave Reggie a pound, we hugged and caught up a bit. He had heard about everything that had happened with Charlie and my weekend in jail.

"I want you to know that I got your back," Reggie said.

BZZZZZZZZZ.

"Uh-huh, for sure, Reggie, I know that," I replied.

"I'm going to ask you a couple of questions, and I need you to keep it one hundred with me. . . ."

BZZZZZZZZZ.

"Do you happen to know . . . ?"

He listed four names. All four were guys from the JBM. Guys I had been gambling with—and not taking cars from—for the past two years.

My heart jumped into my throat. I felt like I had to swallow it back into my chest.

"I *might* know 'em. Why?"

"Willard, do you *know* them, or *not*?" Mom-Mom blurted, cutting through all my bullshit.

"Look," Reggie said, "I'm here to help. You know what they do, right? What they're into?"

I nodded.

"Will, you got a good thing going with your music. Those guys are bad. They're being watched by the FBI. And the Feds are about to shut it all down. Word is that they have photos of them coming in and out of your house, of you driving their cars, and traveling with them. Do you know that it's a crime to give and take money from them?"

I couldn't breathe.

"It *really* doesn't look good," Reggie said. "You need to get away from them. Right now. The FBI is comin' with the thunder and sending a big rap star to prison would just be a cherry on top."

Mom-Mom's face was stone, but the volcano inside was churning and boiling. This was exactly why I needed to take my dumb ass to college.

"You didn't get involved in any of the stuff they did, right? I can't help you if you don't tell me the truth—you clean, right?" Reggie said.

"Yeah, yeah, *totally*. We just played pool and partied," I said.

"Alright, but you need to lay low for a minute. Maybe get out of Philly. It's about to get ugly."

I called Tanya and asked if I could come stay with her for a little while. She was ecstatic.

The problem was, I couldn't afford the plane ticket. My Amex was finally broken—literally. I decided that I needed to take a chance.

I called Bucky.

We met in Fairmount Park, near the Plateau. I pulled up behind his black 325i and jumped into the passenger seat. I loved his car—he had the Alpine CD changer that held twelve CDs; when I got mine, I could only afford the six-changer.

I told him everything—that the Feds were circling, that I was moving to LA, and that he should leave, too. He kinda chuckled, laid his head back on the headrest like he knew that he had been living on a runaway roller coaster that had always been predestined to come to a fiery end. He closed his eyes; we sat in silence.

It was about 6:00 p.m. There was a flight to LA in two hours.

I hated that I had to interrupt him to ask him for money.

"Hey, Buck, I need to hold somethin' to get out to LA," I said quietly.

"What ya gon' do in LA?" Buck asked, not even opening his eyes.

"I don't know for sure. I just love it out there. There's a chick out there I'm feelin'. Our album crashed, so . . . I might try acting."

"You could definitely do that acting shit," he said, smiling as he seemed to replay some of my funniest highlights. "You the dumbest nigga I know for sure." He was laughing out loud now.

"How much you need?" Buck asked.

"Nothin' heavy. I need to get out there, get an apartment, be able to move around a little bit."

"A'ight, I got ten G's here. You need more than that we can run to the spot."

"Nah, that's straight."

Buck had a secret compartment under the driver's seat floor mat. He grabbed the ten G's, reached into the back seat, shook a Tastykake Butterscotch Krimpet out of a brown paper bag, and stuffed the cash into it. He handed it to me, but when I grabbed it, he wouldn't let it go.

He looked straight into my eyes.

"You know you not better than me, right?" he said.

"Of course, Buck, I know that," I said, somewhat confused.

"I'm just like you. We the same." He got quiet for a moment, then said, "I could do *all* that shit you do. I just fucked up. We just born in different spots."

"Yeah, that's real," I said.

Bucky let the money go.

"Just do *right*, man," he said.

"No doubt, Buck. I'm-a get this back to you quick."

He chuckled again, as if somehow, he knew he would never need it.

"When I get my feet, you should roll out to LA."

Bucky chuckled the same knowing chuckle.

"Sure, man, I'll do that."

He gave me a pound.

I made my flight.

Three days later, Bucky was dead.

TEN

ALCHEMY

Tanya had secured us an apartment in Marina del Rey. She knew somebody who knew somebody, and it was only 1,300 bucks a month. I didn't really care.

There were 7,700 dollars left in Bucky's brown paper bag. He had been shot in the head in front of his house. It was a setup. Reggie explained this was the classic playbook—when the Feds close in, everybody turns on each other.

I didn't leave the apartment for weeks. Part fear, part exhaustion—I was in shock. My entire life had collapsed.

I guess my depressed and debilitated state elicited a divine act of mercy from Tanya: We never really talked about it, but we both knew she was my woman now. And she set upon the harrowing task of breathing my spirit back to life. We spent every moment together. Tanya coddled, comforted, and cared for me; she cried with me, and helped me mourn. We would talk for hours; I met her mother and her grandmother. She didn't cook, but she could order the hell out of some takeout.

We fell in love. I coulda hidden in that apartment with her forever.

But then, after a few weeks, as if some cosmic egg timer had sounded—at a frequency just beyond *my* hearing, but well within *her* sonic range—this phase was over. Tanya shifted gears like a drunk trucker crossing the Texas panhandle.

"OK," she said, "that's enough. It's time to get back to life."

"What?" I said, as the cold water of reality flooded our Marina del Rey love nest.

"You've gotta *do* something," she said. "You took a break—that's good. You needed it. But that brown paper bag is almost empty. What are you gonna *do*?"

"What do you mean, what am I gonna *do*?" I said, getting agitated.

"Which part of 'What are you going to do?' is hard for you to understand?" Tanya replied, with equal and opposite agitation. "You have to get out."

"Get out and *do what*? *Go where*?" I shouted.

"I don't fuckin' know!" she clapped back. "But whatever it is, you ain't gonna find it in this kitchen! Just go . . . I don't know . . . go back to Arsenio."

The Arsenio Hall Show was the biggest talk show in America at the time. Everybody who was anybody appeared on *Arsenio*. He was like the Panama Canal of celebrity—all roads to public success ran through *The Arsenio Hall Show*. Charlie had been dragging me there for months.

"We gotta stay where it's happenin'," he said.

Arsenio and I had become kinda halfway friends during the height of me and Jeff's Grammy run. We had appeared on the show and Arsenio had taken a liking to me.

"Go to Arsenio and do *what*?" I yelled.

"Arsenio likes you! Just go to the *show* and hang out. *Meet* people."

"You sound crazy as shit," I said. "So, you want me to go to *The Arsenio Hall Show* and stand around like a dickhead so I could might meet somebody?"

"Yes, exactly—so you *could might meet* somebody!"

"I'm not doing this wit' you. That's dumb, and I'm not in the mood for this shit."

I arrived at *The Arsenio Hall Show* about 4:30 p.m. Five o'clock was showtime. That half hour before was prime mingle time. Charlie Mack was in his world.

"Yo, man, Eddie here tonight! I'm-a go grab him," Charlie said.

Eddie Murphy was appearing on the show that night. He knew who I was—he kept calling me "Young Prince." Arsenio was a lightning rod for magical moments. Many people would argue that Bill Clinton playing the sax on the show solidified his presidential victory. Michael Jackson, Mariah Carey, Miles Davis, Madonna—Magic Johnson even appeared on *Arsenio* twenty-four hours after his HIV announcement.

As I stood backstage, I felt the electrical currents of possibility pulsing and receding—it was like a lush forest with ripe fruit on every tree. The show was a flashpoint, a nexus, a cosmic garden of opportunity that Arsenio knowingly and purposefully cultivated. If Tanya had just said *that*, I wouldn't have been a dickhead.

Charlie and I went almost every day for months. His routine was that he would accost famous strangers and drag them against their will to come meet me. I met everybody—politicians, actors, musicians, athletes, executives.

Benny Medina was an A&R exec at Warner Bros. Records. I didn't know who he was, but apparently, Charlie thought he was important enough to be accosted and dragged. Benny had worked under Berry Gordy at Motown. At Warner Bros., he now oversaw some of their biggest hip-hop acts, including Queen Latifah, De La Soul, and Big Daddy Kane. He was about five foot seven, stocky build, brown skin, curly hair, rockin' hot gear—you could tell he thought he was fly. He knew how to work a room. He was an unapologetic, straight-down-the-middle mover and shaker. Benny could smile when it was time to smile—which was most of the time—but he could get real gully if somebody impeded the movement or desires of one of his artists.

"Hey, Will—this is Benny Medina. Benny, this the Fresh Prince— you know that, though," Charlie Mack said.

Benny knew all about my music. We talked for a bit about hip-hop and the impact technology was having on the music industry, and the future of video on demand, and then out of nowhere, he asked, "Do you know how to act?"

Act? You mean to perform actions in order to elicit joy and passion from those around me? You mean to warp my perceptions of myself as a means to hide myself? You mean to believe deeply in stories that don't exist, that never existed, that could never exist? You mean to play the role of who everyone around me wants me to be, rather than who I actually am?

As a general rule, if someone asks me if I can do something, the answer is always yes.

"Yeah, definitely, for sure, I can definitely act, yes, sir," I said, employing too many words. "Yes."

"I figured you could," Benny said. "I can see it in your music videos. I might have something to talk to you about. Let's keep in touch."

I didn't think anything of it. In Philly, we always clown dudes like this. "Being Hollywood" is like the worst thing you can be—it's the *definition* of insincerity. Moments like that happen all the time in LA. I moved on and forgot about it. Yet, that quick three-minute "Hollywood chat" would turn out to be one of the most important conversations of my life.

Benny Medina is the *real* Fresh Prince of Bel-Air.

Benny was an orphan who grew up with extended family in the projects of East Los Angeles. Then, as a teenager, he was taken in by a friend's wealthy Jewish family who lived in Beverly Hills. Benny was Afro Latino and found himself at Beverly Hills High School. He was a good kid, yet the chasm between the two worlds created a constant culture clash that was a combustible source of tension . . . and humor.

By the time I met him at *The Arsenio Hall Show*, Benny Medina was plotting a move into television.

The universe is not logical, it's magical.

A major aspect of the pain and mental anguish we experience as humans is that our minds seek, and often demand, logic and order from an illogical universe. Our minds desperately want shit to add up, but the rules of logic do not apply to the laws of possibility. The universe functions under the laws of magic.

I was in Detroit a few weeks after my "Hollywood chat." JL had booked a couple of shows to help us to dig out of our collective financial hole. The Joe Louis Arena was always crazy—we loved playing there. We were back down to one hotel room. Strangely enough, it was soothing for all of us to be together again in such cramped quarters. Jeff had headphones on making beats; Omarr was watching TV; Charlie was cutting his toenails. I hated when he did that; I felt like gotdamn *Braveheart* in there—like I needed a Scottish battle shield and to paint my face blue.

None of us knew that this was the last time we'd ever tour together.

JL burst into the room.

"Yo, get up. Quincy Jones wants to talk to you!"

"Quincy Jones? To me? For what? What I do?" I was still shell-shocked from the last chapter.

"Did you meet somebody named Benny Medina?" JL asked.

"Yeah, the Warner Bros. dude."

"Well, he works with *Quincy*," JL whispered, almost knocking my front teeth out jamming the phone into my face.

"I *told* you," Charlie said.

"Hello, Mr. Jones, how are you?" I said with the tone and diction that would have made Mom-Mom, Daddio, *and* Gigi proud. "I'm great, sir, thank you. Detroit. Yup, Joe Louis. We perform tomorrow night."

"Yo, man, what he sayin'? We can't hear him!" Charlie Mack said, pausing his fusillade.

"Shhh!" JL hissed.

"Yo, don't shush me J, I'm a grown-ass man."

"Will you shut your grown-ass *up*?" Jeff chimed in.

"Uhm, sure," I said. "When is it? Oh, wow, OK . . . Uhm, well, yes, definitely. I don't perform till tomorrow night. Thank you. Thank you, sir. Alright. I will see you then."

I put the phone down slowly, the whole squad staring at me, like I just took a pregnancy test.

"Quincy Jones wants me to come to his birthday party," I said to myself as much as to the squad.

"To perform?" Omarr asked.

"Nah. Him and this dude Benny Medina have an idea for a TV show they wanna pitch."

"When do you need to be there?" JL asked.

"Tonight."

Quincy Jones's party fell on the same night as the Soul Train Music Awards. He was being honored with the Heritage Award for Career Achievement and the birthday/after-party was being held at his Bel-Air mansion. JL got me on a 3:00 p.m. out of Detroit and I landed in LA just as the sun was going down.

It all felt surreal, a little head-spinny. I had flown by myself, which was uncommon and uncomfortable, and now, as traffic backed up on the 405, I had a moment to contemplate, *Why the hell am I driving to Quincy Jones's house?*

It was about thirty minutes from LAX to Quincy's. When I pulled up, there was valet parking. Quincy Jones had valet parking *at his house*—twenty red-coated valet parkers *in his driveway*. It looked like the British were coming. It was right up there with Sue Ellen Ewing's fucking breakfast horse.

By the time I arrived, the party was on full bang. *Everybody* was there, from Steven Spielberg to Tevin Campbell; Stevie Wonder and Lionel Richie were arriving as I pulled up. That was too much for me; I knew I didn't belong here. And right before my fragile self-image convinced me to bounce, I saw Benny Medina, a familiar face—a life preserver as I was drowning in yet another sea of insignificance and irrelevance, et cetera.

"Hey man," Benny called out, "you *made* it!"

I *wanted* to say, *Yeah, man, fuck you, I'm out.* But instead, I said, "Yo, man, don't take that jacket off—trust me, you won't see it again."

Benny was wearing one of those Versace, Picasso-looking jackets. He laughed, tugged on the lapel, and said, "If tonight goes well, it's yours. Let's go meet Quincy."

I just thought that was too fast. *Couldn't I at least get a drink first? Or one of them little toast points with some cheese or some salmon or something? Damn. You're jus' gon' rush me to meet Quincy Jones from the* driveway? *I need to stretch; you're gon' have me pullin' a hammy out here.*

The center of the party was in Quincy's massive living room—two-story vaulted ceilings, and a couple hundred of Hollywood's heaviest hitters and A-list rainmakers. Quincy was holding court, a sorcerer in a designer jacket with a piano keyboard embroidered down the left side. Benny and I enter, and before Benny can make the introduction, Quincy and I catch eyes.

"Heyyyy!" Quincy yells out. "The Fresh Prince is here, y'all!"

That would have been embarrassing if anybody had actually given a shit. But it didn't matter to me, because the most important person gave a shit. Quincy is like that—he loves and enjoys people. Every person is a unique work of art to him. He doesn't play celebrity favorites; he genuinely finds something interesting about everybody.

Quincy bounds across the room, arms open, and grips Benny and I in a single embrace.

"Welcome man, welcome," Quincy gushes.

"Thank you, Mr. Jones. This house is *amazing*!" I gush right back.

"Oh, you *like* this? This is Bel-Air! Benny tryin' to set the show in Beverly Hills. I keep tellin' him, man, *fuck* Beverly Hills! Bel-Air make Beverly Hills look like public housin'! Did Benny tell you about the show?"

"Well, a little bit. I mean, uh, he told me he grew up in Watts. And he moved in with a rich family . . ."

"Where you from?" Quincy said.

"Philly," I said with the requisite swag and pride that Philadelphians use to make sure you know that our city is better than yours.

"Ah, man, I *love* Philly!" He leaned in and whispered, "I had some things happen in Philly we not even gon' talk about." Then he laughed and nodded, signifying some unspeakable wilder days in his youth.

"OK, that's it, it's perfect: Your character's from Philly. Will from Philly! Then he goes to Bel-Air!" He was back at full volume now. Quincy had clearly been tastin' a little bit; I figured it was *his* house, and *his* birthday, and *his* Achievement Award, so if he wanted to be drunk and loud, then *gotdamnit, Quincy, you be drunk and loud!*

"Brandon! *Brandon!*" Quincy hollered across the room at a fortysomething-year-old white guy. The guy seemed low-key, understated attire, but everybody was fully attentive while he was talking. Well, until Quincy interrupted him, shouting his name, startling him and pretty much everyone else. Quincy waves him over.

"Brandon! It's Philly to Bel-Air now!"

Brandon Tartikoff was the head of NBC, and the most powerful decision-maker at the network. He decided which shows were financed and aired on the station. He approached with his second in command, Warren Littlefield (Littlefield would ultimately end up running the network).

"Y'all come meet the Fresh Prince!" Quincy said. We all shook hands. They looked at me in a way that I missed back then, but I understand *today*—it's the look that executives have when tens of hours of conversations have gone on about you behind your back. And they still haven't quite decided if they're going to roll the dice on you.

"OK, yeah, can I have everybody's attention?" Quincy bellowed. "We gon' have a audition. Clear the furniture out the living room!"

I was looking around, thinking, *Oh, wow—an audition at a party, that's dope! Quincy is the man! I wonder who's auditioning?*

"Get Will a copy of that Morris Day script, the one we were workin' on," Quincy said. At first slowly, and then painfully, I remember that *my* name was Will. My father had given it to me. And since he wasn't here, and nobody else was moving. . . .

Reality took hold. Quincy Jones was asking me to do an impromptu audition in front of some of the biggest icons, present and past, in all of entertainment, not to mention the top brass at *the* National Broadcasting Company, home to *The Cosby Show*, *Cheers*, *The Golden Girls*, *L.A. Law*, and *Seinfeld*. My knees buckled. Couches were being moved and someone handed me a script.

I grabbed Quincy's arm, probably a little harder than was respectful.

"Quincy, no, wait, no, I can't *do* this now," I whispered in his ear.

Quincy looked at me with an unflinching, tipsy joy.

"Y'all keep settin' up!" he ordered the room. "I'm gon' talk to Will in the library."

Quincy Jones understands magic.

He sees the universe as an infinite playground of magical possibilities. He recognizes miraculous potential in every moment and every thing and everyone around him. His superpower is that he has learned to present himself to the universe as a lightning rod, placing himself perfectly to capture and conduct the ever-present, ever-recurring magical flashes of brilliance surrounding us all.

Quincy Jones is an intuitive, artistic storm chaser. He can sense the subtle flickerings of the *impossible* preparing to strike. He prepared himself for decades, studying music, playing thousands of gigs, learning from masters, surrounding himself with the most accomplished performers and artists. Quincy used to say, "Things are *always* impossible, right up until they're *not!*" He learned how to prepare the environment and invited the energy in; he saw himself as the "conductor," both in the electrical sense and the musical definition. His main job was to keep all of us from missing the miracle, from blocking the subtle magical opportunity that was obviously (to him) presenting itself.

Gigi had a similar idea—she would say, "Don't block your blessings." Even though these possibilities are abundantly and perpetually flowing around us, we can miss them, or even worse, block or repel them.

Gigi used to love to tell the Bible story of the death of Lazarus. Lazarus was a great friend of Jesus, so when he fell ill and died, Lazarus's sisters, Martha and Mary, were devastated. They had sent word to Jesus, begging him to hurry. Jesus had to walk two hot dusty days from the other side of the River Jordan. He was already exhausted—he'd worked all week, preaching during the Feast of Dedication. When he arrived in Bethany, Lazarus had already been dead and buried for four days. When Jesus approached the tomb, he saw that the rock was still in place at the mouth of the cave, as was the burial tradition of the time.

Jesus wept, perturbed, and said—and I paraphrase . . .

"So, lemme get this straight. Y'all made me walk fifteen frickin' furlongs—'scuse my language—to hot-dag'on Bethany, where Pharisees and Sadducees is runnin' around here like roaches just waiting for a chance to take a pop at me, to perform the miracle of raising your patriarch from the dead, restoring your family to blessed wholeness and light, and y'all can't even move the rock from in front of the tomb? If I'm gonna raise this boy from the dead, the least y'all lazy jokas could do is move the dag'on rock!"

This was an idea that Quincy understood fully. Magic demands awareness (faith—you have to *believe* in magic); preparation (move the rock—we must identify and eradicate the poisonous resistances and impediments within ourselves); then, surrender (stay out of the way and trust the magic to do what it does). Quincy helped people get their rocks out of the way of the blessed light that is *always* trying to shine in. The universe *wants* you to have the miracle! Move the damn rock! Quincy was moving furniture, but he was trying to get *all* of us—me, Brandon, Benny, even himself—to move our rocks out of the way.

Quincy's library was dark mahogany. High-back leather armchairs; I don't know if the rugs were from Persia, but they looked expensive. I don't remember much else about the room because I was blinded by the glare from the gaggle of Grammy, Tony, Emmy, and Academy Awards scattered around the place like butter knives in a Swiss Cottage hotel bathroom. A framed poster of Oprah Winfrey's *The Color Purple* hovered over my left shoulder; Michael Jackson's *Thriller* sales plaque loomed over my right—48,000,000 sold. (I could have just written the word "million," but I wanted you to feel how many zeroes that is.) I felt Michael looking at me on his toes in the classic "Billie Jean" pose, as if he were saying, *So what are you gonna do, Will?*

I take a seat. Quincy stands in front of me. He's been here before. This is what he does. He moves rocks for a living.

"Talk to me, Philly," he says. "What you need?"

"Quincy, I'm, I'm . . . not prepared to do an audition," I stammered. "I didn't know, when you called, you know, what we were doing and all that."

"It's only a couple of scenes. I got some people out there who will read with you. You just gotta be you and have fun."

"Quincy, I can *not* do an audition in the middle of a party. I need to prepare, I just need some time, to work on it."

"OK, I hear that—how much time you need?" Quincy asked.

"I mean, just, uh, give me a week, and I'll find an acting coach, and I can study it, so I can do it, not just read it."

Quincy considered my words.

"OK, so you need a week?"

"Yes, a week, a week is *perfect!*"

"OK, so you know what's gonna happen in a week?" Quincy asked. But before I could answer, he said, "Brandon Tartikoff is going to have an emergency on one of his shows and he's gonna have to fly to Kansas to fire somebody. Then he's gonna have to reschedule for the following week."

"Oh, cool, cool! *Two* weeks would be even better," I said, missing the subtleties of Quincy's point.

"Right, two weeks. Then Warren Littlefield is gonna have something at his kids' elementary school that he forgot was on the schedule he can't get out of because his wife's going to tear him a new one if he doesn't show up. And *he's* gonna have to reschedule for two weeks after *that.*"

"Right," I said, slowly starting to glean his point. "So, a month . . . ?"

Quincy leaned in, eyes crystal clear, suddenly sharp, totally sober.

"But right now, everybody that needs to say yes to this show is sitting out there in that living room waiting for *you*. And you are about to make a decision that will affect the rest of your life."

I took it in. I looked at Michael, then to Oprah. They looked right back at me. *We know baby, it's* hard.

"Whatcha gon' do, Philly?"

"Fuck it," I said. "Gimme ten minutes."

I don't remember much about the audition—it's kind of a blurry collage of jokes, laughs, punch lines, and ad-libs—Quincy, then Brandon, Benny—twenty magical minutes culminating in an ovation from the entire room. The applause, like a defibrillator, jolted my awareness back into the moment, reestablishing my mental timeline.

Quincy stands up, aggressively pointing at Brandon Tartikoff.

"Did you like it?" Quincy screamed.

"Yes, yes, I liked it, Q," Brandon said calmly, keeping his cards close to his vest.

"Don't give me that shit! You know what I'm talkin' about! DID YOU *LIKE* IT?"

Brandon knew exactly what Quincy was talking about.

"Yes, Quincy, I *liked* it," Brandon said firmly, and confidently.

"Yes!" Quincy shouted, clapping his hands and turning to point at a different man, who turned out to be Brandon Tartikoff's chief legal counsel, who had been "strategically" invited to Quincy's party.

"You!" he said, to the man who was in mid-mini-pizza bite. "You're Brandon's lawyer. You heard what he just said. Draw me up a deal memo right now!"

I was thinking, *Damn, Quincy Jones got power. That's not even his lawyer! He makin' other people's lawyers do work, on Wednesday, at nine at night, at a party!*

The lawyer looked at Brandon; Brandon attempted to chime in.

"Quincy, listen—"

"NO PARALYSIS THROUGH ANALYSIS!" Quincy shouted. "Draw me up a deal memo, RIGHT NOW!"

Brandon relents and nods to his legal counsel, who steps up, exits to the NBC limousine where he would spend the next two hours drafting a deal memo.

Next, Quincy snaps around with the same aggressive index finger/ magic wand, only this time it's pointing at me.

"You got a lawyer?"

"Well, no, no, not at the party . . ." I stuttered.

Quincy spins again, now in full magical conductor mode, wand pointing at a new victim.

"Get me Ken Hertz on the phone! That's Philly's new lawyer!"

(As a side note, Ken Hertz was in the maternity ward at Cedars-Sinai where his second daughter had just been born. But when you're a young lawyer, with a brand-new family, and you get a 10:00 p.m. call from Quincy Jones, and the maternity ward at Cedars-Sinai is twenty minutes from Quincy's house, you arrive in eighteen minutes. I met Ken Hertz that night; he represented me in the negotiations with NBC, and for every other deal since. He's still my lawyer to this day. He named his daughter Cori.)

I mention that Quincy had been drinking, right? There was no reason for him to be saying everything as loudly as he was saying it—it wasn't that big a room. We could all hear him perfectly well. But, maybe he knew he wasn't speaking to our *ears*—he was bellowing to reach the caverns behind the rocks, simultaneously conjuring and welcoming the magic of the universe. I guess he wanted to be loud enough to make sure that the miracle didn't miss the house.

"NO PARALYSIS THROUGH ANALYSIS!" Quincy shouted again and again. He would intone this mantra nearly fifty times over the next two hours. It was the answer to every question, it was the response to ever stutter, it was the solution to every legal problem. Until, two hours later, when Quincy Jones, Brandon Tartikoff, Benny Medina—and Will Smith—entered into an agreement to shoot a pilot for a television show tentatively titled *The Fresh Prince of Bel-Air*.

Now, this is a story all about how my life got flipped, turned upside down. And I'd like to take a minute, just sit right there—I'll tell you how I became the prince of a town called Bel-Air.

Six weeks earlier, I had been curled up in a ball in Marina del Rey, lost, depressed, and terrified. And just like that, the universe had given me a new family: James Avery. Janet Hubert-Whitten. Alfonso Ribeiro. Tatyana Ali. Karyn Parsons. Joseph Marcell.

James Avery: Uncle Phil. Six foot four, 320 pounds. Shakespearean actor. New father figure. Demanded the highest commitment to my craft. "You're not a rapper here—you're an actor. So, act like it." I spent the greater part of the next six years seeking his approval.

Janet Hubert-Whitten: The first Aunt Viv. Triple threat—singer, dancer, actress. Elite on all levels. Starred in *Cats* on Broadway. The conscience of the show. Fought tirelessly to maintain a dignified portrayal of African Americans on *The Fresh Prince of Bel-Air*. In hindsight, the show suffered after she left.

Alfonso Ribeiro: Carlton Banks. Acting since nine years old. "The Tap Dance Kid." Broadway; television; film. Unflinching ally, great friend—he rode with me no matter what. Gave me the best advice ever ("Hey, man, I hear the producers discussing names for your character. Take it from me: Give your character *your* name, Will Smith. Because people are going to call you that for the rest of your life." —Carlton).

Tatyana Ali: Ashley Banks. Eleven years old and still had more experience than me. Singer, dancer, actress: *Sesame Street*, *Star Search*, Eddie Murphy's *Raw*, performing with Samuel L. Jackson. Would spend her teenage years on set ultimately educating herself to Harvard University. One of the most disciplined people I've ever met.

Karyn Parsons: Hilary Banks. The least experienced next to me. Beat out a slew of Hollywood big hitters to win her role. Was smart enough to tell me "hell no" when I tried to explain that we were not *really* cousins so it would be fine if we dated. ("I swear it won't mess up our working relationship." She knew better than that—good call, K.P.)

Joseph Marcell: Geoffrey Butler. Royal Shakespeare Company; Globe Theater: *Othello*, *King Lear*, *A Midsummer Night's Dream*; Solly Two Kings in August Wilson's *Gem of the Ocean*. Producers of *Fresh Prince* were torn between him and another actor. My first Fresh Prince flex was "I want Joseph Marcell."

In Hollywood terms, the conception, casting, writing, deal making, set design, shooting, editing, and airing of *The Fresh Prince of Bel-Air* hovered on the border of the miraculous. Shows don't happen this fast. Everything went perfectly. Quincy's party had been on March 14, 1990; the writing, auditions, final casting, and deal making was completed by the end of April. Staffing, set design, wardrobe, et cetera, were completed, and we were shooting the pilot in mid-May. The show was edited and tested in late July; we promoted in August, and it aired on September 10, 1990.

There was no paralysis through analysis.

And I *loved* it.

I found my thing. The world of acting unleashed all the artistic impulses within me. It was the first external canvas that felt big enough to hold the landscapes of my imagination. My musical expression always felt narrow and constrained by the limits of my skills and talents. Making music felt like living in a great neighborhood, whereas acting felt like being set free in an infinite universe. As an actor, I would get to be anybody, go anywhere, and do anything: world champion boxer, fighter pilot, tennis coach, galaxy defender, cop, lawyer, businessman, doctor, lover, preacher, genie—I would even get to be a fish. Acting encompasses all the things that I am—storyteller, performer, comedian, musician, teacher.

Don't get me wrong: I really like making music; but I *love* acting.

Mom-Mom was an avid reader. Her every free moment was spent between the pages of everything from Edgar Allan Poe to Agatha Christie to Toni Morrison to Stephen King to Maya Angelou to Sherlock Holmes and Sidney Poitier's autobiography. She would often talk about a book that "spoke to her soul" or "she just couldn't put it down." It had penetrated her and transformed her way of seeing or being, but I had never experienced that. I was well into my twenties before I actually read an entire book cover to cover.

The Alchemist, a novel by Brazilian author Paulo Coelho, was my first literary love affair. The book spoke to my soul, and I just couldn't put it down. It penetrated me and transformed my way of seeing and being.

The Alchemist is the journey of a young Andalusian shepherd boy named Santiago. He has a recurring dream of a hidden treasure buried at the pyramids of Giza, in Egypt. The dream beckons him so profoundly that he sells his entire flock, gives up his life in southern Spain, and sets out to follow the whispers of his heart to Egypt, to pursue what Paulo Coelho describes as his "Personal Legend," his divine calling, what I think of as his destiny, his dharma.

But Santiago's journey is not an easy one. I cheered and feared and jeered every step of the way as he was loved and hated and helped and hindered along his perilous path. I felt like I *was* Santiago, my hidden treasure buried somewhere under the Hollywood sign. *The Alchemist* is probably the most influential book I've ever read. It empowered my dreamer's spirit and validated my suffering. If Santiago could suffer, survive, and claim his treasure, then so could I.

An alchemist is a spiritual chemist, a master of transmutation. The great feat of an alchemist is that they can do the impossible: They can turn *lead* into *gold*. This concept erupted in my mind—the ability to take anything that life gives you and turn it into gold.

Gigi could take the last half glass of Welch's grape juice and mix it with the last swallow of Dole pineapple juice, throw in some Kool-Aid packets, dice up some lemon and the other half of the orange she was just eating, and swirl it all together with a blast of Canada Dry ginger ale—freeze it—and hand you the best damn Popsicle you've ever had in your life. This was *after* you'd looked in the refrigerator five separate times and each time told her that there was *nothing* in there.

Quincy Jones is an alchemist, and he had set my mind on fire; I had never met anybody like him. I wanted to be an alchemist, too. I wanted to be able to transform anything and everything that life gave me into gold.

The universe had given me a second chance, and I swore to God that I would *not* need a third.

ELEVEN

ADAPTATION

JL refused to come to LA.

The whole "TV thing" was disconcerting to him—it was all happening too fast, it was out of left field and outside his expertise. I'd been to Quincy Jones's birthday party, and the next day I had a TV show? There was no plan, no strategy, and we were all still trying to recover from the catastrophic financial and creative collapse of DJ Jazzy Jeff and the Fresh Prince. And *now*, I wanted JL to pack up everything and move to Los Angeles because Quincy Jones is . . . an *alchemist*?

Tanya and I had gotten a new apartment in Burbank, walking distance to NBC. My full focus was clearly now on television. And making this pilot episode *hot*.

"Dude. You need to be in the studio doing what you do," JL implored.

"J, I'm *tellin'* you, our future is out *here*! Our music shit is dead."

"Well, that's not true. . . . But whatever you need me for, I can do it from Philly."

"J, you don't under*stand*—you have to be *out* here. It's not scheduled meetings and structured like that. People make decisions at birthday parties and in fucking *diners*."

JL knows me as well as anybody on this earth. He saw me (and sometimes *still* sees me) as an impetuous artist who needs to be protected from myself. He saw *himself* as the final checkpoint of sanity keeping Will from driving us all off a cliff. JL couldn't stomach the uncertainty and the tornado of change that he felt was endangering our recovery.

Omarr moved immediately; Charlie came out every week.

(Just as a piece of *Fresh Prince of Bel-Air* trivia: In the opening credits of the show, when I get in "one little fight and my mom got scared," the person I get into "one little fight" with, the guy who is spinning me around and precipitating my departure for California? That's Charlie Mack.)

I figured if I could convince Jeff to come to LA, then JL would see that all of us were out here. So, without even telling Jeff, I went to the producers at NBC and pitched them a character for him to play on the show. I told them he was my music partner and that he was a bigger star in the hip-hop community than I was—our fans would go crazy if they saw Jeff on the show.

Obviously, they were worried about adding *yet another* Philly homeboy who had *zero* acting experience into a prime-time sitcom. But this became my second *Fresh Prince* flex. They reluctantly agreed to "test" him in six episodes—or a quarter of the first season.

Excited, I hit Jeff to tell him the news.

"Ah, man, thanks," he said, "but I'm not really feelin' that TV actin' stuff—that's *you*. I just wanna do music."

I was dumbstruck.

"Jeff. You can do music in LA—they got studios out here like we got liquor stores and churches. Plus, they're offering you ten grand per episode. That's easy money, man."

Silence.

"Jeff?"

"I'm just not feelin' it, man. . . . That LA shit's not me. I'm a Philly boy."

I wanted to scream, *What the fuck are you talking about? You are broke. You are back in your mom's basement. You don't have a choice.*

But instead, I just said, "OK. I'll holla at you later."

Change can be scary, but it's utterly unavoidable. In fact, impermanence is the only thing you can truly rely on. If you are unwilling or unable to pivot and adapt to the incessant, fluctuating tides of life, you will not enjoy being here. Sometimes, people try to play the cards that they *wish* they had, instead of playing the hand they've been dealt. The capacity to adjust and improvise is arguably the single most critical human ability.

There's a Buddhist parable that has guided me through many a perilous transition: A man is standing on the banks of a treacherous, raging river. It's rainy season—if he can't get to the other side, he's done. He quickly builds a raft and uses it to safely cross the river. In joyous relief, he high-fives himself, lifts the raft, and heads toward the forest.

But as he attempts to make his way through the dense tree cover, the raft is banging and knocking into trees and becoming entangled in vines, preventing him from moving forward. He only has one chance for survival: He must leave the raft behind—the vessel that saved his life yesterday is the same one that will kill him today if he does not let it go.

The raft represents our outmoded ideas and old ways of thinking that no longer serve us. For example, the same angry, aggressive persona you cultivated as a child to protect yourself from bullies and predators will now destroy every relationship you have if you're unwilling to let it go. Things can be perfectly useful and absolutely necessary during certain periods of our lives. But a time will come when we must put them aside or die.

Simply put, if we don't adapt, we become extinct. I saw JL's and Jeff's choice to stay in Philly as a death sentence for both of them. But I also knew that I wouldn't allow it.

The Fresh Prince of Bel-Air was behind the 8 ball from the beginning. A show of this size would usually have been greenlit nine months earlier. Because of the truncated, damn-near-impossible shooting schedule, decisions were having to be made in real time across the spectrum of the entire production. In JL's absence, Benny Medina stepped up in a managerial capacity. He became the contact for all things "Will Smith." Benny knew what he was doing, and he knew how to get things done. But my heart hurt being in LA without JL and Jeff.

I had to get them out here, so I threw up a Hail Mary at the buzzer: I told JL that I would record another album if he agreed to spend one week out of every month in LA. At the time, I didn't see music as any major part of my future, but I didn't tell him that; I just needed him in LA.

Now, I had to convince Jeff.

"Look, man, just do *three* episodes. If you hate it, you only got three to go. If you love it, you can get a spot out here and we'll go back to the producers and get you more. *And* we can record! The worst-case scenario? You clear sixty grand for being on a network television show, and at a minimum? More pussy."

I wasn't entirely sure which part of that argument sold Jeff, but I didn't care—he was coming.

(*FP* trivia moment: Jeff went on to become one of the most beloved characters on the show, and he loved it. His signature comedic bit was Uncle Phil throwing him out of the house. During the shooting of the pilot episode, no one knew that this bit would catch on, so we only had one shot of Jeff flying out of the house. The interior of the Bel-Air mansion and the exterior are two different locations, and we only had a one-day shoot at the exterior location. So, we had to use the same shot of Jeff being thrown out over and over. Therefore, any time you see Jeff enter with the brown-and-white Aztec-patterned shirt, you know that he'll be thrown out in that scene.)

The Fresh Prince of Bel-Air premiered on September 10, 1990, and was an immediate success, becoming the highest-rated debut show of that season. That meant there were definitely going to be more seasons.

Opportunities were heating up, but despite it all, JL was *still* skeptical. Even a year later and tens of millions of weekly viewers, JL kept his bedroom at his mother's house in Philly. I guess in his defense, it was barely a year ago that he had seen me burn through three million dollars, not pay a single dime to the IRS, collapse DJ Jazzy Jeff and the Fresh Prince over chicken fingers and rum punches, and then blithely move to LA to become a TV star.

When I put it like that, I guess it's amazing that he still took my calls. But even though he was denying it, it was undeniable: the show was a hit, the iron was hot, and it was time to strike.

I was hungry, focused, and excited about the new life I was being blessed to undertake. But my personal and professional crash and burn had taught me a harsh, universal lesson: Nothing lasts forever. *Everything* rises and falls—no matter how hot the summer gets, the winter is inevitable. I promised myself I would never get caught sleeping again. That during the good times, I would plant and nurture the seeds of the "next thing." And if I was truly wise, and attuned to the movements of the industry, I would be able to time the harvest of the next thing impeccably, just before the death of the old thing. In the same way that my music career was scorching hot, then icy cold, I knew the same thing would one day happen in TV. I was about to be on blaze—but one day, I knew I'd be cold again. I asked myself: *After television, what would be my next thing?* There was only one answer: *movies*.

But I also made a deeper, more problematic conclusion: that love and relationships were also subject to the universal law of impermanence. I vowed to never get caught without my eye on my next love. My heart had been crushed, and I was *certain* that it would happen again. I knew there would be a blissful, springtime meeting; a hot summer whirlwind; a melancholy fall; and then an icy winter death. I decided that my only emotional defense against this brutal cosmic certainty was to outcreate the cycle of destruction. In my mind, I knew I had to be like Tarzan: catching the next vine just as I let go of the old one. If I could grab the new thing, while simultaneously releasing the dying thing, I could avoid and escape the harshest elements of winter and indefinitely sustain the vibrance of springtime bliss.

Sitcom television is the individual, undisputed, greatest job on earth.

A sitcom workweek was five days to produce one episode. Monday was the table read—actors, producers, writers sit around a table and read the script aloud. Everybody would give notes, and overnight the writers would deliver a new draft. Tuesday and Wednesday were playtime: the actors onstage trying to breathe life into the words. *This* was the part that made sitcom television the best job. We got paid to laugh, joke, play, create, debate, grow, and love on each other. At the end of each day, we would do a run-through for the writers and show them what we had come up with. And Tuesday and Wednesday night they would make adjustments, improving the script.

Thursday was a technical run-through. Lights, sound, cameras, all figuring out how they would cover the action of the scenes. And then . . . Friday: the live, in-studio audience.

Friday nights on the set of *The Fresh Prince of Bel-Air* were like being at the hottest club in the city—everybody who was anybody made their way to our tapings. The top comedians on the mic, the most gorgeous Hollywood starlets, professional athletes, musicians—a who's who of the flyest of the fly.

And then there was our unique competitive advantage: Everybody in our cast could sing and dance. So, between scenes, Alfonso would perform Michael Jackson; Joe Marcell would sing some obscure, hilarious British show tune; James Avery would demonstrate all the old-school dances; Janet Hubbert-Whitten was an Alvin Ailey–trained dancer, and a Juilliard-trained actor and singer; even Tatyana, at eleven years old, was jumpin' in the game. And then, as if all that wasn't enough to send the studio audience into hysteria, we dropped our nuke: DJ Jazzy Jeff and the Fresh Prince would perform live every Friday night. Our between-scene moments were as iconic as anything we ever put on camera.

This was heaven. A new family, a new home, a new life.

The message read, *I need a cut of that Will Smith business.*

JL received this message from an infamous LA gangbanger with a reputation for shakedowns, violent extortion, and charging "fees" for "protection." JL decided not to respond. We were no strangers to violence and attempted intimidation. We had guys in Philly who were more than prepared to make trips to "handle things" if we needed it.

But LA was different. There was a brazenness and a pervasiveness that made us feel uncertain. In Philly, you could easily discern the dangerous areas and avoid them—you knew if the trash wasn't getting picked up, if there were cars parked on the sidewalk, abandoned buildings on the same block as family homes, you had to be careful in that neighborhood. And of course, the projects—you knew what that was. But in LA, the "worst" neighborhoods would have green grass and palm trees. Carjackings *in broad daylight* were common—you could get caught slipping anywhere. We couldn't work out where to drive or what to wear . . . it all felt dangerously confusing. *None* of us carried guns in Philly; *all* of us carried guns in LA.

There were now five messages for JL. *I need a cut of that Will Smith business. You should probably respond.* We had heard the stories about this dude—he would just take people's money, force them to sign over their publishing, strong-arming people throughout the industry. We were new to LA, and we did *not* want trouble. But if trouble wanted us, we were right here.

JL decided to take the call.

"This is James Lassiter. How can I help you?"

"You a hard man to get in touch with," the dude said. "I'm thinkin' I need to get into that Will Smith business."

"OK," JL responded, taking a pause to measure his next move. "I think we can do that."

"Good, good . . . ," the dude said.

"But I have a partner," JL interjected. "I don't make the final decision. You'll need to speak with him."

"OK, let's set that up."

"Absolutely; immediately. My partner works at the Federal Bureau of Investigation," JL said evenly. "I'll set the call. And any deal that you and he come up with, I'm down for it."

We never heard from him again.

A threat is one thing; violence is something else.

But when you grow up in violent environments, your mind adapts to perceive threats *everywhere*. You reason that you cannot afford to get caught slipping, even once. You begin to respond to a *perceived* threat and to *actual* violence equally, even though they're very different things. There's an old adage: I'd rather be judged by twelve than carried by six.

It was a Wednesday. We were struggling on set, trying to make a scene work. We all felt it—the writing wasn't landing as authentic or funny. So I took it upon myself to begin making changes to the scene. When the producers came down and saw all of the "unilateral" adjustments I'd made, they immediately called the leadership at NBCP (the production arm of the network), who demanded that we stop production and come to the office right now.

Benny Medina, JL, me, and Jeff Pollack (Benny Medina's television partner) headed to the "emergency meeting" in the exec's office. There were two couches facing each other, with a wooden coffee table in between, and a huge etched-glass desk at one end.

The executive was standing, leaning against his desk, facing the two couches. His posture suggested that he was in charge and that he was pissed. We entered and took our seats in front of the "headmaster." JL and Benny sat on one couch, and me and Jeff Pollack sat facing them on the other.

No formalities, no hellos, no hearing our side of the story.

"So, you're a big man, huh?" the executive asked me.

I didn't totally understand the question, so I didn't respond. He begins to circle the perimeter of the two couches. It felt like the scene from *New Jack City* when Wesley Snipes was trying to get somebody to explain to him how the Carter got infiltrated.

"So, you can unilaterally change any of the words you want on a network sitcom, huh?"

At that moment, he's standing behind me. I made eye contact with JL. *Is this dude about to swing on me?*

JL looks at me as if to say, *I got my eye on him—if he even flinches, I got you.*

"Hundreds of millions of dollars, multiple partners, a shit-ton of fucking veterans of the business . . . and *you* get to decide what the words are?"

At this point, he has circled behind the other couch and behind JL. I give J the same look he gave me. *If he even flinches, I got you.*

The executive now circles back behind me. Jeff Pollack, the only white person in our group, begins to explain.

"I'm not sure you've been brought up to speed on the totality and the complexity of the situation. . . ."

"Well, hold on, Jeff, I know what I need to know . . ." said the executive. Now, he's over my right shoulder, and his voice is beginning to rise.

"I've seen this happen a thousand fucking times. You can be gone just as fast as you got here. . . ."

In front of JL, on the coffee table, is one of those five-pound glass snow globes. JL surreptitiously grabs it and sits it in his lap. Our eyes locked. He has a different look this time.

Whatever you wanna do, homie.

I jump up and spin, stepping around the couch, coming face-to-face with the exec.

"What the fuck you wanna do, bitch?" I sneered.

JL jumps up, now fully brandishing the snow globe.

"Hold on, guys, hold on," Benny Medina implores.

"Back up, Jeff," JL says. Since Jeff came with us, he's confused about JL's tone and energy toward him, especially as all he did was stand up. But JL has a five-pound snow globe in his hand, so Jeff does as he's told and quickly backs up.

"Who the fuck is you talkin' to?" I woofed at the executive. In retrospect, I did notice that the man's eyes were completely surrendered and that he had *no* idea what was happening. He clearly had never been called a bitch in his life and wanted no beef whatsoever.

"Who the fuck is you squarin' off on?" I was fully in it now. I could tell he wanted to respond, but he was still stuck trying to unravel the urban koan *What the fuck you wanna do, bitch?*

"Will, uhm, clearly we've gotten off on the wrong foot, here," he said sweetly, his left hand now holding his lower back.

"You damn right! You standin' up screamin' on motherfuckers. Sit *down* when you talk to me."

"But, Will," he said, even more sweetly, "I just had major back surgery and the doctor told me that I should stand up when I'm . . ."

"You gon' sit the fuck down when you talk to me," I growled.

"But, Will, the doc . . ."

"SIT. THE. FUCK. DOWN!"

He gingerly made his way over to the edge of his big glass desk, delicately placing his hand to brace himself. Wincing, he lowered himself painfully onto the edge of the desk.

Benny had seen enough. "OK, we're good. You guys, go," he said. "JL, put the snow globe down."

Jeff steps in front of the exec and gestures for JL and I to leave the room. We comply. As we're exiting, we hear Jeff whisper, "We are *so* sorry."

WHAT THE HELL WAS THAAAAAAT?"

Jeff Pollack is screaming at the top of his lungs in the parking lot. This was the only time I ever heard Jeff raise his voice.

"Dude looked like he was about to swing on me," I said in my defense.

I had heard the term before, people "pulling their hair out," but this was the only time I'd ever *seen* it in real life. Jeff was actually taking two fistfuls of his own hair and tugging on them as if he wanted to rip them out of his scalp.

"A sixty-four-year-old television executive with a bad back was going to 'swing on you'?"

Me and JL kinda looked at each. In the office, we had been certain; but when you hear it in a parking lot, it feels like it *might* not hold up in court.

"Well, why was he standin' up, walkin' around us, like he was gon' do somethin'?" I asked, in a last-ditch defense of my perception.

"WHAT. THE. HELL. WAS. HE. GOING. TO. DO? He's just had major invasive lumbar decompression surgery!"

"OK, guys, let's take a break," Benny said compassionately. "I gotta call Quincy."

Oh, shit, Quincy.

I immediately rushed to try to call Q first.

"Quincy's on a call right now, Will, can I have him return?"

Fuck, no, tell him to hang up with NBC and hear my side of the story first.

"Sure, that would be great, thanks," I said.

After the worst thirty minutes of my life, he hit me back.

"IthinkIfuckedup," I blurted.

"It's fine—people cuss each other out all the time," Quincy said. "Just never put your hands on nobody. I talked to 'em, it's good. What happened on set?"

"I changed some lines in the script because they was tryin' to have me say some whack shit. They tryin' to tell *me* what a dude from Philly would say. And I'm like, that line's not *real. . . .*"

"Oh, so it was a *creative* disagreement . . ." Quincy said.

"I guess that's what they call it in LA," I said.

"You have a script right there?" Quincy asked.

"Yeah, I got one right here."

"OK. What's it say on the cover?"

"Uhhmm," I said, confused, "*The Fresh Prince of Bel-Air*?"

"Right. And who's the Fresh Prince?" Quincy barked.

"Me," I said.

"EXACTLY! Don't nobody know what the fuck you're supposed to say better than you. If they could do what you do, they wouldn't have hired you. You say what you wanna say, the way you wanna say it. And when somebody has a problem with it, tell 'em to call me."

I was barely twenty-two years old, and Quincy Jones had just empowered me to say whatever I wanted to say on a network television show. He took my side over producers, writers, executives, advertisers, everybody.

He bet on me.

"Yes, sir," I said.

JL and I were shook up by how thoroughly we had misread the snow globe situation. We were coming from violent homes and violent neighborhoods and the violent music world. It was not unreasonable to think that an executive might get violent. We felt cornered and vulnerable. JL and I had been 100 percent certain that that executive was going to hit me.

It's amazing how skewed your vision can become when you see the present through the lens of your past. It was a very difficult psychological rehabilitation for us to learn how to put down the snow globe.

As per my agreement with JL, me and Jeff went to work on our fourth album, which would become *Homebase*. But Jeff and I were on TV now, so we were essentially moonlighting from our day jobs to make music. We were used to open-ended creative time; in the past, we'd blocked out months to conceive, write, and record (and consume chicken fingers). But now, because of the specific and limited time frames, we had to be laser-focused and razor-sharp with every single moment of studio time. To quote Daddio, "There was no bullshittin' while we were on the clock." The result was, as opposed to *And in This Corner . . .* , for *Homebase* we made twice as many songs in half as much time for a quarter of the budget. And the songs were better.

Another by-product of our television success was that we were freed from the pressure of *needing* the record to be a hit. If the album bombed, we would be fine—our rents (and our tax liabilities) were getting paid with *Bel-Air* money. We got to have fun again—it was just me and Jeff being me and Jeff, getting back to what made us great. We were getting back to our home base.

It was also the first time we opened up our creative process to new producers and other creative voices. I had been working in Chicago, finishing my vocals on the album with a couple of young Jive Records producers named Hula and Fingers. Jeff was doing the final mixing in New York, and I was booked on a 6:00 p.m. flight from O'Hare to LAX. Me, Hula, and Fingers had partied hard the night before, celebrating the completion of *Homebase*. I had blown my voice out yelling all night in the club. On the way to O'Hare, I stopped by the studio to pick up a couple of CDs of the sequenced album so I could listen on the plane. Hula gave me the CD, I tucked it in my backpack, and headed to the door.

Fingers called after me. "Hey, man, there's one more track that we were messin' with. Jeff said he likes it. He told us to give it to you and see if you wanted to lay something real quick."

I was exhausted, my voice was blown out, I was ready to get home to LA, and plus, the album was finished. Fingers was holding out a CD with the word "Untitled" in Magic Marker across the top. Just seeing the word "Untitled" was exasperating. Even the thought of having to write a whole new song made my stomach hurt. I was done.

"Hey, Fingers," I said, "I appreciate you, man, y'all have done great work. But I'm exhausted; I mean, listen to my voice. I couldn't lay nothin' if I *wanted* to. You would probably have to get *Jesus* to hand me that CD for me to write another song."

The guys laughed, but out of courtesy I took the CD.

I arrived at Chicago O'Hare an hour before my flight to the announcement that Flight 1024 to Los Angeles has been delayed ninety minutes.

Gotdamnit—why is it always *like that? The more you wanna get home, the more delayed your damn flight is.*

I found a quiet corner, put my headphones on, and decided to listen to "Untitled." The track opened with Fingers's voice into a crazy drum drop with a rising crowd cheer.

Druuuuuuumz, pleeeeeease
Aaaaaaaaa, yeah!

And then a sultry female voice:

Summer, summer, summertime
Time to sit back and unwind

"Oh. My. God."

I must have looked crazy in that airport lounge; I had that face that musicians get when a track is bangin'. It's like you smellin' something *nasty*. My head was about to bop off my shoulders.

I quickly grabbed my rhyme book from my backpack, and the next two hours was nothing short of divine intervention. I didn't *write* "Summertime" as much as I *channeled* it. My mind collapsed into the bliss of summertime in Philadelphia. I felt myself floating through my childhood summer memories and my hand was just along for the ride, trying to keep up. "Summertime" is the only song I've ever written from beginning straight through to the end and didn't edit or change a single word. The lyrics, as they appear on the final cut, are *exactly* as they came through. It was a pure stream of consciousness. I would later learn a term that resonated deeply with my experience at O'Hare that night: *psychography*, or automatic writing, is a theoretical psychic ability allowing someone to produce written words without *consciously* writing. (Skeptics call it self-delusion; I call it "another Grammy" and "my first #1 record.")

"Flight 1024 is now boarding. . . ."

"Shit."

I knew this song was crazy. And if I didn't record it today, it wasn't going to be on the album. I could hear Quincy in my head, *Whatcha gon' do, Philly?*

"Fuck it."

I popped up, back in the car, back to the studio.

My voice was wrecked. The pitch and tone of voice I was famous for was high, up-tempo, and wrapped in a smile. But every time I reached for that energy in the studio that night, my voice would crack and fail. Hula and Fingers kept telling me, "Don't worry about it—just work with what you got. Lay down in that lower register. Gimme some Rakim. . . ."

That was exactly the direction I needed. Rakim was hands down my favorite rapper at the time. So, I settled down and decided to play the cards I'd been dealt, rather than the ones I wished I had.

My vocal delivery on "Summertime" shocked the hip-hop world. It was released on May 20, 1991, and within a month, it had hit #1 on the Hot R&B/Hip-Hop and #4 on the Billboard Hot 100 charts. The music video was recorded back home in Philly with me and Jeff's real family and friends.

Homebase went platinum within two months. It won an American Music Award and snatched our second Grammy. (Just as a piece of Jazzy Jeff and Fresh Prince trivia, we boycotted when "Parents Just Don't Understand" won our first Grammy, and "Summertime" was nominated against the monster Naughty by Nature hit "O.P.P." And I was *positive* we were going to lose, so I didn't go. Jazzy Jeff and the Fresh Prince now had two Grammys, and I had yet to make an appearance anywhere near the award show.)

Meanwhile, in my other career . . .

I studied my lines obsessively. In those early days of the *Fresh Prince*, I was so terrified of failing that I would memorize the entire screenplay—not just my lines, but everybody's. It was the only thing that kept my anxieties at bay. If I was going to lose, it was damn sure going to be somebody's else's fault.

I may have overdone it slightly. I was *so* prepared that I was unconsciously mouthing all the other actor's lines on camera *as they said them.*

Fortunately, there's an interesting thing that happens when you watch TV—your eyes focus on the person who's talking. This is a form of something called "inattentional blindness." Daniel Simons, in *Smithsonian* magazine, describes it like this: "This form of invisibility depends not on the limits of the eye, but on the limits of the mind. We consciously see only a small subset of our visual world, and when our attention is focused on one thing, we fail to notice other, unexpected things around us—including those we might want to see."

A perfect example of this phenomenon is in season 1, episode 5, "Homeboy, Sweet Homeboy." Don Cheadle plays my boy from Philly, Ice Tray. If you look closely, you'll see that I'm mouthing Don's lines. But even though I'm front and center, mouthing away like an idiot, you didn't notice at home because your attention was focused on the actor who was speaking: inattentive blindness. Feel free to pull up that episode and watch me nincompoop my way through the scene.

Karyn was nominated to break the embarrassing news to me. Of course, I denied it, and was horrified (and remain so) when I was shown the excruciating evidence. To this day, I cannot bear to watch that episode.

All of these world-class, stage-trained master thespians, and the dumbass rapper is mouthing their words back to them. And the show is named after *him*.

It took me a couple of weeks to break the simian habit. I would be in a scene, damn near biting through my bottom lip. But I got it.

There were very few people in my life I wanted to impress more than James Avery. James had been acting longer than I had been alive, and he was my paragon, the pinnacle of dramatic presence. I desperately wanted him to think I was a good actor.

But nothing I did impressed James Avery.

He played my father figure on the show and slowly assumed the role in real life. He was demanding and always pushing me to "master my instrument" as an actor.

"You can do jokes with your eyes closed," he'd say. "You have that naturally, and it's beautiful to watch. But you have deeper talent in there," he said, tapping on my chest emphatically, "that you can't even imagine yet. And you're never going to find it if you don't *reach* for it. There's a difference between talent and skill. Talent comes from God—you're born with it. Skill comes from sweat and practice and commitment. Don't just skate through this opportunity. Hone your craft."

One of the proudest moments of my career was in one of the most famous episodes of *The Fresh Prince*, "Papa's Got a Brand New Excuse." In the show, Will's biological father, Lou, played by Ben Vereen, comes back into his life and spends time with him again. Will is thrilled to have his father back, but Uncle Phil is skeptical. This drives a wedge between Will and Uncle Phil.

Will's father, a big-rig trucker, invites Will to travel with him over the summer. Will is excited and decides to go against Uncle Phil's urgings. The climax of the episode happens when Will's father comes up with an excuse and cancels the father-son trip and disappears again, leaving Will brokenhearted with Uncle Phil trying to console him.

This was the most demanding dramatic scene for my character of the entire series. It was me going toe-to-toe with James Avery. Master actors revel in the opportunity to go head-to-head in a scene with other masters. But I was not a master—I was a scared little boy in the shadow of a giant. When actors have these types of scenes, you know they're coming for weeks; everybody else knows it, too. The anticipation wreaks havoc on your sleep, on your appetite, on your memory, on your nerves. On set, dramatic scenes have the energy of a prizefight—cast and crew lean forward in their seats to see if you'll bring it home. But the studio audience has no idea, and you want to shock and surprise them.

It was Friday night; the audience was in place and the episode was going along great. And then the final scene.

I had studied day and night. I felt ready. But on the first take, I froze. My mind went blank, and I missed my second line. I was anxious and trying too hard, speaking too fast, stumbling through my words. The director quickly yelled cut to not blow the surprise for the audience. But I snapped.

"FUUUUUUUUUCK!" I bellowed at the top of my lungs. "FUUUUUUUUUCK!" The veins in my neck bulging, my fists balled tight.

"HEY!" James yelled, snapping me back to attention.

"Settle down," he whispered. Then, pointing his index and middle finger to his own eyes, he gave me the universal signal for *Focus on me*.

He leaned into my ear.

"Use *me*. Look into my eyes and talk to *me*."

I fell into his gaze, somehow plugging into his power, our stare, unbroken, until he felt I had been sufficiently fueled. James didn't wait for the director; he called action from the floor.

The next take is what appeared in the actual episode:

Uncle Phil: I'm sorry. I, you know, if there was something that I could do—

Will: You know what, you ain't got to do nothing, Uncle Phil. It ain't, like, I'm still five years old, you know? Ain't like I'm gonna be sitting up every night asking my mom, "When's Daddy coming home?" you know? Who needs him? Hey, he wasn't there to teach me how to shoot my first basket. But I learned, didn't I? I got pretty damn good at it, too, didn't I, Uncle Phil? Got through my first date without him. Right? learned how to drive. I learned how to shave. I learned how to fight without him. I had fourteen great birthdays without him. He never even sent me a damn card! [Screams toward the empty door] TO HELL WITH HIM!

I ain't need him then, and I don't need him now.

Uncle Phil: Will . . .

Will: No, you know what Uncle Phil? I'm going to get through college without him. I'm gonna get a great job without him. I'm-a marry me a beautiful honey. And I'm-a have me a whole bunch of kids. I'll be a better father than he ever was. And I sure as hell don't need him for that, because they ain't a damn thing he could ever teach me about how to love my kids.

And after a beat, Will starts crying and says, "How come he don't want me, man?"

Uncle Phil lovingly gathers Will into his arms. The shot slowly pans away onto a statue of a father and son Will had purchased as a gift. In the embrace, James Avery whispers in my ear.

"Now, *that* is fucking acting."

DESIRE

*hat does he want?*

As an actor, this is the single most important question to ask of the character you are preparing to portray. His "want"/dramatic quest is the first pillar of behavior. What someone desires is a portal into the essential truth of their personality. If you want to understand why someone did something, you need only answer the question, *What did he want?* An actor's overarching focus is to unearth the "system of wants" that intertwine and sometimes collide within the mind of a character to create their psychological driving force. Acting is like building out a new personality for yourself from scratch.

(Once you have a foundational comprehension of a character's central motivation, the real acting fun begins with the second question: *Why does he want it?* But that's for later.)

The war between desire and obstacle is the heart and soul of dramatic storytelling (sometimes, the obstacles are *internal*—those are the fun ones). In filmmaking circles, there is a simple axiom that describes the structure of a great character journey: *somebody wants something badly, and goes for it, against all odds.* (Another variation is, *a person falls into a hole, and tries to get out.*) If you think about any movie you've ever liked, any character you've ever rooted for, it's because they wanted something you could relate to and they struggled, risking life and limb, to achieve it.

What's true about movies is also true about life: You tell me what you *want*, and I'll tell you who you *are*.

What are we doin', man?" JL asked me one day, out of nowhere.

"What do you mean?"

"I mean, everything. There are too many people, there are too many things happening—I can't function like this. If you want me to help you, I need to know what I'm helping you to do."

"Shit is goin' good, J. I think you just not seein' it."

"No," JL insisted, "I *am* seeing it. I'm seeing it all over the place, and unfocused, and I'm seeing us about to do the same shit we did last time. I'm not gonna be out here just winging it. I need to know what the *goal* is."

I didn't really understand his question. In my mind, he was just scared. I knew he didn't do well with disorganization. He was a minimalist, damn near an ascetic—he had very few clothes, his bedroom was always kept in impeccable condition, and everything in his life had a place and a purpose. And when things weren't neatly arranged, in a way he could get his head around, he'd feel disrupted, disturbed, and ultimately would want no part of it. So I was trying to give him a stabilizing, simple answer.

"The goal is to not be broke, J," I said. "To be able to have fun, to be able to travel and live how we want. To not have the IRS taking our shit no more."

"So, technically, that's *five* goals. And that's my problem: What is the dream? What are we trying to build? What do you want?" he pressed definitively.

I had never said this out loud before. I had tried the phrase in my head a few times, but I had never given it voice.

Mom-Mom once laid out about fifty family photos of me and my brother and sisters, all throughout our childhood. She stood smugly over them and asked me if I noticed anything. I scoured the pictures like a detective trying to discover the clue that would break the case. After a few minutes, I gave up.

"I don't notice anything, Mom," I said.

"Look at your brother and sisters. Notice how in some pictures they're looking off to the side, or their faces are twisted, or hidden behind someone. Now look at you. There is not a single photo where you are not looking *directly* into the camera."

I've always had a sense of the camera. I love performing. I like the camera, and more important, it likes me. I had held a secret dream for as long as I could remember. I didn't even feel comfortable dreaming it. I didn't *deserve* to dream this big. But in my quietest moments, alone, there was a consistent yearning, an emotional compass that was always trained on the Hollywood sign.

I wanted to do what Eddie Murphy was doing. I wanted to make people feel how I felt the first time I saw *Star Wars*.

I wanted to be Eddie Murphy in *Star Wars*.

So, for the first time ever, I said it out loud to JL.

"I want to be the biggest movie star in the world."

JL is the type of guy who rarely reacts outwardly. His standard face is: poker. Whether you say, *JL, your mom is on the phone*, or *JL, the oven just exploded, and the whole crib is on fire*, or, *I want to be the biggest movie star in the world*, his countenance remains exactly the same. He never divulges what he's thinking, so you always find yourself leaning in for some tiny hint.

I leaned in, hard.

"Now, *that's* a goal," JL said.

Stephen Covey, in *The 7 Habits of Highly Effective People*, said there are only two human problems: (1) knowing what you want, but not knowing how to get it; and (2) not knowing what you want.

Clarity of mission is a powerful cornerstone of success. Knowing what you want gives direction to your life—every word, every action, every association, can be accurately chosen and harnessed to precipitate your desired outcome. What you eat, when you sleep, where you go, who you talk to, what you allow them to say to you, who your friends are, can all be corralled and launched toward your wildest dreams.

(Desire, however, is a double-edged sword. But that's for later—I didn't know that back then.)

When JL has a goal, his ability to educate and transform his mind is beyond that of anyone I've ever met. He spent the next few months reading every screenplay in Hollywood. Old ones, new ones, bad ones, good ones, successful movies that had already come out, failed movies that were never released, hits and flops and everything in between. He probably read one hundred screenplays, and we would discuss the pros and cons of each.

We had our goal, and the first question we asked was *What makes someone a movie star (as opposed to simply an actor)?*

Movie stars tend to play likeable characters who embody and depict the best of humanity: courage, ingenuity, success against the odds. I loved the idea of being a better person in a movie than I was in real life. I could protect people, I could kill bad things, I could fly, all the women would love me—they have to, it says it right here in the script. I came up with a way to describe what makes a great movie star character: I call it the three Fs of movie stardom: You have to be able to fight, you have to be funny, and you have to be good at sex.

Beneath the three Fs are our deepest human yearnings: fighting equates to safety, security, and physical survival. Being funny equates to joy, happiness, and freedom from all negativity. And being good at sex equates to the promise of love.

And encompassing these qualities, the biggest movie stars make the biggest movies in the world. *Movie stars put asses in seats.*

The next obvious question was *What are the key elements of the biggest movies?* JL grabbed a list of the top-ten-grossing movies of all time to see if we could determine a pattern. And it was crystal clear: Ten out of the top ten films of all time had special effects. Nine out of ten had special effects and creatures. Eight out ten had special effects, creatures, and a romantic storyline.

(We would ultimately discover that *all* of the top ten movies were about love, but we didn't notice that back then.)

We knew what we were looking for. Now, we just had to go find it and convince whoever had it to give it to *us*.

The problem was that the biggest movies in the world were also the most expensive to produce and promote, meaning they were hyper-risky propositions. They were career-making, or career-ending, for everyone involved. I was young, unknown, inexperienced, and Black, trying to convince studios to bet $150 million production budgets and $150 million promotional budgets on my charm, good looks, and modesty.

Tanya used to smoke weed. (To this day, I never have.) I think Daddio's alcoholism made me keenly attuned to all substance use around me. I tried to let her do her, but now with the clarity of my new mission, I couldn't see how my girl smoking weed would be helpful. I was ready for a family; I was ready to start my life. I told her she had to stop.

My demand was not received well.

"You are such a priss," Tanya said. "It's just *weed*. I'm not snorting coke off the bathroom floor."

"Drugs are drugs," I said, like it was deep.

"No, they are not," she said indignantly. "This is not that serious."

"Oh, this shit is *very* serious," I said. "I can smell the weed in your nose hairs.

"I'll make you a deal," I said. "You stop smoking for thirty days. Prove to me you're not addicted. Then we'll talk about it."

She thought for a moment. I got the sense that she could have done it, but something about the inflexibility of my stance seemed to trigger a deep-rooted resistance within her. She loved me, she wanted to please me, but there was no way in hell she was going to let me control her.

I can still see her standing there: Arms folded. Head cocked to the side, knowing she was about to make a big decision. Then, calmly, she said, "No."

When you know what you want, it clarifies what you don't want. And even painful decisions, though not easy, become simple.

"Cool," I said.

Have you ever seen those National Geographic documentaries on the Alaskan salmon migration? The ones where the hungry brown bears stand in the middle of the river, waiting for a salmon to jump out of the water and directly into their mouths?

That's how Alfonso Ribeiro and I used to stand outside of *The Fresh Prince of Bel-Air* casting office.

Every Black actress in Hollywood made the pilgrimage through those hallowed halls. One day in 1990, me and Alf were sitting, having lunch. Alf was waxing philosophical about something. He is deeply passionate and opinionated, and he always felt that if he said things *loud* enough and chopped his right hand into the palm of his left hand *hard* enough, that it made whatever he was saying true.

Then she walked by. I damn near choked to death on my Roscoe's chicken and waffles.

"Who the fuck is *that*?" I whispered to Alf, between his relentless chops. "She is *not* from LA." (East Coast recognize East Coast.)

She was pissed. Apparently, the casting agent had just told her she wasn't tall enough to play my girlfriend on the show. She hated that about Hollywood—that somehow her height (or lack thereof) was of more vital importance to the art than her abundant talents.

Oblivious to all of this, I stepped into the river.

"Whatup, shawty?" I said, poorly choosing my descriptive.

"Whatever, nigga, move," she said, gesturing me away with the swat of her hand. And with that, she was gone.

That was the first time I ever saw Jada Pinkett.

It was love at first sight.

Alfonso found out that Jada had landed a role on a sitcom called *A Different World*, the eight-thirty spinoff of *The Cosby Show*. He knew one of the writers on the show, and he found out when Jada was shooting. It was perfect—we taped on Friday, but *A Different World* taped on Thursday, so me and Alf could head over right after work.

By this point, *The Fresh Prince of Bel-Air* was bubbling hard, and me and Alf were hot in these Hollywood streets. The plan was, he and I would go to the taping of *A Different World*, and we would sit in the audience. That would give me an opportunity to adequately Fresh Prince flex. The audience would, of course, erupt when we showed up; Jada would hear all of the cheering during her scene, and she would look out to the crowd and realize it was because of me. (And Alf.)

So, I pulled out the twenty-four-carat herringbone gold chain, "The Fresh Prince" dancin' across my chest, the "T," the "F," and the "P" gleaming with VVS1 clarity, round brilliant-cut diamonds everywhere, fresh to def, ready to stunt.

Everything was rolling like clockwork. Me and Alf step in, the place goes boom. I didn't see Jada, but she knew I was in the building. I shushed the crowd.

"Come on, y'all, they're tryna shoot," I whispered, magnanimously, as me and Alf took our front-row seats in the right corner. Jada's scene didn't come till about midway through the taping, but there she was, in all her East Coast glory. She was fire—her accent, her mannerisms, her hair, her *attitude*. She felt like home.

Between scenes, Alfonso saw his writer friend, Orlando Jones, who was talking to a gorgeous, caramel-skinned woman in the front-row center. She's clearly not from LA, either—I can tell by her slight discomfort with the grandeur of everything. I make my way over; I say "What's up" to Orlando, and I introduce myself to the woman.

Her name is Sheree Zampino; she is from New York. Not *real* New York—Schenectady (near Albany, damn near *Canada*).

"Now, here's the deal," I said. "We're just meeting, so I'm-a give you a pass on this one. But the next time somebody asks you where you're from, you are *forbidden* to say 'New York' when you know damn well you are from Schenectady."

If she had been drinking water, she would have done a spit take. She begins to laugh uncontrollably, as if I had given voice to one of her own, secret inner whispers. The bell rings, signaling for the audience to settle down so that taping can continue, but she hasn't gotten herself back together yet. She needs to be quiet. But I'm *definitely* not going to allow that. I lean into her ear.

"It's misleading, and an utter misrepresentation of the truth. If you tell people you're from New York, they're thinking the Bronx, Brooklyn—I mean hell, even Staten Island. They're gonna think you're *cool*. Then they find out you're from *Schenectady*?"

At this point, she's nearly choking with laughter, begging me to please be quiet. But there is no chance of that.

"I'm just sayin', you shouldn't be goin' around, *lyin'* to people. Fucking Schenectady is *not* New York. You're sitting here representing . . . *Canada*. You should be wearing a maple leaf sweater and handing out syrup."

Fortunately, the scene ends, and she is free to laugh out loud. Her makeup running, eyes red, totally out of breath, she said the thing that any comedian who has ever told a joke craves to hear—the ultimate in comedic approval:

"You are a *dumb* man."

I didn't meet Jada that night. Sheree and I left together before the show was even over. We laughed all the way through dinner, all the way through that fall, and three months later, we were married.

Willard Carroll Smith III was born on November 11, 1992. From birth we called him "Trey," since he was the third Willard Smith.

From the first time the doctor placed you in my arms
I knew I'd meet death before I'd let you meet harm
Although questions arose in my mind, would I be man enough?
Against wrong, choose right and be standin' up
From the hospital that first night
Took a hour just ta get the car seat in right
People drivin' all fast, got me kinda upset
Got you home safe, placed you in your bassinette
That night I don't think one wink I slept
As I slipped out my bed, to your crib I crept
Touched your head gently, felt my heart melt
'Cause I knew I loved you more than life itself
Then to my knees, and I begged the Lord please
Let me be a good daddy, all he needs
Love, knowledge, discipline, too
I pledge my life to you

"JUST THE TWO OF US"

That is the public depiction of Trey's birth and my introduction to fatherhood.

But that first night was far more emotionally tumultuous than my poetic verse suggests. Sheree was asleep and we had a tiny bassinette for Trey in an adjacent bedroom. I couldn't stop looking at him. I was terrified.

I had wanted this my whole life. And here I was, with *my* son, *my* wife, *my* family. My *turn*. My body was quaking, overwhelmed with the immensity of the responsibility to this tiny human life. I fell to my knees, sobbing uncontrollably, praying to God: "Please, help me do it *right*. Please help me be a good daddy."

My mind swerved and careened like a drone through my childhood. I had talked so much shit about Daddio—now, here *I* was. Would I be smart enough to orchestrate the building of a wall for *my* son? Could I put food on the table and keep the lights on without fail? Would I be strong enough to fend off someone who came to kill him?

It's 3:00 a.m. I'm on my knees. I'm just a little boy. I never wanted my daddy so bad. And then, something clicked, deep in a place where nothing had ever clicked before. A decision, an ironclad conviction. I wiped my tears, I stood up, I gently touched Trey's head. And I knew. There were only two possibilities: (1) I was going to be the best father this planet had ever seen, or (2) I was going to be dead.

I literally can count on one hand the number of times in my life I've been sick—I *never* get sick.

It was a Friday night, tape night at *The Fresh Prince*. I had been vomiting all day. I could barely move; I'm pretty sure it was food poisoning. I stayed in my dressing room during pretape and rehearsals in order to conserve my energy to make one big burst in front of the live audience.

Sheree had come to the set to take care of me. She couldn't understand why we couldn't just tape another day.

"How would you ever respect me if I did that?" I said, between gags.

Working while sick, injured, or under difficult conditions became a badge of honor for me. I wanted to thrive where my competition would fold. I wanted my wife to know that I was invincible. Women (and Europeans) always shake their heads or describe this trait negatively. But on a primal level, it's really hard to not respect a warrior.

Friday nights became major networking events for us. JL would invite sponsors, executives, anyone from the business world we were looking to impress. Our approach was to invite their entire families. When someone's kids and spouse have a great time, they're more inclined to want to be in business with you, and there was no greater time to have than Friday nights at *The Fresh Prince of Bel-Air*. This particular night was a big one, but I was dying. I didn't have it in me to entertain.

Sheree took the reins. I had never seen her in this light. She moved the meetings out of my dressing room and set up space on the stage. She got extra food and asked the rest of the cast to take up some of the schmoozing weight. She wasn't only doing it for her husband—she *loved* it. She moved from couple to couple, family to family, engaging on whatever topic they found interesting. She showed the kids around the stage; she exchanged telephone numbers with the wives and made sure everyone had the time of their lives. She held it down, so I was able to pop in for ten minutes, seal the deals, and get to the taping.

Sheree was the perfect hostess, bringing life to the wife I had seen in my head. Like Tgia with Pooh Richardson, Sheree and I were a team in the "Will Becoming the Biggest Movie Star in the World" business.

We bought a townhome in Toluca Lake, strategically located nine minutes from NBC Burbank, where *The Fresh Prince of Bel-Air* was now shooting. This proximity would give me the maximum time at home and at work. These were prime logistics. The condo was also just seven minutes from the Buena Vista apartments where the whole Philly squad was headquartered, and only fifteen minutes over the hill into Hollywood, making it a perfectly situated staging area for my impending cinematic invasion.

One Saturday afternoon, as I was studying my lines for Monday's table read, Sheree was in the kitchen, cooking, which was just one of the aspects of her creative spirit.

I loved the artist within her. She had gone to the Fashion Institute of Technology (which was *actually* in New York City). She could make her own clothes, she could paint; it was the first time that I had ever seen someone hang their own art in their home. I thought that was hot. She was also a martial artist—her father was a 9th Dan grandmaster and instructor of tae kwon do, and Sheree could defend herself if she had to.

Sheree had a strong nurturing instinct—her father was Italian, and her grandma Zampino had been an expert homemaker. The Italian side of Sheree's family had owned the L&M Supermarket in Schenectady, so they always had tons of food, and the heart of the family was centered around mealtime. When Sheree's parents separated, her mother reentered the workforce so the kitchen became Sheree's domain. Sheree loved to cook and feed people—she was the only person I'd ever met who could turn scraps into a delicious feast the way Gigi could. We'd have viewing parties each week for new *Fresh Prince of Bel-Air* episodes. Sheree took to it instinctively, cooking for everyone and making the house warm and inviting. There were always at least five Philly homeboys in the house, conspicuously stalking around the kitchen, preparing to pounce on the next succulent morsel Sheree tossed into their cages.

Sheree's vision of a happy life was joyful, harmonious nurturing—taking care of people; homemaking. She was happy to live a simple life as a mom and a wife. I wanted to conquer. My definition of love was protection and provision, securing the family's physical and financial future. My belief was: "A meal is a lot less enjoyable if you have to eat it in a tent underneath an overpass."

Omarr was setting up a small portable studio in the garage when the phone rang.

"Yo, Will, it's JL," Omarr yelled.

I ran over and picked it up.

"Whatup, J?"

"Hey, I was just making sure you were home. I need to talk to you. Immediately."

"Why, wassup, what happened?" I said urgently.

"I need to talk to you in person. I'm on my way."

Click.

I always hate when people do that. Don't call me with the fucking emergency voice, get me on the phone, and then not tell me what happened. *We're on the phone—just say it!* Fortunately, the agreeable logistics meant I only had to wait nine minutes—two minutes for him to get to his car, and seven minutes for him to drive from the Buena Vista apartments. (We'd save time on this side because I'd be waiting for him at the front door.)

Nine minutes later, JL pulls up. He seems . . . OK, so it's not *medical*. He looks anxious, but not fearful; he's kinda smiling, but *sad*. This is *clearly* something he could have just said over the phone.

"Whatup, J?" We exchanged a standard Philly half pound, half hug. JL preferred the variation where you clutch the person's hand and keep your arm across your chest, giving *you* the sense of a hug but maintaining *his* personal space at the same time.

He dives right in.

"Alright, look—there's a studio that wants you to costar in a gangster movie called *8 Heads in a Duffel Bag*. They're prepared to pay you ten million dollars."

"GOTDAMN!" I wrap both arms around the top of my head.

I went to give JL a high five, which he returned half-heartedly.

He held on to my hand and said, "And I came here to advise you *not* to take it."

"Wait . . . *what?*"

"I don't think you should accept the part. It's not right."

Still holding his hand, I wanted to rip his arm out of its shoulder socket, and then beat him to death with it. Instead, I said calmly, "It sound right as hell to me, J."

"It's not—it's the wrong look. I read it *five* times. I kept trying to make it be right. It's not. I *was* just gonna turn it down and not tell you. . . . Look, at the end of the day, it's *your* call. I was there with you for these last few years, so . . . I will rock with you whatever you decide to do, but I'm advising against it. If you truly want to be the biggest movie star in the world, do not take this movie."

"J. That's a *lot* of money, dude."

"Tom Cruise wouldn't take this role," JL said.

We turned down *8 Heads in a Duffel Bag*.

JL, as my manager, earned a 15 percent commission. When he advised me to turn down *8 Heads in a Duffel Bag*, he was walking away from $1.5 million for himself. (Have I mentioned that he was still living in his childhood bedroom at his mother's house?) He was taking the risk *with* me, because he believed in the vision—he believed in *me*.

About a month later, JL called me hyped. This time, he behaved as a respectable human and told me what was going on . . . *over the phone*.

"I've got the *one*," he said excitedly. (JL never gets excited.)

I was being offered a supporting role in the film adaptation of John Guare's Pulitzer Prize–finalist stage play, called *Six Degrees of Separation*.

"This is right where we want to be," JL said. "People are not taking you seriously yet as an actor. We gotta go *against* stereotypical roles. We need to make people *forget* that they're watching a rapper. We gotta make them see a movie star.

"Plus, you'll be protected in third bill, surrounded by a veteran cast: Stockard Channing, Donald Sutherland, and Sir Ian McKellen. The pedigree is ridiculous. I want everyone to see you with that level of actor. We gotta shock these people and get their attention. And every single word your character says is brilliant—it's one of the best written things I've ever read. In fact, the movie is about *your* character. This is star-making material."

"Damn, J, you are *hyped* about this one!"

"I'm tellin' you, this is the *one*," he said, punching his fist into his hand.

"Word! How much?"

"Well, this one's different. . . ."

"I get that, J, but, how much?" I said.

I took *Six Degrees of Separation* for $300,000.

JL had done his part. He had found exquisite material powered by world-class artists. Now it was on me.

My military upbringing kicked into gear—I had my mission: I needed to *smash* this role. I immediately flew to London with JL to see the final weeks of Stockard Channing's West End stage performance of the play. And once the shooting schedule was set, Sheree, Trey, and I moved to New York.

Six Degrees of Separation is about a wealthy white couple who live on the Upper East Side of New York City. They are older, and lonely, empty nesters whose kids have recently moved out. They spend their days collecting and dealing famous art. Then, one night, a young Black man shows up on their doorstep. He is cut from being mugged and stabbed on the street. He says he is a friend of their children from Harvard, and the son of Sidney Poitier. The couple takes the young man in, and over the course of the story, Paul (my role) turns out to be a con artist. Yet, despite Paul's victimizing the couple, he and Louisa, played by Stockard Channing, strangely begin to fall for each other.

This character was so drastically different from who I was, and his life experience was so foreign to me, that I felt impelled to employ method acting (something I knew absolutely nothing about). I memorized the words of the entire screenplay, verbatim. I vowed that I would not miss a single line while I was on set.

During the months of my preparation, I would spend four or five days at a stretch without breaking character. Not once, not one moment. I would go to a jewelry store or a bakery and try to discern what Paul's likes and dislikes were. I wanted to get comfortable in real life and real situations, not only *thinking* as Paul would think, but learning to involuntary *feel* the way that he would feel.

It was fun . . . at first. But then slowly, and imperceptibly, I lost touch with my own likes and dislikes, I lost access to the intonation and rhythm of my own speech—I lost touch with Will Smith. Sheree started to say things like, "Why are you *looking* at me like that?" and "Stop talking like that." I was totally oblivious—I couldn't figure out what she meant. In my mind, I was going back and forth between Paul and me, but Will Smith had quietly slipped away. Sheree was suddenly living with a stranger.

We tend to think of our personalities as fixed and solid. We think of our likes and our dislikes, our beliefs, our nationalities, our political affiliations and religious convictions, our mannerisms, our sexual predilections, et cetera, as *set*, as *us*. But the reality is, most of the things that we think of as *us* are *learned* habits and patterns, and entirely malleable, and the danger when actors venture out to the far ends of our consciousness is that sometimes we lose the bread crumbs marking our way home. We realize that the characters we play in a film are no different than the characters we play in life. Will Smith is no more "real" than Paul—they're both characters that were invented, practiced, and performed, reinforced, and refined by friends, loved ones, and the external world. What you think of as your "self" is a fragile construct.

Sheree and I were in the first few months of our marriage with a brand-new baby, and for Sheree, I can imagine that this experience was unsettling to say the least. She'd married a guy named "Will Smith," and now she was living with a guy named "Paul Poitier." And to make matters worse, during shooting I fell in love with Stockard Channing. Not as "Will," but as "Paul." I couldn't turn him off.

After the film wrapped, Sheree and Trey and I moved back to LA. Our marriage was off to a rocky start. I found myself desperately yearning to see and speak to Stockard. I only saw her once, and I never said anything, but she's a vet, and I sensed that she knew what had happened. She probably said the words "Sheree" and "Trey" fifty times.

Fortunately, it was time to go back to work on *The Fresh Prince*.

What the fuck are you doin'?" Alfonso blurted out.

"What do you mean, Alfonso?" I said.

"THAT! I mean, *that*. Why are you talking like that?"

"Talking like *what*?" Paul said.

"Like THAT!" Karyn chimed in.

"The 'w' is *before* the h. It's not *hwat,* Will," Alfonso said frustratedly.

I had lost touch with the Fresh Prince. I couldn't remember how he walked or talked or which Jordans he preferred. This went on for ten full episodes at the beginning of season 4. I had lost my sense of humor, my timing, my swag, my charisma, and my ability to improvise and ad-lib.

Cast and crew alike were terrified. This was the season that Alfonso truly began to shine. For the first few episodes the writers had to write away from my character and toward Carlton. Alfonso stepped up and took the comedic weight. No one knew what was happening; no one was relating my behavior on the set of *Fresh Prince* to my ill-conceived foray into the dangerous psychological world of method acting in *Six Degrees*.

I couldn't tell a joke to save my life. The scary part was that I couldn't see what everybody else saw. But if enough people tell you that you're drunk, then you should probably sit down. So, I immediately hired five or six of my friends from Philly to work on the writing staff, on the crew, and to surround me on set while I relearned how to play the character of "Will."

It worked. Right around mid-season, something clicked. I was in a scene with Karyn, and my character was trying to convince her to go on a date with his teacher, but he had a mole next to his left nostril. And for Hilary, this was an absolute deal breaker. My character was begging her to just give him a chance, and in a moment of career-saving comedic inspiration, I ad-libbed, "Come on, you're making a mountain out of a mole, Hil."

The audience roared; I was back. And method acting was gone forever.

I am not trying to relinquish any of my responsibility for the deterioration of our marriage, but I believe firmly that the early months of our union, being marred by my disappearance into the character of Paul in *Six Degrees of Separation*, created a disconnect between Sheree and me from which we would never recover.

At the end of 1993, *Six Degrees of Separation* came out to widespread critical acclaim. Stockard Channing was nominated for an Oscar for her performance, and critics wrote glowing reviews of my surprising casting as Paul. JL was right—my name started to be discussed in Hollywood as a serious actor.

Achieving goals requires strict organization and unwavering discipline. I began to lean more into structure and order, but Sheree was an artist: she cooks by feel, not by recipe; she was much more fluid, intuitive, and less structured. It drove me crazy. 6:17 is *not* six o'clock.

It was Friday night, tape night. My barber had gotten into a car accident—he was fine, but he wasn't going to be able to cut me for the show. Five hours before the taping of a network sitcom and a young man from Philadelphia is about to be forced to go on network television without a fresh fade.

Never.

I put out the 911 call for a barber. A guy named Slice came back as the blue ribbon of the Philly fade standard. I hit him up.

"Yo, Slice, whatsup?"

"What's happenin', Will?"

"I'm jammed up over here. I need you, brethren."

At the time, my fade was legendary. To cut *my* hair, for *The Fresh Prince of Bel-Air*, was not only a challenge but also a catapult for a young barber in Hollywood.

"Damn, Will, I would love to, man," Slice said, "but I got a cut I have to do in San Diego. The client is paying me cash. And I got my kids for the weekend. . . ."

"San Diego? Man, that's a two-hour drive both ways. You need to come get this local money."

"Oh, trust me, I would *prefer* local money . . . I would not be drivin' to San Diego if I didn't need it so bad. I got my kids, I gotta break my baby mama off somethin'—"

"How much is he paying you? Actually, whatever it is, I'll double it—come get this local money."

Slice was being paid $500 for the San Diego cut; I promised him a thousand to come directly to set. I didn't have cash with me, so I called Sheree.

"Babe, how much cheese you got on you?"

"Probably about two thousand, why?" Sheree said.

"A'ight, I'm gonna send a guy named Slice by in about a hour, so, just break him off a G."

"OK," Sheree said.

"A'ight, I love you, catch you later."

Slice came to set, sharpened me up perfectly—he lived up to his name—I gave him the address to the house and went and shot the episode.

That next week, my barber still wasn't ready to come back to work, so I hit Slice.

"Whatsup man, it's Will."

"Ay," he said coldly.

"I need you again, man. I need that sweet shit you do."

"Yeah," he said, "I don't think so." I could tell something was wrong.

"Why, man, whatsup?"

"That's fucked up what you did."

"What I do?" I said, confused.

"That was some real bullshit. It's fucked up."

Click.

I was trying to replay our last interaction. As far as I could tell, everything had gone perfectly. So, perplexed, I called Sheree.

"Hey, babe, did anything happen with Slice last week?"

"Uhm, oh no," she said, remembering. "I just didn't have the cash that I thought I had."

"Well, what did you give him?" I said.

"Four hundred—I only had a thousand."

"I told you to give him a thousand dollars," I belted out.

At the time, because of my IRS issues, we didn't have credit cards—we were functioning on cash. And it was Friday night; these were the days before ATMs were everywhere and it would be Monday at 9:00 a.m. before we could have gotten more cash.

"That was all I had," she snapped back.

"He had his fucking *kids* for the weekend. I promised him the thousand dollars. I took him off of another job."

"Well, *I* have a baby over here who's going to need to eat this weekend, too. I wasn't giving him all my cash. What do you want me to do?"

"I want you to do what the fuck you *say* you're gonna do. So, you just don't pay the man, you don't call me, you don't say shit? You broke *my* word!"

"Will, I am not your errand girl. . . ."

"Ain't nobody say you was no errand girl."

"Just stop overreacting. He'll live."

This moment is among the handful of times in my life where I hit an absolute ten of fury. In general, I'm a man who measures his words. This was not one of those times.

"You know what—maybe one day you'll be *worth* something," I said, slamming down the phone.

If God were to give me back one sentence from my entire life, to erase it, to make it so I never said it, and the person never heard it, it would be those seven words.

Something broke in our marriage—something we would never get back. (Sheree would later confide that was the most her feelings had been hurt in her adult life.)

Sheree and I deteriorated quickly after that. We argued about everything—nothing was too trivial to fight about: I recall criticizing how she washed a skillet. . . . Sheree and I would go days without speaking to each other. We even invented a "game" that we "played" when people came over called "You Know What I Hate About You . . ?" And the "winner" was whoever could make our guests "laugh" the most.

I found myself yet again in love's death spiral. It was a vicious rip-tide, dragging our dreams into the depths. Sheree took Trey and went to clear her head back home in Schenectady. Our marriage was becoming increasingly unbearable for her. She was going to take a few weeks to decide what she wanted to do.

The Baked Potato was a small lounge in Studio City. Tisha Campbell and Duane Martin, two close friends of mine, invited me to join them there. They were strangely insistent that I show up.

I'm not really a "lounge" guy, but they assured me that I'd be happy I came. A little after 8:00 p.m., I walked through the door, made my way to their table: Duane, Tisha, and Jada Pinkett. And just like that, I was a lounge guy.

Duane was always in the middle of some deal, brokering some take-over of something, managing the band while simultaneously purchas-ing the venue they were performing in. Tisha was the matchmaker; she knew that Sheree and I were on the outs, and she wanted to make sure, just in case, that I had no consideration other than Jada.

They neglected to inform Jada or myself of this planned meeting.

I had seen Jada a few times around town over the past year—nothing too memorable—casual Hollywood hi's and byes. She was still stunningly gorgeous to me. Still swaggy. Still full of that delicious, East Coast energy. But something was different. Something a little deeper, something profound just below my depth of perception. Maybe it was that I was older now; I was a father; perhaps I was more open, or maybe pain recognizes pain . . . but I felt her differently. She was only twenty-two, but her eyes felt like they had witnessed centuries. They seemed to know secrets and struggles far beyond her years.

We talked about everything—she could meet me, ascend, and elab-orate on all topics and subjects, from Tupac to apartheid, from col-lege basketball to Ganesh and eastern mysticism. It was like we went away to a private place alone, content to embrace the joy of our ques-tions, unburdened by the quest for answers. Being together was the answer.

Hours passed like minutes. I could sense the potential potency of our combined energies. Cities and empires were being constructed in my mind as we laughed and pondered and debated. Her body was so tiny, but her spirit was so strong. She was confident, solid, unwavering—a ten-ton cornerstone holding up the Great Pyramid.

Jada would later confide in me that she had heard a voice speak clearly, with no sentimentality, just a matter-of-fact: *That is your hus-band.* For the time being, she rejected the prophecy. I was married, and that was a nonstarter. We gently returned from our private inner so-journ and settled back into our hard metal seats. We said our extended goodbyes; neither of us really wanted to leave. I walked her to her car and watched her drive away. I left that night dazed, smashed, imprisoned between elation and reality. I had met a queen strong enough to bear the weight of my dreams. But it was not to be.

A few days later, Sheree came home from her time in Schenectady, and we decided we'd meet at our favorite restaurant, the Palm. They had the best lobster in the city—they were huge. We always ordered one, the perfect portion size to share.

I guess I had hoped that the time apart and the intertwining of our forks over our favorite meal would somehow rekindle and reconnect our wounded hearts. I had certainly put my faith in the revitalizing power of melted butter and those silly plastic lobster bibs.

I arrived first. Sheree had dropped Trey off at her mother's directly from the airport. She walked in; she was beautiful as always. We hugged and took our seats. I had preordered; she liked when I did that. We talked about Trey and Schenectady and her father's new dojo. He and Trey had had a ball—he had gotten him his own little gi.

Everything was perfectly pleasant, but suddenly I started to feel light-headed. There was a weird, dry, metallic taste forming in my mouth. I tried to breathe through it. I was thinking, *Oh shit, am I about to pass out?*

"Are you OK?" Sheree asked, looking concerned.

A surging wave of dizziness, a shortness of breath, beads of sweat jumping up on my forehead . . .

"Yeah, I'm good," I lied. "Let me run to the bathroom real quick."

I charged into the bathroom and locked myself into one of the stalls. I sat down to try to catch my breath—*What the hell is happening?* I suddenly burst into tears. For the next twenty minutes, I purged, toggling back and forth between sobbing and laughing hysterically. *Am I having a fucking nervous breakdown?*

And slowly, my emotional truth came into vivid, three-dimensional clarity.

I knew with absolute certainty that Jada Pinkett was the woman of my dreams. But I had committed my life before God to Sheree. And there was no version of me *ever* going back on my word. My tears were railing against the harshness of this reality. And my laughter was cursing its absurdity.

But soon, my hysteria subsided. I wiped my tears, and I exited the stall fully prepared to spend the rest of my life with Sheree Smith.

THIRTEEN

DEVOTION

t sucks getting divorce papers. It's like a publicly filed declaration that you're an unlovable piece of shit. And no matter how awful your relationship has been, it's *always* a surprise when you get 'em. I mean, you knew it was *bad*, but gotdamn . . . you never imagined it was *that* bad.

And the divorce gods are merciless: By a fluke of the Los Angeles postal system, I received the papers on February 14. Fucking Valentine's Day.

Sheree was done. I couldn't believe this was happening. The lowest point in my life had been my parents' separation, and this felt worse. I was repeating the cycle. I was blindsided. I was in denial. I was furious. And I was saddling my son with the same burden that had pushed me to contemplating taking my own life.

Sheree said that I wasn't in love with *her*, I was in love with the *idea* of her—what I believed a wife should be like.

"Anybody could be here," she once said.

Sheree used to call herself my "placeholder wife." The woman who was supposed to check the box of "Wife in Will Smith's Perfect Life."

Sheree and I had recently bought a house in Encino that was being renovated. Sheree had already taken Trey and moved there. I felt like she was ruining my life, destroying my family. I had silently promised myself that I would *never* let this happen. And here I was, not even thirty years old, and my family was being destroyed.

I felt like I was dying.

I called Quincy.

"Hey, Philly, what's goin' on?" he said.

"Sheree filed for divorce."

"Shit," he said. "How you doin'?"

"I'm hurt, man. Lawyers 'n' shit. I don't even *want* a divorce—"

"I been there, brother," Quincy interrupted. "Lemme give you some advice."

I leaned into the pause. I'd never needed a good word like I did at that moment.

"Give that woman half your shit and move on with your life," Quincy said.

Huh?

"All my divorces took place in one day. As soon as somebody act like they don't wanna be with *me*, they can take half of this shit and let the doorknob hit 'em. . . . And let me tell you some shit you're not gonna believe right now."

He brought his voice down, like Morpheus trying to make sure I could handle the red pill.

"Y'all gonna be together every fuckin' Christmas anyway," he said. "When you have kids with somebody, you're *stuck*."

Quincy had been divorced three times.

"Man, I got a ex-wife across the street. I got another ex-wife a block away, I got kids in three different houses. We're still family! They think divorcin' your ass will get them away from you. It *won't*. You gonna be on billboards and commercials 'n' shit all the time. . . . Give that woman half, tell her you'll see her on Christmas Eve, and move on with your life. You gonna make all that money back next year anyway. Just write the damn check and move on."

This wasn't exactly what I'd been hoping to hear. I wanted him to tell me how to fix it. How to make her keep her promise. I thought there were only two options: you complete the mission, or you die. Where the fuck did the third option of quitting come from?

And half of *Thriller* is a *lot*.

I would never have gotten married if I thought divorce was an option.

If quitting is a possibility, everyone will pick that—it's the easiest one. Who wouldn't pick *not* running at 5:00 a.m. over running at 5:00 a.m.? If quitting is an option, you'll never finish anything hard. The only way an imperfect mind can be forced to achieve is by removing all of its other options. To me, the heart of all successful human interactions is we look at each other and we know we're about to attempt something that is difficult/impossible. And we look in each other's eyes, and we shake hands, and we both vow to die before we quit.

And that's what I thought we did. This is such a simple idea to me. The vows are "til *death* do us part"—God agrees with me. The vow is not to your partner—the vow is to the *weakest* part of *yourself*. How could you *not* quit if that's one of the options?

The reason you say you're gonna do it or die is because death is what happens when you *don't* do it. Your mind is trying to protect you from hard things, to defend you from pain. The problem is, all of your dreams are on the other side of pain and difficulty. So, a mind that tries to seek pleasure and comfort and the easy way inadvertently poisons its dreams—your mind becomes a barrier to your dreams, an internal enemy.

If it was easy, everybody would do it.

The reason we make vows is because we know we're about to do a hell walk. You don't have to vow to do easy things. No one ever said, "I vow to eat every ounce of this crème brulee—I swear to the wide heavens that I will not leave one speck on my plate! And I vow to skip my run tomorrow morning, and I vow to sleep in!" We wouldn't need to make vows if it was easy. The reason the vows are so extreme—"in sickness and in health, till death do us part"—is because *life* is so extreme. Nothing else can keep us there. That's the *point* of devotion. I'm not against divorce, and I'm not against surrendering in a battle, but it has to be at the *end* of the battle—not while you're putting your armor on, not the first scary moment, not the first casualty. In my experience, most people get divorced too soon, before they've extracted the lessons that will keep them from doing the exact same things in their next relationships.

I'm still not totally sure what I was thinking. Maybe it was pain; maybe it was delirium. Maybe I wasn't thinking at all.

Maybe I didn't need to think, because I was clear. I could see the North Star through the fog.

On February 19, only five days after I received my divorce papers, I called Jada. I hadn't seen her, or heard from her, in months. The phone seemed to ring forever.

Click.

"Hello?"

"Whatup, Jada. It's Will."

"Heyyyy!" she said. Her voice seemed to still echo with the magic of our night at the Baked Potato. "How you doin'?"

"I'm good. Better now that I'm talkin' to you."

In hindsight, I probably could have given her a little more context, or warning.

"Hey, are you seeing anybody?" I said.

Jada hesitated—partly stunned, partly confused.

"Um, no. Why?"

"Cool, you're seeing me now, a'ight?"

"Um . . . OK . . . Yes," Jada said, sensing there was something big at play but knowing now was not the time to question.

"A'ight, I'm at work, I'll hit you later. OK?"

"OK."

What I didn't know at the time was that Jada was in Baltimore. She had been so discouraged and disillusioned by Hollywood that she had left the business and moved back home. She had purchased a beautiful, turn-of-the-century, five-acre farm in Maryland and had begun renovations. She had decided to build a simple, quiet life for herself.

After my phone call, she went directly to the airport and flew to Los Angeles. Jada would never spend a single night in her Maryland farmhouse.

I never really bought into the whole "past lives" thing. I would hear people say, "We must have known each other in a former life." I always thought that was corny. But those first couple of months with Jada transformed me from a disbeliever to an agnostic.

We fit together so naturally, and our energies combined exponentially in a way that felt like old friends more than new lovers. We had an unspoken language, and everything we focused on flourished.

My divorce from Sheree wasn't yet final, so Jada and I decided it would be prudent if we kept our relationship under wraps. (We were both getting pretty famous, and we felt it just wouldn't have been a good look.) The blessed yet unintended consequence was that we spent every single moment together, just us. The first three or four months were as wild a romantic whirlwind as our bodies could have possibly handled. We traveled to exotic secret getaways—Cabo, private Caribbean islands, Aspen, secluded estates in Maui—and we discovered private air travel. We checked in under aliases (I would tell you what they are, but we still use them today). We drank every day, and had sex multiple times every day, for four straight months. I started to wonder if this was a competition. Either way, as far as I was concerned, there were only two possibilities: (1) I was going to satisfy this woman sexually, or (2) I was going to die trying.

But the heart and soul of our union was then, and is still today, intense, luminescent conversation. Even to the writing of this very sentence, if Jada and I begin a conversation, it is a minimum two-hour endeavor. And it is not uncommon that we talk for five or six hours at a stretch. Our joy of pondering and perusing the mysteries of the universe, through the mirror of each other's experience, is unbridled ecstasy. Even in the depths of disagreement, there is nothing in this world that either of us more cherishes or enjoys than the opportunity to grow and learn from each other through passionate communication.

Riiiiiiiinnnnggg.

"Hello?"

"Hey, Lover Boy."

"Hey, Gigi! How you doin'?" I said.

"Oh, I'm good. Do you have something you want to say to me?" Gigi asked, leading the witness. I had no idea what she was getting at. This was unlike our normal interactions. Clearly, she had something on her mind.

"Um, I don't think so," I said cautiously, as I ran through all the shit I might have done. "Do I?"

"Well, somebody said you have a new girlfriend that you've had for a long time."

Damn it. My sister Ellen . . .

"Well, nah, yeah, but . . ."

"We're keeping secrets from each other now?" she asked, melting all my defenses.

"Well, no, Gigi, I just—"

"Well, somebody said she's an actress."

"Gigi, somebody is *Ellen*. Ellen's the only person who would be telling you all my business."

My sister Ellen stays in the mix; she always has. Every party, every piece of gossip, every rumor—she's the girl on the block that when something happens, she has the scoop. If she worked for the police department, she would drop crime by 40 percent in her first week. She knows everything about everybody at all times. Ellen also happened to be a *huge* Jada Pinkett fan; Ellen *is* Peaches from *A Low Down Dirty Shame*. She couldn't believe I was hiding Jada from the family, so she told on me.

"I'm not keepin' secrets, Gigi. . . ."

"OK, well you can just send a plane ticket, and I'll come out and meet her. Tomorrow."

"OK, yes, Gigi. I love you. I'll see you tomorrow."

"Love you, too."

Click.

This next story has been a bone of contention between Jada and me for more than two decades. It's been *so* contentious that I considered leaving it out of this book altogether. But I decided, to let you, dear reader, settle our dispute once and for all. So, please clear your minds. You have been chosen as the Supreme Court of this story. The question to you, learned justices, is a simple one: "Is this prank *funny* or *not* funny?"

Gigi arrived in sunny Los Angeles early the next morning and came directly to my house. I had just purchased a new place in Westlake Village, a suburb about an hour northwest of LA. We had breakfast together; she loved the house. I could tell more than anything that she just wanted to make sure I was OK.

Jada was working that day, so her plan was that she would run to her house when she got off, freshen up, and then head to *my* house to meet my Gigi. Jada had heard all the stories about Gigi that you've been reading in this book, and she was so excited to finally get to know my grandmother.

Gigi wasn't a big movie fan, and she didn't know who Jada Pinkett was. So, I decided to show Gigi one of Jada's most popular movies.

At 3:00 p.m., Jada called me from her home in Studio City, which was exactly forty-four minutes, door to door, from my spot.

"Hey, babe, are you leaving *right* now?" I said.

"Um, in about fifteen minutes," Jada said.

"OK, I'll see you when you get here. I love you."

Jason's Lyric was Jada's current movie. The film is a beautiful love story between Lyric, played by Jada, and Jason, played by Allen Payne. At sixty-three minutes into *Jason's Lyric*, Jada has a graphic love scene that has become one of the most iconic love scenes in African American cinema. So when Jada said she was leaving her house in fifteen minutes, to take the forty-four-minute drive to my place, I pushed play on *Jason's Lyric*, and Gigi started watching.

Fifteen plus forty-four is fifty-nine minutes, and I trusted the comedy gods to do their part with traffic, parking, maybe a hug and kiss in the driveway. The comedic scene had been set.

And boy, did the comedy gods come through. In a moment of unbelievable comedic synchronicity, Jada walked into my family room exactly sixty-three and a half minutes later to find Gigi summoning all the Jesus she could muster as Lyric and Jason roll around butt nekkid on-screen—not even *socks* on—outside on the grass.

Jada freezes. She looks at Gigi, then to the screen. Back to Gigi. Horrified. Then to me. Back to the screen. To Gigi. To me.

"Gigi, I'd like you to meet my new girlfriend, Jada," I said, filled with so much joy I could barely stand.

Gigi sits back on the couch, folds her arms, and says, "When I was young, people didn't have to take their clothes off to make movies."

Jada plastered an uneasy smile on her face, and awkwardly hugged Gigi.

"Will," Jada said calmly, "may I speak to you in the other room, please?"

"We'll be right back, Gigi," I said.

Jada and I went into the bedroom.

"Why. The. Fuck. Did. You. Do. That?" she whisper-yelled.

"Babe, I *promise* you it's funny."

"WHAT?"

"Babe, it's a joke, it's fine. We're gonna get married, we're gonna have kids, it's a *story*. We're gonna tell this for *years*. This is how you met my grandmother. This is how she met you! Please trust me, it's *funny*. . . ."

"IT'S NOT FUCKING FUNNY."

"OK, not today, but . . ."

"NOT EVER! You play too damn much."

"Life is about memories," I said. "You're mad *now*, but that wears off, I'm tellin' you, it's *genius*. This is perfect for us. One day, you are going to laugh and laugh and laugh."

Gigi ultimately loved Jada; they had a beautiful relationship. Years of joy and family laughter—their bond was precious: It grew deeper and wider with every interaction. And it is my ardent belief that my orchestration of that initial meeting laid the foundation for their profound connection.

To this very moment, however, Jada has never even cracked a smile— not even the tiniest chuckle—about that meeting, not even once. So, ladies and gentlemen of the Court, I ask you humbly to search your hearts, and if I'm wrong, I will accept the censure of the court. But I feel honor-bound to pose the question anyway—almost rhetorically—for closure, and final resolution between Jada and me: *Is that shit funny, or what?*

Jada grew up with Tupac Shakur. They were best friends; they went to high school together at the Baltimore School for the Arts. Two young dreamers, fighting their way from under the weight of abuse and neglect to become "Tupac" and "Jada." And though they were never intimate, their love for each other is legendary—they defined "ride or die."

In the beginning of our relationship, my mind was tortured by their connection. He was *'PAC!* and I was me.

He had a fearless passion that was intoxicating, a militant morality, and a willingness to fight and die for what he believed was right. 'Pac was like Harry—he triggered the perception of myself as a coward. I hated that I wasn't what he was in the world, and I suffered a raging jealousy: I wanted Jada to look at me like that.

So when Jada and I committed to each other, and the demands of our relationship made her less available to 'Pac, my immature mind took it as a twisted kind of victory. Jada was the paragon, the pinnacle, the queen of queens. If she chose me over Tupac, there was no way I could be a coward. I have rarely felt more validated.

I was in a room with Tupac on multiple occasions, but I never spoke to him. The way Jada loved 'Pac rendered me incapable of being friends with him. I was too immature.

Will, Martin Lawrence is on the phone."

I had never met Martin; I had no idea how he got my number. I was, however, acutely aware of the burning jealousy in my heart. He is a comic genius. Martin was the people's champ—he was the star of his own Fox television show, *Martin.* In the Black community, he was loved and revered the way I had always yearned for.

We were the two biggest Black actors on TV at the time. *The Fresh Prince of Bel-Air* was higher rated, but Martin's comedy street cred was undisputed—he was the funniest dude on TV. I studied him day in and day out; his physical mannerisms, his vocal inflections, his scene structuring—in my heart, I knew he was naturally funnier than me, and I hated it.

"Marty Maaaar!"

"Big Will-aaaay!"

I'm not sure you can actually love somebody forever from six seconds of a first phone call. But for some reason, we couldn't stop laughing just from hearing each other say each other's names. For nearly three decades, we have greeted each other identically, and laughed every single time.

"Marty Maaaar!"

"Big Will-aaaay!"

He invited me to dinner at his Beverly Hills mansion. Martin was also born and raised on the East Coast—just outside DC—and the second I walked in I was all the way at home. His sisters are just like my sisters; his brother is just like my brother; his friends have Jeff, JL, Omarr, and Charlie Mack written all over them. We understood each other from the jump.

"I got this script I love," Martin said. "It's produced by Don Simpson and Jerry Bruckheimer. It's called *Bad Boys*. I was gonna reach out to try to do it with Eddie, but my sister said, 'Hell, no, you gotta do that with Will.' And I thought about it. Look at what we've been able to do separately—can you imagine what would happen if we collab?"

"Word," I said. "That could be *crazy*. What's the story about?"

"It's about two cops in Miami who have to change roles in their lives to solve a murder. One of the cops is married with kids, a family man. The other is a rich playboy. You can read the script and see which role you want to play. The words and the scenes aren't totally there yet, but if we get in there together, we can freak this joint."

"I'll read it immediately. But even if it's not this one, we definitely gonna work together."

"Don't give me that Hollywood shit, Big Willie—we gonna make this movie or not?" We both cracked up.

"Oh, so I don't get to read it, huh?" I said.

"Ain't none of the words right. We gotta dive in and fix it. Listen to me—the two biggest Black actors on television come together to make a big-time Hollywood movie. People will lose their *minds*. Come on, Big Willie, don't miss the boat!"

Don Simpson and Jerry Bruckheimer had originally slated Jon Lovitz and Dana Carvey to star in *Bad Boys*. (Yes, I know, that would have been a very different movie.) But as things go in Hollywood, the deal fell apart, and Martin took control of the screenplay.

Nobody was 100 percent certain about me—not the studio, not the producers; nobody, in fact, but Martin. He got to the point where he was telling people he wouldn't make it *without* me. I started off looking at him as my competition, and he turned out to be one of the greatest friends and allies I've ever had in Hollywood.

Uncertainties were quelled, deals were hammered out, and we found ourselves at the table read for *Bad Boys*. The director was a first-timer; he had never directed a feature-length film before. He had, however, done an award-winning music video for Meat Loaf. On a $50,000 budget, he managed to shoot a plane crash—with no special effects. He just crashed an airplane and shot it. In a pop video. His visual boldness, cinematic ingenuity, and fiscal wizardry made Michael Bay the unanimous choice.

The table read began. Everyone could feel the potential powder keg of creative possibilities, but there was no spark in the screenplay. The words that may have been perfect for Dana Carvey and Jon Lovitz rang clunky, forced, and unrealistic for Martin and me. The table read ended, and Don Simpson ceremoniously rolled up his screenplay, walked over to the trash can, slam-dunked the script, and announced to cast, crew, studio, and director: "Well, we're not shootin' a fuckin' word of that bullshit."

And with that, he walked out.

You might think that a big-time Hollywood producer slinging a screenplay into the trash, three weeks before shooting, might be unsettling for two young actors and a director who'd never made a movie.

But exactly the opposite occurred. Michael was used to making music videos; he was comfortable behind the 8 ball. He never had enough money, he never had enough time, and he always had to improvise. Martin and I were from the world of television; we were used to making up everything we said anyway. We were used to getting pages five minutes before a scene; we were used to scrambling and ad-libbing and trying to catch lightning in a bottle. In a way, Don Simpson throwing out the screenplay set us free.

It was both a challenge and an invitation. We all combined our collective resources—Don and Jerry grabbed seasoned writers from their Hollywood network; Martin and I pulled in the top dogs from our TV and stand-up teams; Michael Bay secured a nimble crew that knew how to run and gun. We would shoot during the day and then work together every night to create the next day's work.

Martin and I had so much chemistry that Michael eventually stopped concerning himself with the specifics of the dialogue. After a while, he simply trusted that Martin and I would show up with something great. One day, on set, everyone was sitting around waiting while Martin and I were taking a long time to figure out exactly what we wanted to say in a scene.

Michael yelled, "I don't give a fuck what you say, just say it in my shot."

The entire shoot of *Bad Boys* was exhilarating and educational in a somewhat hectic, by-the-seat-of-our-pants kinda way. There was no time for paralysis through analysis; we had to figure it out, shoot it, and move on.

One day, Michael Bay and I had one of our biggest disputes. This was the first time I had ever worked out. I had put on twelve pounds, and for the first time in my life, I had muscles. There's a famous scene where my character chases a car on foot over a bridge. Michael was demanding that I do the scene with no shirt.

"Mike, come on man, that's corny," I said.

"Corny? Are you crazy? It's Miami, dude—you're a badass cop. Take your fucking shirt off!"

I wasn't yet secure with my new body. The thought of standing around all day with no shirt on intimidated me.

"Mike, I hate when I see that in movies," I said. "The dude just all greased up, pretending like it's natural to be in an abandoned church with shafts of light, and doves 'n' shit, and no shirt on."

"You're wrong, you're wrong, you're wrong!" Michael yelled. "No shirt, dude! Just take it off. Trust me and do what I say. I'm trying to make you a superhero!"

"It's not that big a deal. Just let me do a tight T-shirt," I said.

"We've seen that the whole movie! This is your breakout!"

We ultimately landed on a compromise: I would wear a shirt, but it had to be unbuttoned. I felt like I wasn't completely naked and vulnerable, and Michael knew that the shirt would billow like a cape when I ran.

The scene was set. What I hadn't told anyone was that I had secretly been training with the UCLA track coach. For my whole childhood, I had hated how actors ran in movies. Other than Carl Weathers on the beach with Sly in *Rocky III*, I cannot name a single scene from a film where I thought that an actor looked badass running. And I promised myself that the first time I ran on camera, I was going to look like Carl Lewis. I had trained high knees, high elbows, for four months. I was ready.

We set for the first pass; Michael yelled, "ACTION!" A Bronco storms across the Miami footbridge, and in the distance Mike Lowrey, full stride, looking like an Olympic sprinter, comes into frame. Two-hundred-yard sprint, top speed, elbows back, knees up, gun in hand, shirt billowing out behind.

"CUT!"

Michael Bay charges across the street, grinning like a twelve-year-old boy who just found his father's *Playboy* stash. I'm winded; I'd given it all I had; hands on my knees, hunched over catching my breath. As Michael approaches, I slowly stand up.

"How'd it look?" I asked.

He smacks me on my bare chest, and screams at the top of his lungs, "I JUST MADE YOU A FUCKING MOVIE STAR!"

My divorce process was long, silly, and unnecessarily tedious. I did *not* take Quincy Jones's advice. I haggled over every dime, decision, and determination. It's amazing how quickly and grotesquely love dissolves into litigation. But after four grueling months, the final papers were prepared for signature.

Sheree and I hadn't spoken much during this time. So, when she requested a conversation, I was actually a little surprised.

"I've been seeing a therapist for the past few months," Sheree said. "I was trying to figure out how to make all of this less painful for all of us. And I've been taking a really honest look at myself."

"Uh-huh," I said, waiting for the shoe to drop.

"I realized that I didn't do everything I could have done to make this work. Neither of us did. I know we have our divorce papers, but we also have a son. And I think we owe it to him to do everything in our power to keep our family together."

I couldn't believe it. *What am I supposed to do with that? Jada and I are in love. But if there's a chance to preserve my family . . .* How could I say no?

I told Sheree I needed some time to process.

I immediately called Jada. I told her everything. She didn't say a word. I could tell she was crying. The restraining of her sniffles and tears made them all the more agonizing to hear. She steadied her breath, collecting herself; she cleared her throat. And then she spoke.

"Sheree is right. When you have a child with someone, it is your responsibility to do everything you can to create a loving home for them. I grew up without both of my parents. I love you. And I am devastated. But I will never do that to Trey. You and Sheree need to figure it out."

I was overwhelmed by Jada's selflessness. The willingness to put her own needs aside to do what she felt was right. Through tears and a breaking heart, she found resolve in loving kindness.

I picked up a pen, and I signed my divorce papers.

FOURTEEN

BOOM

Me and Jada were knocked out. The previous two weeks had been the biggest grind of my professional career. Sixteen-hour days, no weekends off, for fifteen straight days. I was exhausted.

It was 3:00 a.m. when the phone rang. Those middle-of-the-night calls always suck—somebody's either in jail, the hospital, or worse.

"Yo?" I said, in a groggy, raspy, hopeful whisper.

"MAN. YOU SEE THEM NUMBERS?" The voice bellowed as if it were noon on a football field.

"Huh? Hey, Dad. What?"

"I SAID, DID YOU SEE THESE GODDAMN NUMBERS?" Daddio reiterated.

Independence Day had just opened. It was 6:00 a.m. in Philly, and the film had broken every conceivable box office record; it was world news.

"Dad. It's only 3:00 a.m. out here. . . ."

"I SAID, DID YOU SEE THESE GODDAMN NUMBERS?" He seemed pretty hell-bent on getting his question answered.

"Nah, Dad, I haven't seen 'em yet. JL will—"

"Remember I told *you*! There's no such thing as luck. That you are the creator of your own destiny. Remember I told you that?"

"Yeah, Dad, I remember. But can we—"

"Remember I told *you*? That there was no such thing as luck. Only what you *make*? Remember I told you that?"

"Of course, Dad, you would say that all the time, but—"

"Remember I told *you*—there's no such thing as luck? Luck is when preparation meets opportunity. Remember I told you that?"

"Yes, Dad, absolutely—"

"Well, that's a buncha *bullshit*! You the *luckiest* muthafucka I ever met in my *life*."

This was one of the greatest laughs Daddio and I ever shared— waves of raucous laughter settling back to giggles and then, with no words, and no warning, erupting again into hysteria. Years of discord, not justified, but somehow cleansed with every purifying wave. We probably laughed without speaking for ten minutes.

Though we never talked about it, *Independence Day* represented a significant victory for him, a validation. It put an exclamation point on some story he had been telling himself about himself. Something was finished in his mind.

Not long after, he sold ACRAC—the work of the ice house was done. He started calling himself "the Fresh King."

The next ten years of my professional life were an absolute, unadulter- ated, unblemished rout of the entertainment industry.

Bad Boys; *Independence Day*; *Men in Black*; *Enemy of the State*; *Wild Wild West*; *Ali*; *Men in Black II*; *Bad Boys II*; *I, Robot*; *Shark Tale*; *Hitch*; *The Pursuit of Happyness*; *I Am Legend*; and *Hancock*. Resulting in more than $8,000,000,000 in global box office. And not to be a stick- ler, but that number is from almost thirty years ago, when tickets were less than half the price they are today. Adjusting for inflation . . . you know what, that's neither here nor there.

Two Academy Award nominations: *Ali* and *The Pursuit of Happy- ness*.

Over thirty million records sold: "Men in Black," "Gettin' Jiggy Wit It," "Just the Two of Us," "Miami," and "Wild Wild West" leading the charge. Not to mention the theme song from *The Fresh Prince of Bel-Air*, which technically counts as a record. In which case, it's the biggest rap song in history. But that's neither here nor there, either.

I'm getting ahead of myself. *Independence Day* had just come out. *The Fresh Prince of Bel-Air* was in season six. JL had gotten us a seat at the big table. We were now represented by Ken Stovitz and Richard Lovett at the most powerful agency in Hollywood: CAA. And I had just gotten back to even with the IRS. Now, I was just *broke*—from this point on, I could start *making* some money.

Bad Boys had hit movie theaters in 1995 and had been a solid success. Nothing earth-*shattering*, but a whole lot of earth-*shaking* was going on. I had grown up as the lanky, goofy kid with the big ears. But I snuck into a movie theater on opening weekend of *Bad Boys* and the scene came where I run across the bridge with my shirt open. I heard a fortysomething Black woman purr out loud, "Mmmm. Look at *Will*!"

I wanted to scream, *I'M RIGHT HERE, MISS!*

It was the first time I had ever experienced a woman having a sexual reaction to my manness. Up until this point in my life, I had used comedy to attract women. And now I was being objectified. It was wonderful. All I could think was, *OK, Michael Bay, you were right, I was wrong. Thank you.* From that point forward, directors had to argue with me to keep my shirt on.

We were preparing to go into our sixth season of *The Fresh Prince of Bel-Air*, and I had just signed on to shoot *Independence Day* over the summer of 1995. The sixth season was our final contracted season. The question arose: Would I do a seventh?

The ratings of *The Fresh Prince* had fallen slightly but progressively. The storylines were becoming increasingly hokey and it was difficult to maintain the "Freshness." But we were all making more money than we'd ever made in any previous season.

There is an episode of *Happy Days* in which Fonzie *literally* jumped over a shark on water skis dressed in his signature leather jacket. In the world of sitcom TV, "jumping the shark" is now used metaphorically to signal the beginning of the end, the moment after which a television show has passed its prime—whatever made the show special is now increasingly hard to capture. The problem is you don't know it at the time—you always feel that you can rekindle the magic.

Anyone who has ever been on a sitcom can tell you the episode in which their show jumped the shark. Ours was season 5, episode 15, "Bullets Over Bel-Air," the one in which I got shot and Carlton started carrying a gun.

I had successfully fulfilled a promise to myself that I would never get caught in a cycle of deterioration without having the next thing on tap. The show could easily sustain another season; this was my family; I loved them. But a movie career was now a viable option; I was at a crossroads.

John Amos—the legendary actor who played James Evans on the iconic 1970s hit sitcom *Good Times*—costarred in three episodes of *The Fresh Prince of Bel-Air*. His character on *Good Times* was famously and brutally killed off because of a contract dispute. The show was ultimately canceled mid-season; no final episode, no goodbyes, no beautiful montage of memorable moments—just over. John Amos had heard the rumblings of my consideration of a seventh season. One day between rehearsals, he took me for a walk in the parking lot.

"This is one of the most beautiful sets I've ever worked on," John said. "I can feel that you all really love each other."

"Yes, sir," I said. "We've all fallen into our character roles in real life."

"I may be overteppin' my bounds a bit here," John went on. "But none of these execs, or producers, or businesspeople, give a shit about your family. Do *not* let them fuck off all of your hard work and passion. It is *your* responsibility to make sure these people get to leave this show with some dignity."

I had remembered even as a child being jarred by James Evans's death on *Good Times*. As a kid, I wouldn't have used the word "dignity," but in retrospect there was a sense of disrespect that my heart sensed. As a fan, I felt insulted and abused by the narrative. John's character was unceremoniously killed off, and almost twenty years later the man himself spoke the word that fit the hole in my heart. The whole shit was undignified. I even sensed John's pain, that maybe *he* had failed his TV family.

The next week, I gathered my cast together. I told everyone that season six would be our final season and that they should take the year to make whatever plans or preparations they felt necessary. I promised them that we would go out with style and grace.

The final episode of *The Fresh Prince of Bel-Air* aired on May 20, 1996—a one-hour finale. The week of shooting had been the most emotional week of my professional life. We laughed, we cried, we reminisced, we loved on each other. And we said goodbye.

I sent my television family off with dignity.

Meanwhile, in my *real-life* family, I had to pay my own child support—not to my ex-wife for *my* child. That would be normal, and right. I had to pay *my* child support, *to* my own mother, for *myself.*

Plus, interest and penalties.

Exactly. Let me explain.

Harry had graduated from Hampton University with an accounting degree and had been in charge of all family investments. He was now taking the family into real estate and his first official venture was to help Mom-Mom secure the home of her dreams. They found an old farmhouse in Bryn Mawr, Pennsylvania; Mom-Mom was head over heels, so on Christmas morning 1997, we surprised her with the keys.

In the move from Woodcrest, sifting through ancient boxes, Mom-Mom had found her and Daddio's unexecuted divorce papers. Almost twenty years earlier, they had gone through the whole divorce process, but for whatever reason they never got around to signing the final documents. Mom-Mom didn't realize that technically, she wasn't *actually* divorced. So, she signed her divorce papers . . . and *filed* them.

I'm on set shooting *Wild Wild West* when I get an urgent call from Daddio, demanding a mandatory and immediate family meeting, minus Mom-Mom. Still dressed in chaps and spurs, I joined Harry and Ellen on the call.

"Did any of y'all talk to your mother?" Daddio says.

"Um, we talk to her all the time. Is there something specific?" I said.

"She sent over these divorce papers," Daddio said, "and I want to know what y'all think I should do with 'em?"

Just for a little context: Our parents had been separated for twenty years. And they have barely exchanged three words in the last decade. And two of the words are unprintable. Daddio had even started a new family; I had a beautiful new sister named Ashley. So, as his loving children, we find ourselves legitimately confused. And as his loving children, we have roles we tend to play. Ellen never has time for his foolishness. Harry wants to go head-to-head and challenge every syllable he utters. And I try to be the peacemaker. Therefore, as a rule, I tend to talk first.

"Well, what exactly do you *mean*, Dad?" I say, gently and lovingly, recognizing there's something going on that I don't understand.

This causes my father to repeat slightly louder, and more aggressively, as if tone and tenor were the basis of my misunderstanding.

"Your mother sent over these divorce papers, and I said I want to know what y'all think I should do with 'em?"

Immediately, there is a break in the sibling ranks.

Ellen says, "I don't have time for this, I'll talk to y'all later."

We're losing numbers rapidly. We're suffering casualties—I need to resolve this quickly.

"Well, Dad, we *heard* you, it's just that you and Mommy have barely spoken in twenty years. So, I just—"

"I'm askin' y'all what you think I should do with these divorce papers."

Now, Harry's heard enough and blurts out indignantly, "*SIGN*'EM?"

"Oh, just sign 'em, just like *that*?"

Frankly, Daddio's starting to lose me.

"Dad, I don't understand the question. You and Mommy's relationship—"

"Oh, so *you* think I should just sign 'em, too?" Daddio said.

"Well . . . *yes*?" I said.

"AND THROW IT ALL AWAY, JUST LIKE THAT?"

To this day, I have no idea what Daddio was thinking. Maybe there was some bizarre finality in the signature that was too much to bear; maybe it was why he never signed them in the first place. But the first domino had been tipped.

Mom-Mom's filing of the divorce papers triggered the full weight of the Commonwealth of Pennsylvania. Daddio had taken care of us, but he had never *officially* paid child support, a fact that came to light upon the basic review of the paperwork. Mom-Mom was informed that with interest and penalties, Daddio owed her close to $140,000. And she wanted every single dime of her money. Under Pennsylvania law, if he refused, or couldn't afford to pay, he could be arrested, jailed, and have his assets seized by the sheriff.

"Mom," I pleaded, "don't be like that."

"No, he owes me money, and I want it."

"Mom, he doesn't have $140,000. . . ."

"Well, that sounds like a *personal* problem to me," she said.

"C'mon, Mom, you're in your new house, everything's good. Let's just make this go easy."

"Oh, this'll go *real* easy. He's gonna give me my money, or he's going to jail."

Mom-Mom wouldn't budge. Too many years of Daddio's crap . . .

"And don't you help him out with *nothin'*, Will!" she said, pointing at me like Celie from *The Color Purple*. "Let *him* figure out how he's gonna pay me my money."

I was stuck. Daddio didn't have $140,000, and Mom-Mom was unwilling to make any concession whatsoever. And there was no version of me letting my father go to jail. So, in an underhanded, Ponzi-style, backdoor deal, I transferred $140,000 into Daddio's account; he immediately cut a check to the Commonwealth of Pennsylvania for the full amount, and the Commonwealth of Pennsylvania made Mom-Mom whole on back child support.

This made me the first person in the history of Pennsylvania to pay their own damn child support. (Note: When Mom-Mom found out that I had paid Daddio's debt, she was pissed. And immediately wrote me a check for $140,000, making her the first person in the history of Pennsylvania to pay her own child back the back child support that they had paid for themselves.)

We should tell this story during Black History Month.

Planet Hollywood was launching in Sydney, Australia, in May 1996. It was a themed restaurant that celebrated the history of Tinseltown. Three of the founding members of the project were three of the biggest movie stars in the world, the Three Wise Men, the Hollywood Magi: Arnold Schwarzenegger, Sylvester Stallone, and Bruce Willis. I was invited to attend the grand opening. I canceled everything and cleared my schedule for the opportunity to be in the same room with the three masters who could absolutely show me the road.

The opening of the restaurant was as big as any movie premiere. Red carpets, searchlights, a massive press line, fans screaming and jockeying for autographs. I made my way into a green room set up in the rear of the restaurant. And there they were: all three of them, *together*—Arnold, Sly, Bruce. I channeled my inner Charlie Mack and interrupted their conversation.

"Hey, guys. Congrats on everything with the restaurant. . . ."

They politely acknowledged my youthful enthusiasm with a subtle hint of, *Uh, you don't interrupt the three biggest movie stars in the world when you've only done one film and a TV show.*

Undeterred, I kept going: "Quick question: I wanna do what y'all are doin'. I want to be the biggest movie star in the world. And if there was ever an iconic trio who knew, I *know* it's y'all."

They all chuckled—I guess the audacity of the question qualified me for an honest answer. They all looked at one another, and in some secret, nonverbal, biggest-movie-star-in-the-world language, they decided that it would be Arnold who answered me.

Imagine the following in the Arnold voice:

"You are not a movie star if your movies are only successful in America. You are not a movie star until every person in every country on earth knows who you are. You have to travel the globe, shake every hand, kiss every baby. Think of yourself as a politician running for Biggest Movie Star in the World."

Bruce and Sly concurred.

"Thank you, guys," I said. "I didn't mean to interrupt—y'all can go ahead back to talkin'. . . ."

I walked away like the kid in the "Mean" Joe Greene Coke commercial from the eighties. Mean Joe was a famous football player, and he throws the kid his jersey after the Super Bowl. Arnold had given me the key, the key that would become my secret weapon for the next two decades.

This made perfect sense to me. The movie companies were putting up north of $150,000,000 to plaster the movie posters in every country in the world. I would get to piggyback on their massive financial investment. In my mind, I was *never* promoting a movie—I was using their $150,000,000 to promote *me*. As far as I was concerned, the movie's not the product here; *I* am the product. I was grateful to the movie companies for their investment in my future.

I started to notice how much other actors hated traveling, press, and promoting. It seemed like utter insanity to me. JL and I ran the numbers. We realized, for example, a film that might only earn $10 million in Spain could easily earn $15 to $25 million if you go to the country, do a premiere, a day of press, and a couple of fan events. (It doesn't hurt if you learn a handful of phrases in the local language and say them on the news.) If you multiply that across thirty global territories, actually showing up in the countries could take a $250 million box office global potential north of half a billion dollars.

As a gross participant, a portion of those extra dollars went directly into my pocket. Not to mention, I became a bigger movie star in each specific territory, meaning that the next movie company would pay me more money than any other actor, because they knew I could double or maybe even triple the bottom line through global promotions.

So I would shoot *The Fresh Prince of Bel-Air* during the week, leave the set, go straight to the airport, fly to Europe overnight, land Saturday morning, do interviews all day, do a premiere, sign autographs all night, head straight back to the airport, hop back on the jet, memorize my lines for the next *Fresh Prince* episode on the flight, and land in LA just in time to go to sleep Sunday night. Then I'd wake up Monday morning and do it all over again.

I had been given the Holy Grail of movie stardom. I scanned the field of my competition to see who else *knew*, who else held the secret . . . and *Tom Cruise* was the head of the pack.

I started quietly monitoring all of Tom's global promotional activities. When I arrived in a country to promote my movie, I would ask the local movie executives to give me Tom's promotional schedule. And I vowed to do two hours more than whatever he did in every country.

Unfortunately, Tom Cruise is either a cyborg, or there are six of him. I was receiving reports of four-and-a-half hour stretches on red carpets in Paris, London, Tokyo . . . In Berlin, Tom literally signed *every single autograph* until there was no one else who wanted one. Tom Cruise's global promotions were the individual best in Hollywood.

How could I beat him? What do I have that he doesn't have?

And it hit me.

Music.

I started setting up stages and doing live performances, free music concerts outside the movie premiere for the fans who couldn't get in to see the film. We once had ten thousand people fill the streets in

Piccadilly Circus, London. It was so wild that the police had to ultimately shut it down. Same in Berlin; Red Square in Moscow was the biggest-ever Hollywood premiere up until that point. Tom couldn't do that—neither could Arnold, Bruce, or Sly. I'd found my way out of the entertainment news segment and into *headline* news. And once your movie moves from entertainment to news, it's no longer a movie—it's a cultural phenomenon.

The special effects in *Independence Day* were beyond anything anyone had seen up until that time. The promotions for the film simply showed an alien ship hovering over the White House and blowing it up in a single laser strike. People lost their damn minds.

Independence Day earned $306 million in the United States. The movie company was happy and had broken even. But then the global promotions kicked in. $72 million in Germany, $58 million in the UK, $40 million in France, $23 million in Italy, and $93 million in Japan alone. Within a month, it was the second-highest-grossing film of all time, topping out at $817 million—an unheard-of number at the time— and all on a $75 million budget.

We had found the formula. *Independence Day* had special effects, creatures, and a love story, and when we added our global promotional sledgehammer, two words: Scorched. Earth. I had gone from being poor to rich to broke with no acting experience, to starring in the highest-grossing film in the world. And I was only twenty-seven years old.

I felt invincible; but I had felt that before. I knew what it was like to have the wind at my back. But this time, my foot was on the gas, and I wasn't letting up until the wheels fell off. Full beast mode.

It is very difficult to tell this next story without either cloaking its graphic nature in euphemism and inuendo—and thereby diluting its potency—or being so explicit as to offend the delicate reader and fuck up my book sales. But this is such a pivotal and astonishing experience in my life and my relationship with Jada that I feel impelled to roll my literary dice.

We were in Cabo San Lucas, Mexico. It was one of our favorite hideaways. We had rented a beautiful hacienda in the hills. Jada and I had spent a raucous evening in the company of our dear friend, Jose Cuervo. (That's a euphemism.)

Jada was on top of me as the sweet crescendo simultaneously crept upon us. (Innuendo.)

"I'm crescendoing," she said. "I'm crescendoing!"

"I'm crescendoing, too!" I said.

And as the majestic movement reached its culmination, a shock wave shudders through Jada's body. And then panic—a look of abject terror washed over her face.

"I'm pregnant," she said.

"What?"

At first, I thought she was joking, so I began to snicker.

"Oh no, oh no, oh no, this can't happen. This can't happen!" she said, rocking back and forth, with two fistfuls of her own hair.

Now, I'm cracking up.

"It's not *funny*, Will. It felt like a lock on a vault, one of those big wheels that spins and bolts into place. I felt it. I'm tellin' you, I'm pregnant."

"Babe, I'm no fertility expert," I said, choking back laughter, "but I'm pretty sure they're not even finished swimmin' yet. I think *scientifically* you can't be pregnant."

"I know my body, Will," she snapped. "I'm pregnant!" Then she rolled over and burst into tears.

I couldn't figure out what the hell was happening. But she was serious and genuinely scared. I wanted to be helpful, so I rubbed her back and said, "Babe, just stand up and jump up and down."

"WILL! Stop it! What are we gonna do?"

I felt like this was now going too far and she needed tough love.

"Jada, stop trippin'," I said sternly. "I understand that you're experiencing something right now. But you are *not pregnant*. It doesn't happen that fast. It's impossible."

Jaden Christopher Syre Smith was born on July 8, 1998, pretty much nine months to the day. . . . In our family, we affectionately refer to his conception as "the Miracle."

But the road to his birth was a rocky one.

Jada didn't believe in *conventional* marriage, and despised the traditional ceremony. She also had questions about the viability of monogamy as a framework for successful long-term relationships.

Jada had dreamed about a simple, *alternative* ceremony: She saw herself on a mountaintop in a white dress, just she and I. No preacher, no family, no witnesses—just us and God. She had studied the evolution of marriage law from slavery through Reconstruction, and this had given her a serious aversion to the idea that she had to ask the government for permission to pledge her life to her beloved. Jada wanted to look into my eyes, devote her undying love before God, and then get on with the difficult business of building a life together.

Jada had no illusion that love and family would be an easy endeavor; this was another reason she hated traditional wedding ceremonies. She thought that the fluffiness and the pageantry of a classic wedding ceremony was flawed symbolism and gave a false sense of the true gravity of the undertaking. She would say, "A *real* wedding ceremony should be a marathon—we should have to run an *actual* marathon together. And if we're both still there at the finish line, then we've earned the right to get married. You gotta *know* that that person is a survivor."

While I understood her point, I would always think to myself, *That's some real unromantic shit right there. Would we have them shiny tinfoil blankets awkwardly slung over our shoulders to prevent hypothermia, and crap running down the back of our legs?*

I did not say this out loud.

I got an emergency call from Jada's mother, Gammy. She was near tears.

"Will, you and Jada *have* to get married," Gammy pleaded. "I hear all this newfangled foolishness y'all are talkin' about, but you have to have a wedding. Like regular people. Like normal people—with an aisle, a pastor, and some cake."

"Gam, I'm with *you*," I said. "I already gave her a ring. And you think I want to tell *Gigi* I'm having a baby and I'm not getting married?"

"Will, this is my only child," Gammy said. "Please please please convince her to have a wedding. I want to *see* y'all get married! The family wants to be there to support you."

"I hear you, Gam. Have you told Jada how you feel?"

"Yes, I have," Gam said, "but she is *not* trying to hear it."

"Alright, I got you, Gam. We'll figure it out."

Jada held her ground as long as she could, but pretty soon, the "wedding pressure" became too much. She was in her second trimester, she was tired and uncomfortable, and didn't want to argue. She also couldn't bear the thought of breaking her mother's heart, and deep down inside—even though I wasn't saying it—she knew I wanted a wedding, too. So she agreed to have a traditional ceremony in Baltimore on New Year's Eve under one condition: Gammy had to handle *everything*. Jada agreed to show up, walk down the aisle, eat some cake, yell "Happy New Year!," and be *out*.

Gam was ecstatic. To this day, Jada refers to our ceremony as "Gammy's Wedding."

It was beautiful. It took place in a historic castle just outside the city. It was a very small ceremony—not as small as Jada would have preferred; about one hundred friends and family. There was a pastor, and it was government sanctioned. And while the event itself was joyful and heartwarming, this would be the first of many compromises Jada would make over the years that painfully negated her own values.

She had boarded the Will Train, and there was no way off.

Not all forms of fame are created equal.

Music famous is fast, current, and immediate. It's quick-burning, and hard to sustain. But when you touch someone's heart with music, it's forever. Once one of your songs fuses with an experience in somebody's life, there's damn near nothing that could break that bond. And when you make *party* music, your fame becomes synonymous with fun—you become the center of the party. That's probably why popular musicians are often associated with sex, drugs, and alcohol. If you're *having* sex, drugs, or alcohol, you probably want some music to go along with it.

Television famous is a little different. When you're on TV, people are used to you being in their living room or their bedroom or their kitchen. They are used to watching you in their underwear; they think of you as a friend. When you're music famous, people will scream and cheer, but they're used to being kept at a distance—if Beyoncé or Kanye doesn't sign your autograph, you are like, *Well, of course not, they're Beyoncé and Kanye.* But when you're TV famous, people expect you to honor that "friendship." TV fans are much more insulted by being denied access.

But movie famous is a whole different beast. There is something about the forty-foot silver screen that exalts those projected upon it. Movie famous borders on worship . . . and not always in a good way. Crowds literally part when you're movie famous. Other times, they can flood and nearly drown you.

There's a reverence when you're a movie star. When I was music famous, fans called me "Fresh Prince." When I was TV famous, people yelled out, "Hey, Will!" But the Monday morning after *Independence Day* opened to record-breaking box office receipts was the first time anyone ever referred to me as "Mr. Smith."

Movie stardom also had effects on my relationships. When I was music famous, my family and friends saw it as cool and fun. When I was TV famous, there was a subtle distance growing between us, but

Friday nights at *The Fresh Prince* felt so family-oriented that we would reconnect and feel as bonded as we always had. But when I became movie famous, something fundamental changed. Some friends and family I had known my whole life shifted into one of two camps: Either so respectful and deferential that it felt like we were strangers—I couldn't find my loved one within their new behavior. Or, in the second camp, they became disrespectful to try to show me that I'm not no damn movie star round here.

I've got another one," JL said.

I was recording in New York. JL interrupted a studio session. He never does that.

"I really like it," he said. "It has all the ingredients—great script, great director, Steven Spielberg producing. But there's one major issue. . . . I don't want to poison your read. Just read it and call me right after."

The script was for another sci-fi film. It was about a "secret bureau that licenses, monitors, and polices alien activity on the planet Earth." The director, Barry Sonnenfeld, had asked for me by name; it wasn't an audition—it was an offer.

I read the script that night. Everything about it sounded great. Comedy. Creatures. Space. But I had JL's same concern: back-to-back alien movies. I was worried that the film would be too similar to *Independence Day*. And then, because *Independence Day* had been such a gigantic hit, it felt like going back to the same alien well could only set us up to look smaller and less successful. It seemed to me that at best, this would be a lateral move. *Bad Boys* was a buddy-cop movie; *Independence Day* was an alien movie; and this new script was a buddy-cop alien movie.

I told JL I wasn't feeling it. We thought about it over the weekend, and on Monday we passed.

Steven Spielberg is on the phone for you, Will."

I was in New York City recording with a studio full of hard rocks and hip-hop heads.

My ego could not have been more on swole than in that moment.

"Oh . . . Steve is not calling for any of y'all?" I said.

I dipped out to take the call, and in the ten yards from the studio to the phone, I got real unswole, real fast.

"Hello, Mr. Spielberg, sir," I said, in a least swole tone of voice I could muster. I had just turned down his movie; I would hate to have burned this bridge.

"Hey, Will, call me Steven. How are you?"

"I'm great, Mr. Spielberg, sir, thank you so much for asking."

"Better yet, *where* are you?"

"New York," I said.

"OK, perfect," he said. "Then we can do this in person."

Uh-oh.

"Do what?"

"Well, you turned my movie down and I'd like to talk to you about that," he said good-naturedly. We shared a laugh. The tone of his chuckle registered to me as, *Fool, you know I made* Jaws, *right?*

"Well, no, it wasn't like that . . . you know," I said, saying absolutely nothing.

"I just want to show you some images and talk about it. Barry and I are neighbors. Can you come to the Hamptons?"

"Um, sure. When's best?"

"How about today?"

What is it with these guys and the "right now, today, no paralysis through analysis" shit?

"You can chopper up. You'll be here in an hour, you'll be back in three. How's that sound?"

I've been to this dance before.

"Yes, sir, Mr. Spielberg, sir. Yes, that works for me," I said.

Less than an hour later I landed at Steven Spielberg's Hamptons estate. There he was, dressed casually in jeans and an old T-shirt, looking like he didn't realize he was Steven Spielberg.

His house was a Cape Cod–style cinematic temple: original posters of classic films, pictures of him with Hollywood greats, an office with the actual model of E.T. used in the film, concept drawings of the mechanized shark from *Jaws*.

Everywhere I looked, I saw film greatness, but I was struck by Steven's complete absence of flexin'. Here he was, Steven Spielberg, director of four of the top ten films of all time, but what stood out above all was his childlike joy for cinema. He was anxious and excited to show me the vision for *Men in Black*.

We sat down in his office. He served homemade carbonated lemonade; I wasn't sure I'd ever had *carbonated* lemonade before; I was damn sure I'd never had *homemade* carbonated lemonade before. It was so good it caught me off guard.

"So, why don't you want to be in my alien movie?"

"Well, it's not that I *don't* want to be in it. I mean, I love the script. And I was really, *really* flattered that you thought of me."

He could feel my hesitancy.

"Just tell me what the problem is. Let's see if we can fix it."

I laid out all of my thoughts and concerns about *Bad Boys* and *Independence Day* and similarities and repetitiveness and my fear around getting pigeonholed into being the "Alien Guy."

He listened intently; in retrospect, I recognize his skill set as that of a master director—he spends his life listening to actors, cinematographers, writers, studio executives, producers—determining the problem, and finding a solution to synthesize everyone's brilliance into a single creation.

He took a long pause, deeply pondering my reservations. Finally, he spoke.

"OK, Will, I understand. Completely."

Thank God.

"Ahh, OK, I'm so glad because, you know, I have so much respect for you," I said. "This whole decision is making my brain hurt."

We share a laugh.

"Then don't use *your* brain for this decision. Use *mine*."

He said it jokingly, but it rang like the Liberty Bell in my mind . . . that time it cracked.

Indiana Jones, *Jurassic Park, Close Encounters of the Third Kind, Jaws, The Color Purple, Schindler's List, Saving Private Ryan*, oh, and *E.T.* It dawned on me that if one of us had to make the decision of whether or not I made this film, who should it be?

We spent the rest of the afternoon together. I met the director, Barry Sonnenfeld. We drove around the Hamptons; we went to their kids' school. I went full fanboy on Spielberg; we talked about his process, choosing concepts, developing screenplays, his opinions about story and character and what makes a hit movie and the differences between actors and movie stars. Barry is quite possibly the silliest man on the face of the earth. His sense of humor is as sharp and layered as anyone I've ever known. We are polar opposites, yet our comedic harmony was perfectly calibrated instantly. We cracked each other up; I loved how he saw me.

They gave me a list of movies to watch and things to read and turned me on to what would become the central conceptual framework for how I chose and made movies for the rest of my career: Joseph Campbell's theory of the monomyth, the hero's journey as laid out in *The Hero with a Thousand Faces*.

Published in 1949, *The Hero with a Thousand Faces* became my second literary love affair. It would not be an overstatement to say that I bet my entire movie career on this book.

Joseph Campbell's work reveals a hidden story structure embedded in global mythology, folk tales, and classic storytelling. This pattern, this narrative template, has appeared across all cultures and across all time. Campbell theorizes that the reason these ideas, archetypes, patterns, and themes are so universally embedded in our stories is because they are universally embedded in the human experience.

The human mind is a storytelling machine. The creation of narrative is hard-wired into us. What we call "memory" and "imagination" are essentially just stories that we program into our minds as a survival mechanism to protect ourselves and to help us thrive. We are what Jonathan Gottschall called "storytelling animals." Our minds abhor abstraction—from the beginning of time, humans have used character and story to make sense of the mystery of life. We need our lives to *mean* something. It is a kind of mental illness if we cannot shape our experiences into a story that gives our existence a sense of purpose.

Campbell laid out seventeen stages that encompass what he called the "monomyth," or "the hero's journey." (Christopher Vogler, in his landmark interpretation of Joseph Campbell's work, *The Writer's Journey*, refined the stages to twelve. Chris's book has become a Hollywood standard and a classic screenwriting textbook throughout the world.)

The fundamental narrative pattern of the hero's journey is as follows: A hero receives a "call to adventure." Something happens in his life that forces him to embark upon a journey that takes him into a world of danger and wonder. He faces a series of challenges, tests, and trials; he encounters allies and enemies (maybe even falls in love), all culminating in a "supreme ordeal." And if he proves himself wise enough, and strong enough, to overcome his internal wounds (traumas), and external obstacles, and survive this near-death ordeal, he comes away with a "treasure"—what Campbell calls the "elixir," a rare wisdom and insight. He is now empowered to "return home" with "the boon" and do the only thing that makes a human life worth living: help others find their way.

Some stories just bounce off us; we don't get it, we don't feel it, it doesn't mean anything to us. But some stories penetrate; they get past our defenses and plunge into our secret spaces, bypassing our brains and inducing physical reactions: tears, chills, laughter, gasps. They light us up, creating ecstatic pleasure; they inspire us; they make us want to strive. Great stories illuminate truth, and ultimately make us want to see the movie again and again and again.

The list of Hollywood blockbusters that conform to the hero's journey paradigm is almost innumerable. Just off the top of my head? *The Wizard of Oz*; *The Matrix*; *Jaws*; the Star Wars films; *Titanic*; *Braveheart*; the Harry Potter series; *Rocky*; The Lord of the Rings; *The Lion King*; *Finding Nemo*; *Forrest Gump*; *The Incredibles*; *Silence of the Lambs*; *Mulan*; *Gladiator*; *Aladdin*; Indiana Jones; *Beauty and the Beast*; and *Dances with Wolves/Avatar* (watch them back-to-back).

The hero's journey became my road map to creating riveting characters and centering them in universally resonant stories, films that transcend language, age, race, religion, culture, nationality, education, economic status. Joseph Campbell/Christopher Vogler had codified the story elements of universal struggle, transformation, and rebirth as one's greatest self—to me, this was cinematic gold, and the key to global human wish-fulfillment. The movie star represents the warrior in the life-or-death battle against the brutality of the human condition.

It is the path of the caterpillar becoming a butterfly; it is the story of Christ, Buddha, Mohammed, Moses, Arjuna; it is the story of Cassius Clay becoming Muhammad Ali; it is the universal arc of transformation; it is the story of Santiago in *The Alchemist*.

Men in Black checked all the boxes. It was a special-effects movie with creatures, a bromance (a love story), and a perfect hero's journey. This would be a major test for the efficacy of the "Will Smith Cinematic Success Formula."

Men in Black was slated for release on July 2, 1997. This was the same weekend that *Independence Day* had hit cinemas the previous year. In Hollywood, all weekends are not equal—the Fourth of July was the most coveted slot of the year. It was where the studios put all of their make-or-break films. Because of the summer holiday, every day was like a Friday, meaning your box office numbers could be 200 to 300 percent bigger on the Fourth than any other weekend. When the studios put your movie on that date, they're betting the farm on you. I decided I wanted to publicly lean into the pressure. In all of my press interviews, I began referring to the Fourth of July weekend as "Big Willie Weekend."

They ate it up. It made headlines everywhere. (In the UK, it had an added though unintended media benefit, because "willy" is slang for the male reproductive organ, and "big" means big. It was as if I was inviting my British fans to join me for "Big Dick Weekend.")

The release of *Men in Black* took on the energy of a prizefight. It was me versus the box office. I was trying to bring to the world of film openings the same anticipation that Muhammad Ali would bring to a title fight. I wanted to come to town like Barnum and Bailey, parading into countries and cities, near and far, the ringmaster galvanizing and unleashing the global circus. I wanted to orchestrate size, scope, and spectacle, the likes of which had never before been witnessed. We were teed up, and Big Willie was coming with the thunder. (That wording was just for my British friends.)

Omarr was the youngest in our crew. He'd started out as my dancer, and now that me and Jeff were performing a lot less, I had brought him in as a wardrobe consultant on *Fresh Prince*—Omarr has a great sense of style, and he helped establish my overall fashion flavor.

But he had been quietly and secretly plotting his career shot: With JL and my attention moving more and more into the direction of television and film, he wanted to be in charge of the production and management of my music career. He'd been courting the Trackmasters, up-and-coming New York–based music producers. They'd worked with Nas, LL Cool J, Foxy Brown, and they had a vision for my return to music.

Omarr was anxious to break out of his "Little Omarr" status. He felt things bubbling, and he wanted his shot to contribute.

"Big bro, I'm tellin' you," Omarr said, "how the theme song for *Fresh Prince* popped off crazy? We *gotta* link a song to *Men in Black*. Trust me, fam, it'll be outta here. Everything in music is dark right now. You can counterprogram the whole culture."

When you're famous, everybody has an idea. Everybody has a new business, a demo, or a better way that you should be doing things. It's even more extreme with friends and family because they feel entitled, and you feel obligated. So I listened patiently to Omarr's pitch.

Then he played me an idea, using a sample of Patrice Rushen's "Forget Me Nots." The demo singer comes in on the hook, "Here come the Men in Black." I turned to Omarr with that classic musician face, bopping my head and looking like something stinks.

We jumped into the studio with the Trackmasters. They modernized the drums and the orchestration—it was bangin'. I wrote and recorded the lyrics to "MiB," and as we listened back to the rough two-track mix, I turned to Omarr and said, "I think you may have just gotten yourself a new job."

(Omarr would later run the same play with Jaden and Justin Bieber on *The Karate Kid* with "Never Say Never"—number one movie, number one record.)

There are very few things in entertainment that are more combustible than a hit movie combined with a hit record. Think about Whitney Houston's *The Bodyguard* and "I Will Always Love You"; Prince's "Purple Rain"; Rocky and "Eye of the Tiger"; *Saturday Night Fever*; *Footloose*; *Grease* . . . Y'all get it. The alchemy of the story and the soundtrack together is like a self-perpetuating tornado sucking all the cash out of the weekend.

The symbiotic relationship between movie, song, and music video was a perfect promotional storm. The song works as massive radio promotion for the movie that is essentially free. The music video acts like a trailer for the movie, and the movie sends fans to buy the album and request the song and video.

We were now locked and loaded. All there was left to do was to wait for the Fourth of July . . . I mean, Big Willie Weekend.

FIFTEEN

INFERNO

The boy and his father had been unjustly imprisoned. The Greek King who jailed them was an asshole—the charges were trumped-up, no bail, not even a public defender. They were looking at life.

Father and son decided they were going to escape. Dad was a master craftsman, a genius inventor—he could design, build, or fix anything. And he refused to let his son rot in this stank-ass jail cell. So Dad engineered two sets of wings made of wax and feathers to effect their daring escape. But before their flight, the father sternly cautioned his beloved child: "Do not fly too close to the sun, as the wax will melt. And do not fly too low, as the feathers will get wet in the sea."

But the son, Icarus, wasn't hearing *none* of that. He was off, over the thick stone walls, past the towers—freedom!—rising into the vast blue ether. As he was getting higher and higher, he was getting *higher* and *higher*. The bliss, the intoxication, the rush of flight, pumped a torrent of adrenaline through his immature veins, the proverbial moth to the flame. The sun ever closer, the inferno scorching and blinding, but still he climbs, flying higher and higher, until his delicate wax wings start to soften and begin to melt, disintegrating and dripping back to the sea. Icarus begins to lose altitude, slowly at first, imperceptibly, then he's falling. The sea looms; the sun recedes; the disaster is upon him. Icarus burns, crashes, and then he's gone.

The thing is, I was totally comfortable flying so near to the sun; it was just that everybody else around me was my wings.

> Will Smith was named Hollywood's most bankable star in a survey of movie industry professionals. . . . The stars were ranked on ability to attract financing for a project, box office success, appeal to different audience demographics and other factors. . . . Smith was the only person to receive a perfect score of 10. —REUTERS

> Smith ranks first . . . of more than 1,400 working actors [edging out Johnny Depp, Brad Pitt, Leonardo DiCaprio, Angelina Jolie, Tom Hanks, Denzel Washington, Meryl Streep, Jack Nicholson, Tom Cruise, Matt Damon] when it comes to ensuring the financial success of film projects. —FORBES

> "We can safely say now that Will Smith owns the Fourth of July weekend," said Jeff Blake, president of worldwide marketing and distribution for Columbia Pictures. —THE NEW YORK TIMES

Big Willie Weekend was madness—*Men in Black* opened to $51 million in the first three days in the United States alone. It was #1 in more than forty countries around the world, ultimately steamrollering to $250 million domestic and topping out at almost $600 million worldwide. (The soundtrack ended up selling more than five million copies. To capitalize on the momentum, we followed immediately with *Big Willie Style*, which sold more than twelve million worldwide.)

It was now official; it was unanimous; I was the undisputed biggest movie star in the world.

But just to be clear, this is not about me; this is not some narrative ego trip; it's not about flexin' or identity inflation. This is purely for historical context, a background, a framework, all in order to give you, dear reader, greater perspective and deeper insight into just how much I was actually smashin' on muthafuckas.

Something changed when I saw her.

I'm not even going to try to explain it. But I was never the same again. We knew we were having a girl, but I had no idea what that was going to do inside of me.

I had been in varying degrees of terror and confusion for the births of my sons. Trey was born of an emergency cesarean section and was immediately rushed into the NICU. My first image of him was of an IV tube inserted into the center of the top of his skull. When Jaden was born, Jada was in distress and my attention was fully on her, not on the delivery of my new son. My memories of both births are laced with fragmented, fearful flashes.

So, this time, as a veteran of the maternity ward, free from all of those novice, new jack parent phobias, I vowed complete and total attention. I wanted to be present and involved, every step of the way.

Willow Camille Reign Smith was born on Halloween 2000. Her due date had been November 11, which is Trey's birthday, but even in the womb, she knew she wasn't sharing no birthday with nobody. She showed up two weeks early, in dramatic fashion.

I was the first person to hold her. She was so tiny; her whole body fit in one hand, her limbs dangling off the edges of my palm. Within fifteen seconds she had her nickname, something I call her to this day: My Bean. Her beautiful emerald eyes trying to focus. She couldn't quite see me, but some part of her seemed to know I was hers.

I always enjoy recounting the stories of my children's births—partly to depict the harrowing journeys to parenthood, but mainly to embarrass my kids in front of their friends. The punch line to Willow's story is: she came out, I held her, I gazed in awe at her, and then screamed at the top of my lungs, "OH MY GOD, WHERE'S HIS PENIS?"

Willow hates it when I tell that story, which only makes it funnier to me and makes me want to tell it all the time (in, like, books and stuff).

Saving the world in *Independence Day,* with the help of Judd Hirsch (left) and Jeff Goldblum (right). At the Bonneville Salt Flats it was 110 degrees and the glare off of the white salt was giving people sunburns under their chins. (Not to mention one of the crew members who was wearing baggy shorts and didn't have no drawz on.)

New Year's Eve 1997. Every time I see this picture I think, *Y'all better eat big pieces of that cake—you're going to need to carb up for the run that's coming.*

Jaden Christopher Syre Smith was born on July 8, 1998.
If it was up to Trey, his name would have been Luigi.

Trey and baby "Luigi."

Jaden has always been my most calm child.

Willow Camille Reign Smith was born on Halloween 2000.

Jaden, Sheree, Willow, Trey, and Jada.

With Jada and the children.

Mom-Mom and Gigi, Black excellence.

Me and Darrell running at nine thousand feet in Colorado. "Write his name," Darrell said. Darrell snapped a picture. "You need to remember why we're suffering," he said.

Landing in Maputo, Mozambique, for the final sequence of *Ali*. With JL, Charlie Mack, Darrell Foster, and Bilaal Salaam.

I was shocked by how much I innately understood Muhammad Ali. I clocked how similar our senses of humor were. Our banter was fluid and comfortable. The actor in me thought, *Oh shit. I might be able to do this.* . . .

One of the highlights of my life: Daddio, Trey, and Sheree meeting Nelson Mandela.
On the right, director of *Ali*, Michael Mann, and his wife, Summer.

"What's that look?" I once asked Nelson Mandela. He peered into me as if trying
to discern whether or not I had accidentally asked a good question, or, if I had
asked in earnest, was I ready to hear the answer. "If you will come and
spend some time with me," Madiba said, "I will show you."

Me, Jada, and JL in Aspen.

During the year, Jada was Peaches from *A Low Down Dirty Shame*—a ghetto superstar—but at the first jingle of sleigh bells, she turned into a Midwest, middle-aged white lady. With Jada and Mom-Mom; I'm holding baby Willow.

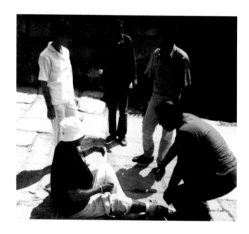

The moment right after Mom-Mom tripped and broke her ankle in the ruins at Ephesus in Turkey.

Jada on stage at Ozzfest with her band, Wicked Wisdom—#abs.

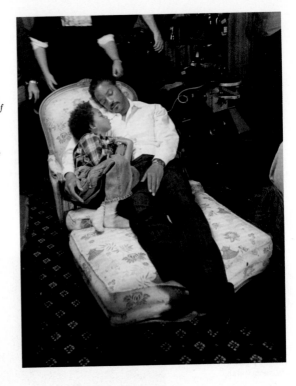

Me and Jaden knocked out on the set of *The Pursuit of Happyness* in San Francisco in 2005. Is that the best sleep-acting you've ever seen or what?

Me and Willow on the set of the "Whip My Hair" video shoot.

On stage at the fortieth annual Grammys in 1998; there are very few things in entertainment that are more combustible than a hit movie combined with a hit record.

Jay-Z, Jada, Willow, me, and Beyoncé the day Willow
signed her first record deal with Roc Nation.

In case you were wonderin', I was playing Snoop's "Gin and Juice."

Scoty Sardinha was the first "security" I'd ever had who was wearing flip-flops.

With Michaela Boehm. She is a single red curly hair over five feet tall. Her Austrian accent makes everything she says ring with psychoanalytical authenticity.

This is my no-big-deal-I'm-at-the-Taj-Mahal pose. All I need is a couple grand laid out on the ground in front of me.

Me and Daddio on the set of *Men in Black 3*.

Daddio at his waterfront condo in Philly.

Father's Day 2021.

Mom-Mom with all of her kids and most of her grandkids. From left: Jade, Ashley, Trish, Jaden, Dominic, Skylar, Mia, Willow, Langston, me, Mom-Mom, Caila, Pilar, Kyle, Pam, Trey, Sabrina, Ellen, Dion, Eddie, Harry, Sheree, and Tyler.

Something strange happened in our family dynamic after Willow was born. Up until then, we had maintained a fragile equilibrium—Sheree and I had one child, and Jada and I had one child. We'd all worked very hard to cultivate a sense of a singular family. It was rough in the beginning, but Jada and Sheree agreed that Jaden and Trey must think of themselves as full brothers. Jada even refused the term "stepmom." To this day, Trey refers to her as his bonus mom.

When Jaden was born, we tried to make sure that Trey was involved every step of the way. We had spoken to a psychologist to help us make the transition through Jaden's birth. The psychologist suggested that we allow Trey—who was six at the time—to be a part of naming the new baby. She instructed us that if Trey was part of the naming process, he would think of the new child as *his* brother. The choosing of the name would create a sense of ownership and connection.

Jada and I came home excited to involve Trey. Trey was in his room playing *Mario Kart* on his new Nintendo 64. He was displaying the standard catatonic stare of the video-game-addicted prepubescent male.

"Trey!" I said excitedly.

"Hey, Dad," Trey said, never taking his eyes off the TV.

"We got a surprise for you! We want you to help pick a name for your brother."

"OK," the little caveman said, in a semi-comatose, unresponsive response.

"Trey, stop playing for a second," Jada said.

"OK," he said, "gimme one minute."

"Trey, this is *important*," I said, getting frustrated that my psychological master move was being thwarted by a six-year-old. "We need you to pick a name for your brother—"

"LUIGI!" he shouted, continuing to play.

Jada and I look to each other in abject horror, both of us thinking the exact same thing: *Have you ever met a nigga named Luigi?*

Jada jumps in.

"Trey, is that the *only* name you like?" she said, in her best fake, singsongy mother voice.

Trey, apparently feeling a sense of rejection, immediately pauses the game.

"But you said *I* get to pick my brother's name!"

"Well, yes, Trey," I say, invoking my best fake, singsongy father voice. "But we're only asking if you have *another* name. In case maybe he doesn't look like a Luigi. . . ."

"I WANT LUIGI! IT'S MY FAVORITE NAME!" Trey wailed.

"OK, OK," Jada said calmly. "It's your choice."

I'm going to happily choke the hell out of that lady!"

"I'm callin' her now, Will, just relax," Jada said, dialing frantically.

I'm pacing around our bedroom, fuming, imagining having to introduce my new son as Luigi Smith because some damn four-hundred-dollar-an-hour shrink made up some shit about naming kids.

"We're gonna have to move to fuckin' Palermo!"

The psychologist apologized profusely, but she had a new solution: She instructed us to quickly buy Trey a puppy. She theorized that if "Luigi" is Trey's favorite name, he won't want to wait until his brother is born to use it—he'll want to name the *puppy* Luigi. Then, we'll be able to ask him for *another* name for his brother, this time being careful to lead the witness a little more effectively.

We immediately rushed out and purchased a beautiful, fluffy, gray Lhasa apso.

"Trey, we got another surprise for you!" I said.

"WHOA!" Trey cheered, running over to hug his new puppy.

"What do you want to name him?" Jada stage-whispers, verbally tiptoeing back into the Afro Italian minefield.

And sure enough, Trey yells, "LUIGI!"

Jada had successfully completed phase one. Now, I was up.

"But wait, Trey, your brother can't have the same name as the puppy," I said.

Jada snaps around on me, uncomfortable with the open-endedness of my promptings.

"I wanna name the *puppy* Luigi!" Trey said emphatically.

Phase two, nailed. Now, for the third, and most critical phase.

"So, you'll have to pick another name for your brother," I said. "I have an idea—we'll *all* pick a name. I'll pick one, Jada will pick one, and you'll pick one! And we'll give your brother *all* three names."

Trey had just made a new friend at school named Christopher. So, by the grace of a benevolent creator, Trey yells out, "CHRISTOPHER! I want to name my new brother Christopher."

"YES!" Jada shouts, damn near fist pumping.

In the end, I picked "Jaden"; Trey picked "Christopher"; and Jada picked "Syre": Jaden Christopher Syre Smith. (For the historical record, JL refused to call Jaden anything but "Luigi" until Jaden's fifteenth birthday.)

Willow's birth had tipped the scales of our precariously balanced blended family and suddenly, for the first time, from within, and from without, there was a sense of my "new" family and my "old" family. In the press, when people would refer to "Will Smith's family," they would often times use pictures of only myself, Jada, Jaden, and Willow, leaving out Sheree and Trey. The media preferred the symmetry and conventionality of the nuclear grouping.

As the heat of my global fame came to a boil, so did the cauldron of public scrutiny. My family's already fragile wax wings began to soften. Sheree and Trey started to retreat from the spotlight, but the spotlight was where I lived. I took their withdrawal personally. *What do you mean you don't want to go to the premiere of* my *movie? My family has to walk the red carpet with me. That's how* we *eat.*

"I want our son to have a normal life," Sheree said one day. "I want him to go to school; I want him to go to church; I want him to have regular friends. . . ."

"That's not his life!" I said.

"That's not *your* life, Will—it can absolutely be Trey's life. That's why he has a mother *and* a father. I don't want him bouncing around from city to city, set to set, with no stability."

"My son has to be with *me*," I said. "I'm the man you had a baby with. So, I'm the father that your son has. In order for me to parent, he has to have the freedom to move when I move."

"What about school, Will?" Sheree said.

"Tatyana had a tutor on the set of *The Fresh Prince* and got accepted to Harvard. Of course he needs to be educated, but school is not the only place that kids get educated."

"Will, I've seen you on set," Sheree said. "You're not even going to be paying attention to him. He's gonna be left with whatever tutor or nanny you hire. Some people do make movies in LA, you know—did you ever think about maybe staying in LA and raising your son?"

The emotional wall I keep crashing into while writing this book is that *today*, I know the right answers to many of these questions. But in the confusion of yesterday, I created so many unnecessary messes.

Did you ever think about maybe staying in LA and raising your son?

Here's what I *should* have said:

"First of all, I love you. I realize that this is not the life either of us envisioned, but this is where we are. I know it's scary. But I am devoted to you and to Trey with all of my being for the rest of my life. Now, in order to secure resources for our family, I have to be mobile, and I have to be global. But I hear you and I understand your concerns; it's scary to go against prevailing wisdom. I know that I'm asking you to come with me down an uncharted, dangerous, rocky-ass road. It's terrifying to not send your kids to traditional schools, or to not know what city they're going to be in month-to-month. Now, I'm not sayin' I have all the answers right now, but I promise you, if you ride with me, and support me on this journey, I will *die* before I allow our family to not flourish."

Now, here's what I actually said:

"Sure, then we'll just sell everything and live on whatever *you* can earn."

Hey, man, if you say you heard it from me, I will deny it," Harry said under his breath. "I showed the property to Jada, and she said it was too big. But I've known you my whole life, and you've only ever talked about Southfork. I found it."

Harry, as head of our family real estate office, had been charged with finding my Southfork. Even as a child, he knew of my obsession with *Dallas* and my fantasy of having a property with a name. He had found a 256-acre ranch, forty-five minutes northwest of Los Angeles.

"Jada asked me not to show it to you," Harry said. "So, out of respect for her, I can't. But here's the address. It's everything you ever dreamed about."

Harry's like JL—there's no sauce on his descriptions. If he said it was "everything I'd ever dreamed about," that meant "sneak away to see it today."

There were five existing houses on the property; a beautiful lake; horse stables; hiking trails; extensive chaparral flora and fauna. A gorgeous doe walked up to the front door on my first tour; I took it as a sign. I loved it. I had the perfect wife, three beautiful children, and I was the undisputed biggest movie star in the world. The final triumphant brushstroke on my lifelong dreamscape would be "Her Lake," a house with a name.

Jada loved horses; I was shaking with anticipation. I could see her, just like Sue Ellen, coming to breakfast on a stallion. This purchase would serve as the physical manifestation of my love for Jada. This land would nurture the seeds of our hopes and shelter our flowering aspirations. As soon as I saw the lake on the property, I knew it was for her: Her Lake. (I considered the Spanish translation—*Su Lago*—but ultimately remembered that I was from Philly and she was from B'more.)

Jada didn't want the property. All she could see were the fifty people it would take to manage, upkeep, secure, and operate 256 acres, horses, five buildings, and a bunch of bold-ass deer continually ringing your doorbell. On top of all that, she knew that I would be away six months of every year working, saddling her with the full responsibility of Her Lake.

She hated the whole idea.

I had just visited India for the first time. Harry and I had stood in front of the Taj Mahal and marveled, not only at its aesthetic detail and beauty but also at the loving intention behind its construction. Many people don't realize this, but the Taj Mahal is a single mausoleum, designed, constructed, and maintained for one woman: Mumtaz Mahal, the favorite wife of Emperor Shah Jahan. The emperor was so distressed by the death of his beloved that he commissioned the construction of the Taj Mahal. He preserved her body for the more than twenty years it took to build (from 1632 to 1653); he spent thirty-two million rupees (nearly a billion dollars in today's currency), and employed twenty thousand of the world's greatest artisans, imported Italian marble (which was not an easy thing to do in seventeenth-century India—and not to mention that India had its own makrana marble he could have been using), all to create a *private* tomb worthy of his lost love.

I related to Emperor Shah Jahan—I wanted anything I was involved with to stand the test of time. I wanted everything around me to be the grandest and most magnificent that anyone had ever seen. Powered by burning passion, my creative impulses would forge the finest expression of anything I touched: movies, music, family, children, businesses, marriage.

I was inspired and consumed by the dream of the Smith family. And Her Lake was an imperative.

"Will, I don't like it," Jada said. "I don't want it. It's too big, it's too expensive. And you're not gonna be here. It's too many people, it's too much space, it's too much noise. No!"

"Babe, I promise you," I said, "you're not seein' what I'm seein'. You're looking at it as it is right now. You can't see what's in my head."

"I don't know what you want me to say. I don't like it; I don't want it."

This was Jada's second great compromise, the next stop on the ever-accelerating Will Train.

Hindsight? Twenty-twenty. To all of my young male readers: no means no. Nothing good comes from spending your hard-earned money on a "family home" that your wife doesn't want. You are putting a down payment on discord and for years you will be paying off a mortgage of misery.

Or worse.

One of the greatest arguments Jada and I ever had was in a therapy session around priorities. Jada and I were both given a sheet of paper and a pen, and the exercise was to list our priorities, ordered from most important to least. Jada and I feverishly scribbled away, and after a few minutes, we were instructed to hand our sheets of paper to each other.

Surprisingly, we'd both only written four priorities each. As I read Jada's, a look of confusion spread across my face. And as she read mine, her eyes swam with tears. In the twenty-five years we've been together I've never felt her more injured than in that moment. Jada had listed her priorities as:

1. The children
2. Will
3. Myself
4. Extended family and friends.

I had written:

1. Me
2. Jada
3. The children
4. My career

The therapist reminded us that this was an opportunity to get to know each other better. He said that we should reserve our judgments of each other and remain open to the process of exploration and discovery. Then he asked which of us wanted to respond first.

"Babe," I said, "I can see you're struggling with something. What was it that I wrote that's bothering you?"

Jada could barely speak.

"I cannot believe you put yourself above our children," she said, her voice quivering.

"What do you mean?" I said, "I love our children as much as you do. I was actually surprised that you put yourself third. That doesn't make any sense to me. It's like the airlines: You have to put your mask on first before attempting to assist others. Of course I will take care of all of y'all, but *by* taking care of me."

"This explains a lot," Jada said.

"I feel like you're taking it wrong, babe."

"Oh, no, I'm taking it exactly how you wrote it on this paper."

"Jada, all I'm saying is that if you don't go to the gym, if you don't eat right, if you don't take your mental and emotional condition as *primary*, you're not going to be as good a mother. You take care of your kids *by* taking care of yourself."

I tried to recover and clarify, but her heart was shattered. She didn't even wipe the tears.

I have spoken over the years to many artists, musicians, innovators, athletes, thinkers, poets, entrepreneurs, big dreamers from all walks of life, and there is a secret conversation that always seems to arise: *How can we fully pursue and realize our visions while at the same time culti- vating love, a thriving family, and fulfilling relationships?* And here's the harsh reality for everyone who loves a dreamer: Everything comes second to the dream.

The attainment of my dream became an act of survival. In my dark- est nights, my dream saved my life—it was my light, my food. My vision of brighter days sustained me. It was my whole purpose. I saw my hopes as the ticket to a better life—to joy, fulfilment, security, safety. I saw the realization of my dream as my *only* road to love and happiness. Failure equaled death. My belief was, *When I get to the top of this moun- tain, I will never be scared again. I will never be sad again. I'll never be abused or disrespected or unloved. Everything worth living for is at the top of this mountain. And there is nothing I am unwilling to leave or to lose to get there. And anyone who opposes or impedes my progress is my enemy.*

But here's the dichotomy: My wife *was* my vision; my family *was* my vision. My picture encompassed joy, fulfillment, and prosperity for *all* of us. It's *my* vision, but it's not selfish because I'm doing it for everyone around me. (Spoiler alert: it's a little bit more complicated than a di- chotomy.)

I never understood the term "embarrassment of riches" until "Gettin' Jiggy Wit It" went to #1. It was my first #1 on the Billboard Hot 100 chart. And so much shit was going so absolutely perfectly in my amazing life, that, well, I was legitimately embarrassed.

I always remember the image of Michael Jordan shrugging, palms up, after dropping his sixth three in the first half of game one of the 1992 finals against the Portland Trail Blazers. He couldn't miss—he wasn't necessarily even a three-point shooter. And even though he was choosing the shots, he had practiced the shots, and he was taking the shots with every intention of making them, he was just as shocked as we were that they were all going in.

Just for a sense of the timeline, *Independence Day* was July 1996; the "Men in Black" song was mid-June 1997, and the movie was two weeks later; *Big Willie Style* was November 1997, right after I started filming *Enemy of the State*.

I married Jada on December 31, 1997.

"Gettin' Jiggy Wit It" was released in January 1998, to a decent response. Then it labored a bit through February—that month I received my third Grammy, for "Men in Black," so we were sort of OK with "Jiggy" not being a hit. Then, the wheels of serendipity began to turn: In an episode of *Seinfeld*, Jerry is attempting to woo a woman who is not feeling him at all.

He asks her, "What is the problem?"

To which she responds, "What do you want from me, Jerry?"

"I'm trying to get jiggy with you," Jerry says emphatically.

Fans appreciated Seinfeld's risqué redefinition of the word "jiggy." That next week, Stuart Scott, on ESPN, over the countdown for NBA shots of the week, yelled out, "And he is gettin' jiggy with it!" over the top dunk. Immediately, we saw a spike in single and album sales, and by March, "Gettin' Jiggy Wit It" was #1.

I was embarrassed. But I was just warming up.

Oh, by the way, during this time, Jim Carrey became the first actor to earn $20 million per movie, setting the A-list fee for the top of Hollywood. So, it was obvious that if Jim was worth twenty, the conversations with me started at . . . twenty-one.

Being a great father was central to my vision of the perfect life. I loved the idea of teaching and crafting and molding and nurturing my children's hearts and minds. Boys need man training. It was my responsibility to teach them how to "hunt," how to survive and navigate the material world. I began to see Sheree as an impediment to my forging of Trey as a young warrior. My father raised me on the ice truck, mixing concrete at the shop. I was forged in the heat of daily battle.

"My son is going to be with me wherever I am because that's the only way I can teach him," I said.

Sheree and I deteriorated into almost daily parenting disagreements. She wanted me to enforce her bedtime rules for Trey. But I didn't care what time he went to sleep as long as he woke up and did his chores. He would learn about going to sleep by waking up and having shitty mornings. She wanted me to limit his video game play, but I was thinking, *What if he's a video game genius and he's going to invent the next PlayStation?* I wanted to align with his love of video games and introduce him to coders and designers and fan the flames of his excitement about video gaming.

Sheree wanted me to pressure him about school and getting good grades, but I didn't view conventional schooling as mandatory for success. I was more concerned with his commitment to critical thinking. I saw school as getting in the way of me having time with him to teach him the *real* shit. I wanted him to see the entire world as school, and every person as a teacher, every place as a classroom.

These conflicting parenting and worldviews landed us in a custody battle. Trey was about nine years old, and now his parents were both demanding full custody. The emotion of these types of disputes is so extreme that very little sanity prevails. It becomes a strange game of chicken, with the child in the middle. How aggressive are you willing to be against your ex with the risk of injuring your child if you miss? And the answer is tainted with the delusion that your behavior is strictly and only for the protection of the child, so you feel justified in higher

levels of emotional violence because after all, it's your ex's fault anyway—
they are causing the whole thing. It's obvious, and *everyone* can see it's
their fault, except them.

I called Daddio. He listened calmly, patiently, a veteran of a very
similar petty war.

"Hey, man, look," Daddio said, with an uncharacteristic delicacy. He
understood where my mind was, and he knew he had to be careful.
"You can't win. You can't fight with a kid's mother. The kid will hate
you forever."

Daddio had hit a bull's-eye in my heart. I knew that to be true first-
hand.

"So, what am I supposed to do?" I asked. "Just let her mess up
my son?"

"You have to wait. When he turns thirteen years old, she ain't gonna
be able to do nuthin' with him. He's gonna reach for you. It'll be your
turn then. But for now, let her do whatever she gonna do. You just get
in where you fit in."

When I look back on my life, I'm still torn about the pros and cons of
my decision. But I stopped fighting Sheree. I agreed to shared legal
custody, but Trey's primary residence would be with her. But it also
meant that he could not leave the State of California without her per-
mission, permission that she was unlikely to grant anytime during the
school year. The result was, three- and four-month stretches where I
didn't see Trey. And this was pre-FaceTime. The other unintended con-
sequence was that because Willow and Jaden were homeschooled, they
were with me at all times.

But true to Daddio's hard-earned insight, three weeks after Trey's
thirteenth birthday, he asked if he could move in with me. Just as
Daddio had said, it was my turn now. It was joyful and exciting—Jaden
and Willow were ecstatic to have their big brother living with them full-
time. But the chasm between me and Trey was deep and wide. Dark
seeds of misunderstanding, resentment, and distrust had taken root.
Though it would be years before their flowers would fruit.

Will, it's an emergency, call me right now!!!

Ellen's text was like defibrillation paddles to my chest. She lives with Mom-Mom.

"Yo, what happened?" I said.

"MommywasonacruiseinTurkey . . . ," Ellen said hysterically.

"Ellen," I said, icy calm. "We're gonna handle whatever it is. But I need you to take a breath so I can understand what's going on."

I surprised myself with the calmness and steadiness of my reaction. I wanted to be in charge; I wanted to be responsible; I liked being the only person Ellen wanted to depend on to fix it. And for the first time, I had an inkling I might be good at it.

"Mom-Mom was on a cruise in Turkey," Ellen wailed, "and I don't even know what happened, but she's in the hospital."

"OK. It's all good. Just relax. Who's she with?"

"Aunt Florence," Ellen said.

Mom-Mom's greatest joy over the past few years had been to travel and explore. Every birthday, Christmas, holiday, I'd surprise her and her friends with another adventure—they had even nicknamed her "the Trip Tester." In Turkey, she's been traveling with Florence Avery, James Avery's mother. They'd become travel buddies, and James would always joke, "Your mother is dragging mine around the world on a Will Smith budget! I can't afford it—you're responsible for both of 'em!"

On the first stop of their Turkish cruise, they were walking through the ruins at Ephesus. Mom-Mom had been so excited to see the columns that she didn't notice a step that was worn away—she slipped and her ankle slammed onto the jagged concrete.

Mom-Mom was rushed to the nearest hospital, which was understaffed and ill-equipped to deal with her injury. By this time her ankle was badly swollen, and she was sent back to the ship. The ship doctor determined that the ankle was broken, and she needed to go to the American hospital in Turkey to get a cast placed properly.

Ellen and I were in London at the time. Mom-Mom is diabetic, and with her condition worsening and the medical barriers to travel increasing, I arranged a medevac to the UK, and within ten days we were all back in Philly.

Mom-Mom's diabetic condition caused significant complications in the healing of her ankle. It decreased blood flow, which was necessary for her ankle to heal. Her ankle had been pinned through the tibia with an external fixator, or stabilizing cage, after which she had developed osteomyelitis, an infection of the bone, which with progression can cause a loss of bone integrity and necrosis (bone death). And while the doctors were attempting to do everything in their power to heal her ankle, for the first time, the word that all diabetics fear—"amputation"—was being mentioned.

Mom-Mom had been in the hospital for nearly two months, and for a woman who had discovered the great joys of globe-trotting, this immobility was becoming too much to bear.

"How much longer am I going to be in this bed?" Mom-Mom said.

"Well, we're trying to increase blood flow to your ankle, but it'll probably take at least three months to be able to determine if the procedure will be effective," the doctor said.

"And in three months, what are the chances that you'll be able to save my leg?" Mom-Mom said.

"We're looking at fifty-fifty."

"So you're saying that I could lay in this bed for the next three months and then you could still have to amputate my leg?"

"Well, yes, that's a possibility, but . . ."

"Cut it off now," Mom-Mom said sharply.

"Wait, Mom, just let him finish what he's saying . . . ," I said.

"I'm not wasting my life away in this bed," Mom-Mom said. "Cut it off now. I've got a cruise I'm planning on in June."

That is the most gangsta sentence I have ever heard.

Mom-Mom's leg was amputated just below the knee. Within seven weeks, she was fitted for her first prosthetic limb. And within four months, she'd set out to finish her cruise with Florence Avery.

Three days after Mom-Mom had left Turkey, a massive, 7.8-magnitude earthquake hit the country, killing twenty thousand people. The doctor treating her in Philadelphia told her that the hospital she'd been in in Turkey had been destroyed.

"All I lost was a leg," Mom-Mom said. And then she bowed her head, and lowered her voice. "Thank you, God."

SIXTEEN

PURPOSE

o! Hell no. Absolutely not; no way. Never—not gonna happen. Uh-uh, nope."

That was my reaction when JL told me that Michael Mann wanted me to star in his forthcoming Muhammad Ali biopic. The thought of it literally ran a chill down my spine. Ali was one of the most recognized and beloved human beings on earth—a living legend. I was not about to be the dude who ruined the cinematic portrayal of his life and legacy.

Besides, everything was going great—I was already the undisputed, undefeated Hollywood Box Office Heavyweight Champion of the World— why roll the dice? Why risk my title? The degree of difficulty in portraying Ali bordered on stupidity. The risk-reward proposition was catastrophically imbalanced toward abysmal global failure and universal, eternal embarrassment. In a nutshell, I didn't like my odds.

Not only would I have to learn how to fight, but I'd have to learn how to fight like the greatest fighter of all time. *Great* fighters can't fight like Ali. I had never boxed before. He was over 220 pounds; I barely weighed 190. The dialect and cadence of his voice was singular—no one sounds like Ali. People throughout the world have such fond memories of this revolutionary icon of social justice. There was more video of Muhammad Ali than damn near any other person ever—and not just any old video: classic, era-defining images seared into the hearts and minds of boxing fans and non-fans alike. Everybody knew Muhammad Ali.

"Not this one, J. I'm not feelin' it."

"I think you should just meet with Michael Mann," JL said.

"I don't wanna be in the room, hear him pitch for an hour, and then have to tell him no. I definitely wanna work with him—just not on this."

"I think you should take the meeting," JL said, as if he hadn't already said it, and as if I hadn't already said no.

I paused, and then attempted to clarify my position: "No! Hell no. Absolutely not; no way. Never—not gonna happen. Uh-uh, nope."

We hung up, and I went about my safe, challenge-ducking, risk-averse little life.

About a week later, JL called again.

I would have to guess that I have spoken to James Lassiter on the telephone over the past few decades somewhere north of twenty thousand times, with an average call lasting between seven and twelve minutes, give or take, which comes out to about 171,000 minutes. This means I've spent roughly 118 days on the phone with JL. So, just as a point of reference, if it were a *single* call, and we started it by wishing each other a Happy New Year, by the end of the call I could ask him what he was doing for Easter. We've talked on the phone about *everything*—births, marriages, movies, kids, accidents, music, money, not money, death, dumb shit, and sports.

But this twenty-six-second call is definitely in the Lassiter top five. In his standard, unfazed monotone flair, he said: "Muhammad Ali asked to speak to you personally."

There are rare individuals among us who just know *who* they are, they know *what* they are, and they are crystal clear about what they are here to *do*—Gandhi, Mother Teresa, Martin Luther King Jr., Nelson Mandela, and even budding change agents like Malala Yousafzai and Greta Thunberg. Each accepted their divine duties and are willing to suffer for what is right and to benefit others. There's an intoxicating power in their conviction—they are calm, they are decisive, and they are loving, even in the midst of conflict and the worst of storms. Just being in their presence inspires your heart toward higher purpose. You want to follow them; you want to serve them; you want to fight along-side them.

Muhammad Ali, at the height of his fame and fortune—and in the prime years of his athletic capabilities—gave up everything to oppose the war in Vietnam. He refused induction into the US Army on religious grounds as a conscientious objector, and in 1967, Ali was convicted of "draft evasion" and sentenced to five years in prison. His passport was seized; he was heavily fined; and he was punished with a three-year ban from boxing.

I ain't draft dodging. I ain't burning no flag. I ain't running to Canada. I'm staying right here. You want to send me to jail? Fine, you go right ahead. I've been in jail for four hundred years. I could be there for four or five more, but I ain't going no ten thousand miles to help murder and kill other poor people. If I want to die, I'll die right here, right now, fightin' you, if I want to die. You my enemy, not no Chinese, no Viet Cong, no Japanese. You my opposer when I want freedom. You my opposer when I want justice. You my opposer when I want equality. Want me to go somewhere and fight for you? You won't even stand up for me right here in America, for my rights and my religious beliefs. You won't even stand up for me right here at home.

I meet with the champ; his wife, Lonnie; and his daughters, Laila and May May, in Las Vegas.

Ali is seated in front of a bowl of chicken noodle soup. Even though I had no intention of portraying him in the film, I couldn't help but clock his hair, the shape of his lips around the spoon, his left hand balancing himself on the table while eating with his right, and the surprising fluidity of his physical movements. He looks up and sees me, his face collapsing into the iconic Ali scowl, his top teeth comedically biting into his bottom lip.

"Who let that sucka in here?" Ali yells, as he jumps up from the table. Clearly the family has been here before. Everyone falls into their roles. May May steps in front of her father.

"Come on, Daddy," she says, "let's not do this today."

Ali pretends to struggle to get past her.

"This sucka think he can just walk up in here. Let me at him," he said, sounding just like Muhammad Ali.

It's Lonnie's turn to step in. She and May May are now trying to both hold Ali back.

"Come on, honey," Lonnie said kindly, "just finish your soup. Can we have *one* day when you're not trying to fight somebody?"

Not to be outdone, I decided to play along.

"Listen to your wife, champ," I said. "Just eat your soup. You don't want none of what's over here."

This puts Ali into a mock rage.

"That's it! That's it! Y'all move out my way! I wanna hear how he talk with my fist in his mouth!"

Everyone is roaring with laughter. Who knows how many times the family has played out this scene? But this time, it was Ali's gift to me— he knew I would talk about it for the rest of my life.

That's how Ali was. He was always trying to create something that would make you smile forever. He knew he was Muhammad Ali; he knew what that meant to people; and there was no length he was unwilling to go to in order to autograph your heart with a loving memory.

Once he's "calmed down," he hugged me. He began checking my biceps and my abs and feeling the bone structure of my hands. He held his hands up like boxing mitts.

"Let me see your jab," said Muhammad Ali.

"Well, I haven't trained or anything yet, champ. . . ."

"Come on, now, you can't jab wit' your lips! Let me feel it," the greatest fighter of all time insisted.

I didn't know anything about how to box or land a punch. I was a southpaw at the time. But I reach out and tap Ali's hand with the saddest right-hand jab. And Ali scares the hell out of me as he screams in pain, doubles over, clutching his hand.

"Did y'all see that?" he said, pointing at me. "That boy just hit me! I was mindin' my own business and he struck me! You're gon' to jail tonight, sucka!"

The room once again erupted in joyous laughter. Ali then announced to Lonnie, "He's almost pretty enough to play me."

We talked for hours.

"They got me on a diet," Ali said. "Lonnie thinks I'm gettin' too fat."

I peer comically at his stomach.

"Yeah, look like you got a lot goin' on over there, champ," I said.

Ali put two hands on his belly, looked down at it, and shakes it.

"Aw, man, this ain't nuthin' but a young girl's playground."

I clocked how similar our senses of humor were. Our banter was fluid and comfortable; there was a deep childlike core to him that harmonized with my own. His heart was transparent to me. Ali told me about his childhood; how his life changed when he learned how to fight; his Olympic win; his difficulties with women; the strained relationship with his father. I was shocked by how much I innately understood him. The actor in me thought, *Oh shit. I might be able to do this. . . .*

"I don't want anybody else to do this movie," Ali says. "I've been tellin' people no for years. But I would be honored if you would tell my story to the world."

Michael Mann is one of my all-time favorite filmmakers: *Heat*; *The Last of the Mohicans*; *The Insider*; *Manhunter*; *Miami Vice*. The meeting was in a small warehouse that he'd converted into his office in LA. The main section was a three-thousand-square-foot Muhammad Ali war room: thousands of pictures, books, memorabilia, magazine articles, stacks of overstuffed color-coded binders, videos on multiple televisions—interviews on one, Ali's jab on a loop on another. A heavy bag, weights, wraps, gloves, and jump ropes surrounded a perfectly lit boxing ring in the center.

It looked like an FBI Quantico situation room—the level of detail was mind-boggling. When I arrive, Michael is midconversation with an elderly Italian man. Four black leather jackets hang on mannequins in front of them. They're in some dispute. Michael wanted an identical jacket to one he'd seen in a picture of Ali from the late sixties. The Italian man was the now seventy-five-year-old tailor who had made the original jacket. He had sent four versions of the jacket, none of which had met Michael's approval, so Michael flew the man in from Chicago to discuss the problem. The tailor is vehemently defending the precision of his work, pointing back and forth between the 1960s picture and the jackets. (All four jackets were identical to my eye, by the way.)

"Michael, with all due respect," the tailor says, "I made the original jacket. And I made these four replicas. Everything is sourced and constructed exactly as it was forty years ago."

"Something's off," Michael says, "it's not right."

As the debate intensifies, it suddenly hits Michael.

"I see the problem," Michael eurekas, pointing to Ali's collar in the photo. "The stitching on the collar of the replicas is single thread; but look, in the photo, the stitching is double thread."

The tailor squints and realizes that Michael is correct. He then remembers that in the mid-1970s, the fabric of the thread changed, and he stopped using the double-stitching technique. He shook Michael's hand and set off to make the jacket . . . *right*.

As it turns out, Michael Mann is a savant-level researcher. I had never before (nor since) met a more thorough cinematic scientist.

We sat at Michael's desk.

"I met Malcolm X in 1963," Michael said. "I'm one year younger than Ali. So, generationally, I was pissed off about the same things he was pissed off about. I'm not looking to idolize him; that would diminish his humanity. This is not a story about boxing—it's about politics, war, religion, and rebellion. I want to create an inside view, an intimate perspective. I want to see his despondency when his fortunes are at their absolute most abysmal."

"I have no idea how to become Muhammad Ali," I admitted.

"Well, fortunately, you don't have to worry about that," Michael said. "I will create the curriculum that will render you *as* Ali. All you have to do is follow the syllabus."

Michael explained that he would do all of the research, build a world-class team of teachers, experts, trainers. He would be in charge of my schedule; he would surround me with people who had actually been there with Ali. He would pick my clothes, he would build a cast, he would even choose the music I would listen to.

All I had to do was commit.

I loved the sound of that recipe: take one firm commander, mix in some clear orders, just add discipline, and shake thoroughly. I could definitely do that.

"But it's not gonna be easy," Michael said. "It's going to take everything you've got. And then just a little bit more than that. Do you have any boxing experience?"

"None whatsoever," I said.

Michael, unfazed, maybe even a little inspired by that damning revelation, reaches for the phone on his desk.

"Is Darrell still here?" he asks, knowing damn well that Darrell was still here. "Good. Have him come in."

Darrell Foster is the individual hardest man I've ever met in my life.

Born and raised on the streets of Washington, DC, Darrell survived a horrific childhood marred by violence and abuse.

"Shit—it's a damn miracle I ain't dead or in jail," he'd say. "If it wasn't for boxin', man, ain't no tellin' . . . these gloves saved my life."

Darrell was an athletic prodigy. He started boxing at age ten, and within a few years he was the best amateur boxer in the country at his weight class. At thirteen, he won the Golden Gloves, the equivalent of the Super Bowl for amateur boxers. He was undefeated. He had college scholarships lined up. His coaches were even eyeing the Olympics.

Then, at seventeen, Darrell Foster nearly killed a guy in the ring, pounding him after the referee had told him to stop. Just like that, the sport that Darrell owed his life to was taken away from him. He was banned from competition.

Darrell became a trainer. There, too, he excelled. He had grown up with Sugar Ray Leonard—one of the best boxers of all time—and had been his training partner, helping him win an Olympic gold medal and become world champion in five different weight classes. Once Sugar Ray retired, Darrell moved out to Hollywood and began consulting on films. There, he helped train Woody Harrelson and Antonio Banderas in the 1999 film *Play It to the Bone*. And in 2000, when Michael Mann needed someone to do the heavy lifting of turning Will Smith into Muhammad Ali, Darrell was Michael's top choice to carry that load.

Darrell enters the room—five ten, 190 pounds. Imagine if you could crossbreed a pit bull with a brick. The omega symbol is branded proudly on his upper left arm—he's a Que Dog (a member of the Omega Psi Phi fraternity). They're as hard as they come. His posture is rigid, straight up and down, head high, shoulders back, like a soldier. Like a general. His hands, at their default setting, halfway to a fist, just in case.

His presence is intense.

He's already looking me up and down. Unconvinced. He holds his hand out to greet me—not a handshake, a closed fist. We pound.

"How tall are *you*?" Darrell says.

"I'm six two."

"What you weighin' right now?"

"I'm probably one ninety. . . ."

"Yeah, that's not enough," he says, almost to himself, making his way to the boxing ring. "Take your shoes off, hop up in here."

What? I have jeans on. And jewelry. I'm fly right now.

But Darrell is already in the ring, waiting for me. Michael Mann is grabbing a video camera. Darrell slides the focus mitts on, and he claps them together, an explosion echoing through the cavernous warehouse. The reverberation seems to say, *Hurry the fuck up, bling boy. . . .*

Darrell didn't give two shits that I was the biggest movie star in the world. In fact, he almost saw it as the biggest problem.

Michael Mann helps me on with the fourteen-ounce gloves, and I step into the ring.

This dude better not hit me.

"Ninety percent of the people on earth are right-handed," Darrell said in a voice that seemed to be louder than necessary. "That means that if you're gon' get knocked out in the street, most of the time it's gon' be with a looping overhand right. In order to deliver that punch, a person's right foot gotta be set back—that's how they gon' get the leverage to throw it. You see that shit in the street all the time when niggas is beefin'. So, when you see them shift their weight, you know what's comin'. Your rear cranium bone's the hardest bone in your skull, so all we gon' practice today: put your left ear down to your shoulder, and we gon' break their hand on the top of your head. Then you gon' fire your right hand straight back."

For about thirty minutes, we repeated that sequence. Darrell was pretending like we were in the street. He would talk shit, then shift his right foot back, throw the overhand right; I would time it so that I caught the mitt on the back-left section of my cranium—"the hardest bone of my skull"—and then I'd fire my right hand back at the center of his mitt.

"You master that," Darrell said, "you gon' stretch most muthafuckas in the street."

"Is that a move Ali did?" I said.

"Don't you worry about Ali. I gotta teach you how to fight first."

Something about that promise rang deep within me. He was going to teach me how to fight for *real*. The thought of being able to physically defend myself induced reverence and surrender to Darrell's leadership.

Michael and Darrell share a silent look. They've seen enough—clearly, they need to talk about me behind my back. Darrell begins to remove the mitts and steps out of the ring.

"I'll see you tomorrow," Darrell says.

"What are we doin' tomorrow?" I say.

"Five at five. We only got a year—we need to get started."

Darrell's style of training is full immersion: He doesn't ask anybody to do anything that he doesn't do. Over the next year, he ran every mile, jumped every rope, lifted every weight, sparred as many rounds—every moment of training, right by my side. He ate when I ate; he slept when I slept; he worked when I worked. Often, he would quote Edgar Guest's poem "The Sermons We See":

I'd rather see a sermon than hear one any day;
I'd rather one should walk with me than merely tell the way.
The eye's a better pupil and more willing than the ear,
Fine counsel is confusing, but example's always clear . . .

This was not a dude I thought was going to quote poetry.

Darrell had a "no actors" rule—he set up an authentic fight camp. Every boxing role in the film would be cast with active, professional fighters: former heavyweight champ Michael Bentt as Sonny Liston; James "Lights Out" Toney—a three-weight-class champ—as Joe Frazier;

IBF cruiserweight champ Alfred Cole as Ernie Terrell; and 17–1 heavy-weight contender Charles Shufford Jr. as George Foreman. These would be the anchor fights of the film.

"We ain't doin' no Hollywood bullshit around here. This a real fight camp," Darrell said. "We are preparing for a title shot. Fuck a movie."

Everybody knew we were doing this for Muhammad Ali. Every fighter felt indebted and dedicated to the champ. There was an energy around the project that I had never experienced before. The *purpose* of the film had a unifying and electrifying effect on all of us.

That first week was brutal. I had just finished a thirty-minute foot-work drill, and I was exhausted, so I laid down in the ring.

Darrell saw me from across the gym and snapped.

"Hey! Get the fuck up!"

I stood as he made his way over to the ring.

"Do not get comfortable with your back on that canvas," he said. "You fight how you train."

You fight how you train was one of Darrell's central axioms. "You do *everything* how you do *one* thing," he'd say. Darrell didn't want me to get comfortable with my back on the canvas in case I ever got knocked down. He wanted lying down in a boxing ring to feel utterly foreign to me, just in case I ever found myself lying down in a boxing ring.

His position was: dreams are built on discipline; discipline is built on habits; habits are built on training. And training takes place in ev-ery single second and every situation of your life: how you wash the dishes; how you drive a car; how you present a report at school or at work. You either do your best *all* the time or you don't; if the behavior has not been trained and practiced, then the switch will not be there when you need it.

"Training is for the purpose of habituating reactions to extreme cir-cumstances," Darrell said. "When situations get hot, you can't rely on yo' thinkin' mind. You must have habituated reflexive responses that kick in without the necessity of thought. *Never* de-train your killer instincts."

The Sonny Liston and Joe Frazier fights feature early in the movie, so Michael Bentt and James Toney were the first fighters I trained with. Darrell and I had spent the first three months with just the two of us, working on the fundamentals: footwork, posture, cardio, and developing the fluidity of the classic Ali jab—what Ali called the "snake lick" because it mimicked the strike of a cobra. Michael Mann brought in a brain scientist to help with what he called "burning new neural passages." The scientist created a twenty-minute loop of the quintessential Ali footwork and jab. I would sit in a pitch-black room, watching the loop twice a day, staring at the repeated movement until it was seared on my brain stem.

The first few months of training were in front of mirrors, in empty gyms, and in solitary locations. We ran at altitude in the snow in Colorado, in combat boots. I could barely breathe; Darrell had run the same distance but looked like he had just awakened from a refreshing nap. I had to take a knee. Darrell didn't care much for my little breaktime in the snowbank.

"Write his name," Darrell said.

"What?" I said, struggling for a sip of oxygen.

"Ali. Write it."

I leaned down and slowly began to write.

A-L-I.

Darrell took out his phone and snapped a picture.

"You need to remember why we're suffering," he said, as he began to run.

When the group training camp began, it was no longer just Darrell and me. For the first time, I was gloved up across the ring from seasoned boxing champions.

Darrell whispered to me as he laced my gloves, "These are not actors. These are instinctual fighters. Their hands will just fly before they even know it. The first rule of boxing: protect yourself at all times."

In the mirror, I was starting to look like Muhammad Ali. I was 223 pounds of muscle now, with a one-rep max bench press of 365 pounds. But as soon as another fighter stepped in the ring, my fear wouldn't allow me to maintain my forward posture. I began leaning back at the waist too much.

"Don't compromise your spine angle! Lean in!" Darrell yells from outside the ring. "Just stay off the train tracks! Create angles."

But Michael Bentt was not inspiring me in the least to lean in toward him. I decided, *Fuck it, just lean in!* And my simple, two-inch spinal adjustment triggers Michael Bentt's right hand. I see it coming, but it's too late. I only have enough time to put my chin down a little and brace for impact. Bentt's right hand lands high on my forehead, but because of my forward posture, my head doesn't snap back—instead, it compresses down onto my spinal column. I feel an electrical shock shoot from the top of my spine down both arms, ending at my elbows. I have an alkaline, metallic taste in my mouth like I've just licked a nine-volt battery. Fortunately, Bentt sees that I'm hurt and doesn't follow with the left hook he hit Tommy Morrison with to become heavyweight champ.

This was the first time I'd been truly hit. Every fighter in the room knew that this was a make-or-break moment—fight or flight. Everybody went silent. Darrell calmly stepped up into the ring and sat me in the corner.

"You good?" he said, knowing damn well I was not good.

Michael Bentt appeared over Darrell's shoulder. "You a'ight, Gawd?" he said in his thick Brooklyn accent.

All I could think was, *Where the fuck are my car keys?*

As I look back on my life, I see funny stories, beautiful experiences, tragic losses, magnificent victories—all held together by a handful of pivotal moments, critical choices that completely altered the trajectory of my journey. In that ring with Michael Bentt, a switch got flipped that would take a decade to get unflipped. The warrior within me took complete command of everything in my life.

I stood up off the stool, looked at Bentt, and said, "Good shot. Let's work."

The one year of training and the five months of filming of *Ali* was the most grueling mental, physical, and emotional test of my entire career, but also the most transformative.

The filming of *Ali* spanned seven cities and two continents. We began in LA, did two weeks in Chicago, quick shoots in New York and Miami, and then it was time to bring it home. We were heading to the motherland. We were heading to Africa, a place I'd never been.

The final sequence of *Ali* was shot in Mozambique. Michael Mann is a purist—he wanted to shoot in the Democratic Republic of the Congo, where the actual "Rumble in the Jungle" took place. But the raging civil war there redirected the production to Maputo.

Michael wanted the cast to feel what it was like to fly together and arrive together—Jamie Foxx, Jeffrey Wright, Nona Gaye, Mykelti Williamson, Ron Silver, Mario Van Peebles, Jon Voight, and Michael Michele; and me, JL, Charlie, and my whole squad. Michael was trying to orchestrate a similar emotional experience to the one that Ali and his crew had had. This was a part of his cinematic genius.

And it worked.

It is difficult to overestimate the power of a first experience in Africa. Two steps off the airplane, and I'm already crying. I'm not sure if it was my cells or my soul that recognized their origin, but it was visceral and overwhelming. We found a quiet place just outside the airport in Maputo, Mozambique; we all huddled, held hands, knelt down, and kissed the ground. One of the airport workers yelled out from the other side of the fence, "Welcome home, brothers!"

Nelson Mandela has invited us to dinner," JL said, in his regular-ass JL voice.

I couldn't even respond.

"His current wife is Graça Machel, the former first lady of Mozambique," he said, as though he was reading from Wikipedia. "They have a house near here."

"J, you *gotta* start putting some expression on it when you tell me shit like that," I said.

I had felt the world moving differently around this film. Ali's name alone opened doors in a way I'd never experienced. It engendered the goodwill of every person we approached. His legacy lubricated the logistical wheels of the production; deal negotiations, permits, locations, casting—everything and everybody wanted to serve Ali. Whatever we needed to tell his story properly, the answer was always yes. It wasn't because of his fame, or his boxing titles; it wasn't about success, or money; the always-positive reaction was about people's deep recognition and reverence for a life lived in integrity. In the face of grievous injustice, profound prejudice, and financial devastation, he never wavered from the convictions of his principles. He was the greatest fighter of all time yet would always say, "My religion is love."

Everybody wanted to be a part of honoring him.

I had experienced the magnetism of fame, I knew well the allure of celebrity, the attraction of money, but this was my first dose of the power of *purpose* and the radiance of service.

Nelson Mandela had spent twenty-seven years unjustly imprisoned for opposing the South African apartheid regime. His eyes had been damaged from hard labor in the lime quarries. Upon the toppling of the apartheid system, he was released from Victor Verster Prison and was subsequently elected president of South Africa.

One of his first official undertakings was to commission the Truth and Reconciliation Commission hearings, where the architects and the perpetrators of the heinous system of racial segregation and brutality were put on trial. And in a controversial and extraordinary act, Nelson Mandela offered forgiveness and amnesty to those who would confess their atrocities. He was, however, widely criticized for this stance, but as he wrote in 2012:

In the end, reconciliation is a spiritual process, which requires more than just a legal framework. It has to happen in the hearts and minds of people.

The night of the dinner came. Twenty cast and crew members made our way to his suburban home in Maputo. As I entered, Charlie Mack and JL by my side, my eyes once again welled with tears.

"You don't need to cry, man," Charlie Mack said, "you belong here."

"Hallo, Willie!" Mr. Mandela said, joyfully bringing me into his arms. "Come—you will sit with me."

"Madiba"—as he's known among his closest friends and family— grabbed my hand and walked me around his home. We must have held hands for a full ten minutes. Men didn't hold hands like this where I grew up; the show of affection was overwhelming.

I introduced him to everyone; he, in turn, introduced me to his wife, Graça, and his family. He took his seat at the head of the dining room table and sat me to his right hand. We all ate and talked and laughed, and he praised us for honoring Ali. Then, as the meal wound down, Madiba began to recount in vivid detail the horrors of apartheid and his twenty-seven years in prison, eighteen of them on Robben Island.

"As inmates, once a month we were shown a film—movies from all over the world—but American cinema was my particular favorite. There was a film called *In the Heat of the Night*, starring Sidney Poitier. And in the middle of the movie, there was a strange glitch. I could tell that the film had been edited. I was so intrigued. I used all my angles and connections on the outside to determine what had been taken out. It took weeks, but finally I was informed that Sidney Poitier had slapped a white man in the face. Something in my spirit was energized. If Black men in American cinema are standing on equal ground with their white counterparts, then it was only a matter of time. The film empowered me, it inspired me."

And then he paused, he looked directly into my eyes, and said, "Never underestimate the power of what you do."

After dinner, cast and crew are milling about. The evening is winding down. Madiba and I are sharing a quiet moment. He sits calmly, taking in the room. I catch myself staring. He has the same little smile and trancelike countenance that Gigi displayed every Sunday in Resurrection Baptist Church—the soft rise in the corners of his mouth betraying an invincible serenity.

My heart jumped at the recognition. He soon feels my gaze and turns his attention to me. I ask him, jokingly, but in all seriousness, "What's that look?"

He peered into me as if trying to discern whether I had accidentally asked a good question, or, if I had asked in earnest, was I ready to hear the answer?

"If you will come and spend some time with me," Madiba said, "I will show you."

If you will come and spend some time with me, I will show you.

Madiba's words lingered as we prepared to film the final scenes of *Ali*—the "Rumble in the Jungle," Ali versus Foreman. In a perfect example of art imitating life, this was the most difficult fight of Ali's career, and also the most difficult fight to capture on film. The sequence took two weeks to shoot; Michael Mann had an entire stadium refurbished and over 20,000 extras in the stands. With the lights and the humidity, it was over 105 degrees in the ring, and I lost eleven pounds on the first day of shooting. That meant I had to double the portions of chicken breast, broccoli, and brown rice I'd been "enjoying" for months.

One weekend, everyone was sitting around in the house we had rented just outside Maputo. I had been training with Darrell and the other fighters for more than a year, and everything was coming down to this final sequence.

The Africa experience was the culmination of the entire journey. My boys Bilaal Salaam, Dave Haines, and Mike Soccio flew in and brought a spark of new energy that I desperately needed at the time. But while everyone was thinking of this as a regular movie shoot, Darrell saw it as a fight camp.

My boy Bilaal ended up losing one hundred pounds during the training and filming. Dave Haines was my stand-in—in Hollywood terms, that means he would stand in the spots that I would eventually be so the crew could set the lights and the shots and get everything ready. Dave so impressed Michael Mann that Michael gave him the role of Ali's brother, Rahman, in the movie. I accidentally gave Dave a concussion during a sparring session.

My boy Mike had been a writer on *The Fresh Prince*. I had hired him to video document our entire African experience. As far as he was concerned, he was here in a domestic capacity, and accordingly, he had had a case of Snickers shipped in from Philly.

Darrell exploded.

"Nigga, you eatin' a fuckin' Snickers?" he said, which for Mike was confusing on two levels—one, in his mind he was just a videographer, and two, he's white. "Will is about to be in a ring with a 235-pound muthafucka punchin' at his head. This is the challenge of his lifetime. We all benefittin' from his suffering and you stuck in the fuckin' pleasure principle. He don't need to be seein' yo ass chompin' on no fuckin' candy bar! You either helpin', or you hurtin'. And if you not committed to helpin', then you need to take your ass the fuck home."

(Africa side note #1: Mike ultimately trained into the best shape of his life, and thank God, because as great a writer as he is, as a videographer, he failed bad: One time on safari we were chased by an elephant, and Mike was so terrified he couldn't pick the camera up, and all we got was the audio . . . of Mike screaming, and Charlie Mack saying "That's a motherfuckin' elephant!" eleven times in a row.)

Darrell and JL were perfectly in sync. JL knew the magnitude of this endeavor. He had been fighting for that kind of order for years. Charlie's father had been a boxer; Charlie had been around boxing gyms his whole life—he understood the idea of supporting the champ to secure our collective win (Charlie and Dave even started calling me "champ"). Omarr never trusted anybody anyway, so he loved that Darrell was defending the space.

This fight-camp, support-the-champ mentality became the new law of our group. *Everybody* had to run five at five; *everybody* had to work out in the gym; *everybody* had to eat right; *everybody* had to read and study and offer new ideas. *Everybody* had to live a disciplined life, to reach for the best version of themselves, otherwise they had to go the fuck home. The unified mission of telling Muhammad Ali's story established a new fundamental way of being that would extend within our group far beyond the completion of *Ali*.

The infrastructure in Mozambique was not equipped at the time to sustain a production the size of *Ali*. We literally had to rebuild and refurbish hotels and residences to accommodate cast and crew. Most of that crew and assets had to be brought in from neighboring South Africa. This created a subtle tension: a mostly white South African production contingent, working for a mostly African American cast and crew, backed by a 100 percent Black Mozambican support staff. The racial and nationalistic frictions were simmering from day one.

But there was an immediate camaraderie between the African American cast members and the Mozambiquans. Jamie Foxx damn near became a local—he went out every night; Jeffrey Wright spent every free moment with artists, poets, and musicians—he was always bringing somebody to the set who had blown his mind. (Africa side note #2: My barber, Pierce, ended up falling in love and getting married to a beautiful Mozambiquan girl named Iva. They have two gorgeous children, Madiu and Gaelle.)

We all took a liking to a young production assistant named Jorge Maciel. He was in his early twenties and had one of those personalities that you never forget. Everybody liked him, which made him the de facto leader of the Mozambiquan PAs. (Africa side note #3: Jorge told us he wanted to move to the United States. We told him, "Sure, Jorge, if you get there, we got you." Six months after *Ali* wrapped, Jorge appeared in Los Angeles; he moved in with Pierce, and I financed a cleaning company that he owned and operated for five years, until he felt he had gathered sufficient business knowledge to return and build in his native Mozambique. We finance the trucking company that he owns and operates to this day.)

The experience of Africa was spiritual, transformative, and deeply emotional for all of us.

One day, Jorge came to Charlie Mack and informed him that one of the white South African crew members had assaulted a young Mozambiquan PA. The South African crew member was responsible for cleaning and maintaining the bathrooms on set; apparently, the Mozambiquan boy had allegedly left urine drops on the toilet seat. The crew member chased him down, grabbed him by the scruff of his neck, took him back to the bathroom, and allegedly wiped the toilet seat with his face.

Charlie comes to my trailer in a rage.

"Yo, come with me right now, motherfuckas is trippin'."

I didn't know which motherfuckas and what kind of trippin', but I've known Charlie long enough to know it wasn't good. News of the incident was building on set, and a crowd was forming around the bathrooms. By the time we reach the scene there are ten of us. To the left are fifteen Mozambiquan PAs, and to the right, thirty white South African crew members. Charlie Mack walks right into the middle.

"Who did it?" he says.

The Mozambiquans point to the accused crew member. We all turn and face him.

"Yo, you put somebody's head in the toilet?" Charlie says, towering over the guy.

"This doesn't have anything to do with you," the man says.

"Oh, it got *everything* to do with me. I want *my* head in the toilet," Charlie said, now invading the man's personal space.

Feeling uncomfortable with the proximity, the man takes two steps backward, which prompts Charlie to take three steps forward. Now we are fully squared off with the South African crew members, each of us picking who we're going to stretch if it kicks off.

"What I gotta do to get *my* head in the toilet?"

Other crew members attempt to deescalate the situation.

"Let's all just turn it down a little bit . . ." Which only prompts Charlie to turn it up.

"I WANT MY HEAD IN THE TOILET! WHAT DO I HAVE TO DO TO GET MY HEAD IN THE TOILET? YOUR MOTHER'S A MOTHERFUCKING BITCH! WILL THAT DO IT?" Charlie says, screaming directly into the face of the accused.

"YOUR MOTHER'S A HO-ASS FUCKING BITCH! WILL THAT GET MY HEAD IN THE TOILET? YOU LIKE PUTTING MUTHAFUCKAS HEADS IN THE TOILET! PUT *MY* HEAD IN THE TOILET! JUST TELL ME WHAT I GOTTA DO! IF I KNOCK YOUR FUCKING FRONT TEETH OUT, WILL *THAT* GET MY HEAD IN THE TOILET?"

Just then, Michael Mann walks up. He had heard of the incident brewing. He was probably the only person in all of Mozambique (except probably Nelson Mandela) who could have gotten water on this fire. Michael pointed to me and then to the head of the South African crew.

"You, and you, in my office, please. Everybody else, go back to work."

That guy needs to go home. Right now," I said.

"It doesn't work like that," the appointed crew spokesperson said. "And, with all due respect, this doesn't have anything to do with you. We will handle it internally."

"You can handle it wherever you wanna handle it," I said, "but you gonna handle it with your racist friend gone. He's fired. He cannot be here."

"I agree with that," Michael said. "That kind of behavior will not be tolerated on my set."

"You arrogant Americans and your foolish racism," he said. "Every confrontation doesn't fit into your childish conception of race."

"So, wait a minute," I said, "let me understand: You're saying that he would have done the same thing had it been a *white* crew member?"

"I'm saying that you couldn't possibly comprehend the complexity of what's going on here."

"OK," I said, "well how about this: That motherfucka's fired just for being a dickhead."

"Well," the man said, "if *he* goes, we *all* go."

The "all" he was speaking of was about one hundred members of our South African crew. If they were to leave, that would shut our film down—tens of millions of dollars down the drain. This was a potentially catastrophic threat. My heart pounded; my mind raced; I had promised Muhammad Ali that I would bring his story to the world. If I let the crew quit, the project could be doomed.

And then it hit me like a left hook from heaven: This is Ali. This moment is the whole point. Muhammad Ali gave up *everything* for this very purpose. Fuck this movie. Ali would never want his film to come to the screen on the back of a seventeen-year-old boy's head in a toilet.

I was crystal clear.

"Then all of you motherfuckers can go the fuck home," I said. "I will spend every dime of my fee to fly a crew from the US. But what we're not gonna have is people's heads getting shoved into toilets on Muhammad Ali's movie. Go. Home."

With that, I left Michael's office.

Michael was 100 percent behind me. Ultimately, only about 20 percent of the crew left. Michael and I ended up splitting the overages. It was a few million dollars between us, but it felt like a no-brainer. I was coming into an understanding of the power of purpose.

Purpose and desire can seem similar, but they are very different, sometimes even opposing forces.

Desire is personal, narrow, and pointed, and tends toward self-preservation, self-gratification, and short-term gains and pleasures. Purpose is wider, broader, a longer-term vision encompassing the benefit of others—something outside of yourself you're willing to fight for. There have been many times in my life where I was acting from a place of desire but I'd fully convinced myself that it was purpose.

Desire is what you want; purpose is the flowering of what you are. Desire tends to weaken over time, whereas purpose strengthens the more you lean into it. Desire can be depleting because it's insatiable; purpose is empowering—it's a stronger engine. Purpose has a way of contextualizing life's unavoidable sufferings and making them meaningful and worthwhile. As Viktor Frankl wrote, "In some ways suffering ceases to be suffering at the moment it finds a meaning, such as the meaning of a sacrifice."

A noble aim engenders positive feelings. When we pursue what we believe to be a profound and valuable goal, it stirs the best parts of ourselves and others.

I am not a man who is prone to regrets. But every year for the rest of his life, Nelson Mandela sent me a message urging me to come spend some time with him. *I am an old man, don't delay.*

But some deep part of me felt unworthy; the *world* needs Nelson Mandela—who was I to take up one more second of that man's time? I'd seen Madiba many times over the years—a charity event here, an awards presentation there, only five and ten minutes at a time.

On December 5, 2013, I was on a promotional tour in Sydney, Australia. I was watching the TV when the current South African president Jacob Zuma appeared on the screen.

"Fellow South Africans," Zuma said, "our beloved Nelson Rolihlahla Mandela, the founding president of our democratic nation, has departed."

Nelson Mandela died in Johannesburg, South Africa, just before 9:00 p.m. local time. He had been surrounded by his family and closest friends; he was ninety-five years old.

Madiba was gone. This was one of the greatest moments of regret in my entire life.

How could I not have taken him up on his offer? Over the years, I've done deep soul-searching around that question. He held me in the purest affection and highest regard. It was scary to me. He saw something in me that I hadn't yet seen in myself. I think subconsciously I didn't want to spend extended time with him for fear that I wouldn't live up to his impression of me. Maybe I thought he'd ask me to do something or change something about my life that I'd be unable or unwilling to change.

Madiba thought I was special—I didn't want to prove him wrong.

He has since appeared to me multiple times in dreams, always wearing that same knowing smile—his energy seems to communicate,

I'm still here whenever you are ready.

SEVENTEEN

PERFECTION

YEAR	MOVIE	OPENED	DOMESTIC (USD)	GLOBAL (USD)
2002	Men in Black II	#1	190,418,803	441,767,803
2003	Bad Boys II	#1	138,540,870	273,271,982
2004	I, Robot	#1	144,801,023	348,629,585
2004	Shark Tale	#1	161,412,000	371,741,123
2005	Hitch	#1	177,784,257	366,784,257
2006	The Pursuit of Happyness	#1	162,586,036	307,311,093
2007	I Am Legend	#1	256,393,010	585,532,684
2008	Hancock	#1	227,946,274	624,234,272

was gonna put the totals, but I thought it might be fun for y'all to add it up with the kids.) What you're looking at is arguably the greatest individual hot streak in the history of Hollywood. (Note: My editor forced me, against my will, to add "arguably.")

I was running my life like a fight camp. Darrell became not only my trainer but my mentor and my protector. Ali had been my first

Academy Award nomination—and validation of the fight-camp way of life.

(Smith family trivia: The *Ali* nomination would be yet another award ceremony that I would miss. Willow was one year old and was at home with Gammy and had to be rushed to the hospital with a 103-degree fever. [She had an ear infection.] Jada and I sprinted from the Oscars six minutes before the announcement of Best Actor. As we drove away, I saw Denzel win my award on the jumbotron.)

For the next ten years, Darrell never left my side. He pushed me, motivated me, and defended my psychological space for the whole of my cinematic heyday. And he would check *anybody*.

During this run, my team was on fire. Nobody moved how we moved. People in Hollywood were trying to figure out how we managed to be so productive and so successful so consistently.

My core group—Harry, JL, Charlie, Omarr, Darrell; my chief of staff Jana Babatunde-Bey; my nephews Kyle and Dion; my brother-in-law Caleeb Pinkett; family manager Miguel Melendez; my executive assistant Danielle Demmerella—everybody embraced the philosophy of the fight camp. We were building our lives, we were striving for perfection, we demanded excellence from each other and everybody around us, and like the Junior Black Mafia, you could either get down, or lay down. From corporate relationships to extended family and friends— Mia Pitts (property manager), Fawn Boardley (creative director), Judy Murdock (makeup artist), Pierce Austin (hair stylist), Robert Mata (wardrobe)—and all the way to the guys who detailed the cars, everyone had to strive and climb or they couldn't be here.

I am a dreamer, and a builder. I picture grand visions, and then I build the systems to make them real in the world. That is my love language. I want to help the people I love build extraordinary lives for themselves. But it demands that they be willing to grind and sacrifice and most importantly, they have to trust me. And if they don't, it registers as a complete rejection of my love.

The team started referring to themselves as "the Lifers." They were ride-or-die. It's impossible to build something that is of a higher quality than the quality of the people around you.

There's a strange and perturbing success paradox. When you have *nothing*, you suffer the fear and pain of grinding to achieve your goals. But when you have *everything*, you suffer the brutal recurring nightmare of losing it all.

I had the wife; I had the family; I had the property with the name. I was the biggest movie star in the world, but I started to notice the "subtle sickness," a sort of sneaky poverty mentality. I was more anxious and fearful than ever. It all seemed so fragile—one injury, one scandal, or one flop movie away from having to move back to Philly. *What if the financial crash of 1929 happened again?* There's only one fear worse than the fear of not attaining the object of your desire: and that's the fear of losing it.

And opening weekends are the worst of all—pure hell. It's like a presidential election night, everybody scrambling around, trying to cross-reference the 6:00 p.m. numbers out of Miami with the 7:45 numbers out of Pittsburgh. The East Coast numbers come in first—then you hold your breath for Chicago, then Houston, and no matter how good the polls looked, or how confident you are, deep down inside you know anything can happen: a snowstorm in the Midwest on a Thursday night shuts down hundreds of theaters, killing 12 percent of your opening-weekend box office. And depending on the genre, Siskel and Ebert trash your movie? Another 6 percent gone.

The axiom used to be *opening weekend is about the movie star, final gross is about the movie.* So, while there are plenty of other factors involved, and many people are going to get fired if the movie doesn't open, the face on the poster takes the biggest hit. It doesn't matter how big your previous movie was, if this one doesn't open bigger, that means you're over; that means moving trucks outside Her Lake, and all the incoming boxes are labeled "Robert Downey Jr."

When I was about nine years old, Daddio took me on a job with him into the basement of Forty-Eighth and Brown Shop 'n Bag supermarket. I'm sure most of you have never been into the basement of a supermarket. I'm not sure I can quite communicate what it's like down there, but let me give it a shot: imagine an old, creaky wooden staircase, one or two steps are always missing. Daddio points them out, but to my young mind, these bottomless gaps are not just a tripping hazard, they are gateways to hell.

The stairs lead down to a very poorly lit dungeon where out-of-date food goes to die. I'm in charge of the flashlight—we need it because the string of single light bulbs is erratic and flickering ominously. This is the stuff that horror movies are made of, and both Daddio and I are Black, so one of us is definitely not coming out alive. Our shoes squeak and squelch as every step sticks to the gunk-caked floor. Decades of broken bottles of ketchup, leaking canned goods, rotted bags of long-since-thawed peas: a repository for the unsalable.

These cellars are generally poorly ventilated and oppressively hot. The smell gets into your clothes and your hair . . . but Daddio likes it. To him that's the aroma of hard work. *That's how you fucking smell when you are doing what has to be done to feed your family.*

Two lines of compressors—the engines that power the refrigerator and freezer cases upstairs—run down either side of this basement abyss. I point the flashlight to the barely visible dust-covered numbers above the compressors.

"There it is, number 19," Daddio says.

There are d-CON trays everywhere. D-Con is a powerful rat poison— rodents eat it, and it essentially burns away the interior of their stomachs and intestinal tracts, leaving a pretty disgusting disemboweled carcass. And directly under compressor #19 was the top half of a rat that had clearly overindulged on d-CON. Without a single moment of hesitation, Daddio bent down, grabbed the dead rat with his bare hand, and tossed it aside. Two slaps of his hand on the side of his jeans—presumably to fully disinfect it—then he lay down, placing his head into the exact spot where the half-a-rat had spent the last month of its life. Choking my lunch back down, I distinctly remember understanding that this act was for *me*, for my brother and sisters, for my family. But I also distinctly remember thinking that if the roles were reversed, my kids would not have eaten that night.

I believe that the stress and uncertainty of Daddio's lifelong financial struggle was a major part of what kept him from being able to emotionally sustain a family. After you've just discarded a dead rat with your bare hand and laid your head down in the same space, you're not trying to hear shit from nobody about how hard their day was.

Witnessing my parents' struggles branded me with the impression that financial stability was an *imperative* for love and family to have any chance whatsoever to thrive.

I was on a tear—the biggest winning streak in Hollywood history. I was working seventy to eighty hours a week; holidays, weekends, even "vacations" became a time to advance. I noticed that most people came back from Christmas vacation heavier and out of shape. So, the holidays, for *me*, became an opportunity to extend my lead.

I made it a point to come back every New Year in better shape than I left the last. I would work out and sometimes even abstain from Christmas dinner as act of personal discipline. Darrell loved and praised my austerity. "If you not eatin', then I'm not eatin'," he would say. I would spend the days studying and writing, reading a book, or rewriting a script, touching in and out of whatever holiday festivities others were enjoying.

I decided to throw lavish Christmas and New Year's parties—it was a win-win-win. Jada and the kids would have all of their friends and cousins and family in town for a week of mountain fun. I would lure my business associates to beautiful ski destinations that I paid for. That meant they had an all-expenses paid trip for themselves and their families. And I got to have my whole team in a remote location—a captive audience—for daily strategy meetings that helped me get a jump on the year and on my competition.

I was killing it, I was winning at everything, and winning, to me, meant everything else in my life should be perfect and everyone around me should be happy.

But it wasn't, and they weren't.

Throughout our relationship, mornings had been Jada and my bonding, building, and connecting time. We would wake up before sunrise and talk for hours. We would share the dreams we'd had during the night, revelations, new ideas; we'd discuss the kids and any issues in our family.

But these days, I could tell something was shifting. Jada was having almost daily crying spells. Now, in our mornings, she would wake up sobbing. During one stretch, she cried for forty-five days straight.

So, Will, to what do you attribute your meteoric success?"

"Well, I consider myself to be fairly average in talent. Where I believe I excel is in my unflinching, unyielding discipline and work ethic. While the other guy is eating, I'm working. While the other guy is sleeping, I'm working. While the other guy is making love . . . well . . . I'm making love, too, but I'm working really hard at it."

Reporters used to love that response, and while I was "joking," the reality of the math was very simple to me: If I could wake up and start an hour earlier than everyone else, *and* stay an hour later than everyone else, *and* work through my lunch break, I would be gaining fifteen extra hours every week on the competition. That works out to 780 more productive hours in a year than the next guy—that's the equivalent of one month. If you give me a one-month start on anybody, they'll *never* catch me. And if they need their weekends and vacations, so they can get their beauty rest and recover and maintain their little punk-ass "work-life balance," then they will always be looking at my taillights.

It was Christmas Eve.

We had rented a house in Aspen, Colorado. The two weeks either side of Christmas were Jada's entire reason for enduring the rest of the year. She had two nonnegotiable demands: the whole family had to be there for the whole two weeks, and it must be spent where there was snow. We would move around year to year, depending on the probability of frozen precipitation. There was no holiday, no celebration, no gathering or event that got anywhere near the emotional value Jada placed on family time at Christmas. Her Christmases as a child had been "less than festive," to say the least. And she was going to make up for it with her own family. (Note: Sheree has spent every Christmas with us for almost two decades. Quincy was right.)

Everyone had to wear the Christmas clothes that Jada picked out. One-piece pajamas with footies; ugly sweaters; reindeer ears; special one-horse-open-sleigh rides; singing Christmas carols. All mandatory. Black Santa Claus lamps in every bedroom, motion-activated Rudolphs scaring the shit out of you when you just want a Christmas cookie in the middle of the night; and a forty-foot Christmas tree wedged in the corner of our living room looking like Shaq in a Prius.

During the year, Jada was Peaches from *A Low Down Dirty Shame*— a ghetto superstar—but at the first jingle of sleigh bells, she turned into a Midwest, middle-aged white lady.

This year, Jada decided that we were going to enjoy a family game of Monopoly. Just for a little context, I am a *master* Monopoly player.

This is not a joke; I'm not saying it to be facetious; this is not hyperbole. I have studied, I have worked with professional instructors—I fully intended to play international Monopoly tournaments. When the dice hit, I don't have to count squares; I know that States is six squares to New York—I just pick the piece up and move it. I also know that if you land on Go when you have a lot of property, you don't want to roll a 7 because you'll hit Chance, and you always know the Property Assessment card is coming; and you hate that 9 from Kentucky because it throws you back to jail and you have to walk the gauntlet again without collecting your $200.

We all sat down, and the game began. I found myself in the unenviable Monopoly position of being stuck with Boardwalk and Park Place. Amateurs think that Boardwalk and Park Place are prime real estate; what they don't realize is that they are actually priced out of the range of manageability. The property values increase as you move around the board from Go—Boardwalk and Park Place are the most expensive to buy, and the most expensive to build. And, because there's only two of them, you lose a 40 percent probability of getting hit as other players move around the board. You invest all of this money, they take longer to build—so you're hitting other players' properties before yours are set up to be hit—and then people skate past them for the whole of the game. In a nutshell, Boardwalk and Park Place are sucker properties. They force you into a Hail Mary toward the end of the game, praying for a big hit.

In this lamentable Monopoly purgatory is where I found myself this night.

Willow was seven—she established the first monopoly: Illinois, the red properties. I have Virginia and States (the purples), Boardwalk and Park Place, and three of the railroads. But I'm broke. Jaden is leery of my Monopoly skill set, so he's squeamish about doing deals with me. He's nine, and he's refusing every angle and offer I present him with to get St. Charles from him and complete my purple monopoly. Jada has the Pacific line—that's the greens—but she doesn't have any cash to

build, either, so she's no threat. Trey has Baltic and Mediterranean—
that's the plum color right next to Go—and the full Connecticut line,
the baby blues. He has an entire block; he burned most of his cash to get
it, but he's the guerilla on the board. (Note: Having an entire block or
corner is the holy grail of Monopoly—you get hit every single time
around the board and by every player.)

As the houses and hotels begin to come up on the board, the frailty
of my Boardwalk and Park Place position is being exposed. The com-
petitive noose is tightening around my neck; the Hail Mary is now or
never.

Jada lands on Pacific.

"YES!" I scream, clapping my hands, causing the motion-activated
Rudolph to slowly turn and see what the noise was. Pacific is *Jada's*
property, so no one can understand why that was such an exciting mo-
ment for me. To the untrained eye, she just landed on her own property.
But they are novices, and I am a master. I think I may have also star-
tled Jada with my elation.

"Why was that so exciting to you?" she said.

"Well, you just landed on Pacific!" I said joyfully. I was excited to
explain my logic and usher them into my elevated sphere of Monopoly
understanding.

"Pacific is six spaces from Park Place, and eight from Boardwalk.
Other than 7, 6 and 8 are statistically the most common numbers rolled
on a pair of dice. 6 has six potential possibilities: five–one, four–two,
three–three, three–three, two–four, and one–five. As does 8: six–two,
five–three, four–four, four–four, three–five, and two–six. When you
pick those dice up next time, there's a 13.89 percent probability that
you'll throw a 6—same percentage for 8, which comes out to nearly
30 percent probability that when you throw those dice, you're going to
get a 6 or an 8! And when you do, I'm going to have three houses on
each, and you, young lady, are toast—you can't afford the hit."

I busily set to mortgaging all of my other properties—$100 each for
the railroads, $70 for States, $80 for Virginia—just enough to go from

two houses to three on Boardwalk and Park Place, which in Monopoly is the exponential increase: When you go from two to three, you maximize the return on investment.

"Are you sure you wanna do that?" Jada asks calmly.

"Hell yeah!" I say, my eyes widening with anticipation. I hand Jaden—who is the banker—the $400 necessary to complete my Hail Mary transaction. "You are *definitely* rolling a 6 or an 8!"

Jada remains steady, not breaking her gaze upon me.

"So, you are *sure* that you want to put your *wife* out of the *family* Monopoly game with your *children* on *Christmas Eve*?"

I finally turn and catch eyes with her. I was *totally* certain I wanted to do that *before* she put the emphasis on those key words—*wife, family, children,* and *Christmas Eve*—but now, I was down to *mostly* certain.

"If you can't stand the Monopoly heat, you gotta stay out the Monopoly kitchen, Jada," I said jokingly.

Jada nods her head, slowly palming the dice, shakes them way too many times, clearly trying to give me a chance to change my mind. But I am dug in.

She drops the dice into the center of the board. The mystical 13.89 percent probability becomes a 100 percent stone-cold actuality.

Four—two.

Jada turns her property into the banker (Jaden), kisses Willow, touches Trey's hair, and heads off to bed.

Yes, dear reader, it's obvious *today*. But I was functioning at the time on a very different operating system. My mind-set was: *You fight how you train.* I felt like Jada and my family needed me to think like that. They needed me to cultivate and maintain a winner's mind. They needed me to never de-train my warrior instincts. I am a Black man in Hollywood—in order to sustain my position, I can't get caught slipping, not even once.

I had to be perfect at all times.

It took me years to realize that Jada wasn't actually playing Monopoly. She was bonding and connecting and enjoying family time. Apparently,

I was the only person who was actually *playing* Monopoly. I have since upgraded my software and developed a new axiom: *Never get caught playing Monopoly.*

Daddio taught me how to play chess when I was seven years old. In the summers, we would play almost every night. He would set the board up on the back porch and go back and forth between the game and the grill. He would play our next-door neighbor Mr. John sometimes; he played me no differently. Daddio didn't believe in taking it easy on kids. He thought that giving children false wins did a vile disservice to their growth and development—even to their ability to survive in the world. He smashed me game after game, month after month—checkmate after brutal checkmate—year after year, until I was thirteen years old.

I will never forget the moment. He had taught me the Giuoco Piano opening. I had faithfully played that opening and response for years. But on my own, I started practicing the Ruy Lopez variation, and he was less familiar with that. The game moved calmly from the opening to the middle game; my position was strong. And Daddio knew it. No trips to the grill, no sips of his Chivas Regal. His Tareyton 100 burned untouched in his ashtray.

Total silence. Total attention upon every move.

Daddio's style was unrelenting attack.

"Put the pieces down their throat, ram them down their throat," he'd say, But not tonight. First, he pulled his bishop backward, and then scrambled his knight back to defend his king.

It was my move. And I saw it.

But he didn't.

I was frozen.

I sat over the board, my heart pounding, minutes burning away. I couldn't bring myself to make the fatal move.

"Aw, shit," Daddio says.

He saw it.

Daddio looks directly into my eyes. He knows my hesitancy is not because I don't see it. He knows it's because I'm scared to make it.

"Go ahead, move it," he said.

I picked up my knight, setting it gingerly into its final position. The felt on the bottom of the chess piece like a soft guillotine.

"What's that?" he said.

I couldn't even bring myself to say the final words.

"Uhhmm, check . . . ?" I said.

"You know goddamn well that ain't no check. What is that?"

"Checkmate?"

"Why you puttin' a question on it? Say it!"

"Checkmate."

"Yup, good game."

Daddio shook my hand, grabbed his cigarette and his drink, and went inside.

We never played chess again. For years, I thought it was because he was a sore loser. But as I got to understand him better, I saw that he wanted my final memory of playing chess with my father to be perfect. He wanted my mind to be programmed to winning and to savor victory. His training of me on the chessboard was complete; it was a mythological rite of passage, and he didn't want to tarnish it.

Nothing in our world is mine," Jada said. "I didn't want to live like this. I wanted a small farm and a quiet life."

"I get that," I said, "but we're here. So, how do we fix it? You can do anything, babe, so what do you wanna do?"

Jada had loved metal music all through her teenage years. She has one of the most eclectic ears I've ever known. She'd always dreamed of having a band, but she caught me off guard when she announced she was putting together a heavy *metal* band.

Jada is a brilliant poet and thinker. The depth of her lyrics has always captivated and moved me. I was trying to love and support her, so I was quietly going along with her journey, and then she handed me a book called *Women Who Run with the Wolves* by Clarissa Pinkola Estés. Jada had marked a story titled "*La Loba*" ("The Wolf Woman"):

> *The sole work of* La Loba *is the collecting of bones. She collects and preserves especially that which is in danger of being lost to the world. . . . When she has assembled an entire skeleton, . . . she . . . raises her arms over it, and sings out . . . so deeply that the floor of the desert shakes, and as she sings, the wolf opens its eyes, leaps up, and runs away. . . . The wolf is suddenly transformed into a laughing woman who runs free toward the horizon.*

> *A dismantled skeleton that lies under the sand. It is our work to recover the parts . . . to look for the indestructible life force, the bones. . . . [It is] a miracle story . . . a resurrection story. . . . If we will sing the song, we can call up the psychic remains of the wild soul and sing her into vital shape again.*

> *To breathe soul over the thing that is ailing or in need of restoration by descending into the deepest mood of great love and feeling, then to speak one's soul. . . . This is singing over the bones. We cannot make the mistake of attempting to elicit this great feeling of love from a lover, for this woman's labor of finding and singing the creation hymn is a solitary work, a work carried out in the desert of the psyche.*

The idea that *La Loba* had to sing over the bones to resurrect the dead parts of herself was intensely resonant to me. If you kill one aspect of a woman, you kill the whole woman. *La Loba* gathers the "dismantled skeleton" of the shattered feminine and begins to sing it back to life. Jada had killed parts of herself to sustain our family. And her band, Wicked Wisdom, was how Jada would unleash *La Loba* to resurrect the whole of herself.

But I was not ready for Ozzfest.

I can do that, Daddy."

Jaden used to lay in bed with me when I would read screenplays, deciding which new world I would inhabit next. He loved to *hear* the stories as much as I loved to tell them to him. He'd stare and watch me as my mind danced, trying the characters on for size.

"You can do what, man?" I said.

"I heard you on the phone with the man earlier."

"The man" was Gabriele Muccino, an Italian director who had just been hired to make *The Pursuit of Happyness*. Gabriele didn't speak English—we needed a translator for our initial meeting. The leading directors in Hollywood were being considered for this film, but Gabriele was the top choice. . . .

Todd Black, a major Hollywood producer, had sent JL a *20/20* piece about a guy named Chris Gardner. Chris had gone from homeless, and living with his young son on the streets of San Francisco, to becoming a successful stockbroker. The screenplay was stunning; it was a perfect hero's journey.

We had our choice of the top of the top of directors, but I loved *L'ultimo bacio* by a director named Gabriele Muccino, so I asked JL to set up a meeting. I was pretty sure that he wouldn't ultimately direct the film, but I had long ago learned the power and importance of exploration. General meetings with world-class artists had become standard operating procedure.

The meeting was awful. Gabriele didn't want to use the translator; he was trying to speak English, but he didn't speak English. JL and I didn't even try to speak Italian, because we don't speak Italian. But Gabriele's artistic passion culminated in two game-changing moves: one, he gave us an Italian film, Vittorio De Sica's *Bicycle Thieves*, which won the Academy Award for most outstanding foreign language film in 1950, and through the translator, said, "This is the movie I want to make." And then, he got me: he said, "If you don't choose me to direct this film, please don't choose an American filmmaker, because Americans don't understand the beauty of the American dream."

Gabriele was in.

So what makes you think you can do this, man?" I said to Jaden.

Jaden was six years old at the time, and other than elaborate home movies, he'd never shown any interest in the business.

"The man keeps saying to you that he can't find a little boy to play your son. That's because *I'm* your son, Daddy."

"Well, that's true, man," I said, laughing. "But this would be acting, pretending."

"Pretending to be your son, though, Daddy. Duh! I be your son every day!"

Gabriele Muccino had been struggling to cast the perfect actor to play my son. He had seen nearly five hundred kids. Gabriele is an instinctual, intuitive artist—things have to *feel* right for him. Jada and I decided that we would let Jaden audition.

"Grazie, grazie, grazie!" Gabriele exclaimed. "I wanted Jaden for this role from the first moment I met him, but the studio forbade me from asking you."

"What? Why?"

"The studio felt like it was a death sentence for the film from a marketing standpoint. They felt that people wouldn't be able to suspend disbelief seeing Jaden and you on camera as father and son."

The studio also felt that it would seem like nepotism, and just put us in the hole from the first announcement. At Gabriele's pleading, they agreed to allow him to put Jaden and me on camera as a chemistry test.

It was such a touchy subject at the studio that Jada and I removed ourselves from the decision-making process. We allowed Gabriele to run with his vision and cast whoever he wanted. Because we were producers, and I was starring, there were conflicts of interest everywhere we looked. So Jada and I agreed that we would not speak on the subject—we would be parents only.

Jaden ultimately was asked to audition an unprecedented nine separate times. The studio simply didn't want the problems that came along with casting him. But audition after audition, in all of his innocent, six-year-old glory, he proved himself the right actor for the role. After his ninth audition, though, the studio requested a tenth.

Jada had had enough. She informed Gabriele and the studio that Jaden was no longer available for the role. At which point, Gabriele— the bleeding, passionate artist that he is—decided that he was emotionally incapable of making the film without Jaden.

The studio relented and offered Jaden the role of Christopher Jr. in *The Pursuit of Happyness.*

For me, this was perfection—on the set, at work, with my son. That was how I wanted to parent: on the battlefield of life, real stakes, real outcomes, real hunting. I could correct errors in real time, and I could teach in real-life scenarios.

This is how I defined parental love.

Ozzfest is a traveling heavy metal festival. Established by Ozzy Osbourne and his wife, Sharon, it began in 1996 and featured all the metals: thrash, industrial, hardcore punk, deathcore, metalcore, posthardcore, alternative, death, gothic, and nu. Sharon had seen Jada's band and some part of her understood. She and Jada became friends, and Sharon put Wicked Wisdom on Ozzfest in summer 2005.

Ozzfest is the least African American event outside of that broom-and-big-ass-hockey-puck thing they do at the Winter Olympics.

"Babe, are you sure you don't wanna do some R and B?" I asked softly, but I meant it hard.

"This is the music I feel," Jada said softly, but she meant it hard. So we packed up our children and headed down the black brick road to the land of Ozz.

I had never seen this side of Jada.

La Loba was raging. Ozzfest is a purist audience, and what began as skepticism and dismissal, with every show was transformed first into silence, and ultimately into respect. Jada's creative energies were being revived. She was coming up with ideas for TV shows and movies she wanted to write and direct; she was filling journals with poetry and artwork. It was breathtaking to see the bones struggling to reanimate. With every spit, curse, and growl, Jada seemed to come alive.

Jada and I had agreed early in our marriage that we would never work at the same time. One of us would always have to be available full-time to the children. *The Pursuit of Happyness* was slated to begin principal photography in fall 2005. Jada's appearance at Ozzfest was so successful that Guns N' Roses asked her to open for them on their upcoming tour. But the tour was set smack-dab, dead center in the middle of *Pursuit*.

At the time, I felt like Jada had options—we had Mom-Mom and Gammy, and I was going to be there every step of the way. Jaden and I would be sharing a trailer—all his scenes were with me.

In retrospect, I can see the truth: Jada was faced with a horrific reality, and there was no version of her leaving her six-year-old son without his mother on his first movie gig.

Jada turned down Guns N' Roses.

The Pursuit of Happyness came out in 2006 and was a critical success and box office smash, and garnered my second Academy Award nomination. If I felt invincible before, now I *really* felt it. I just made a movie about a homeless Black guy who gets a job in the eighties, and *still* crushed every other movie at the box office that season.

I couldn't miss.

The streak continued: *I Am Legend* roared out the first weekend with the largest-ever box office gross for a movie in December. It was a movie that featured me, on-screen alone—with a dog—and it grossed around $600 million.

Then *Hancock,* written by Vince Gilligan of *Breaking Bad* fame, about an alcoholic superhero, came out and grossed another $600 million plus within six months of *I Am Legend.*

I was unstoppable. It was the greatest streak of smash hits of any movie actor in Hollywood history. I became the highest-grossing film actor *ever.* And I still wasn't even forty years old.

The problem was, I'd conflated being successful with being loved and being happy.

These are three separate things.

And since I'd conflated them, I ended up suffering from an even more insidious version of the "subtle sickness," which I can best describe as "more, more, more, more."

If I am more successful, I'll be happier, and people will love me more.

I was trying to fill an internal emotional hole with external, material achievements. Ultimately, this kind of obsession is insatiable. The more you get, the more you want, all the time never quite scratching the itch. You end up with a mind consumed by what it *doesn't* have and what it *didn't* get, and in a spiraling inability to enjoy what it *has.*

I Am Legend had opened to the biggest December opening ever. When JL called to give me the weekend grosses, he was uncharacteristically ecstatic.

"The three-day was $77,211,321 in 3,600 theaters. That's over $21,000 *per* venue. Nobody's ever done that, ever."

I was quiet for a moment and then I recognized a subtle dissatisfaction.

"Why do you think we missed eighty?" I asked.

"What?" JL said.

"I'm sayin', do you think it was the ending? I feel like if we had made the adjustment to the final moment, you know, if we could have made it feel more like *Gladiator* at the end. . . ."

"Are you fuckin' serious right now?" JL said. "It's the biggest opening ever. *Ever.*"

"I get that, J, I'm just asking you a question," I said.

This is the only time that James Lassiter has ever hung up on me. *Ever.*

I am sitting with Wayne Gretzky and Joe Montana. Their sons, Trevor and Nick, respectively, are on the field with Trey. And over the loudspeaker the game announcer shouts, "Montana, deep to Smith . . . touchdown!"

Trey is a wide receiver on the number one high school football team in Southern California, Oaks Christian. And the son of football legend Joe Montana just threw a touchdown pass to my firstborn. If my life were a movie, I would have looked directly into the camera, broken the fourth wall, and said, "Who wrote this bullshit?"

So let me get this straight: You want us to believe that my character grew up bagging ice in West Philly, wins the first Grammy ever given to a rapper; becomes a TV star, then the biggest movie star in the world, breaking box office records every time he releases a damn movie; marries a beautiful actress, artist, performer, and poet; has three spectacular children; and the greatest hockey player in the history of the sport, Wayne Gretzky, just patted him on the back because his son just caught a touchdown pass from the son of the greatest quarterback in the history of *that* sport, Joe Montana?

That's unrealistic; I'm not filming a word of that bullshit; get me Aaron Sorkin on the phone. We gotta rewrite this crap immediately. And somebody see if Robert Downey Jr. is available!

I'm not sure if it's because of my lack of athletic fulfilment in my youth, or the magical energies of the Friday night lights, or the surprising development of Trey's physical abilities and talents, but there was nothing in life that I enjoyed more than watching that kid play football. Trey was being courted by the top college scouts—Wayne and Joe were guiding me through the process. As our children were getting older, it seemed like Jada and I used to play a man-to-man defense, but now we were having to switch to a zone. Every kid had something important happening all the time. Just as Trey was preparing for his senior-year football season, Jaden was approved by the studio to star in *The Karate Kid* with Jackie Chan. The family was ecstatic.

Then we realized: shooting would mean three months in Beijing. Trey's games were in Southern California. We all agreed that this was an opportunity that Jaden couldn't pass up. We as a family would support him. But the previous year, every family member had been at every single one of Trey's games. And the thought of Trey playing without his family in the stands was unacceptable.

During this time, it was becoming clear that the likelihood of Wicked Wisdom returning to the stage was dwindling with every moment of Smith Family Perfection™. But in my mind, there was still a solution for every problem. We would have to grind, we would have to sacrifice, we would all have to suffer a little bit, but I had the vision, and if everybody followed my lead, we would continue to win, and we would all be happy. We were even winning in the stands: I had Jada to my right, and Sheree to my left. We were the picture of the perfect blended family. Nobody could do what we were doing. (Not even us.)

My way of problem-solving was to prioritize. I would decide which problems on the list were most pressing and focus on those—but what I missed was that everybody's list was different.

Jada, Willow, Jaden, and I left for Beijing in June 2009; Trey went back to school that September. All ten of Trey's football games would fall during principal photography of *The Karate Kid*.

And then the grace of God revealed itself in the form of the international date line. Beijing to Los Angeles is a twelve-hour flight. A 10:00 p.m. flight out of Beijing on Friday crossed the date line, landing in Los Angeles at ten Friday morning, just in time to get to the house, get some rest, and make it to Trey's game at six Friday night. A 4:00 p.m. flight on Saturday going the other way arrives at 4:00 a.m. Monday morning, just in time to get back to work. Jaden and I commuted ten straight weeks, Beijing to Los Angeles and back, never missing a single one of Trey's games.

I was loving life. I felt like a master.

Oprah Winfrey asked us to come on her show—me, Jada, Trey, Jaden, and Willow, even Sheree and her husband, Terrell. An entire episode dedicated to the Smith Family Perfection™. I was the biggest movie star in the world. *Karate Kid*, Jaden's first feature with him as the star, was about to be the number one movie in the world. The first season of Jada's new show *Hawthorne* had premiered, with her as the lead role. Willow had just signed to Roc Nation to record her first album. Trey was the star of his high school football team. And to top it all off, here was my ex-wife, talking about how much her and Jada collaborate to raise the kids.

I finally had it—my own version of *Dallas*. The picture was complete, and it was perfect. I had built a family empire—this was beyond anything I'd ever dreamed.

"I feel like J.R. Ewing," I said to Jada jokingly.

She said, "You know J.R. got shot, right?"

EIGHTEEN

MUTINY

Hop up out the bed, turn my swag on
Pay no attention to them haters
Because we whip 'em off . . .

 hip My Hair" was a platinum, global hit record. Michael Jackson and Stevie Wonder were the only artists in history to have a higher-ranking single at a younger age than Willow Smith. The record was released two weeks before her tenth birthday. Little girls around the world were whipping their hair—the iron was hot, and it was time to strike.

Jada and I never pressured the kids into show business. It was true that fame and fortune made Jada uncomfortable—she felt ambivalent about her kids being celebrities. But part of my vision for Her Lake was that it would be a creative campus, an artists' haven. I wanted to shorten the distance between anyone having an idea and being able to create art. I built a music studio; there were video cameras and editing bays; there were sketch pads in every room, painting supplies and pencils everywhere; and eventually, even our living room became the studio for Jada's *Red Table Talk*. The fact is, the kids simply grew up in it, so there was nothing to pressure. I grew up working in Daddio's shop. It struck me as normal that kids do what their parents do. My father sold ice, so I bagged it. Similarly, for Trey, Jaden, and Willow, there was nothing unusual about being on a film set or in a recording studio. It's the family business—it was their normal experience.

So no, I did not push my kids into show business because I was an insane, overbearing father. It was only *after* they decided to be in show business that I became an insane, overbearing father.

In the case of Willow, when she was about eight years old, she got really into singing. This is not unusual for an eight-year-old girl. Eight-year-old girls all over the world love to sing and dream about singing onstage.

The only difference was that most dads would put her in the church choir, or maybe sign her up for a voice lesson or two.

I'm not that kind of dad.

My mind-set at the time was that there is no reason to do *anything* unless you are prepared to take a shot at being the best on earth. My belief was, you should always be aiming at the pinnacle, always striving for the very top of the mountain. Nothing should be done half-heartedly.

Willow landed a thirty-day European tour opening for Justin Bieber. This was a huge moment for our family. The baby was now throwing her hat (hair) into the ring. The frenzy around "Whip My Hair" was madness. Television appearances, magazine covers, red carpets, orange carpets, photo shoots—she was on *Jimmy Fallon*, *Ellen*, blanket coverage across Europe. The entire family flew for Willow's sold-out opening night at the Birmingham National Indoor Arena in the British Midlands. She absolutely smashed.

Next up was Dublin, Ireland. Same deal. Same set. Once again, she slayed. Another sold-out arena, a synchronized tsunami of ginger tresses—never-before and never-since has that much hair been whipped in the Republic of Ireland.

The tour continued—night after night I watched her grow. Her voice was getting stronger, her stage presence coming alive, she started to learn how to work a crowd, she was able to pop in and out of dance sequences.

I felt like a genius.

Jada had flown back to LA, so I was on daddy duty. On the last night of the tour, Willow comes offstage, in full post-performance bliss, and jumps into my arms.

"Baby, you *ripped*!" I said.

"Thank you, Daddy!" she squealed.

"Was it fun?"

"Yes, Daddy, I saw all the little girls in the front and all the way to the top! They knew all the words!"

"Yes, they did, that's crazy, right?" I said, remembering the feeling in Detroit when the crowd sang "Parents" back to me. "Alright! We're going to go home for a couple of days, then we're gonna start the album. And Justin's team loves what you're doing so much that they want you to do the same thing . . . *in Australia*!"

"I'm finished, Daddy!" she gushed, with so much glee that I almost missed what she'd said.

"What you say, Bean?"

"I said I'm *finished*, Daddy—I'm ready to go home."

"Well, yeah, you're finished for a few days, sweetie, but really you just started. You have a few more weeks to go," I said in the standard parental not-taking-my-kid-seriously tone.

"No, no, Daddy, I'm finished."

"Yes, for this part, Bean, you made a promise to Mr. Jay-Z that you would do the whole album and more videos. . . ."

"No, Daddy, *you* made a promise to Mr. Jay-Z . . . ," she said, smiling that she scored a point off her daddy.

"Honey, *we* promised *together*. And when you start something, you have to finish it."

"It doesn't matter to you that I'm done, Daddy?" Willow said.

"Well, of course it *matters*, baby, but you *can't* be done."

"Why, Daddy? I had fun, and I'm finished."

"I get that, but you can't be finished until you complete what you promised to do."

This was such a foreign idea to her. She stared at me with no malice, no anger—just a delicate confusion. And then she relented.

"OK, Daddy."

We flew home.

The Smith Family European Conquest had been a mega success. I set out busily organizing the next phase: world domination. One morning at Her Lake, I had just finished a call with Jay-Z when Willow came skipping into the kitchen for breakfast.

"Good morning, Daddy," Willow said joyfully, as she bounced to the refrigerator.

My jaw nearly dislocated, dislodged, and shattered on the kitchen floor: My world-dominating, hair-whipping, future global superstar was *totally bald*. During the night, Willow had shaved her entire head. My mind raced and scrambled—how was she going to whip her hair if she didn't have any? Who the hell wants to pay to watch some kid whip their head back and forth?

But before I could respond, I felt something slowly turning, shifting, until it clicked into place: In a moment of divine connection and revelation, she had reached me. I wasn't angry; I was *shaken*, the feeling you would have if you were absentmindedly looking at your cell phone and you stepped off the sidewalk into the path of an oncoming bus and at the last second someone snatched you back to safety.

Willow was my little catcher in the rye. I leaned down, peered deeply into her eyes, and said, "I got it. I am so sorry. I see you."

As strange as this may sound, in that moment I discovered *feelings*.

It doesn't matter to you that I'm done, Daddy?

I know it sounds crazy, but Willow's question put a Liberty Bell–sized crack in my worldview. It was just an innocent question from a daughter to her father, but somehow, I knew that it was more than that: What she was really asking me was, "Don't you care how I *feel*?" It was the deepest, existential human question. It may be the most important question that we as humans ever ask each other. *Does it matter to you how I feel?*

Even though she was only ten years old, and my choice to abandon the conquest had sufficiently answered her question in the affirmative, I asked myself *What is my* honest *answer?* I took a deep, hard, self-reflective look at my belief systems around feelings. And my truth startled me.

I would have never said this out loud, but a truthful answer to "Does it matter to you how I feel?" would have sounded something like this:

Not exactly, sweetheart—feelings are *seventh* on my list.

1. Food
2. Shelter
3. Security
4. Intelligence
5. Strength
6. Productivity

First and foremost, I care that you eat . . . every day. Second, I care that you have somewhere to live; third, I care that you're safe. Fourth, I care that you are intelligent, and your mind is trained to solve the problems of your life. Fifth, I care that you're strong, because the world is hard. And sixth, I care that you're productive—I want you to contribute to the human family. And I believe that if you have all of those things, they will add up to you feeling great.

I believe that if I take care of one through six, number seven will take care of itself.

This is not something I just apply to you: I don't even care how *I* feel. Many of my feelings have been enemies to my dreams and to our prosperity. I don't *feel* like running five miles at 5:00 a.m.; I don't *feel* like working eighty hours a week; I don't *feel* like getting booed onstage, and feces thrown, and M-80s hurled at my head. And I know that if I worry about how I feel, I won't be able to feed, clothe, house, and protect my family. When I determine a right action for our survival and prosperity, it doesn't matter to me that I don't feel like doing it. If it's obviously an action of supreme benefit, then to hell with my feelings. When people are too worried about how they feel, they'll never feel how they want to feel.

Note: To any of my horrified readers, I don't care how you feel.

Just kidding, folks. That was a joke.

Here's the thing: I watched my father's negative emotions seize control of his ample intellect and cause him over and over again to destroy beautiful parts of our family. I also sat in church one time when Miss Mamie caught the Holy Ghost, and she was so overwhelmed by "positive emotion" that she leaped from the pew in joyful ecstasy and swung her left hand so wildly that she damn near broke my nose. (And didn't even notice.)

While my feelings about feelings have evolved and elevated, I still struggle to this day when extreme emotion arises in myself or others. Feelings are extremely valuable tools for maneuvering and manifesting in the world. They are like fire—they can be used to cook and heat and cleanse. But when extreme emotions go unchecked, my experience has been that they will incinerate your dreams.

Unfortunately, at the time, I was neither wise enough nor articulate enough to prevent the many gruesome wildfires that were about to consume my life.

Willow's act of protest kicked off a period in our family that I refer to as "the Mutiny." The pressure had been building for years; I was trying to head it off; but it was all about to unravel.

We were sitting in the kitchen. Me, Jada, Willow. Willow was eating dulce de leche ice cream, her left hand playing with my beard, a spoonful of Häagen-Dazs in her right.

She said it so sweetly, but sometimes from the mouths of babes . . .

"Mommy?

"Yes, sweetie?"

"It's so sad," Willow said.

"What is, honey?"

"Daddy has a picture of a family in his mind. And it's not *us*!"

I was at the top of the mountain. I was living beyond everything I had ever dreamed. Every goal had been attained, every obstacle conquered. And then some.

Yet, everybody around me was miserable.

Daddy has a picture of a family in his mind. And it's not us!

Willow looked me in the eye with so much compassion. She genuinely felt bad for me, dulce de leche dripping down her arm. Jada mercifully looked away, pretending she'd seen something of critical importance in the lower freezer.

Willow just kept rubbing my face.

"It's OK, Daddy. You'll be OK."

To this day, dulce de leche ice cream is forbidden in my house.

I started noticing feelings everywhere. I'd be sitting in a business meeting, and someone would say, "It's nothing personal . . . it's just business." And I realized, *Oh, shit, there's no such thing as "just business"—* everything *is personal*. People get furious, excited, frustrated, hopeful, hope*less*, disappointed, fearful, embarrassed, all in the confines of "business" meetings. Everybody is caught up in their feelings, making all their decisions all the time based *only* on how they feel. Even my aversion to extreme feelings . . . *is based on how I feel about feelings*. I felt like Christopher Columbus who had discovered this "new" place where people was already at (sorry about that preposition, Mom-Mom). All of politics, all of religion, all of sports, culture, marketing, eating, shopping, sex—everything is centered on how people feel.

Then the truth hit me like a 90 mph fastball; Nobody gives a shit about anything *except* how they feel. Feeling good is the most important thing to everyone, everywhere, at *all* times. We are choosing our words, actions, and behaviors in order to achieve a feeling that we deem positive. There's nothing more important than feeling how we want to feel. And people determine whether or not you love them by how well they *feel* you honor their feelings.

This has been a precarious conundrum in most of my adult relationships. I have always been less concerned about someone's immediate feelings than I have been about their overall well-being. People in my life have consistently complained about feeling unconsidered by me, and when left unaddressed, this has sometimes festered into their feeling unloved.

I would walk through fire for the people I love. I am fully prepared to die for my family. But no—I haven't always focused on their feelings. I don't trust feelings; feelings come and go and change like the weather. You can't plan anything around them. And just because somebody feels something, doesn't make it true; just because your feelings are extreme, doesn't mean that you're right—in fact, the more extreme your feelings are, the more likely it is that they're skewed.

People care less about facts, truth, probabilities, or intentions than they do about how they *feel* and how well you have displayed that you care about those feelings. So, when we open sentences with "The fact of the matter is," the other person is thinking, *I just talked for ten minutes—I told you what my fact of the matter is*. Or if we say, "Look, here's the reality," the other person is thinking, *Asshole—I just told the reality*. Other classic offenders include "Truth be told . . . ," and "At the end of the day . . . ," and "I get it—but in all likelihood . . . ," and "I get it—but here's the thing . . . ," and "Can I be honest?" Use any of those, and you're dead in the water. People take it as a total negation of what they just said and a complete disregard of their feelings.

Nobody cares what *you* think and what *you* feel. They care what *they* think and what *they* feel. That's why they said it.

There are other inherent questions attached to *Does it matter to you how I feel?* If the answer is yes, then the next unspoken question is *How much?*

And then, *What behavior alterations are you willing to make to show me how much?*

And what parts of your personal agenda are you willing to let go of in order to apply that energy to my agenda?

Are you willing to put your thoughts and feelings aside in order to care for mine?

In essence, people want you to behave differently so they can feel better. How much you're willing to change will prove to them how much you love them.

Trey was twenty years old; Jaden was fourteen; Willow was twelve. I began to experiment with my parenting by reassessing my relationships with my children in terms of my care and concern for their *feelings*.

I was a master provider and protector. I was a world-class teacher. But I began to be able to perceive the subtle, and not-so-subtle, emotional injuries of their childhoods. The one consolation I afforded myself was that at least I saw I was getting better. Trey had gotten the most ignorant version of my parenting; Jaden got Will Dad 2.0, which was a slight upgrade, and even though Willow had had to shave her head, she had stopped me before her point of no return.

At eleven years old, Willow, for all intents and purposes, retired from the entertainment industry. I knew a part of it was the intrinsic pressure of the business, but I also knew a bigger part of it was that she had felt unprotected. She couldn't articulate it, but it was clear that she didn't want any part of anything that took my focus off her heart.

I could feel my family turning away from me, questioning my leadership and even my love. Trey asked me at dinner one night, "Dad, what do you worship?" Sheree had recently rediscovered the church; she'd found comfort and transformation in Christ—it was beautiful to watch, and it was real. And while I was happy that she had kindled a new faith and direction, I deeply resented that she began questioning and judging my choices and my decisions in my life. In the Black community, when someone discovers faith as an adult and begins to point out your transgressions and detail your only path to salvation, we call that "holy-rollin'." And there are very few things more incensing than one of your ex–sin partners pointing out your current sins.

I loved how Trey took to the Bible; he has one of the purest hearts of any human I have ever met. I was excited to discuss Abraham and Isaac and to debate the righteousness of David and what the story of Lazarus really meant. I was wide open to ponder the life of Christ in the spiritual context, and the historical, even the mythological if his mind could handle it. What I was neither prepared nor willing to do was to debate the scriptural inadequacies of my life decisions.

"I worship God," I said.

"Are you sure?"

"So, here's the deal. Your Bible is brand-new, with pages you haven't even looked at yet. Mine is tattered and worn, with no page unturned. So why don't you rough your Bible up a little bit, then we can have this conversation in a few years?"

I had brushed off his question, but I couldn't stop thinking about it. I do interviews for a living; thirty-five years of questions in fiftysome-thing languages. And the number one greatest question that I have ever been asked is "What do you worship?"

And the second greatest question is "Are you sure?"

I decided we needed a family project. We tended to rally around one another when one of us had a significant endeavor. Trey playing football, Willow with her music, Jaden during *Karate Kid*, Jada or myself on a film set—there was something galvanizing when we worked together. *After Earth* became the project that was going to rejuvenate and reconnect us.

I had seen a TV show called *I Shouldn't Be Alive*. It featured different stories about harrowing, life-threatening ordeals and jaw-dropping brushes with death. One of the stories was about a father and son who had become stranded in the wilderness, miles and miles from civilization. The father was injured in an accident, and the teenage son had to travel alone through dangerous terrain to find help and save his dad.

As I watched, I kept imagining myself injured and helpless and Jaden climbing through the wilderness, trying to get to civilization to save me. The scenario stuck in my mind—a coming-of-age story about a young man trying to save his father. The idea morphed into a movie— it would also be about a father learning to trust and depend on his son. It would be a metaphor, a means to healing their relationship.

At the time, I was also experimenting with migrating story through time and setting: Can you take a 1940s Berlin nightclub, with all of the core human themes and conflicts, and set it twelve hundred years in the future and maintain the fundamental human truths? I sent the episode of *I Shouldn't Be Alive* to M. Night Shyamalan. He felt great about the episode and thought there was a movie in it. When Night felt the idea, I took it as providence. Night had vowed to shoot the interiors of his films in only one city: Philadelphia.

Night lived just outside Philly; I had never worked on a film in my hometown. My immediate family and my extended family would be together for three whole months. My foot was on the gas.

I had also just agreed to mentor Jada's brother, Caleeb Pinkett, in the process of script development. He is a world-class history buff, and historians tend to have profound insight into character and story. He was a perfect pupil, and he was my brother-in-law. Family, family, family.

JL hated the idea. JL hated the treatment. JL hated the timing. JL hated everything about it.

"It's just a concept," JL said. "Finish the script. Complete the story. Let's not pull the trigger until we know what we're pulling the trigger *on*."

But I wasn't hearing it. I needed this to save my family. And then there was the secret vow, my hidden agenda: I was going to make sure that Jaden felt loved, protected, and cared for, every step through the process. He was going to know, unequivocally, that his father cares about his feelings.

After Earth was set one millennium in the future, after humankind had rendered the planet uninhabitable. Father and son crash-land in the most dangerous place in the universe: Earth. The interiors of the film had been shot in Philly, and the exteriors would be captured in Moab, Utah, and Costa Rica. Jaden's character, Kitai, would have to make his way through jungles, rivers, plains, canyons, and volcanic streams in order to save his injured father.

I was determined to create a joyful and loving environment for Jaden on set. Costa Rica was hot (slangily and temperature-wise). I had giant, air-conditioned tents set up at every location so Jaden could chill between shots—ping-pong tables, food, music, somewhere he could take a nap.

"What the fuck is this tent shit?" Darrell said, pulling me to the side.

"It's hot, D, I just want him to be comfortable."

"Comfortable? You gon' make this little nigga *soft*. Your character is the top general in the universe. How he supposed to save your ass comin' out of a fuckin' *tent*? Let his ass wait in the sun like everybody else."

Darrell had been my mentor, my coach, and confidant for a decade now. He had prodded and pounded and propelled me into my wildest dreams. He knew how to build winners; he had been there with Sugar Ray versus Marvin Hagler; he knew how to design soldiers. I'm not sure why I didn't just tell him what I was going through and what I was doing; I was probably embarrassed, or maybe I just concluded that he wouldn't understand. But Darrell saw my actions as a form of sabotage. I was breaking all the rules that had defined our successful conquest.

This drove a wedge between us that eventually grew into a chasm and ultimately estrangement. We stopped working together. At the time, I couldn't muster the courage to communicate with him directly. Our decade-long, hyper-successful partnership just ended without even a conversation.

Darrell would later confide, "You broke my heart, and you never even told me why."

In terms of my relationship with Jaden, the filming was perfection. When I would come on set on *The Karate Kid*, Jaden would deflate and lose his energy—it was as if the enemy had arrived. I was the person who was going to push him, to make him do another take, to extend the movie shoot another month in China because I wasn't happy with a scene. But on *After Earth*, I didn't allow production to go one minute beyond his allotted shooting schedule. I was his protector.

One day on set—in what was my highest parenting moment with Jaden—he was shooting an action sequence on one soundstage, and I was producing a shot on another. I wasn't onstage with him, but I had a monitor where I could see everything he was doing. One of the coordinators was asking him to do a move that Jaden was uncomfortable with. He tried a few times to explain that he didn't want to do it, but the man wasn't taking no for an answer. I could see on the monitor that they were in dispute, so I turned on the sound.

"That doesn't seem realistic to me," Jaden said respectfully.

"Well, let's just get a few takes," the coordinator insisted.

And then, the individual greatest words I've ever heard from Jaden's mouth: "Can someone go get my dad, please?"

It makes me teary every time I think about it. I had transformed our relationship; I had purified his perception of me; I was no longer the ogre who was going to push and punish him. I was the person he called for in his time of need. I can still see him standing there, confident. It was as if he knew he had a lion that would protect him—he didn't want to sic it on anybody, but he knew he could if he had to.

When I grew up, I knew I had a lion, but I hated that sometimes he'd bite *me*.

The shooting of *After Earth* was a magical bonding experience for Jaden and me. He was fresh into his teens—the mythological timing was perfect. I had succeeded in illustrating the depth of my care and concern. But in my preoccupation with his well-being, I had diverted my usual hyper-intensive focus away from the storytelling, the screenplay, and the overall sculpting of the film. As a result, our father-and-son honeymoon was short-lived. *After Earth* was an abysmal box office and critical failure. And what was worse was that Jaden took the hit. Fans and the press were absolutely vicious; they said and printed things about Jaden that I refuse to repeat. Jaden had faithfully done everything that I'd instructed him to do, and I had coached him into the worst public mauling he'd ever experienced.

We never discussed it, but I sensed he felt betrayed, misled, and he lost his trust in my leadership. Jaden likes to win, and he doesn't mind a little suffering to secure a victory. (This is also an inherent parenting problem—there is no "one size fits all." They all need different things.)

I've read enough to know that a critical stage of a boy becoming a man is the moment of individuation from his father, that instant when you realize your father is not Superman. He's a flawed human. That moment when you make the scary decision to separate from him and live and die by your own hand.

Just like Daddio on the chessboard, as a father it's what you hope for. But at fifteen years old, when Jaden asked about being an emancipated minor, my heart shattered. He ultimately decided against it, but it sucks when you hurt your kids.

Back then, I made the troubling conclusion that questing with empathy was an oxymoron, and you could either worry about how people feel, or you could win.

But you had to pick *one*.

On the night of Jada's thirty-seventh birthday, I had a vision. I saw her fortieth birthday party—it was huge, it was wild. It would be the Taj Mahal of birthday parties. Something she would never forget: a public display of my love and affection that would fix everything.

I planned it for three years.

I love planning events, orchestrating spectacle and emotion. In my mind, the sum total of a happy life is the quality of your memories, so I'm always looking for the most vivid memory that I can create.

Growing up, Jada had been close to her grandmother who had passed a few years earlier. Secretly, I contacted Jada's aunt Karen, who was the default family archivist. Karen had pictures, videos, and letters from Jada's grandmother, and she had recently discovered microcassettes on which Jada's grandmother had recorded her thoughts during the final weeks of her life. No one in the family had heard the tapes. They would be the centerpiece of my birthday presentation to Jada.

The vision was ablaze. I would do a documentary short film about Jada's life. I hired a production team to research her family's genealogy, tracking her grandmother's lineage all the way back to slavery. Then I hired a director to compile the information and make the film.

But the film, by itself, wouldn't be Taj Mahal enough.

Jada loved Santa Fe, New Mexico, and the art scene there. It would be a surprise three-day birthday weekend. I shut down an entire hotel in the city, invited dozens of our closest friends and family. We'd have gourmet dinners each night under the stars, followed by a surprise event. Friday night would be a private art show; Saturday morning would be a spiritual pilgrimage (a hike to Picacho Peak). I got Jada's favorite painters to come and do custom paintings and family classes. Mary J. Blige loved Jada and agreed to give a surprise performance on Saturday night. And the crown of the weekend would be the unveiling of the documentary about her life.

This was going to be my big triumph, how I would win my way back into my wife's heart.

That first evening was blissful—an intimate candlelit dinner on an outdoor rustic terrace. There were maybe twenty of us. I wanted it to be small enough for Jada but big enough for me. A cellist played as we dined; the mood was calm and loving. Everyone recounted their favorite Jada stories. Everything went perfectly. Friday night set the stage; now Saturday was gonna bring the house down.

Saturday morning the rest of the guests arrived. I had multiple activities planned—golf, hiking, brunch, spa treatments. I wanted everybody to have the freedom to move around as they pleased until the sun set, then it was *my* time to shine.

Dinner was at 6:00 p.m. There were forty of us now.

The dinner went off without a hitch. Everyone remarked on how beautiful the decor was, how delicious the food had been; I even overheard some of the women teasing their husbands.

"When I turn forty, you better plan me a Will Party."

"Well, you blew my fortieth, but if I decide to stay with you, you make sure my fiftieth is like this."

"I wonder if Will and Jada need a wife."

I was the perfect husband. And they didn't even realize I was just getting started. The dinner had been more than anyone could have asked for—an exquisite show of love that Emperor Shah Jahan himself would have approved of. And just before dessert, I gently began tapping my spoon on my wineglass. (I had seen that in movies, but I'd never done it in real life. It works!)

"Well, first I would like to thank you all for coming to celebrate forty years of Jada. If you will now all follow me, we will be having our dessert in the garden."

I ceremoniously led the way. A twenty-yard-long flowered archway had been hidden from view for the entire dinner. The reveal drew oohs and aahs from the crowd. The inside of the archway was lined with photos of Jada, a gallery in celebration of her power, her beauty, and her contribution to all of our lives, perfect lighting illuminating not only the pictures but also the quality and the abundance of my love.

The far end of the archway spilled into an open-air theater. Again, the crowd reacts in awe. Jada seemed to be enjoying herself, but she was quiet—I couldn't get a good read. But it didn't matter because I knew the documentary would be a hands-down grand slam emotional home run.

I escorted Jada to her front-row seat. Gammy hadn't seen or heard any of this footage of her mother, either, so I sat her right next to Jada. The rest of the guests scrambled to get the best possible seats. They could feel something special was about to happen.

I had traced Jada's family lineage back to slavery. I had found pictures and stories of Union Army war heroes, Black Wall Street businesspeople, enslaved people, doctors, artists, all of whom had been her ancestors. I had secretly flown with Jaden to the church in Jamaica where her great-grandparents had met and married.

The comedic high point of the film was a meeting between me; Jaden; Jada's brother, Caleeb; and a descendant of the family who had owned Jada's family during slavery. So, imagine you're a sweet sixty-seven-year-old accountant from a tiny suburb outside Cleveland, Ohio. It's a normal Wednesday in your normal life; you're watching a little

Jeopardy! with your loving wife. You've just complimented her on her pot roast, there's a knock at the door, and there stands Will Smith and the Karate Kid. And the Karate Kid's uncle.

And a camera crew.

The man and his wife were great sports. He just so happened to be his family's historian; he knew the stories and the names and the people we were talking about. He showed us pictures and paraphernalia, and we ultimately got him to formally apologize on camera.

"Happy birthday, Jada," he said. "Sorry for the misunderstanding!"

The audience was roaring. People could not believe the lengths I'd gone to. I heard folks saying, "Will is a damn fool" and "I've never seen anything like this!" and "What the hell is he going to do *next* year?"

I still wasn't finished.

The room goes silent as Jada's beloved grandmother begins to speak. The recordings had been directed to specific family members, many of whom were in the crowd. For the first time since her passing, Jada was hearing the voice of her grandmother speaking directly to her.

I had seen the video a hundred times at this point, so I was only watching Jada. The entire place is in tears—her family, my family, everybody. All except Jada. She sat motionless, refusing to make eye contact with me. The video ends—family and friends erupt in a standing ovation.

Then, the screen rises, revealing Mary J. Blige.

We went back to the hotel room. Jada still hadn't said anything: not a "thank you," not an "I loved it." Nothing. She took a shower. I was sitting there, waiting.

After about thirty minutes, Jada emerged from the bathroom.

"I don't want to do anything tomorrow," she said. "So you can cancel whatever you had planned."

I was dumbfounded.

"OK," I said, stifling my growing disappointment. "It's late, we'll just wait until tomorrow and see how you feel."

The next day, I had scheduled a group painting lesson with one of her favorite painters, Beth Ames Swartz, who I had flown in specifically for this event.

"I'm telling you how I feel. I don't want to do it," Jada said.

"Well, you don't know what it is, so you can't know if you want to do it or not."

"It's *my* birthday—just cancel it!" Jada snapped.

"I'll cancel it *in the morning.* Just go to sleep and see how you feel," I snapped back.

"CANCEL IT NOW!" Jada shrieked.

"What the hell is your *problem*?" I asked.

"That was the most *disgusting* display of ego I have ever seen in my life!" she said.

"Ego? *Ego?* You are the most ungrateful . . . I ain't *never* doing *shit* for you *ever again.*"

"Good. I don't *want* shit from you anyway!"

At this point, we are both screaming at the top of our lungs, which was very uncharacteristic. We had struggled to transcend the verbal killing fields of our childhood homes. This night was unlike any before, or since. The pressure cooker of our perfect picture was cracking.

We were so heated that we forgot that we were sharing the hotel suite with Willow. There was a tiny loft above our bedroom. Willow had been listening the whole time.

Willow slowly emerged, frightened, shaking, crying, both hands clutching her ears.

"Just stop! Stop! Please stop!"

This is the worst I've ever felt as a parent. I immediately calmed down and moved to comfort Willow. She recoiled, refusing to let me touch her.

"Just FIGURE IT OUT! Both of you, figure it out!"

With that, Willow left and went to sleep with Jaden.

Jada and I didn't speak anymore in Santa Fe. We didn't speak on the flight back to Los Angeles. We didn't speak for a few days after we got home.

Our marriage wasn't working. We could no longer pretend. We were both miserable, and clearly something had to change.

"I retire," I said. "I retire from trying to make you happy. You are free. You need to go make *yourself* happy and prove to me that it's even possible. But I quit—you go do you, and I'm-a go do me."

Jada and I were suffering the brutal death of our romantic fantasies, the burning away of the idealistic illusion of the perfect marriage and the perfect family.

Neither of us wanted a divorce; we knew we loved each other, and some aspects of our union were magical. But the *structure* of the life that we had established was strangling both of us. We'd gotten married in our twenties; we were now in our forties. Our unhealed inner children were choking the shit out of each other. And that had to stop. We both had work to do, and we agreed that this phase would not be together. The painful awakening was to the reality that we were two separate people on two independent, individual journeys. We had simply chosen to walk this portion together.

We cried like crazy, hugged, and agreed to let each other go.

Give your hearts, but not into each other's keeping.
For only the hand of Life can contain your hearts.
And stand together yet not too near together:
For the pillars of the temple stand apart.

Jada sent me this quote from Kahlil Gibran and repeated over and over, "What's true will remain."

We had concluded that no one can *make* a person happy. You can make a person smile; you can compose a moment that helps a person to feel good; you can deliver a joke that makes a person laugh; you can create an environment where a person feels safe. We can and *must* be helpful and kind and loving, but whether a person is *happy* or not is utterly out of your control. Every person must wage a solitary internal war for their own contentment.

We agreed that Jada's happiness had to be her responsibility, and my happiness had to be my responsibility. We were going to seek our distinct, innermost personal joys, and then we were going to return and present ourselves to the relationship and to each other already happy—not coming to each other begging with empty cups, demanding the other person fulfill our needs. We felt that this vampiric relational model was unfair, unrealistic, destructive—even abusive. To place the responsibility for your happiness on anybody other than yourself is a recipe for misery.

NINETEEN

RETREAT

had achieved everything I'd ever dreamed: career, family, businesses, health, megastardom, a house with a name. In fact, it was *better* than I had dreamed it. More money, more fame, more property, more success. *And* I did everything the right way. I had reached the mountaintop—then discovered that the clouds had hidden an even higher peak, and then I'd scaled *that* one. Short of raising jokas from the dead, what else do y'all want me to do? I did it as big and as bold and as brightly as anyone had ever done it. Or probably ever *will* do it.

What the fuck is everybody so upset about? How is it even possible that my life is falling apart . . . *again*!

What am I missing?

Is it just me, or does *everybody* who's going through a breakup or difficult times during a relationship call their exes?

I guess it somehow brings relief to talk to somebody who hates you less than they used to. They've processed their disappointment and disgust, refracted it through distance and time, subtracted the 12 to 15 percent they *now* see was their fault (it's actually closer to 50 percent), resulting in the "good times" being bronzed in their memories and a pleasant nostalgic twinge when your number pops up on their caller ID. (And not to forget: They hate their *current* man now, so you don't look so bad.)

Tanya had moved to Trinidad after we broke up. She wanted out of LA—too much noise, too much history, probably even too much Will. But we stayed on good terms, and I had helped her move. I hadn't seen her in a few years—she was married now, with two beautiful little island-toasted babies, Marley and Sekai.

On the phone, her voice sounded different, beach-life kind of different: a sun-sweetened softness, a calmness, a transformation all the way to her name: She now went by Tyana, Ty for short—an outward gesture of maintaining the essence of who she was, while signaling a purging of past poisons.

Ty and her family were back in LA for the Thanksgiving holiday.

"You have to meet Scoty!" Ty said. "I'm tellin' you, y'all would vibe." She had been saying this to me for years.

Her husband, Scoty Sardinha, was an artist from Trinidad and Tobago, and a far cry from the executives, Lakers, and rappers-turned-actors she was used to dealing with. Scoty was different (oh, and she didn't hate him yet—in fact, quite the opposite). I'd been hearing about him, and the beauty of Trinidad, from mutual friends whom Ty had been hosting in her new island haven. Queen Latifah had just come back, and she was raving. Queen has exquisite tastes, and is very particular about her accommodations, so when she says some place is hot, you know it's hot.

"I need to borrow your husband," I said.

I'm not sure why I said it like that—I think I may be a drama queen. I love the shock value and the amusing bullshittery of tattooing a sentence on someone's memory. I think it also breaks the ice for me; if I land it right, it's so shocking that it takes away the shock of the shocking shit I just said.

"Well, damn," Ty said, "how long you need him . . . and more importantly, what you gonna *use* him for?"

We always laughed easy.

"I've never been to Trinidad," I said. "Queen said it's hot."

"Oh, that's perfect,". Ty said excitedly. I could tell she was already seeing the beach parties and art exhibits they were going to take me to.

"We're going next month, for Christmas," she said.

"I want him to take me tomorrow," I said firmly. "I gotta get out of LA."

"Well damn, nigga, tomorrow is Thanksgiving!"

Ty's known me long enough to know when something's going on with me. And she's loved me long enough to want to help.

"I mean, shit, y'all can *eat*—we'll leave *after* dinner," I said reassuringly.

"I can't go tomorrow," Ty said.

"I just wanna go with Scoty."

Beat.

Beat.

Beat.

"Hello?"

Scoty Sardinha had never been on a private plane before. And it had been almost fifteen years since I went anywhere without security.

"Yeah, man," he says in his easy Caribbean accent, dreadlocks tied back behind his head, "No problem, man. Dis is *my island*. I know *plenty* people there. Trust me. Everyt'ing will be cool. Don't study it."

Scoty was definitely *not* the type of guy I was used to hanging out with. He was laid-back and comfortable with just letting things happen around him. I was used to wrestling and bending the universe to my will through sheer discipline and exertion. Scoty seemed pleased to let the universe bend whichever way it wanted, and then sit back, *inhale*, and laugh about it.

"I'll show you a true Trini experience," Scoty said somewhere over the Gulf of Mexico.

It had been decades since I had gone anywhere without the place being prepped and briefed.

"Are you sure it's going to be OK when we land? I'm kinda famous," I said.

"No way, man! I'm telling you: Trinis are cool people. Most laid-back time of your life! They don't really study people. They're not even going to care that you're Will Smith. It's gonna be fine, trust me."

We landed at Piarco International Airport in Trinidad around 2:00 p.m.

Bedlam ensued.

The entire airport staff was on the tarmac. Airport security surrounds me and escorts us to a private room. Scoty is in shock—he's never seen anything like this in his life.

"I don't know why they're gettin' on like this, man. They come like it's never-see-come-see. It's just unruly!"

Scoty takes out his cell phone to contact his friend Jason, who was picking us up.

Scoty didn't know any of the Movie Star Rules™, particularly, rule 4a, section II: *Plan ahead for all departures and arrivals.* It's difficult to move film stars through crowds. Note: You should call your friend who's picking you and the movie star up *before* you land at the airport.

"Jason! Nah, maaan," Scoty yelled into the cell phone. "I told yuh we wuz on the whey! Nooo, Jason! I meant on the plane—I called yuh from the plane. Come nah, man! It was a personal, *private* plane! Where you, man? How far you reach? Jason! Nooooo. That's too loooong. Drive fasta than that!"

The center of Scoty's charm is he doesn't see people as "somebodies and nobodies"—everybody's somebody. I couldn't remember the last time I had carried my own luggage. As prosaic as that might sound, no security, no assistants, in a foreign country, for me was an intimidating, epic adventure.

Forty minutes later, airport security escorted us to Jason's SUV. We got safely into the car and off to Scoty's childhood home.

I wasn't sure what I was seeking, but I had told him, "No hotels, no car services, no formal plans." I wanted to be in *his* life, in *his* house, with *his* friends, doing whatever they would ordinarily do if the Fresh Prince wasn't here.

One of his childhood friends, Che Lovelace, was a forty-three-year-old painter from a prominent Trini arts family. He had an exhibit that night. We dropped our gear at Scoty's mom's house and rolled over to Che's show at the Aquarela Galleries. Scoty was driving.

"You just relax and make yourself at home, man!" Scoty said. "*My* crew won't give you no trouble. Everybody here will be respectful of yuh space."

"I don't know, Scoty," I said, "I've never been here before, but we may want to be prepared for people being excited."

"Noooo, man, not here. Diff'rent scene! These are *my* folks, and they're not on all that. My people not like that."

We arrived at the art show—two steps out of the car, and it was a massive, chaotic mob scene. A couple of hundred people cheering, pushing, grabbing, screaming. It was all love, but as the saying goes, sometimes, love hurts. Excited crowds can be dangerous. Scoty is now in full security mode, trying to get me through the electrified crowd of "his folks."

It was the first time that I had ever had "security" who was wearing flip-flops.

It was also the first time since I had become famous that I didn't have backup. No security, no one to call; I didn't know where I was, where the exits were, where the US embassy was. Nothing. It even felt like I didn't speak the language. It's what a baby must feel like being expelled from the safety of the womb.

I was a forty-two-year-old newborn.

We make our way through the gallery. Safe now in the artist's VIP, I meet Che and his family: his younger sister, Asha "Lulu" Lovelace; Che's son, Roscoe; and Lulu's daughters, Ila and Eva. There is something about the Trini sun that bakes children to perfection—these were the most beautiful kids you can imagine.

Che is a figurative artist—his work mixes realism with abstraction. He typically paints figures from the local Carnival, on board using pastel paints and powered pigments, vividly capturing the vibrancy of Caribbean life. I got lost in the eyes of his depiction of a young woman in a painting he called *Dancehall Queen*. I felt her welcoming me to the island. The exhibition was well attended, and the varied cross-section of Trinidad's melting pot was a canvas in itself.

Eventually, we headed back to the Lovelace family home. A covered porch; music, food, conversation. Nestled in a lush area known as Cascade, the home's green exterior caused the house to almost disappear into the surrounding forestry. The "limin'" (the Trini word for hanging out/partying) happened on the covered wooden veranda, which was open on three sides to the sloping garden and the Cascade Valley. There was a dining table, Morris chairs, and my favorite spot, the standard Trini hammock.

The Lovelace family is a family of artists, poets, intellectuals. Earl Lovelace, the patriarch, is a renowned novelist, journalist, playwright, and poet. Lulu is a professor of cinema at the University of the West Indies; Walt, the older brother, is a cinematographer; the house itself was filled with Che's artwork. The conversation was vibrant and expansive.

"What is that sweet scent?" I asked.

"That's called the ylang-ylang tree," Lulu said. "It's best this time of the year when the breeze comes in off the west."

I had never heard the music of Lulu's playlist—Senegalese singers Ismaël Lô, Baaba Maal, and Youssou N'Dour, all harmonizing with the ylang-ylang tree, transporting me into a sweet wistfulness. Delicious food, Caribbean breezes, toasted-caramel children scattered and scampering.

"Are you spending the night?" Ila asked, in her six-year-old innocence. I laughed that adult laugh that adults laugh when they're not really laughing.

Well, Ila, apart from one night in the Lincoln Bedroom after Bill

Clinton's inauguration, I haven't stayed over at anyone's house since I was twelve years old. I don't even stay at my parents' spots when I go back to Philly. I know you're only six, Ila, but you need to understand that there are significant logistical difficulties to safely transporting a "global icon" around the world. For starters, I travel with a minimum of ten people, meaning we need a minimum of eleven rooms. And if it's at all possible, for security purposes, my entourage will take a whole floor of the finest hotels in the world. Of course, my room is always the one all the way at the end of the hallway; the room with the double doors. . . .

Not to mention, I don't really know any of you; I barely know Scoty. I'm here alone, and I've never been alone. So, the thought of staying over with strangers—even strangers as kind and as beautiful as your family— scares the livings daylights out of me.

So, yes, Ila, yes, I'm spending the night.

"So, where's my room?" I asked her.

My room was nicknamed "the Dungeon." It was a storage area with a garage vibe that had been converted into a guest room. Books, old vinyl records, and pottery were strewn about. The only piece of furniture was a handcrafted, wooden platform bed that I would later find out Scoty had made. A white sheet billowed over the wrought-iron, glassless window: the eighty-degree Caribbean nights left no need for anything else.

My luggage was still at Scoty's mom's house.

"I'll come tru tomorrow wit' it," Scoty said, as he *drove away*, leaving the biggest movie star in the world with no toothbrush at a stranger's house. When I agreed to stay, I thought it was clear that I was agreeing for me *and* Scoty. *I can't believe this joka left me here . . . Charlie Mack's gonna shove Scoty's head in a toilet when he finds out.*

I always know my direction. It was a Daddio prerequisite. At any moment, during my childhood, he would ask, "Which way is north?" or

"Point east." He had made it very clear that the passenger in any vehicle is the navigator. The driver gets the last word on the radio and the temperature—the passenger/navigator is in charge of the map and the call on left or right (and snacks—we would have to feed Daddio while he was driving).

This night, though, I couldn't see the moon, and I had been distracted during the drive to the house. I wasn't really up on my star constellations. As I lay twelve inches off a concrete floor somewhere in the Caribbean, I began to chuckle—my lifelong reaction to trauma and anxiety. My chuckle upgraded to a giggle, my giggle escalated into a guffaw, and my guffaw bloomed into full-on hysterics.

Where am I? What am I doing? What is going on? How did my life get here? I don't even know where here *is. Nobody I love knows where I am. This would be the perfect time for someone to kill me; not that anyone would* want *to kill me—I mean,* Wild Wild West *wasn't that bad.*

What if a woman walked in right now? What if she was wearing a long, white see-through nightgown. What if she put her finger to her lips—Shhh. What if she kissed me? What if she told me I was on the right path?

What if I believed her?

I slept for about twelve hours.

I went to sleep at forty-two years old—when I woke up, I felt like I was about twenty-eight. I would have slept longer, but the aroma of the tomato choka, smoked herring, sada roti, homemade bread, and local fruits I didn't even recognize hit me like a dose of sweet smelling salts. After I embarrassed myself by eating three plateful and finishing off Ila's half-eaten bread, Scoty finally pulled up.

Still no toothbrush.

"My boy Jonathan has a Bertram yacht," Scoty announced. "We're lookin' to go DDI."

The entire Lovelace family oohs and claps—clearly DDI is something good.

"What's DDI?" I ask.

"Down de islands."

We set sail at about 9:00 a.m.—me, Scoty, Che, Lulu, Roscoe, Ila, Eva, and Jonathan. After about forty minutes, we tucked into a secluded cove, off Chacachacare Island. Scoty, Che, and Jonathan are in the water before the anchor hits the sea floor. I was trying to stay awake, but either the soothing sway of the Bertram or my gluttonous assault on Ila's leftovers sent me back into the land of nod.

Two hours later, I awake to find the boat empty. Everyone's in the water now except Roscoe, Che's five-year-old son. He's eating a ripe mango, or, more accurately, it looks like he's wearing it, or it's eating him—he's drenched in the flesh and the juice.

I yelled to Scoty and crew, "Yooooo! What's the plan?"

"Whatcha mean, man?"

"I'm saying, the plan, for today—what we doing?"

"We here," Scoty said, gesturing to the horizon.

"I know, but what are we *doing*?"

They all kind of look at one another. *What does he mean?*

"I'm sayin', y'all got some Jet Skis or something?" I say. "Like, what's around here? What we gettin' into?"

"Look around, man," Scoty called from the water, "we reconnectin' and limin'."

What the fuck is "reconnectin'" and "limin'"?

Roscoe and his mango had been watching the whole exchange. I went back inside, lay down on the couch, closed my eyes for another thirty minutes.

These jokas are really about to sit around and do nothing, all day. I was dying. There was no service on my phone, so no texts or calls. We were an hour from land, and ninety minutes from an airport. I was trapped; I felt like a caged animal. I was getting . . . angry. *How dare they waste my valuable time like this?*

I stand up and head back out on deck. They're still in the same spots, just floatin' and yappin'. I couldn't understand what they were doing. I was jittery, I was pacing, checking the time on my phone. And then I caught myself: I noticed the turbulence of my thoughts and feelings, which stood in stark contradistinction to my surroundings, and I thought, *Oh shit, this* is *crackhead behavior.* I could *not* sit still. My mind was agitated—I needed an activity, a target, a mission, an activity, an adventure. Something, *anything*, to *do*.

I caught eyes with Roscoe, peeking over the curvature of yet another mango—this one's bigger than his head. He was just looking at me sweetly, as if to say, "You know you look *crazy*, right?"

It all slowly drifted into focus: Am I an addict? I don't do drugs, I don't really drink, I'm not hooked on sex like some ghetto hyena. But I did *not* know how to stop, or be still, or be quiet, or alone. I'm addicted to the approval of others, and to secure their approval, I became addicted to *winning*. And to guarantee and sustain my stream of massive victories, I became addicted to working, to grinding, and obsessively pursuing perfection.

But there was a deeper issue at play. I saw downtime as the enemy, a place where you lose things. When I had left space between Melanie and me, she had cheated. Daddio saw the space between tasks at the shop as laziness. Darrell never wanted me to sit down in the gym—he saw downtime as the crack where the pleasure principle would poison all our hard work. I never wanted Jeff to put interludes on our albums because I saw the lull between tracks as the empty space for the audience to stop listening. I didn't want to leave space between my TV show, the next movie, and my next record, because I didn't want to give people an opportunity to fall in love with The Rock during my absence.

But the most perturbing aspect of my need to fill every second was that it kept me from having to feel.

My mind drifted to my *I Am Legend* phone call with JL. The film had broken global box office records, but still I was dissatisfied. The subtle sickness was becoming a whole lot less subtle. I asked myself, *How much did* I Am Legend *need to make for me to be happy? How much would have been enough? How many more consecutive #1 movies do I need? How much money would it take for me to feel safe and secure? How many Grammys or Academy Awards do I need to feel loved and approved of? How much healthier do my kids need to be? How many more times does Jada need to say, "I love you"? When will enough be enough?*

The problem is, the more you get, the more you want. It's like drinking salt water to quench your thirst. We develop a tolerance that makes us need more just to get the same high.

I started to recognize the game, the trick, the insanity, the carrot on the stick. I had never liked vampire movies, but I suddenly understood their mythology—they are a metaphor for insatiable human hunger, unquenchable thirsts, and chronic dissatisfaction—the attempt to fill a spiritual hole with external things.

If unparalleled winning and achieving everything I've ever dreamed of does not secure perfect happiness and ultimate bliss, then what does?

I looked at Roscoe. As far as he was concerned, the key to life was mango.

Come on in! The water warm!" Lulu shouted.

"I don't know how to swim," I said.

Clearly, they had never heard an actual human say that before. First, they laughed, then came the realization that I wasn't joking with them. And then they all looked at me like I was starring in a UNICEF commercial: "Please help this stereotypical Afro American urban homeboy—just one dollar a week will help this joka learn how to swim."

I had always feared the ocean—it seemed so vast and unpredictable. It could be calm and beautiful one minute, and then violent and monstrous the next. Even as a child, I stayed far from the water on family trips to Atlantic City.

I remember being at the Grand Canyon and Mom-Mom saying, "This entire canyon was created by water."

That was a terrifying proposition to me. The ocean and water—we just didn't vibe.

One of my most traumatic childhood memories was of nearly drowning in a public swimming pool. I can still see myself underwater, disoriented—I couldn't figure out which way was up. I'm choking and I know I'm dying. Mom-Mom leaps from her deck chair and dives into the pool. I can see her hand coming toward my face. She grabs me under my arms and lifts me out of the pool onto the side.

Years later, as I recount to one of Mom-Mom's friends my harrowing brush with death, Mom-Mom's face contorts into confusion. She's trying to read me. We've been here many times, but she can tell something's different.

"You know that never happened, right?" Mom-Mom gently asks.

"What do you mean?" I say.

"Willard, that never happened," she says, a little more urgently.

"I remember the whole thing, Mom," I say.

"You never got in a pool, you never got in the ocean. We sent you to swimming class once, and you wouldn't even put your feet in the water."

"But, Mom, I can see it all. You had an Afro, and you were wearing a blue bathing suit."

"Well, it must be your *other* mother, because this one never had that experience."

I begin to forensically examine my memory. And then it hits me: *If I was under the water, disoriented, how did I see Mom-Mom jump into the pool?* Then my cinematic experience kicks in: I realize that the angles of my visual recollection are not from my point of view. In my mind's eye, I'm seeing the incident as if I were on the side of the pool. The two-shot of me and Mom-Mom in my mind is impossible—this is a false memory. But all my anxiety about the ocean, my fear and aversion to water, is 100 percent real.

This revelation shook me. Is my memory really that unreliable? Did I dream it? Did I make it up? Is it a past-life experience? If it was, what the hell was Mom-Mom doing there, and why did she have an Afro?

Either way, it didn't really matter: I still hated the ocean.

Memory is not a flawless recording of what actually happened. It's not a video of your experience. It's not even a photograph. It is your psychological, artistic rendering. It is more like an abstract impressionist painting of what happened than it is a pure, unfiltered depiction. *And* it's not fixed—the painting morphs, it fades or expands over time. Sometimes you add colors to a memory that weren't there a year ago, or five years ago, or even collapse multiple memories and paint them into one.

The problem is that most of us trust our memories implicitly. Our memories are the basis for our perception of reality. We then commit to these conclusions, unlocking the requisite emotions and the corresponding actions and behaviors. We move into the world clinging to our flawed assumptions, unleashing upon ourselves the cosmic consequences of wrong ideas.

I *trust* the memory that I nearly drowned—in fact, I'm fully committed to the truth of that story. Water is dangerous, and it tried to kill me when I was little. So, when my brother and sisters are playing in the ocean, I'm by myself halfway up the beach. As an adult, I don't let my kids go in the ocean by themselves. The fear and anxiety take hold in my mind and then constrict my ability to be able to enjoy the beauty of 70 percent of the earth's surface.

Jus' relax, man!"

I'm barely ten yards from the shore, but the sea is choppy. The water is up to my waist. As Scoty sits down, the water is up to his neck.

"Take a dip and chill," he says. "It won't go over your head."

"Yo, man, shit is touching my legs," I say.

"Seaweed, man! Sargassum! It's a problem we workin' on. Just come in."

Scoty reaches down and grabs a handful of whatever sargassum is and slings it away from me—apparently, the fact that it's now eight feet away is supposed to make me comfortable. I take a deep breath, and I sit. The sea is almost translucent, and as warm as bathwater. The waves are knocking and jolting and tossing me around.

"Don't fight it, man," Scoty says. "It's a flow. It'll carry yuh out, but it'll bring you back."

Scoty is calmly floating in complete harmony with the rhythm of the sea, and I'm bangin' around like a monkey fuckin' a football. And while I never got fully comfortable, I began to understand the human relationship with the ocean.

Reconnectin' and limin'.

The ebb and flow of the tide is the heartbeat of the planet. When they sit in the ocean all day, they are tuning themselves in to the frequency of the earth. This alignment, to Scoty, was the highest human experience. When he spends time with anyone he loves, he wants to spend it in the ocean—surfing, fishing, boating, water-skiing, swimming, reconnectin', and limin'.

When I left Trinidad, I was clear about one thing: I knew I was missing something—something about life, something about relationships, perhaps even something about me.

I just didn't know what it was.

But I was no longer fully defending my old belief systems. I was open to the idea that *maybe* fight-camp mentality, in the domestic realm, isn't quite the optimal relating paradigm. I didn't yet know what the new ideas were, but I was certain there would have to be some.

Why are you so afraid of silence?

Silence is the root of everything.

If you spiral into its void a hundred voices will thunder messages you long to hear. —RUMI

I hate it when people send me Instagram quotes that are supposed to be deep. They always come with a little fancy border, and the background's always mauve, and in some woke-ass, illegible, calligraphy font—and when they truly wanna get you, they add a picture of a really, really old Asian man.

Silence is the root of everything made absolutely no sense to me whatsoever. I make noise for a living. I was so confused, I texted back, "WTF?????????"

My phone rang immediately. It was my boy Antoine.

"Man, don't be sendin' me your little pseudo-inspirational Buddha-babble," I said. "If you gon' send me quotes, send me lyrics from Talib Kweli."

"I just got back from India," he said, cracking up, knowing he had no business sending me that Rumi bullshit.

"That is no excuse," I said. "What were you doin' in India?"

"I did a thing called 'Vipassana.' It's a ten-day *silent* retreat—no television, no phone, no talking. It was wild. You *have* to do it."

"No talking for ten days? What's it called again?"

"Vipassana—it means 'to see things as they really are.'"

Antoine and I hadn't spoken in over a year, but I guess he just needed somebody to talk to.

It's weird how people can feel when you're seeking—higher curiosity seems to emit energy at a different frequency. As soon as you truly open to something different, it's like a cosmic shout into an energetic megaphone: *YO! Where y'all at? You see I'm strugglin' over here?*

"Yeah, man, I'm not sure I'm ready for India," I said. "But I do like the idea of seeing things as they really are."

My entire childhood I shared a bedroom with Harry. If you drew a timeline that stretched from that day I met Melanie, when I was fourteen, all the way to my marriage today, I have only been single for a total of fifteen days. I hated being alone.

I wanted to give Jada her space in LA, so I decided to spend a couple of weeks alone, just I, myself, and me—I wanted to see if the three of us could get along. No television, no phone, no people.

No talking.

I went to our Utah house in the mountains. Totally secluded; at 8,400-foot altitude. I'd organized to have food left at the door, but no human contact. Other than a solitary morning walk, I wasn't going to leave the house for fourteen straight days.

Antoine had only done ten, so I *had* to beat him.

Day one was exciting. No texts, no email, no calls. I was preparing my own meals for the first time in thirty years—they were nasty, but I felt good about the attempt. No television, or computers other than my iPad, which I'd filled with books to read. This was the first time in my life I had ever read a whole book in one day: Pema Chödrön's *When Things Fall Apart.*

Day two and day three each felt like they were about thirty-nine hours long, which would have been almost bearable if it weren't for the incessant chatter of the entourage in my head.

Days four and five almost broke me. I was crawling up the walls. I was even thinking about taking sleeping aids during the day so I could get some relief. I just somehow knew NyQuil wasn't an approved Vipassana substance. I had committed to myself that I would do fourteen days, and I'd learned a long time ago, I might break my promise to you, but I'll never break my promise to me.

Day six, I caught myself in the mirror with a pair of tweezers, plucking my eyebrows. I knew I was in trouble.

By day seven, I had beautifully sculpted eyebrows, and I discovered that there's a name for this condition: trichotillomania, a.k.a. hair-pulling disorder. I knew I didn't have it, but there was always day eight!

Day eight:

That's it, I gotta call somebody.

Shit, nope, not gonna do that.

Why do I feel like I wanna cry?

Vipassana's fucking stupid.

Wait, what time did I start? Am I counting a day from midnight, or from the exact hour I started? So, this is day eight, or nine?

Antoine's a fucking moron.

So is Rumi.

By day nine, I noticed that my dreams were becoming more vivid, and creative ideas were flowing. I started filling up notebook after notebook with rhymes and songs and thoughts and opinions and movies and poetry.

I also started reading about meditation and became intrigued with the idea of "watching my mind." It was my introduction to words like "self-observation," "self-investigation," "consciousness," and "awareness." I tasted a tiny, fleeting moment of what I would later come to recognize as "peace." It didn't last too long, but it was a scent that I would learn to follow.

This time alone in Utah launched the greatest period of reading in my life, a period that would last for the next several years. As a very partial list, I devoured *The Autobiography of Malcolm X*; *Bhagavad Gītā As It Is*; *The Road Less Traveled*; *Don Quixote*; *The Untethered Soul*; *Teachings of the Buddha*; *The Odyssey*; *Moby-Dick*; *How to Win*

Friends and Influence People; *The 5 Love Languages*; *As a Man Think-eth*; *Oneness*; *Zen in the Art of Archery*; Plato's *Republic*; *The Way of the Superior Man*; *Iron John*; *Aspire*; *I Know Why the Caged Bird Sings*; *The Power Path*; *Man's Search for Meaning*; and on and on and on and on. I must have read at least one hundred books over the next few years.

Day ten was the first time I tried to meditate.

Day eleven, I gave up meditation. It literally felt like my mind was attacking me.

Day twelve, I gave meditation another shot.

I read Chödrön's *How to Meditate: A Practical Guide to Making Friends with Your Mind*.

I like making friends, I thought. I began trying to listen to and observe what was going on in my head, and a painful realization washed across me: I wasn't enjoying being with myself. In fact, I wanted to get away from myself as fast as I could.

And it dawned on me, *If I don't want to be with me, why the fuck would anybody else wanna be with me?*

SURRENDER

hat would make you happy? I'm not talking about 'Will Smith,' because he comes with a lot of baggage. But *you*—if *you* could be master of the universe, and you could snap your fingers and have any life you wanted, what would it look like?"

That was a really heavy question.

Michaela Boehm is a single red curly hair over five feet tall. Her Austrian accent makes everything she says ring with psychoanalytical authenticity. She's an author, public speaker, and counselor, with more than three decades and 35,000 client hours in the trenches. Her in-depth training in Jungian psychology, trauma, and relationship therapy is seasoned with an expertise in tantric sexuality.

The Google search alone had me feeling exposed and vulnerable, so when she walked in carrying a silver-spangled Moroccan camel saddle-bag, with indeterminate fur, and her first question was "What would make you happy?" I was instantly off balance. *What does she mean by that? What makes her think I'm not happy?* (Apart from the whole, "Can you come and help me because I'm not happy" thing.)

To me, it was blasphemous to even *imagine* something other than the life I'd created. My imagination is usually a white-water-rapids ride of possibilities and potential. But for some reason, this question led me into an area of my inner world that had danger signs all over it, yellow police tape everywhere I looked. The answer would have to be extracted from the place where only the "bad kids" go, the murky, swampy, shadow regions of my psyche. I don't even let myself *think* from inside that neighborhood, so I'm damn sure not going to *speak* from there.

I mean, what if I rip down all the boards and barriers and barricades, and whatever demon is in there takes over? What if I can't put it back? What if I like it being out?

But I approached the dark place. I wanted to see what was in there. I ducked under the first layer of yellow tape. What is she really asking me?

What life would I create if I didn't give a fuck?

And then the shadow spoke: "I would have a harem."

The vulnerability of exposing my unprocessed, unfiltered fantasies first seized me with embarrassment, then filled me with anger—like she'd tricked me.

Maybe Michaela's a witch. How could she get me to reveal my filthy shadow world that fast?

Michaela didn't flinch. She retrieved a journal and a pen from her multicolored enchanted satchel and said, "OK, a harem. Interesting. So, who's in it?"

"What do you mean?" I said.

"Who is in your harem? The women. Tell me their names."

Michaela is holding her pen over her journal, awaiting my answer to her question.

This is some Jedi-mind-trick shit, some Jungian psycho tantric embodiment voodoo. She ain't gettin' me with this.

"Don't sit there like you don't have an answer," Michaela said. "You know exactly who the women are, this is not the first time you've thought about this, you've played this out over and over again in your mind. . . . What are their *names*?"

"I just don't . . . I mean, I just don't understand why you need to know who they are."

"I need to know because I'm going to run your harem," she said, as if I was supposed to know that this was an actual job people did.

"Look, you are Will Effin' Smith. You are one of the richest, most beloved people on earth. If *you* can't have the life that *you* want, the rest of us are screwed."

"Misty Copeland," I said, calling Michaela's bluff. "She's that Black ballerina. . . ."

"I know who Misty Copeland is," Michaela said, as she jotted down her name. "Who else?"

"Halle," I said, stone-faced. *Let's play, witch lady, what else you want?*

"You know harems are not just for sex," Michaela said. "Harems are convened for inspiration. You need a doctor, you need a painter, an architect, a couple lawyers, a musician, a poet. And not just Americans—you should be hearing multiple languages. Your harem should be made up of the most brilliant, unique, and powerful women from around the world. Your responsibility will be resources, and devotion to their individual growth and blossoming. And in return, they will feed you and shower you with their feminine gifts and send you into the world, full and inspired."

For the next two hours, Michaela wrote feverishly. She took out her laptop—*I guess she's a modern witch!*—and showed me pictures and videos and TED Talks of the most dynamic and talented women from across the globe. I'm pacing and laughing and inspired. I was dancing in the shadow zone. And somehow, the demons within me that had seemed too dark and evil to even consider, didn't seem so scary in the light of Michaela's acceptance. When all was said and done, we had about twenty-five names; we had trip routings; global events to attend, like Carnival in Rio and Holi, the Hindu festival of color in India; we had a list of people who my harem and I should meet. Michaela and I high-fived, and I agreed to start making contact with the women first thing Monday morning.

I had a couple of nights to sleep on it, and by Tuesday, close of business, I was out. With every hour, my enthusiasm waned. Every single harem equation in my mind kept adding up to a hellscape. If I can't figure out how to nurture and nourish one extraordinary woman, what the fuck made me think I could care for twenty-five?

"I don't want a harem," I said.

"Of course you don't," Michaela responded. "But why did you think you did?"

"I guess I felt if I had enough women, I'd always be able to find at least one of them who liked me."

"As long as you do things for the approval of a woman," Michaela said, "you will never be free. That is a descending hell. And I'll tell you—when a woman sees that she can bend you, she loses trust in you. We need you to be solid; we need your 'yes' to be a yes, and your 'no' to be a no. As long as you are twisting and contorting and selling yourself out for the affection of others, you will always be untrustworthy."

Michaela began to refer to my nice-guy persona as "Uncle Fluffy." He was "the pleaser" in me, the part of me that had to smile no matter how I was feeling—doing things I didn't want to do just to keep the peace. He wasn't allowed to be in a bad mood or have a bad day. Uncle Fluffy hated conflict, so much so that he'd even lie to avoid it. He signed *every* autograph, shook *every* hand, kissed *every* baby. Fluffy was jovial, talented, smart, generous. Uncle Fluffy needed everyone to like him.

I am so good, I am so nice and resourceful, you don't have to worry; I'm harmless, you can trust me. I'll take care of your every need.

Uncle Fluffy was born as my strategic childhood persona. If I was funny enough, sweet enough, harmless enough, entertaining enough, then I wouldn't be hurt, my mother would be safe, and my family would be happy—no one would ever leave me.

Fluffy wants to be approved of. It's the only safety he can conceive. As an adult, he became my armor and my shield. I was strangling my truth in the hopes of feeling safe, gaining approval, and being loved.

"I want you to have an experience of yourself minus the need to be approved of," Michaela said. "Who are you *really*? What does your heart *truly* want? What are your *deepest* values and *authentic* goals? The problem with Uncle Fluffy is that you are never free to make a pure decision, one that is honest and true for you. You are always forced by Fluffy to compromise and to do the thing that gets the most approval, likes, or sales. Will's creativity is thwarted by Fluffy's need for approval. What are *Will's* feelings, *Will's* opinions, *Will's* needs, *Will's* ideas?"

I could see her point that as a child I had crafted a certain identity—that I had decided that there was a specific way that I had to be to survive and thrive in my environment. I could also see that the behavior was often in conflict with the truth of what I was actually thinking and feeling.

But Uncle Fluffy did some beautiful things. He built Her Lake. He let Willow stop whipping her hair when she was done. He begged Jeff and JL to move to LA. He doubled Sheree's child support when Trey moved in with Will. He auditioned at Quincy Jones's house when *Will* was too scared and he wanted to leave. Uncle Fluffy was swayed by his admiration for Muhammad Ali to make a movie that *Will* was too afraid to make.

"Uncle Fluffy has been a wonderful friend," Michaela said. "He just needs to work for *you*, not the other way around."

Uncle Fluffy was created based on a lie, designed on the false premise that something was wrong with me, that I was a coward. His job was to perpetually apologize for my shortcomings and guarantee that I was always safe and loved. And even as the awareness dawned that perhaps he had outlived his usefulness, the fact still remained: Uncle Fluffy paid the bills.

Fluffy was further complicated by his shadow counterpart, whom Michaela named "the General." When Fluffs had exhausted his reserves of charm and magnanimity, and yet was still unsuccessful in his attempts to secure adoration, he summoned the General. The General's job was to get the flag to the top of the hill by any means necessary, and to covertly (and not so covertly) punish those who dared to dissent, even myself. Basically, when I had suppressed my real needs so thoroughly for so long, and still didn't get the adoration and approval I'd sought, my anguish would express itself as the General.

Because Uncle Fluffy is masking my true feelings (which I'm not even in touch with), when the General shows up, people are shocked and confused. It was sweetness, sweetness, sweetness, and then sour, sour, sourness.

"These personas weave a universe in which you are trapped," Michaela said, "a spiderweb of demands, obligations, and expectations. And if you dare to step outside of these constructs, you receive exactly the disdain and disapproval you fear most. But neither of these identities is *you*. The question is, can you find safety in yourself and not from some external source of approval? Can you become a Freestanding Man?"

Michaela and I worked together over the next few years. Her curriculum centered on the idea of becoming a Freestanding Man. Essentially, a Freestanding Man is self-aware, self-reliant, self-motivated, self-confident, and utterly unswayed by people's approval or disapproval. He knows who he is, he knows what he wants. And because of this, he surrenders his considerable gifts into the service of others.

"You have to sensitize to your own inner landscape and map out the terrain of who you really are, your true desires and true needs," Michaela said. "When someone asks how you feel, don't just throw out a Fluffy answer—think about it. Narrate your feelings, at least internally."

Michaela was trying to get me to put honesty and authenticity *above* my need for approval, as a means of cultivating trust in myself and becoming trustworthy to others.

In the beginning, I found myself still collapsing in the face of disapproval; it was hard to see disappointment in people's eyes or feel their anger toward me if I refused to fulfil their desires. I was trying to learn to be true to myself and not betray myself and override my own feelings. It was excruciating trying to stop saying yes when I meant no, and to stop saying no to things that I actually wanted.

One of the first things we set out to dismantle was my fame belief system that if I was in public, I wasn't allowed to say no to any fan request. If someone wanted a picture, an autograph, a handshake, a hug—it didn't matter if I was eating or talking or not feeling well; I had obligated myself to fulfilling the promise of my image.

In 2017, I was on the jury at the Cannes Film Festival alongside Spanish director and screenwriter Pedro Almodóvar; German film director Maren Ade; Chinese actress Fan Bingbing; South Korean auteur Park Chan-wook; actress Jessica Chastain; French actress and director Agnès Jaoui; Italian director Paolo Sorrentino; and Gabriel Yared, a Lebanese-French composer. During this time, I was practicing the behavioral change of setting and honoring my personal boundaries. I was going to tell people the truth of how I was feeling; I was going to say no when I meant no, and yes when I meant yes.

It was day five, and we'd already watched fourteen movies, ten of which were subtitled, and six of which were "experimental." The jury deliberations were the greatest cinematic education of my life, but watching and debating three movies a day was physically and intellectually exhausting.

With one more movie to watch before dinner, I needed a beat to be quiet and reset. I had thirty minutes to hit the gym before rejoining the jury. I had told myself that this was *my* time, for me, and I had promised myself that I would not allow anyone to infringe on it.

I entered the gym, and it was totally empty. *Thank the blessed heavens.* I headed over to the ab crunch machine—I was going to do fifteen minutes of core, fifteen minutes of cardio, and be out. *Perfect.*

Midway through my second set, a thirtysomething Black dude with a British accent entered and immediately noticed me. He whipped out his phone as he approached, scrambling to start recording.

"Hey, Will," he said, flipping into landscape mode, "say hi to my cousin!" As he got within a couple of feet of my face, I reached up, putting my hand over the lens of his camera and pushed it down.

"Hey, sorry, man," I said, "I'm training now."

"It's just a quick video, Will," he said. "My cousin has Down syndrome. He loves you. I promise it will be quick. *The Fresh Prince* is the only thing that makes him smile."

Uncle Fluffy: Will, just do the video. It's not even for him. It's for a kid with Down syndrome.

Me: But I promised myself: This is my private time. And he can't just start filming me without asking first.

Uncle Fluffy: He was excited. He's clearly a big fan. Fresh Prince *is the only thing that makes the kid smile. Don't be a dick.*

Me: I'm not being a dick. I'm trying to honor my promises to myself. I'm allowed to not do a video if I don't want to. Is there no sacred space for myself?

Uncle Fluffy: Sure, there is—your mansion, your limousine services, your penthouse suite, your private jets: All the shit we wouldn't have if I let your newfangled "sense of self" run our lives. . . .

"Will, there's nobody in here," the guy said. "It's just us. Please, just say hi. . . ."

I know I looked crazy as shit to this dude. I'm still holding his camera down with a thousand-yard stare in my eyes, as the war within me raged.

"I'm sorry, man," I said, "but no."

The pain in this man's eyes is burned in my memory. It brings tears even to this day. He looked at me with such disbelief—*This is not Will Smith. . . .*

"But why not?" he said.

I paused. I searched for the deepest, most honest answer.

"Because I don't want to," I said.

The man shook his head in disgust, turned, and left the gym. I knew I had done right by myself, but I hated that someone else—an innocent—had gotten caught in the cross fire of my internal war.

I never made it to the cardio. I went back to my room and could not stop crying.

Over the next two years, Michaela and I were joined at the hip. She repeated over and over again, "Explore. Experience. Experiment. Expand." She set free the wild-minded pathfinder within me, whose vision had been narrowed by the obligations and expectations of being "Will Smith." Michaela encouraged me to "try new things" and "meet new people"—rekindle my spirit of exploration and adventure. I began to take a fresh sampling of the fruits of the human experience.

"As you break out of the narrow boundaries of 'Will Smith,'" Michaela said, "let's really examine all the beliefs and constructs and paradigms that you've bound yourself to. There's a thing I've heard you say a few times: 'Ninety-nine percent is the same as zero.'"

"Yeah," I said, "Daddio used to say that all the time."

"Well, you know, mathematically speaking, ninety-nine percent is about as far from zero as you can get."

I had used that phrase thousands of times in my life, but for some reason, when Michaela said it, I truly heard it for the first time. This has been a stable, foundational axiom that had driven my operating system. But its falsity was so obvious it opened me up to reevaluating and reexamining *all* of my assumptions. If 99 percent is not the same as zero, what is 72 percent, or 23 percent, or 84.69 percent? Hell, what's zero? Rather than seeing every situation as binary, all of a sudden, the possibilities became infinite.

I realized that I had seen the world but never on vacation. So, I began to travel, with no agenda. I spent time with people I admired who I just wanted to get to know, with no financial or business outcome attached. I visited with famed British-Iraqi architect, the "Queen of the Curve," Zaha Hadid. I became friends with jazz-rock pianist Eric Robert Lewis. He told me he'd been trained as a classical pianist and the rigid confines of that discipline had sent him into a nervous breakdown. While in a mental hospital, Bruce Lee had spiritually visited him and told him to use the piano to fight his demons. "ELEW" as he's known, developed a martial-arts-style of piano playing. He got rid of the stool, he armored himself with steel forearm sleeves, assumed the kata stance, and began to play in his own liberated, one-of-a-kind style.

But Michaela's most important initiative came when she found out that I couldn't swim.

"Not on my watch," she said, in one of the only times I managed to surprise her. When I'd told her I wanted a harem she didn't flinch—but me not being able to swim sent her to feverishly texting my publicist, Meredith O'Sullivan-Wasson, who is friends with the four-time Olympic gold medalist in swimming Janet Evans.

"You are going to develop a relationship with the ocean, the Big She," Michaela said. "The ocean is the ultimate woman, a magnificent feminine environment. If you can understand her, you'll understand us all. The ocean holds all the chaotic glory of Mother Nature, and no amount of power or intellect will ever be able to control or manipulate her. She doesn't care how you're feeling, or how you want her to be. All of the things that happen in a woman's psyche and body are analogous to the ocean. The beauty, the storms, the nourishment, the danger, the moods and weather patterns, birth and death. The Big She will not be conquered or subdued; your only hope to truly enjoy her is to love her, respect her, and surrender.

"I really like this for you because you will be forced to have a beginner's mind. You'll have to navigate her moods and emotions, and you'll have to know when to bow out."

I began to woo the Big She. Our first date was one hour off of Lizard Island, on the Great Barrier Reef.

I learned to swim, and I took up scuba diving. When we got a little more serious, I went to the Maldives and found myself in something out of *Finding Nemo*. When I wanted to explore her feisty side, I dove with fourteen-foot, seven-hundred-pound tiger sharks on Tiger Beach in the Bahamas. And when I felt I was ready to taste her depths, I took an OceanX Triton submersible beyond the midnight zone, below the bioluminescent band, three thousand feet down, to what looked like another planet. There were deep-sea creatures hidden in her fathoms that defied my definition of life, that seem to have been created by another God.

I began to see the personality of the Big She as an instructive embodiment of the flow of life. I realized that if I am to enjoy her beauty and her bounty—and avoid being destroyed by her—she demands that I'm fully attuned, attentive, and committed to understanding her. I settled into the acceptance of my powerlessness, which strangely liberated me.

"Surrender" had always been a negative word for me—it meant losing or failing or giving up. But my burgeoning relationship with the ocean was exposing that my sense of control was actually an illusion. Surrender transformed from a weakness word to an infinite power concept. I had had a bias toward action—thrusting, pushing, striving, struggling, *doing*—and I began to realize that their opposites were equally as powerful—inaction, receptiveness, acceptance, non-resistance, *being*. Stopping was equally as powerful as going; resting was equally as powerful as training; silence was equally as powerful as talking.

Letting go was equally as powerful as grasping.

"Surrender" to me no longer meant defeat—it was now an equally powerful tool of manifestation. Losing could be equal to winning in terms of my growth and development.

I began to understand a perplexing phrase that Gigi used to use: "Let go and let God." That had always seemed wrong to me. It felt like absolving yourself of your responsibilities, like something that people say when they're too lazy to do what's necessary to build the life they want. But all of a sudden, it took on new and magical meaning.

There is an energy that's at work while you're asleep—the energy that fires the sun, that moves the ocean, that beats your heart. You don't have to *do* everything; in fact, most of the things that get done, you didn't have anything to do with them. Actually, it's a great thing that you were asleep, because if you'd been awake, you would probably have messed it up.

And then, a new wording of Gigi's axiom came into my mind: It's not just "Let go and let God"—it's "Let go and let God *work*." The surfer and the ocean are a team; the mountain and the climber are partners, not adversaries. The Great River is going to do 99 percent of the work—your 1 percent is to study it, to understand it, to respect its power, and creatively dance within its currents and its laws.

Act when the universe is open, and rest when she's closed.

I had never heard of it before. I've never smoked weed, never done cocaine or taken any pills, and other than a vodka and cranberry once in a while, I will pass a piss test at the Tour de France. So when my friend Veronica suggested it, I laughed politely, and said, "Thank you, but no thank you. I don't mess with drugs."

"Neither do I," she said. "Ayahuasca is not drugs. It's *medicine*."

I've known Veronica for years. We never had sex, but we argued like we did. We disagreed about everything; I was incensed by her pessimism, and she, in turn, scorned my optimism. It never dawned on either of us to just talk to other people. I guess we kinda used each other to crash-test our theories about life. We knew the other would never easily agree, so when an idea got past, we knew it was a keeper.

But something was new. Her eyes were different, her energy was nonresistant, flexible. She'd had a rough childhood, which I'm sure contributed to her combative disposition. But now, she was calm, stable—there was an undeniable joy about her. She was filled with fresh insight and the passion of someone who'd been somewhere extraordinary and had been utterly transformed.

I found myself hanging on her every word. She embodied a new wisdom. Her heart had always felt closed and impenetrable, but now she was open, warm, reachable. In the past, I'd always felt like her parent trying to wrestle a hardheaded child into reality. Today, I felt like Matt Damon listening to Robin Williams in *Good Will Hunting*. I was riveted. I was intrigued. I was curious.

"Well, whatever you did, I wanna do that," I said.

Veronica laughed the laugh of the initiated to the uninitiated. She paused, and then began to try to explain the inexplicable.

"Ayahuasca changed my life," she said.

"So how does it work?"

"Well, it's a ceremony that goes from sunset to sunrise. It traditionally takes place in the jungles of South America—mostly Peru, now. But wherever you do it, it's led by a shaman. It begins with drinking the most disgusting tea you can possibly imagine. After about an hour it kicks in and then . . ." She shakes her head and shivers, like she's seen things she'll never be able to unsee.

"And then . . . what?" I said.

"Well, it traps you with your mind."

"That doesn't sound fun *at all*," I said.

"Any issues you may be struggling with, the medicine goes right to them," she said, "and brings them to the surface, making you look at them, experience them, and ultimately heal them. I never told you this before, but when I was a teenager, I had an abortion. It was the most devastating choice I ever made. I've been haunted and crippled—I've done therapy for decades but have never been able to shake the shame.

"In my ayahuasca ceremony, I met my child. He was in heaven. He was so happy, so sweet, so beautiful. I wailed and purged for hours. He forgave me—he even asked me to *name* him. I named him Zion. And in one night, I got free from a lifetime of guilt."

I could sense her yearning to share the fruits of her journey, but there was a hesitation.

"It's fucking brutal," she said. "It ultimately ends in revelation and healing, but the bus trip winds through the darkest parts of your mind. It's rough, but it'll help you find what you're looking for."

Ayahuasca is a "sacred brew." It has been used for millennia by the indigenous tribes of the Amazonian jungle during spiritual ceremonies and shamanic rituals. It's a kind of tea made from the bark and stems of a tropical South American vine, sometimes mixed with other psychotropic plants.

The name comes from the Quechua language, where *aya* means "soul" and *huasca* (wasca) is "vine" (translation: "vine of the soul"). Ayahuasca contains a mind-altering compound called dimethyltryptamine (DMT) and is considered a sacred medicine, employed by serious spiritual seekers, not for recreational use.

Ayahuasca's healing properties are currently being used in the treatment of PTSD, drug addiction, depression, and anxiety, among many other physical and psychological ailments. (I do not condone, nor do I suggest, the use of ayahuasca or any substance without professional medical prescription and supervision. I struggled with the decision of whether to even share my journey with ayahuasca in this book—the only reason I'm writing about it here is because it's the truth of my experience.)

The room was dark. A small cabin—one room and a bathroom. Ancient Peruvian tribal chants and sacred melodies drone ethereally from a small speaker in the corner. Images of deities cover the walls. Handmade instruments are strewn around a wooden altar. Blankets, cushions, mats, pillows, cover the floor.

The shaman lives here. Her name is Beata; mid-forties. She reminds me of Meryl Streep (if Meryl had moved to Peru on her twenty-first birthday to study botany and spiritual healing). She hands me a bucket and a small clay cup.

The smell of the ayahuasca preempts my inquiry about the bucket.

Beata takes her seat in front of the altar. We've had very little conversation, and I'm beginning to feel concerned that she may not be aware that I've never done anything like this before. I'd followed the basic instructions—no medications, drugs, or alcohol for two weeks prior; no food after 2:00 p.m. day of, no drinks after 5:00 p.m. Arrive at seven thirty, in loose-fitting clothes, and ceremony at eight. But it seemed like she needed to be talking more. This feels too big for her to be just setting shit up casually. *Hey, lady, I'm a little shook over here.*

"I don't really know much about ayahuasca," I said. "I did some personal research, but is there an orientation of the process or procedure . . . ?"

Beata smiled the smile of the initiated to the uninitiated.

"No," she said sweetly.

To put it mildly, that answer left me somewhat unsatisfied.

"I just wanna be clear about how . . . and what I'm supposed to expect," I stumbled.

"The vine will lead you," Beata said reassuringly. "Just surrender. Let yourself be guided. I'm only here to help you navigate the journey."

"I get that," I said, totally not getting it. "So, what's my next thing?"

She pointed to the burnt-orange clay cup.

"When you're ready . . ."

I drank the brew.

Ten minutes . . . nothing.

Twenty-five minutes . . . nada.

Forty minutes . . . zippo.

Maybe it doesn't work on me.

At an hour, the novelty of waiting had worn off—I figured I was immune. It was 9:00 p.m., and I realized I had agreed to do this stupid shit till sunrise. My little mat on the floor was comfortable, so I said fuck it, and went to sleep.

When I woke up, I was floating deep in outer space.

As I regained my bearings, I realized that I was trillions of light-years away from earth. I was so far away that I knew I would never see anything, or anyone I loved, ever again. This is where I would be for eternity.

As I digest the magnitude of my predicament, I begin to glide through the infinity of stars. I notice that they are not stars, as we know them. It is as if Picasso had painted outer space. Colors and cubes and angles—I am suddenly overwhelmed by the majesty of my surroundings. This is the most beautiful place I've ever been in my life. As I am distracted in awe, I can sense a presence behind me.

It's a woman. I turn to see her, but she is unseeable. I can feel the warmth of her energy, close behind me, as close as she could be without touching. She's happy I'm here, and I can tell she will never leave me. Somehow, I know she's been waiting for me.

Her voice centers directly behind my right ear as if her lips were only millimeters away. I turn again, craving just a glimpse of this beatific goddess, but as I move, she moves—I can tell I'm not meant to see her. But I'm OK with that, because every second with her quenches my lifelong thirsts.

She is everything: lover, teacher, mother, protector, guide. She is all I've ever dreamed of, and everything I've ever wanted. I can tell she knows everything I need to know and how to get everywhere I want to go. She is my goal, my solution, my answer. She is the top of the mountain, and the sky beyond.

"Where are we?" I say to her softly.

"What do you mean, silly?" she says, in a tone that melts away everything but bliss.

"This place is beautiful!" I say.

"This is not a place, silly." She kept endearingly calling me silly.

"I've never seen anywhere more beautiful than this," I said.

She laughs.

"Why does that make you laugh?" I ask.

"This is *you*, silly!" she said.

"Huh? What do you mean?"

"This is not a *place*, this is *you*."

My heart begins to race as I look around, bearing witness to the grandeur of this infinite paradise.

"Wait a minute," I say. "All of this is *me*?"

"Yes, silly."

"I'm *this* beautiful?"

"Of *course* you are," she says.

Her words unlock the emotional floodgates within me. I begin to sob and purge—a lifetime of insecurities, self-doubt, and inadequacies violently flushing out of me. Simultaneously, the revelation of my inner beauty fills my heart and mind with possibilities.

"If I'm this beautiful, I don't need #1 movies to feel good about myself. If I'm this beautiful, I don't need hit records to feel worthy of love. If I'm this beautiful, I don't need Jada or anybody else to validate me. If I'm this beautiful, and I have this internal sanctuary I can always return to, then I don't need anyone to approve of me. *I* approve of me. I am enough."

This was my first tiny taste of freedom. An invisible yoke had been lifted from my neck. All of my needing and grasping and clinging and lusting and demanding and maneuvering and reaching and craving— all of the insatiable desires that had kept me on my hamster wheel of misery were falling away. I no longer needed to chase the proverbial carrot on the stick.

I wasn't starving anymore.

In my fifty-plus years on this planet, this is the unparalleled greatest feeling I've ever had.

In the following two years, I did fourteen ceremonies. In eight of them, the woman I would come to know as "Mother" showed up, each time with detailed advice and instructions. (Three of the times that she did *not* appear were among the most hellish psychological experiences I've ever endured.)

In my second ceremony, Mother repeated, for what felt like five hours straight, "Stop talking." She said it so many times I wanted to bang my head on the floor. She was referring to the constant inner chatter that runs incessantly in my head—planning, strategizing, debating, assessing, critiquing, self-judging, questioning, doubting. She pummeled me with the phrase, thousands of times: "Stop talking."

And at some point, just before sunrise, I noticed it: silence. My inner roommates had stopped talking. It was euphoric. Mother let me bathe in the peace of my inner quietude for about forty minutes. Then, without words she conveyed *why* I needed to stop talking:

In essence, she told me I should be still, and I should be quiet, in order to better observe and understand the people and circumstances around me. She had watched me batter myself for so many years trying to impose my Will on the world. Her point was, if I stopped talking and thinking so much, I could see and sense the universal tides and I could align my energies to them and achieve twice as much with half as much effort. I heard an echo of Gigi's words to me so many years before: "You know, if you stopped talking so much, maybe you could see some of those hits coming."

Minimizing my talking became my practice for maximizing my awareness. I had always seen the world as my battlefield; I now understood that the true combat zone was my mind.

TWENTY-ONE

LOVE

Chronic obstructive pulmonary disease. Idiopathic heart failure. Coronary artery disease. Atrial fibrillation. A normal heart ejection fraction is fifty-five to sixty percent. Daddio's is down to ten percent. His long history of smoking, inhaling refrigerant, and exposure to toxic chemicals, combined with a lifetime of excessive alcohol use . . ."

"So, how long?" I said.

"You should come home."

Dr. Ala Stanford had been our family physician for a few years now. She'd been wrestling with Daddio to make aggressive life changes to preserve and extend the quality of his golden years. Daddio had survived two heart attacks during my childhood; he would tell the stories as a badge of honor. For his second heart attack, he said he felt it coming on. His left arm gave out, so he drove himself to the hospital using only his right arm. When Dr. Ala would plead with him to change his habits, he would say, "Shit, if I stop smokin' and drinkin', I'll probably walk outside and get hit by a bus."

"So, how long, Ala?" I asked.

"Six weeks."

I had just finished shooting *Collateral Beauty*. It is a film about a father who has to cope with the death of his daughter. As a part of my character research, I had spent the last five months doing a deep dive on the spiritual, psychological, cultural rituals and healing practices that help people face the profound suffering of losing someone. I met with priests, imams, shamans, rabbis, gurus; I read a ton of books on death:

On Death and Dying by Elisabeth Kübler-Ross; *The Tibetan Book of Living and Dying* by Tibetan Buddhist teacher Sogyal Rinpoche; *Tuesdays with Morrie* by Mitch Albom; *The Year of Magical Thinking* by Joan Didion. Going into the role, I felt totally prepared and confident that I could accurately depict the triumphant arc from tragic loss toward perfect healing. I had been trying to find the solution to the agony of loss for my character, but now I was being forced to find it for myself.

Daddio knew he was dying.

His body was frail; his muscle had deteriorated. His skin draped over his bones like a shroud, his blueish-gray recliner set to its halfway position, Don Lemon muted in the background, Tareyton 100 in hand, less than a carton of cigarettes left in his life. Daddio had told Dr. Ala that he would either quit smoking *or* drinking, and she could pick. Based on his medication profile, she picked drinking.

"Hey, man," he said, perking up as I walked in.

"Whatup, Daddio?" I approached him to perform what had become our ritual greeting: He leaned forward, I palmed his bald head, and I kissed him where his bald spot used to be. (Five years earlier, Daddio's bald spot had become so prominent that I begged him to shave his head—"Come on, Dad, you rockin' a Homie the Clown, that's not a good look." He fought me for over a year, until one day I cornered him on the set of *Men in Black 3*, wrestled him into a barber's chair, and cut his entire head bald. He loved it and wore his head that way for the rest of his life.)

The Tibetan Book of Living and Dying lays out the most critical tenets to supporting and soothing the transition of a dying loved one. The first idea that jumped off the page for me was that a dying person often needs "permission to die." The book posits that sometimes a dying person will fight and struggle to stay alive if they don't have the sense that you are going to be OK without them. This can create horrific and painful final days. In order for our loved one to let go and die peacefully, they need to be explicitly reassured that we're going to be OK after they are gone, that they did a great job with their life, and that we can handle it from here.

Similarly, Rinpoche states, "A dying person most needs to be shown as unconditional a love as possible, released from all expectations." These concepts crystalized the mission in my mind. I was going to put aside all of my agendas, traumas, questions, and direct my full energies toward the most compassionate and merciful transition that I could tender.

Around week three, I arrived; standard head kiss. I took my seat on the floor. Chris Cuomo was muted today. Daddio's ability to eat was deteriorating. He had macaroni and cheese, braised beef, and broccoli, untouched in front of him. If Daddio isn't eating his mac and cheese, he must really not be feeling well.

"Hey, Dad," I said nervously. "You did good."

"What you mean?" he asked.

"With your life."

I don't think he was expecting to hear that. He took a pull of his Tareyton 100, turned his eyes back to the TV. He didn't seem like he was ready to go there just yet. But I was.

"I'm sayin' you did great with your life. And when you're ready to go, I want you to know that it's OK. You raised me well. And I got it from here. I'm gonna take care of everybody you love."

Daddio nodded his head, maintaining his stoic demeanor. His eyes welled yet never broke from CNN. But I knew he'd heard me.

The soldier was gone.

The ogre barely had enough strength to lift his spoon. He even needed my help to go to the bathroom. As a final attempt to maintain a semblance of his military dignity, he gave me detailed instructions on locking the wheels of his wheelchair, setting it into the perfect position adjacent to his recliner, being careful to close off the left footrest, leaving the right open for him to put his foot on, and the critical importance of placing my left knee outside of his right knee and my right knee straddled between his legs in order to safely lift and maneuver him, my right cheek positioned to his, stepping back at forty-five degrees to turn him and deposit him into his wheelchair.

One night, as I delicately wheeled him from his bedroom toward the bathroom, a darkness arose within me. The path between the two rooms goes past the top of the stairs. As a child I'd always told myself that I would one day avenge my mother. That when I was big enough, when I was strong enough, when I was no longer a coward, I would slay him.

I paused at the top of the stairs.

I could shove him down, and easily get away with it.

I'm Will Smith. No one would ever believe I killed my father on purpose.

I'm one of the best actors in the world. My 911 call would be Academy Award level.

As the decades of pain, anger, and resentment coursed then receded, I shook my head and proceeded to wheel Daddio to the bathroom. Thank God we're judged by our actions, not by our trauma-driven, inner outbursts.

I came to see him every week for the next month and a half. There is something strangely clarifying and cleansing about looking into the eyes of someone who has accepted their pending death. The awareness of death bestows profundity and clears all the bullshit out of the way.

The finality of it all makes every moment feel infinitely significant. Every hello felt like a gift from God. We were both overwhelmed with gratitude that we got to see each other one more time. And then, every goodbye was complete and perfect because we were saying goodbye with the full knowledge that this might be our last. Every laugh, every story takes on weight and meaning in that simple fact. Death has a way of transforming the mundane into the magical.

Hellos and goodbyes should be that way in our everyday lives because the reality is tomorrow is not *promised*. I began to embrace every hello with gratitude and to never take a goodbye for granted. The level of devoted focus, honesty, and compassion that Daddio and I shared became the aspirational model for love in my life.

Daddio had been given six weeks, and he ended up living for three months. I remember on week nine I made my trip to see him. Our meetings had been joyful and poignant, but today he is in an uncharacteristically despondent mood. Shirt off; Tareyton 100 in hand; hunched over his brown wooden folding tray; food untouched.

Standard bald-head kiss.

"Daddio, what's goin' on?"

He puts his cigarette down, pensively gazed out at the Ben Franklin Bridge arcing over the Schuylkill River.

"Man," Daddio said, "you tell motherfuckas you gon' be dead in six weeks, and nine weeks later you still hangin' around. This shit is embarrassing."

This was probably the second biggest laugh Daddio and I ever shared.

CUT!"

About ten days later, I was on the set of *Bright*, a Netflix fantasy-action cop film directed by David Ayer. We were shooting in downtown Los Angeles. Joel Edgerton, my costar, was behind the wheel of our patrol car; he was my partner in the movie.

David Ayer approaches the window.

"Bro, you need to call your father immediately," he says softly. "It's an emergency."

Even when you're expecting these phone calls, it doesn't make it less jarring. My heart was racing. I dialed Daddio's cell. He answered.

"Hey, man."

"Hey, Daddio, what's up?"

"I think it's tonight," he said.

His words hit me like a thousand volts.

"OK," I said calmly. *The Tibetan Book of Living and Dying* had stressed the importance of making a calm space for the transition of loved ones.

"Do you want to FaceTime?" I asked.

"Yeah. But shit, I don't know how to do that . . ."

"I got you—I'll FaceTime you," I said. "You just have to answer."

"Ellen, come do this FaceTime thing, Will about to call . . . ," he yelled to my sister who had just arrived. My cousin Ricky, a Philadelphia fireman who had been caring for Daddio, is holding the phone.

It's 2:00 a.m. in an empty downtown LA parking lot. I stand under the brightest streetlight I can find. I want him to be able to see me.

We simply look at each other. Twenty minutes of silence.

Finally, I hear my sister Ellen in the background whisper to Daddio, "Dad—you're just looking. You don't have anything you want to say to Will?"

Daddio searches for one last piece of wisdom. One final brick. But he's empty. He slowly shakes his head, a final surrender.

"Shit, anything I ain't told this muthafucka already, he sure ain't gonna get it from me tonight."

We shared a final laugh, we said goodbye, and forty-five minutes later, Daddio was gone.

One of the central and most critical tenets of filmmaking is "know your ending." When you understand the emotional, philosophical, and moral conclusion of your movie, you can better craft everything that leads up to it. The comprehension of the physical plot and thematic endpoints allows you to reverse engineer a more resonant and enjoyable journey for the audience. The end of a film is similar to the punch line of a joke—you want the meaning to erupt in the hearts and minds of the audience. Imagine beginning to tell a joke without knowing the punch line.

Life is like that. You're born into a bunch of characters, everyone's looking at you, you can't communicate, you can't walk, you can't feed yourself, yet everybody seems to be excited to see what you're going to end up doing. So, you begin telling your joke, with no fucking clue what the punch line is going to be. You're watching the audience—sometimes they chuckle, sometimes they boo, but deep down inside they hope you land the punch line. Some of us are born into loving and supportive audiences, and some of us land onstage in front of a crowd of hecklers. Most of us land somewhere in between.

In his final days, Daddio wasn't worried about ACRAC. He wasn't worried about money; he didn't even care about food anymore. He had a single burning question about his ending: *Was my life useful?* Daddio needed to know that our lives were better because he was here. He wanted to be reassured that in spite of all of his shortcomings and fumbles and mistakes, that in the net analysis his assets outweighed his liabilities, and his life had been valuable.

When Gigi died, it was a completely different experience. She had been so certain in her loving service and contribution to her family and her community and her commitment to God's children, that she was *excited* to go to heaven. To Gigi, "God" and "love" were synonymous; they were inseparable, and indistinguishable. She worshipped God by loving others. Love was the only commandment that mattered—to her, if you were being loving, you wouldn't need all the others.

There was no negative energy around her passing whatsoever. Gigi was so completely fulfilled that I never even cried. She was ready to go and felt that her work here was finished.

I got my first true glimpse into the secret of "the Smile." I had held a miscomprehension around the physics of ultimate happiness. I had thought that I could gain and win and achieve and conquer and acquire and *succeed* my way to love and happiness. Eight consecutive number one hit movies, thirty million records, four Grammys, and hundreds of millions of dollars makes you happy, right? Makes people love you, right? The fundamental flaw of this theory is the belief that "the Smile" comes from outside, that it is acquired or achieved from external sources or conditions. That someone will love you so much, they will adore you so deeply and thoroughly, that they will fill you with the bliss of "the Smile."

Spoiler alert: There are no relationships, careers, or houses with a name that can fill the hole. There is nothing that you can receive from the material world that will create inner peace or fulfilment. The truth is, "the Smile" is generated through *output*. It's not something you *get*, it's something you cultivate through *giving*. In the end, it will not matter one single bit how well *they* loved *you*—you will only gain "the Smile" based on how well *you* loved *them*.

The physics of love and happiness are counterintuitive. As long as we are stuck in the need to receive—in the cycle of grasping and clinging and demanding that people and the world around us meet our needs—we will be locked into disappointment, anger, and misery. The sweet paradox is being fulfilled by giving, that your output precipitates the input—giving and receiving become simultaneous. To love and to be loved is the highest human reward and ecstasy. Allowing the best within you to serve and unleash the best within others is the most intense of human pleasures.

When I say "love," I mean discovering, cultivating, and sharing your unique gifts for the purpose of uplifting and empowering your loved ones. "The Smile" is a combination of the *recognition* of the unique treasure within yourself and the *realization* that the treasure is multiplied through giving it away.

Everyone is struggling. Everyone is having a hard time. Life can be brutal, chaotic, confusing, and excruciating. Our hearts are starving. Loving, giving, helping, serving, protecting, nourishing, empowering, and forgiving are the secrets of "the Smile." Can you imagine what it would feel like if someone loved you, gave you all you needed, helped you, served you, protected you, nourished you, empowered you, and forgave you?

For many of us, the answer to that question is no. But what Gigi knew, and what Nelson Mandela knew, what Muhammad Ali knew—and what Daddio knew in his final moments—is that you must give it to receive it.

Daddio had poured all of his gifts into me. And at the end of his life, he saw that I had used them to build my life. He was fulfilled through his giving, and warts and all, he was content in how he had loved me. And then, by the grace of a benevolent creator, in his final days—when he had nothing left—I was blessed to pour my gifts into him.

Births, weddings, and funerals have a way of sifting the gold out of the dirt and the rocks. Daddio's death served as a wake-up call for me. As Jada and I sat at his funeral, I became chillingly aware of the fact that one day, one of us would be saying goodbye to the other, and I questioned: *What did I want our ending to be?*

Our time apart had helped us both to discover the power of loving in freedom. We are simultaneously one hundred percent bound together, and one hundred percent free. We agreed that we were both imperfect people, doing our best to figure out how to be in this world joyfully. What we needed from each other was unconditional love and support—not judgment, not punishment, but total, unbending devotion to each other's growth and well-being.

We came to see our marriage as a spiritual discipline—what Bhakti Tirtha Swami called the ultimate "school of love." This relationship is our classroom—we are learning to cultivate care, concern, and compassion in the most intimate and difficult of circumstances. There are few things in life more challenging than being married. The intimacy tends to stir up and expose our most poisonous inner energies.

If we can learn to love here, we can love anywhere.

The question is, can we love each other *unconditionally*, or is our love contingent upon the other person acting *exactly* as we need them to? It's easy to "love" somebody when they do what you want them to do, exactly how you want them to do it. But how do you behave when they step outside of your picture? How do you treat them when they hurt you? Those are the times that determine whether or not or not you actually love somebody.

Love is hard. It takes enormous courage to open a wounded heart over and over again to the possibility of love's bliss. Like Charlie Mack always says, "Scared money can't make no money." Love demands bravery, a willingness to risk it all.

But bravery does not mean the *absence* of fear. Bravery is learning to continue forward even when you're terrified. Jada and I agreed that we would ride together for this lifetime, no matter what.

THE JUMP

**W**e're about to witness something that has never been done before. You've read about it, you've tweeted about it, and it's finally here. I'm Alfonso Ribeiro, and this is 'Will Smith: The Jump,' coming to you [from] the Grand Canyon.

"Today, on his 50th birthday, he will face his fears and heli bungee jump over this jaw-dropping gorge. Now, to be clear, he is bungee jumping out of a helicopter 1,800 feet above the ground. I just got chills thinking about this. This is crazy. . . ."

"Yo, Alfonso, stop sayin' that shit like that!" Charlie Mack barked.

"Charlie, I'm on the air right now. Live," Alfonso hissed.

"I don't give a fuck, Alf, stop making it sound like it's gon' go bad! Like it's too dangerous."

"But also, the weather here can be tricky at the Grand Canyon. We had lightning storms all day yesterday, but we have an experienced stunt team and aerial crew who is keeping track of the winds and the temperature."

"OK, we're out Alfonso!" the producer yells.

"Seriously, Alf, I don't like your whole energy—"

"Charlie, I'm doing my job! Will asked me to host!" Alfonso said, chopping his right hand into his left. "He wants me to build the suspense!"

"Don't build no suspense that make it seem like he gon' die!"

"That's where the suspense comes from, Charlie!"

So why are you heli bungee jumping over the Grand Canyon?

When I first heard that question out loud, I thought, *It's obvious! I'm in the wicked clutches of an anaconda of a midlife crisis.* But I was live on YouTube, so I couldn't say that.

Here's what I actually said:

"I've had an interesting relationship with fear my whole life. I've traversed the spectrum of fear reactions, from complete debilitation through inspiration and sometimes slipping into outright foolishness. But when the idea of heli bungee jumping over the Grand Canyon came up, I wasn't debilitated, and I sure wasn't inspired—all I could think was, *This shit is stupid.*"

My childhood Grand Canyon trip was a deeply meaningful experience. I've always remembered how beautiful it was, but I also remember how terrified I was to walk up to the edge. Harry even got close enough to drop his drum in it, but I stayed back, too scared to take in the full majesty.

I've realized that for some reason, God placed the most beautiful things in life on the other side of our worst terrors. If we are not willing to stand in the face of the things that most deeply unnerve us, and then step across the invisible line into the land of dread, then we won't get to experience the best that life has to offer.

So I've been making a conscious effort to attack all the things that I'm scared of. And this is scary. When Yes Theory challenged me to heli bungee, my heart jumped. And I've learned to recognize that feeling as a signal that the great gift has presented itself. As soon as my heart jumps, I'm in—I gotta do it. But I also can't be outdone, so when Yes Theory said "Heli bungee," I added, "Over the Grand Canyon . . . and on my 50th birthday."

Everybody is here: Mom-Mom, Jada, Sheree, Trey, Jaden, Willow, Harry, Ellen, Pam, Ashley, Kyle, Dion, Gammy, Caleeb, JL, Charlie Mack, Omarr, Scoty and Ty, and on and on. As I took in the dueling landscapes of friends, family, and Grand Canyon, and saw the faces of the next generation—Harry's kids, Ellen's kids, Pam's, JL's, Charlie's, Omarr's, Caleeb's, Scoty and Ty's—I realized: I'm standing in the middle of my dream. This is what I've always wanted: Everyone I love is here, together, as a family, and I had brought them to the Grand Canyon to witness the senseless and horrific death of their uncle Will. I could hear the news reports: "Will Smith, in what is presumed to have been a drug-induced psychosis, leapt to his death in a bizarre heli bungee accident over the Grand Canyon early yesterday afternoon. He is survived by his wife, his baby mama, three children, a smorgasbord of nephews and nieces, extended family and friends, and a day-hiker wondering what all the sirens were about.. He was just 50. In a statement released by YouTube executives, Smith was described as 'a true American lunatic.' End quote."

But another thing happened: The kids *got* it. They seemed to understand the necessity to confront and overcome the things that most terrify them. My niece Caila held on to my leg as I approached the helicopter. And beyond the point where she could no longer follow, she screamed, "I'm gonna be brave like you when I grow up, Uncle Will!"

Alfonso: Willow, how do you feel about your dad going to do this?

Willow: I just want him to do what makes him happy. And obviously I'm nervous, but this is what he wants and we're all here to support him, and I just want him to do what he loves.

Trey: I'm just really happy he's doing what he wants to do. I mean, bungee jumping out of a helicopter over the Grand Canyon . . . I couldn't say I've ever heard of that done in history, so I'm looking forward. [He] taught us [to] just conquer fear.

Jada: Are you trying to terrify your children?

Will: No, no, no, no. My kids don't get scared. . . .

Alfonso: What's dad's biggest fear?

Jaden: His biggest fear is having any fears.

Alfonso: Will, you've been in this business for a really long time. And you have a lot of fans, and you also have some very famous fans, and they all wanted to say a little something to you. So, check this out . . .

LeBron James: You about to bungee jump out of a helicopter into the Grand Canyon. Man, you got too far in life to be doing shit like that.

Michael Strahan: Just because you turned 50 doesn't mean you have to lose your mind. If you need to talk to somebody, you can talk to me any time.

Jimmy Fallon: I don't want you to do this. You still have time. You can back out of this. Throw a dummy out of the plane. Do anything.

Quincy Jones: Happy 50, bro.

DJ Jazzy Jeff: Now you got to go to the doctor and let them stick their thumb up your ass. Because that's what happens when you're 50. I know.

Alfonso: Yes. Alright. Always inspiring words from Jazzy Jeff.

I didn't want to know anything ahead of time. I wanted to walk up to the chopper, get briefed, and do the jump. I wanted to find out in real time, along with the audience, how it was all going to go down.

"Hey, Will, I'm T.J., your stunt coordinator. Let me run you through the basics: You're going to be jumping on a two-hundred-foot active bungee cord. We've got multiple redundant safeties—chest, two to the waist. This cord is an engineering marvel, made from hundreds of individual strands of rubber coated to reduce friction and wear. More strands, more safety. Your body weight is two hundred pounds, right?"

Well, minus the eighteen pounds of fluid and other matter I'm currently shedding due to the crippling terror I'm experiencing, yes.

"You're going to put three Gs into the cord, which when you multiply it by your weight, means you're going to put about 600 pounds of force on it. At the point of maximum stretch, you'll have fallen 550 feet, then you'll bounce several times before ending up hanging about 325 feet below the helicopter. Then we'll bring you back to the crash pad, unhook you, everybody sings 'Happy Birthday,' and we head home. Any questions?"

"Wait, hold on—I just had a terrible thought," I said. "After this bungee cord stretches, isn't it going to throw me back up into the rotors of the helicopter?"

"I hope not!" T.J. said, chuckling. "Just kidding—that's impossible. As you accelerate under the force of gravity, you gain kinetic energy. The bungee cord stretches, absorbing that energy, but only *some* of it. The rest is lost as heat, due to friction and air resistance. This means the rebound can *never* be as high as the initial fall."

"A'ight, cool, I figured it was totally safe . . ."

"Well . . . there are fundamentals to bungee jumping, but this is heli bungee jumping, so there are subtle peculiarities that make it potentially a little more dangerous. For a start, instead of a stable position, the chopper is moving. The weather conditions have to be just right, and we can't be too close to any walls or ledges. But *you* are the x-factor I'm most concerned about. This bungee cord weighs over two hundred pounds. When we get up in the air, there will be three guys holding the weight to keep it off of you. But when they let it go, there's going to be about eight hundred pounds of pull, so you are going out of this chopper whether you like it or not. The only way you can get hurt is if when they let that cord go, you don't get away from this bird. I'm gonna count down from five, and when I get to one, you *must* jump. If that cord snatches you, it's *all* bad."

I'm not jumping. But I'm probably going to get sued. I wonder how much the judgment will be. The average movie costs probably $40 million, so there's no way YouTube is paying more than two or three million to put this event on. Plus, what, a million in damages? So, when I walk away right now, it's probably a $4 million decision.

I can live with that.

But by then, T.J. was attaching the bungee cord to my chest.

"Wait a second—it's not going to be attached to my back or my legs?" Every bungee I'd ever seen was attached to people's legs.

"We're about the same age," T.J. said. "Do you remember the Nestea plunge commercial, where the people would jump backward, arms out, into a swimming pool?"

"Yeah, I remember that one from when I was little," I said.

"When I get to one, I need you to give me your best Nestea plunge."

"I HAVE TO JUMP BACKWARD???"

I'm harnessed up, double and triple checks have been completed. The whirr of the chopper blades slowly increases. I move to take my seat in the helicopter.

T.J. stops me.

"Because of the weight of the bungee cord, I'm going to keep you on the outside, on the ski," T.J. says.

"So, I'm going to be standing ON THE OUTSIDE? When it takes off?" I say, catching myself, realizing I'm an international action hero.

"Yes. Just get your feet firmly planted on the ski. You grab these two handles, hold on to them, and I've got you on a tether," T.J. says, as if that was supposed to make me feel better about being on the outside of a helicopter while it takes off and then flies over the Grand Canyon.

My next and perhaps most startling surprise came as the chopper began to lift off. There is something wildly disconcerting about hanging on to the outside of a helicopter as it takes off. We are eight feet off the ground as the chopper gently banks to the right. I look down to make sure my feet are firmly planted on the ski when suddenly the ground disappears, and the eighteen-hundred-foot gorge reveals itself. My knees buckle under me. I tighten my grip on the steel handles bolted to the helicopter floor.

"Meant to tell you not to look down!" T.J. shouted, with a smile. I thought, *What else has he forgotten to tell me?*

There's a red light just to my left. A cacophony of military gibberish squawks over the multiple open radios. Everybody is shouting over the thunder of the chopper blades and the percussive timpani that is my heart. I can make out a word here and there—"altitude," "copy," "over," "wind," "check," "storm."

Storm? It would be terrible to nail the jump and then get struck by lightning. . . .

And then, "green light."

The red light in the chopper, which had been the Hoover Dam holding back the flood of this collective insanity, gives way and turns green. T.J., six inches from my face to be certain that there are no miscommunications, gives me the universal go sign: thumbs-up. And then he shouts, "We are go! Do you copy? We are go!"

I give him one nod in the affirmative. And T.J. begins the countdown.

"FIVE!" T.J. commands, aggressively showing five fingers.

It really is true that your whole life flashes before your eyes when you think you're going to die.

What if I leap to my death in front of my children? This would be a whack-ass way to go out, and the worst birthday ever. It would be the biggest YouTube special in history, so there's that. I probably should have thought about all this before now.

I wonder what my kids would say at my funeral.

"FOUR!"

Me and Jada just started playing golf together. She loves it—she gets dressed for a round before the sun even comes up. After all of these years, we found something new we love doing. We're supposed to be playing tomorrow. I enjoy playing with her more than anybody.

She's the best friend I've ever had.

THREE!

Why is he counting so fast?

TWO!

Look, I'm either gonna die, or I'm not. If God wants me today, ain't nothin' I can do about it anyway. If I die, I'm not even gonna know. So, the real question is, how do I want to live?

ONE!

ACKNOWLEDGMENTS

This is the most difficult page of the entire book. The number of people I would want to thank is astronomical. Countless angels have carried, shielded, nourished, rescued, and empowered me along my journey. In an effort to do my tiny part for environmental conservation, if I missed you in the book, I will keep a running list of acknowledgments on my Instagram. See you on IG.

ILLUSTRATION CREDITS